# THE RED FOX

# The Red Fox

H.G. LLOYD

B. T. BATSFORD LTD · LONDON

I fy Mam, Meiriona, Huw, John a Mannon,
heb anghofio am y llwynogod – gwyllt a dôf.

First published 1980
Second impression 1981
© H. G. Lloyd 1980
ISBN 0 7134 1190 2
Photoset in Plantin, 11 on 12pt
Printed in Great Britain by The Anchor Press Ltd
and bound by Wm Brendon & Son Ltd
both of Tiptree, Essex
for the publishers
B. T. Batsford Ltd, 4 Fitzhardinge Street,
London W1H 0AH

# Contents

# Acknowledgment

Many colleagues, friends, correspondents and others in diverse walks of life in Britain, Europe, North America and Australia have helped during the course of the collection of information presented here.

I am particularly indebted to my immediate colleagues, David Cowan, Bernard Davies, Daf Evans, Ian Gray, Desmond Isaakson, I. B. Jones, Ian Keeble, E. N. Nicholas, R. J. C. Page, Bernard Price, Frank Thomas and John Woods, for their expert knowledge and help given over many years, and to my immediate boss, H. V. Thompson, for support and encouragement throughout. Veterinary colleagues, especially John Loxam, Peter Marshall, John Macdonald, John Ockey, Peter Swire and Bernard Williams, have, with their specialist knowledge, helped to sort out many difficulties; also I have benefited much from discussion on agricultural matters with W. A. Prowel, H. P. Thomas and John Griffiths. I thank them all. I must also thank the many students who, with the rain in their faces or the blood of dissected foxes on their hands, toiled without complaint. Alas, I can only record my indebtedness to my colleague and friend the late Gordon Ashwell, whose contribution to the development of radio-tracking devices has been of immeasurable help to me, to my colleagues and to many others.

It is a pleasure to thank my European biologist friends, Jan Englund (Sweden), Birger Jensen and Jorgen Muller (Denmark), Jan van Haaften and Frederick Niewold (Holland), Alexander Wandeler (Switzerland) and Dave Johnston (Canada), for their generous advice and information and for their company here and overseas; to Dr Konrad Bogel, WHO, Geneva, for his advice on the chapter on diseases, and to Professor Franz Steck, Berne, and Dr Louis Andral, Nancy, for discussions on rabies.

I am indebted to Kim Taylor for his many hours of painstaking work in correcting the final draft, which ascribed some curious behaviour to foxes, such as 'they hunt mainly by hearing, pursuing unseen prey in tunnels beneath the matted surface layers of fields. . . .' Fortunately, he has, I hope, detected all oddities of this kind. If not, Elizabeth Bland will have rectified this and I am indebted to her for her expert editorial work. H. V. Thompson and Ray Hewson also read the drafts, Dick and Biddy Williams, the chapter on control, and Gwilym Lloyd, that on the fox's relations with man; their comments are greatly appreciated.

Other groups studying foxes in Britain have provided a stimulus to research effort, and I have benefited from, and am grateful for, discussions and freely given advice from James Fairley, Stephen Harris, Ray Hewson, Hugh Kolb and David Macdonald – all of whom are promoting exciting research on the fox in their respective fields.

A large part of the fieldwork mentioned in this book was undertaken on common land in Breconshire and Radnorshire, an area of many hundreds of square kilometres to which access is readily available; much of the fringe of open hill is forested, however, and I am grateful to the local and regional officers of the Forestry Commission and the Economic Forestry Group for their assistance and for *carte blanche* to pursue the study of the fox in their woodlands. In addition, although my activities and those of my colleagues may have been an embarrassment to many farmers and others, I must thank the many Joneses, Hughes, Williamses, Thomases, Prices, Richardses, Pritchards, Pughs, Powells, Lloyds, Protheroes, Lewises, Roberts and Davies and three Hopes, one Bourdillon, one Thrupp, one Raisen and one Lavack for their tolerance, interest and help.

I must not forget to thank my neighbours, in particular Mrs Mathews, for ignoring the smell and riotous clamour of my foxes, and all who have provided the remnants of weekend joints to help feed them.

Finally, it is a pleasure to thank Felicity Gay, Cynthia Mainwaring, Pauline Penney and Susan Smith, among others, for their perseverance with my handwriting. Having finished the book, I can renew my duties within and about the *ménage* and, weather permitting, relegate my wife to a fishing widow once again. My thanks to them all.

The author and publishers would like to thank the following for kind permission to reproduce the black and white photographs: Syndication International Ltd (1), Dorothy Cloynes (2), Jane Burton (3), Aquila Photographics (4, 17), Helge Walhovd (5), Prof. H. N. Thandrup (6), Frank W. Lane (7, 28), Astrid Bergman Sucksdorff (12, 18, 22, 23), Radio Times Hulton Picture Library (13), Paul Popper Ltd (15, 20, 21), Bruce Coleman/Jane Burton (19) and Tony Weir (29). The rest are from the author's own collection. The author would also like to acknowledge the use of Crown copyright material in the preparation of several of the tables and figures.

# List of Photographs

*(between pages 160 and 161)*

# List of Figures

# List of Tables

# Introduction

This account of the life and biology of the fox is not intended for any specific readership. Its purpose is to provide a source of information about the fox which may be of interest to all those in our community who are concerned about it – from parliamentarians engaged in framing legislation to school pupils involved in a fox project. For those who need to know more, I need hardly add that this book can only be the *hors d'oeuvre* and that the main course lies in the bibliography.

The fox is one of the few predatory mammals thriving in Britain today. Its unspecialized way of life and its unique ability to adapt enables it to live in a wide range of habitats and to withstand man's best efforts to contain it. Very numerous today, it probably finds conditions more suited to it now than at any time in the past.

It is variously regarded as a killer, a pest, a rogue, a nuisance and an occasional rascal; as a harmless and beneficial animal and an honoured object of the chase. Whatever our attitude, the fox is a fine animal which commands admiration for its tenacity, intelligence and its handsome appearance. It is the subject of considerable research internationally – much of it being precipitated by its role in the epidemiology of rabies. Fortunately for me, biologists in many countries have studied many aspects of its biology; were it otherwise, and this book based entirely upon personal experience, it would be very thin in places.

With a simple organism the biologist is able to describe many of the animal's requirements fairly easily by studying its distribution, and by field and laboratory experiments on such features as its chemical and physical requirements. But with higher animals, especially the more adaptable mammals, the biologist is faced not only with the difficulties associated with precise, or even loose, description of the animal's requirements but also, more important, the problem of defining the environment in which it lives. The reader will find herein such phrases as 'rich habitat' without any precise explanation of what is meant by this, simply because it is not based upon a scientific appraisal but upon a subjective inference drawn from some knowledge of the fox's way of life and requirements. Thus, many inferences made here may be inaccurately or inadequately founded and may pertain to certain situations only. The reader is invited not to take every statement on trust but, where possible, to apply his own judgement and consider whether or not the inference is sound, and whether it is likely to apply universally.

And a final word about the fox. Perhaps it deserves its reputation as a rascal, but it does not deserve to die the squalid death that so often is its fate – and in this context I am not referring to hunting with hounds, most participants of which observe a code of practice, I have in mind other methods not subject to control.

Gwyn Lloyd
*March 1979*

# 1

# Fact and Fable

For centuries the fox has attracted the attention of the natural historian. Until the seventeenth century most accounts of the natural history of animals were apocryphal or could be traced, with variations, to the observations of Aristotle in the fifth century BC and Herodotus two centuries later. The *Physiologus*, or *The Naturalist*, written in the early Christian era, was an account of natural history widely translated from one language to another even as late as the eighteenth century. Together with other traditional sources, it was the progenitor of the bestiaries, which were compilations of the 'known facts' of natural history. These were not superseded until Gestner and others in the sixteenth century began to seek information at first hand, and Sir Thomas Brown in the seventeenth century subjected the 'known facts' to scrutiny in his *Vulgar Errors*.

Many of the ancient accounts of the behaviour of foxes are so quaint that they are presented here without apology.

Aelian, writing in the second century BC, describes how foxes cope with wasps' nests. To avoid being stung, the fox presents its rear quarters to the nest and lets down its tail to agitate the wasps. The wasps become entangled in the fur, and the fox then beats its tail against a tree to kill the wasps. The process continues until all the wasps are dead and the fox is able to eat the comb. To catch his prey, the fox adopts cunning expedients, according to Aelian. In order to entice bustards to approach close enough to be caught, the fox allegedly simulates the silhouette of a bustard by elevating its tail and pressing its head and shoulders to the ground. The fox is said to catch small fish by trailing its tail in a stream. The fish are trapped in the fur and thrown out on to the ground. Aelian recounts that the impregnable hedgehog is easily dealt with by the fox — it simply urinates into the hedgehog's mouth.

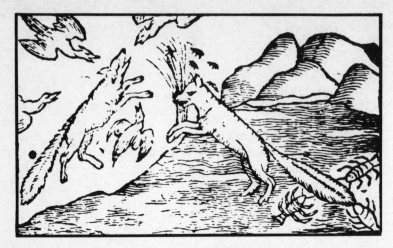

**1**   Three aspects of fox behaviour illustrated by Olaus Magnus (1555) showing a fox feigning death to attract birds, disinfesting itself in water, and catching crabs with its tail.

In the sixteenth century Olaus Magnus depicts, in a single illustration, three facets of the behaviour of foxes which had been observed some two thousand years earlier. Foxes are shown fishing for crabs with their tails, feigning death to attract birds (this ruse is described in a bestiary — the fox rubs itself in red mud to simulate blood, then lies down to await scavenging birds) and disinfesting themselves. The fox's unique method of disinfesting itself of fleas is recorded in writings from many countries, from Hellenic times onwards. The fox is said to wade into a pond or stream, usually backwards, with a bouyant object in its mouth. The substance the fox carries varies from account to account — some suggest that it is wool, others that it is grass, bark, wood or teasels. (Seton, 1929, corroborates this observation. Not only did he witness the procedure — the foxes were using pine bark or corn silk — but he claims that lice, not fleas, were later found in the floating corn silk bundles.) According to some accounts, the fox whips its tail against a teasel to gather its own fur as a substitute for the wool, moss or sticks referred to in other descriptions. The practical objection to the story is that the skin of the fox would not become wet through by this rather gradual immersion, so the fleas would not be in any danger of drowning; however, this method of disinfestation has apparently been recorded in other species (the grey fox, *Urocyon*, for example: Wetmore, 1952).

According to many ancient authorities, the fox is able to improve its health and prolong its life by eating the resin of pine trees, and Topsell, who translated Gestner in 1607, mentions another form of natural protection available to foxes — a herb called a 'sea onion'. This herb is said to have wolf-repellent properties, and affords the fox protection from wolves if it is placed by the fox at the entrance to its den. But the fox allegedly labours under one physical disadvantage: one reads that the right legs of the fox are shorter than the left, so it can go around a hill in one direction only. (Even today countrymen occasionally ascribe a similar deformity to badgers.)

Advice on how to escape the predations of foxes was abundant. A fox repellent, first described by Pliny, was believed to protect poultry. Poultry that was fed the dried liver of a fox was deemed immune from attack, as were hens which had mated with a cock adorned with a collar of fox skin around its neck. In Elizabethan times hens and geese were fed pieces of fox, but this immunity only lasted two months. Wild rue leaves hung 'secretly' under a hen's wing afforded the same protection.

Various organs of the fox were used in popular medicine as both cures and charms against accidents. In the Middle Ages it was believed that the penis of a fox tied to the head relieved headache; its testicles tied around the neck of a child eased teething troubles; its blood promoted the growth of hair, if the balding head was anointed with it; its fat cured gout and, if rubbed on a pomegranate stick, attracted all the flies in a house (Stephenson, 1928).

In the time of Elizabeth I it was claimed that the wearing of a brooch made of a fox's tongue prevented blindness, and fox's blood, drunk and applied externally, was regarded as a remedy for bladder stones. Cramped muscles were relieved by fox fat, and movement was believed to be restored to paralytic limbs by a concoction of fox and duck fat roasted in a goose. Young children were rendered safe from the 'falling disease' (epilepsy) if they were fed on the brain of a fox.

Later generations relied on the tongue of a fox, dried or fresh, to draw foreign bodies from the flesh, and dried fox liver or lungs in wine were believed to ease breathing. Fox bile cured pains in the ears. The testicles of the fox were recommended for the removal of pimples and spots from the face, and a mixture of vinegar and the faeces of the fox 'by anointment cureth the Leprosie speedily' (Topsell, 1607).

While popular belief in the legendary powers and properties of the fox persisted, huntsmen acquired considerable first-hand information about their quarry. Hunting was almost a *raison d'être* among noblemen in the fifteenth century, and their knowledge of the behaviour of the animals they sought was probably deeper and more comprehensive than the literature of the period records. Edward, second Duke of York, in *The Master of Game* (1420), his translation of Gaston Phoebus's book, *La Chasse*, makes many interesting observations, then familiar perhaps to all huntsmen but subsequently forgotten and only latterly rediscovered. He describes, for example, the protuberance of the ulna in hares which 'had not passed a year' – an ageing technique used by biologists today. He describes, too, what seems to be the notch in the epiphyseal cartilage of the tibia or the humerus as a means of distinguishing young hounds, wolves and foxes.

Having treated the legends associated with the fox somewhat lightly, I feel a cautionary note should be introduced. I have mentioned that many early accounts of the fox describe its habit of feigning death to attract scavengers. Whilst I am sceptical of the authenticity of such observations, it seems that in 1961 a Russian naturalist filmed a Caucasian fox capturing an inquisitive crow by this ruse, and a film sequence of the event appears in *Reynard the Fox* by Kenneth Varty (1967). Moreover, I was present, shortly before writing this, while cubs were being dug from an earth in the Kerry Hills, Montgomeryshire. A 'dead' fox cub was taken from a hole and thrown to one side whilst the live cubs were extracted. When the time came to examine the cub it was not to be found. Sceptics like myself, beware!

## Classification

Fossil records suggest that the canids evolved some thirty to fifty million years ago in the Eocene period, probably in North America. The earliest fossil canids such as *Hesperocyon* (about twenty-five million years before present, in the lower Oligocene) possess characteristics which suggest that they might have been ancestral to other carnivores, but Déschambre (1951), in a study of the evolution of canids, considers them to be a diphyletic group – a group with two branches evolving independently – the foxes and jackals descending from their ancestral form *Cynodictis*, and dogs and wolves from *Amphicyon*. Although not confirmed beyond doubt, the direct antecedent of the red fox is considered to be *Vulpes alopecoides* (Zeuner, 1963; Kurten, 1968), found in deposits dated to 650,000 to 400,000 years ago. Contemporaneously, *Vulpes praecorsac*, considered to be ancestral to the corsac fox of the Russian steppes was also described, but there must be some uncertainty about the relationships of these two forms to present-day species since one of the diagnostic characteristics used to distinguish these early Pleistocene species was their small dimensions, which could be misleading. The red fox is found from the middle Pleistocene of Europe – between 400,000 and 180,000 years ago. Its remains are frequently found in profusion in cave dwellings, perhaps because foxes used caves as lairs, or because man exploited foxes for food or fur.

In neolithic lake dwellings in Switzerland dog remains are less common than those of red fox. Hauk (1950) suggested, on rather slender evidence, that foxes must have been domesticated by lake dwellers – and there is no doubt that foxes were eaten, since knife, or axe, and human tooth marks (!) were found on many fox bones. Some of the remains are of very small foxes which, it has been suggested, might indicate domestication, since captive animals would probably not have been as well fed as their wild brethren. Remains of foxes of the same size as present-day ones do also occur occasionally in these lake dwellings. (Davis, 1977, has used fossil fox remains to correlate fox size with ambient temperature as a basis for estimates of temperature changes in the Pleistocene-Holocene period.) Bouchud (1951), studying Quaternary period cave deposits at Bayonne, France, considered that wolves, red fox and arctic foxes were not eaten at that time but were hunted for skins. The long bones of foxes in these deposits were seldom broken, as were deer bones, and they were usually found outside the caves whilst the metacarpals lay inside, which suggests that foxes were roughly skinned outside the cave and taken in for finishing; but there could be other explanations. The foxes of these deposits were larger and had stronger bones than present-day forms. Remains from Jericho Tell show clearly that foxes were eaten.

In later Pleistocene times the red, corsac and arctic fox co-existed in Europe. As the ice receded to the Arctic at the end of the last glaciations, the arctic fox withdrew to higher latitudes and the corsac fox to the steppes of Russia, whilst the more adaptable red fox advanced widely. At various times during the past 6,000,000 years, the British Isles formed part of the European mainland. The last separation, 6,000–7,000 years ago, represents the time of severance of British and European fox populations.

The broad classification of the carnivores and canids is shown on p. 22. The family *Canidae* (the canids) contains about forty-one species. The sub-family *Caninae* contains most of the canids (about thirty-seven species); these are more widely distributed than the four species of the two other sub-families, and they are clearly more successful. The genus *Canis* is represented by about nine species (seven according to Stains, 1967), and genus *Vulpes* by ten or eleven, with a natural worldwide distribution not less than that of the wolves, coyotes and jackals; thus, the genus *Vulpes* can be regarded as being as successful as that of the larger members of the sub-family. Of all the canids, however, *Vulpes vulpes* (the red fox) has the widest distribution. It has about forty-seven recognized sub-species.

Some members of the genus *Canis* and of other genera in the sub-family may outwardly show greater resemblance to the red fox than to the wolf and jackal, and the local or vernacular names for some species can cause confusion – for example, *Canis simensis*, a rare Ethiopian canid with a fox-like head, is known variously as the Abyssinian wolf, the Simenian or Seymen fox and the Ethiopian red fox. Whilst at present included in the genus *Canis*, some taxonomists suggest that this species should be accorded generic status on its own. There is little information on the taxonomic relationship of the *Caninae* to each other, and in particular on the closeness of relationships of the true dogs (the wolves, jackals and coyotes) and red foxes. The absence of red foxes in South America led to the evolution of the thirteen species of fox and dog-like canids found only in that continent. The way of life of most of these South American species is characteristic of the red foxes. One species, *Dusicyon australis*, exclusive to the Falkland islands, became extinct in 1875 as a result of a deliberate campaign to eliminate it by sheep rearers. With the possible exceptions of *Dasycyon hagcnbecki, Canis simensis* and the red wolf (*Canis niger*), the members of the sub-family *Caninae* are not endangered – though the distribution of the larger canids is shrinking, as is, for example, the grey wolf in Europe. The bat-eared fox, *Otocyon megalotis*, should, it is suggested by van Valen (1964), lose its generic status and be included in the *Caninae*.

*Broad Classification of Carnivores and Canids*

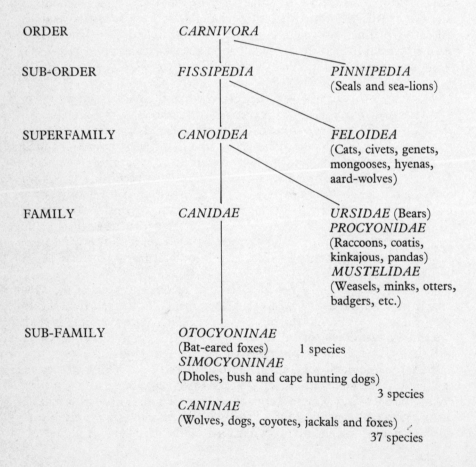

| ORDER | *CARNIVORA* | |
|---|---|---|
| SUB-ORDER | *FISSIPEDIA* | *PINNIPEDIA* (Seals and sea-lions) |
| SUPERFAMILY | *CANOIDEA* | *FELOIDEA* (Cats, civets, genets, mongooses, hyenas, aard-wolves) |
| FAMILY | *CANIDAE* | *URSIDAE* (Bears) *PROCYONIDAE* (Raccoons, coatis, kinkajous, pandas) *MUSTELIDAE* (Weasels, minks, otters, badgers, etc.) |
| SUB-FAMILY | *OTOCYONINAE* (Bat-eared foxes)   1 species *SIMOCYONINAE* (Dholes, bush and cape hunting dogs)   3 species *CANINAE* (Wolves, dogs, coyotes, jackals and foxes)   37 species | |

*Genera of the Canid Sub-families*

SUB-FAMILY OTOCYONINAE
Genus            *Otocyon* (Bat-eared foxes. Africa)
           Muller, 1836           1 species
SUB-FAMILY *SIMOCYONINAE*
Genus            *Cuon* (Dholes. India)
           Hodgson, 1838        1 species
           *Lycaon* (Cape hunting dogs. Africa)
           Brookes, 1827        1 species
           *Speothos* (Bush-dogs. S. America)
           Lund, 1839        1 species

SUB-FAMILY *CANINAE*
Genus            *Alopex* (Arctic foxes. Circumpolar, north)
           Kaup, 1829        1 species
           *Atelocynus* (Zorros. S. America)
           Cabrera, 1940        1 species
           *Canis* (Wolves, jackals, coyotes, dingos, domestic dogs. Africa, India, Asia, Europe, North America, introduced Australia)
           Linnaeus, 1758        9 species
           *Cerdocyon* (Crab-eating foxes. S. America)
           H. Smith, 1839        1 species
           *Chrysocyon* (Maned wolves. S. America)
           H. Smith, 1839        1 species
           *Dasycyon* (Andes wolves. S. America)
           Krumbiegel, 1953        1 species
           *Dusicyon* (Pampas foxes, etc. S. America)
           H. Smith, 1839        *ca.* 9 species
           *Fennecus* (Fennec foxes. N. Africa)
           Desmarest, 1804        1 species
           *Nyctereutes* (Racoon-dogs. Asia, Eastern Europe)
           Temminck, 1839        1 species
           *Urocyon* (Grey foxes. N. America)
           Baird, 1821        2 species
           *Vulpes* ('Red' foxes, N. America, Africa, Europe, Asia, India, introduced Australia)
           Bowdich, 1821        10 species

*Species in genus Vulpes*
*Vulpes vulpes* The red fox
*Vulpes bengalensis* The Bengal fox
*Vulpes cana* Blandford's, or the hoary fox
*Vulpes chama* The cape fox, or silver-backed fox
*Vulpes corsac* The corsac fox
*Vulpes ferrilata* The Tibetan sand fox

*Vulpes fulva* (considered to be conspecific with *V. vulpes*)
*Vulpes macrotis* The kit fox
*Vulpes pallida* The pale or sand fox
*Vulpes ruppelli* Ruppell's fox
*Vulpes velox* The swift fox

## Distribution

**World distribution**
The red fox, *Vulpes vulpes*, is indigenous to the northern hemisphere
only. It is distributed throughout most of the Palaearctic region, from
Ireland to the Bering Strait. In the north it occurs on the south island of
Novaya Zemlya and on islands off the Yamal peninsula. It has been
recorded at about 74°N on the Tamyr peninsula and at the delta of the
Lena River and has been seen 100km north of land on the sea ice in the
region of the New Siberian islands. It ranges southward from the Gulf of
Anadyr to the Kamchatka peninsula and on the Kuril Islands, Sakhalin
and Japan. It occurs throughout China, north Vietnam, north Burma,
Bangladesh and Pakistan, central India and throughout much of Arabia
except the large central desert areas. Its range extends up the Nile valley
– perhaps as far as Khartoum – along the south Mediterranean coast to
the Gulf of Benghazi, along the martime regions of Tunisia, Algeria and
Morocco, perhaps as far as Cape Blanc in the Spanish Sahara. At the northern limits of its range it can survive intense cold and arctic darkness; at
the other climatic extreme it can survive in areas which enjoy no more
than 76mm of rain a year, in the deserts of Australia, for example.

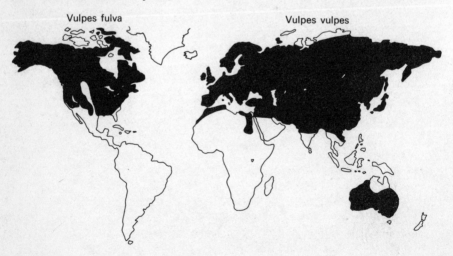

**2**  World-wide distribution of the red fox

Three foxes were undoubtedly introduced to Victoria, Australia, from Britain in 1864. According to Rolls (1969), in a fascinating account of the introduced animals of Australia, some foxes may have been introduced earlier, perhaps from 1845 onwards. These earliest introductions may not, however, have survived to breed, and the progenitors of Australian foxes may have been among several foxes released at two places in Victoria in 1870 and 1871. It seems that introduced foxes were intended to provide sport, not to control rabbit numbers. Hunting with hounds in Australia began with the importation of deer in the early 1800s. Later, for a period of perhaps fifty years, dingoes were hunted, some as 'bagmen' (captive animals released immediately prior to the hunt), a practice sometimes adopted with foxes in England (see page 189). By 1880 foxes were widely distributed in Victoria and, according to Rolls, occupied an area of about 13,000 square kilometres. They were slow to spread at first, but by the turn of the century they were gaining ground rapidly. The map of the known spread of foxes in Australia (Figure 3) is based on information derived mainly from Rolls's enquiries. According to Talbot (1906), two dog foxes and one vixen were introduced into Australia by a George Watson for the Melbourne Hunt, but when this was done is not recorded.

The Australian desert seemed to be no barrier to the spread of foxes westwards, and the first records of foxes having reached western Australia was in 1916 at Esperance on the southern coast. From there on they spread rather more slowly through western Australia, but their numbers began to cause some alarm among sheep rearers and over a period of thirty years, following the introduction of a bounty in 1929, 893,000 foxes were killed in western Australia alone. Payments were discontinued in 1960, because the bounty was not having the desired effect of limiting the distribution and numbers of foxes (Crawford and Veitch, 1959).

The introduction of the fox into Australia may have done more harm to Australia's native fauna than to the sheep industry, and many consider that it has had a greater impact on Australian fauna than the dingo, which was probably also introduced. Foxes were absent from Tasmania. In New Zealand an Act of 1867 wisely prohibited their import.

The enormous geographical range of the fox (Figure 2) is an indication of the adaptability of an unspecialized mammal. Its ability to live in the barren tundra of the northern latitudes, in deserts, in mountains up to 4,200m, in densely populated agricultural areas and in towns is not due entirely to its way of life and physiological adaptations, but partly to its size. A smaller animal than the fox would not have the mobility necessary for survival in barren lands or in near-desert conditions, and a larger carnivore would have problems in obtaining food in populated places, because it would probably need to take larger items of food, thus attracting the attention of man. Its large size would make concealment difficult and would adversely affect its survival. In areas of deep winter snows the fox is able to move through soft snow by virtue of its long legs and physical strength, yet it is light enough to walk on thinly frozen snow.

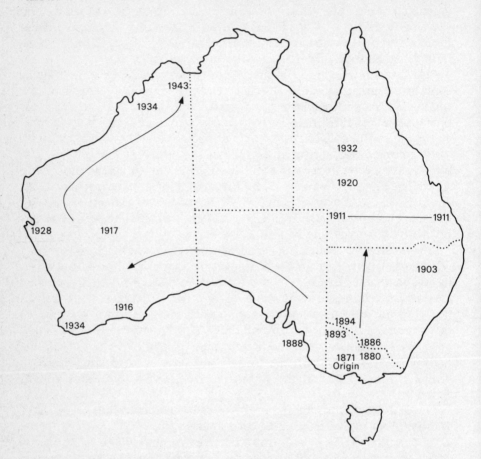

**3**   Spread of the fox in Australia

If, as suggested by Churcher (1959), the North American red fox, *Vulpes fulva*, is not a different species but yet another race or sub-species, its distribution in North America has to be mentioned. Twelve races have been described. Foxes from Britain introduced to Maryland in the middle of the eighteenth century and later to Long Island, New Jersey, Virginia and other eastern States may have had some influence on the genotype that exists there today. Whilst it was, and still sometimes is, the practice to translocate foxes to augment numbers and to provide better sport, there is considerable anecdotal evidence to suggest that these introductions were not made to supplement native fox stocks but to establish foxes in areas where they were absent.

Seton (1929) examined historical evidence of the distribution of the native red fox in North America and concluded that it was common north of latitudes 40°–45°N but scarce in unbroken forests south of these latitudes. As woodlands were felled in eastern areas and gave way to agriculture, the successfully introduced European red fox spread westwards until it encountered the range of the native red fox, probably south of the great lakes. Archaeological evidence shows that the native fox was present in large numbers in Ontario just prior to and during the introductions of the European form in the east, in the middle of the eighteenth century (Gilmore, 1946, 1949; Peterson *et al.*, 1953), but the southernmost limit of the range of the native fox at that time is not known. The North American red fox now extends from the coast of the eastern states to the western seaboard, with the exception of southern Florida, most of Arizona and a band roughly north–south from Alberta in Canada, through much of Montana, down to north-west Texas and Mexico. Seton suggested in 1929 that the distribution of the red fox in North America was still increasing, and certainly in the North West Territories of Canada it has continued to spread over the last fifty years. During that time its range has extended to Baffin Island and, in 1962, northwards across the ocean ice to Ellesmere Island (about 76°N) (Macpherson, 1964). As with many northern mammals, the red fox in Canada shows cyclical fluctuations in numbers, with a periodicity of about ten years south of the taiga (tree belt) (for example, Cross, 1940) and four years in the taiga and tundra (Butler, 1947). The red fox occurs throughout most other mainland areas of North America, but is absent from Greenland.

In South America no foxes of the genus *Vulpes* occur, but its place is taken by other canids. Most of these are solitary species and resemble foxes more than dogs in behaviour and appearance.

Two nearly related species of animals occupying similar kinds of niches do not usually compete with each other for the main essential of life, food. In recent years, however, there have been reports from northern Russia (Skrobov, 1960) of the retreat of the arctic fox with the northward advance of the red fox. Skrobov felt that the red fox was competing with the arctic fox, especially for its denning places in the tundra, but Chirkova (1967) suggests that the amelioration of the climate in the north has affected the distribution and numbers of the two main species of prey and that competition is not involved. The arctic fox preys predominantly on the tundra lemmings, whilst the red fox feeds predominantly on the vole *Microtus*. The warming of the arctic climate has permitted a northward extension of some southern plants, and there is a consequent shift in the distribution of rodent species, with *Microtus* extending further north. The change in distribution of the two fox species is a result of this shift in the prey species, a good illustration of the dynamic instability of the ecology of mammals.

### Distribution in Britain

Foxes are found almost throughout the British Isles. Apart from the mainland, they are present on the Isle of Wight, Anglesey, Skye, sometimes Scalpay and other small islands like Eilean Shona which lies close to the mainland, but not on the Orkneys, Shetlands or the Isle of Man, or on other islands. On Scalpay, separated from Skye at low water by some 150 metres of water, eleven foxes, all males, were killed in six years in the 1960s. They are numerous on Skye and the Isle of Wight.

The fox situation on Anglesey is interesting. Foxes were present there, and subject to the Church-administered bounties, as elsewhere in England and Wales, until some time in the nineteenth century. There was also at least one private pack of foxhounds there in the middle 1800s. For unknown reasons foxes died out in the last century and the island was free of foxes until 1960, when three were released near Holyhead Island in August. In the following year there were complaints of damage to poultry, which Henry Lloyd Owen, the then Pests Officer recognized as characteristic of fox. Within three weeks he had killed one vixen, two adult dog foxes and a litter of seven cubs near Valley. Nothing further was heard of foxes on Anglesey until 1967, when there were further complaints of poultry losses, this time near Mynydd Parys at Rhosybol; again the damage was characteristic of fox. A vixen and seven cubs were killed. Eight well defined placental scars were visible in the uterus of the vixen, which suggested that one cub (almost ten weeks old) was still at large. It was not found. A second litter was located at Mynydd Parys and destroyed – but this left at least one adult vixen, one cub and one dog fox. There were strong indications that foxes had been released in the previous year in the derelict copper mines in the Parys area, but how many is not known. No further reports of foxes were received until May 1968, when two litters were again found at Mynydd Parys and another near Llanelian. A dog fox and two vixens were shot. One was a yearling (the missing cub from 1967?), the other an older one.

The yearling had been killed with seven cubs, and my examination of the uterus revealed that she had given birth to seven cubs, so none was missing. The other vixen had given birth to nine cubs, but only five had been killed. A further search secured two more cubs nearby, but two others remained outstanding. Of the litter at Llanelian only one cub was killed. Thus at the end of June there were at least two cubs, part of a litter of cubs of unknown number, one adult vixen and at least one dog fox still alive in the area, altogether possibly between nine and thirteen foxes.

In November 1968 foxhounds hunted the north-west part of the island in an attempt to rid it of foxes, but none was killed. Fox pad marks were found at Dulas and a dead fox was found in a nearby disused mine shaft (into which the huntsman's terrier also accidentally fell). In 1969 a fox was found dead on the road at the other side of the island at Brynsiencyn. Fifteen more foxes were killed in the north-west sector of the island in 1970 and 1971, and six near Llangefni, some sixteen kilometres distant. In 1973 over 100 foxes were killed, all north of a line from Pentraeth to Malltraeth, but sitings had been reported to the south of this line. In 1974 over 340 adult and juvenile foxes are known to have been killed on Anglesey, and few parts of the island are now free of foxes. The island provides a very suitable habitat for them, and all seems ready for a rapid expansion of numbers. Since 1973 farmers have vigorously attempted to reduce the number of foxes, but more are being killed each year and a climax level of population does not yet (1979) appear to have been reached. Foxes are common on the Caernarvonshire shore of the Menai Straits, even near the two bridges linking Anglesey to the mainland, and it is odd that they did not colonize the island sooner unaided. (In 1971, a fox was seen on the middle span of the Severn Bridge over the Bristol Channel.)

Foxes were scarce in some parts of Britain in the 1920–55 period. Middleton reported that foxes were scarce in Norfolk in 1935. They were absent from Gilbraltar Point (A. E. Smith, pers. comm.) and scarce throughout much of north Pembrokeshire from 1920 to 1955. They were almost unknown in the Lleyn Peninsula of Caernarvonshire up to the 1950s, and in Scotland, Hewson and Kolb (1973) have shown that they were absent from many coastal areas of Aberdeenshire, Kincardineshire, Banff and Nairn before 1955–60.

At the present time foxes are becoming common and locally numerous in Norfolk and Suffolk. From 1911 to 1955 in Pembrokeshire a flourishing commercial rabbit-trapping industry all but eliminated foxes in the northern part of the county, where rabbit trappers used to be engaged annually on almost every holding. The rabbiters set traps to catch foxes and buzzards in order to prevent the mutilation of trapped rabbits, because at that time mutilated and dogged rabbits fetched lower prices. Open trapping (that is, the setting of gin traps just outside the rabbit burrow, but not within the overhang of the burrow entrances, which was legally permitted only during the war years 1939–45) also intercepted foxes visiting rabbit burrows. There was little need to set traps specifically for foxes after the early part of the 1920s when 'a pair of foxes per parish' summed up the situation. The advent of myxomatosis in

1954 put an end to the rabbit-trapping industry and foxes (and badgers) were left in peace. In 1960 foxes were reported to be common throughout the county, including the northern part, and by 1962 they were exceedingly numerous. They seemed to reach a peak in 1965–6 and appear to have declined slightly since then – possibly because action is being taken by many farmers to contain their numbers, but perhaps also for some other, natural reason.

In Scotland much the same pattern of spread was reported by Hewson and Kolb,(1973) but they assigned an increase in food supply as the cause – see page 198. They reported that foxes were to be found throughout much of Scotland except parts of the counties of Aberdeen, Kincardine, Banff, Moray, Nairn and Ross and Cromarty. In the first three of the counties mentioned foxes were known to have been killed in 54 out of a total of 123 parishes between 1959 and 1961. From 1967 to 1971 foxes were killed in 117 of these parishes, and in Moray and Nairn there had been a spread towards the coast. Furthermore, foxes were recorded throughout many parts of Ross and Cromarty where they had been absent previously. Movement of foxes into the Black Isle was reported in 1962, and their numbers reached a peak in 1970. Further north, foxes have not been reported from Nigg to Tarbat Ness and, according to Hewson and Kolb, this is now the largest fox-free area of Scotland. They are also absent from a few coastal parishes of Nairn, Moray and Kincardineshire.

Most cities are not without their foxes. W. G. Teagle (1967), in a thorough survey of the distribution of foxes throughout much of Greater London from 1959 to 1965, showed that foxes were very common in suburban areas but were also to be found comparatively near to the geographical centre of Teagle's study area, St Paul's Cathedral. Several foxes were seen at Greenwich port, and three were shot there in 1965. Foxes were also reported to be present regularly at Highgate and Leyton. The old cemetery at Highgate still seems to be attractive to foxes, and their diggings there reportedly sometimes bring long-buried human bones to the surface. Railway embankments and cuttings in Greater London provide foxes not only with places of refuge but also with easy travelling routes along the railways, and it is very likely that foxes seen near central London – in Hyde Park and along South Lambeth Road, for example – found their way along these avenues. Built-up areas are not, it seems, unsuitable habitats for foxes, providing there is cover for them in the daytime (see Appendix 4). Waste ground, hospital and factory grounds, cemeteries, allotments, household gardens, and so on, also provide this cover. Parks are not usually so attractive, since they provide little cover, but if suitable daytime harbourage is situated nearby, foxes will often use park land at night. (A friend who walks his dog in a Surrey park tells me that he and his dog are often

stalked by a fox who follows and watches them at distance of about 10l
metres.)

Foxes are common in the outer suburban fringe, in such areas as
Bromley, Croydon, Chessington, Hillingdon, Barnet and Chigwell, and
by all accounts they are not uncommon nearer to London at such places
as Wimbledon and Hampstead, where they seem to have been present
for many years. Teagle's account of suburban foxes gives a good insight
into their way of life in close proximity to man, and he recounts some
amusing encounters between fox and man, such as that concerning a fox
which leapt off an electricity transformer when someone, who had mistaken it for a large ginger cat, tried to stroke it. Beames (1972) tells of a
family of suburban fox cubs which played with a small girl in her
garden, and of a fox which stole oven-ready chickens from an early
morning delivery van. (The urban fox's traditional fare remains the
same as its country cousins', though pre-packed, oven-ready and
wrapped.)

Other large conurbations in Britain also have their foxes. Bristol has
its share, as have Bournemouth, Nottingham and Birmingham. Indeed,
for a large town or city to be without foxes anywhere within its limits is
the exception rather than the rule. However, there are fewer reports of
urban foxes at the present time, from about Nottingham northwards,
though they are common in the suburbs of Glasgow and Edinburgh.


## Description of the Fox

The caricaturist's outline of the fox is unmistakable – the long, bushy
tail, slender muzzle and pricked ears and, viewed head on, the slanting,
expressionless eyes and the somewhat inflated white bib at throat and
neck. These features need little exaggeration by the artist if the intention
is to suggest slyness or cunning, yet the impression inevitably is one of
daintiness, a feature characteristic of all species of fox.

In Britian the fox is considered one of the larger mammals, but in
reality its appearance often belies its small physical dimensions. Some of
the smaller adult vixens weigh only slightly more than a large brown
hare, and the long, lean carcase of a fox, as seen on the dissecting table,
seems disproportionately small for the enormous store of energy and
stamina with which the fox is endowed.


### Body proportions
The external conformation and basic skeletal characteristics of all canids
are very similar. However, the relative proportions of the skeletal units
such as the tail, limbs or neck vary from one species to another; these

differences have probably evolved in most cases through the process of natural selection, as adaptive features which have enabled the animal to exploit its environment to greater advantage. The adaptive significance of such features as the short length of the neck in the arctic fox relative to the length of its spine (as compared with other canids) is not demonstrated as readily as the adaptive function of the length of the neck of the giraffe, for example. With the evolution of overall body size, some features such as the limbs, spine or head may have assumed different proportions in the evolved form, because all elements may not grow at the same rate. If the human ear grew from infancy at the same rate as the femur, the adult would have ears like Snow White's seven companions, but the ear has a lower rate of growth than the femur. Any feature with a higher or lower rate of growth than others shows an increasing disproportion as the animal increases in size. Thus it is difficult to determine whether it is change in body size alone which is adaptive, or change in proportion, or both. This is especially true in the case of the canids, since the differences in proportion in most species are rather slight. Milton Hildebrand (1952) examined the body proportions of eighteen living and one extinct canid species to elucidate the differences in body proportions and to examine their possible adaptive significance. He showed that generally those with longer legs were better runners, with the exception of the maned wolf of South America (*Chrysocyon*), which has enormously long legs, enabling it to exploit small prey in long pampas grass. The red fox does not appear to have any exceptional proportions, but its fore- and hindleg lengths relative to the length of its spine are greater than those of most species, suggesting swiftness and endurance. Its tail, however, is exceptionally long and might be an adaptation to facilitate balance and turning capacity when hot in pursuit of small, elusive prey. The tail length of the red fox is 70 per cent of that of the head and body, and in the wolf (*Canis lupus*), jackal and arctic fox the proportions are 28 per cent, 24 per cent and 53 per cent respectively.

### Size and weight

Linear dimensions of foxes in England, Wales, Scotland and Northern Ireland are shown in Table 1. These data suggest that the Irish foxes are larger than all others in the United Kingdom, but the body weights given in Table 2 show that Scottish foxes, and perhaps those of the fells of Cumberland, are heavier than others. In addition to having the largest body frame of British foxes examined, the Irish fox is also distinguished by having a shorter tail. Skull measurements of samples of English, Welsh and Scottish foxes are shown in Table 3.

Mean live weights of foxes in Europe, Australia and North America are shown in Table 2. Compared with the Scottish fox, the North American fox is very small. Seton (1929) affirmed that foxes of the northern latitudes of North America are larger than those of the central states, the fox of Alaska reputedly being the largest, but no data are available to support this possible example of Bergmann's rule, which states that individuals of particular species increase in size with increase in latitude. It is quite clear that in Britain foxes collected from three distinct areas of Scotland are the largest and those of Wales probably the smallest. Tetley (1941) recognized that the Scottish fox was larger than the English fox by linear dimensions and by weight. He considered it to be very similar to the Scandinavian fox on these counts and in similarities of tooth form, and for these reasons Tetley suggested that the Scottish fox should be regarded as *Vulpes vulpes vulpes*, the type species described by Linnaeus in Scandinavia. Norwegian foxes, however, are significantly smaller than the Scottish fox (see Table 2); thus evidence of lumping the Scottish fox together with the Scandinavian fox is rather doubtful, though foxes in Denmark are indeed very large. Hattingh (1956) considered that the Scottish fox, as a race, should be distinguished from the English fox. Until more data on body size and other features of foxes in different parts of Britain, Scandinavia and Central Europe are available, further consideration of possible relationships cannot be undertaken.

It is not known if there is a cline or gradient of body size and weight from Scotland to lowland or southern England, but in Wales there seems to be a gradient of increasing weights of male and female foxes from Pembrokeshire into the five Welsh counties lying to the west and northwest (see Table 4). Unfortunately, linear body dimensions were not recorded for foxes from all six counties, so it is not known whether these body weights represent inherited differences or are due to such environmental features as population density or food abundance. Samples comprising the heavier foxes (Montgomery and Radnorshire) were not collected exclusively from hill land (which is extensive in these counties but of negligible proportions in Pembrokeshire), and in spite of affirmations by countrymen that hill foxes in Wales are larger, the available evidence suggests the hill foxes may be smaller than those caught in the valleys. But since the mean distances dispersed by juvenile males in mid-Wales is 13.7km, most foxes born on the hills are well within dispersal distance of lowland areas, as the topography is highly variable, unlike much of the hill land of Scotland. Huson and Page (in press) have examined the linear dimensions of skull features of my sample of Welsh foxes and, whilst they are unable to confirm a cline from Pembrokeshire to Montgomeryshire and Radnor, the indications are that there are significant differences in some of the dimensions of skulls of foxes between those of the six counties. They suggest that ecological features determine the differences.

Much was made in the older literature of the claim that the so-called bulldog, mastiff and greyhound foxes owed their shape to their habitat, but there is little evidence to substantiate, for example, that the hill fox (greyhound) is more slender and longer in the leg than the foxes occupying lowland areas in the same locality. Certainly foxes, like dogs (even pedigree breeds), show variations in the shape of the head, such that to the experienced observer even a small modification in the length and breadth of the muzzle or angle of the brow alters the proportions of the head significantly. Observers with a keen eye for conformation may indeed see small differences in proportion which may be overlooked by the biologist measuring dimensions with a caliper gauge. To the shepherd every ewe may be individually recognizable, but the caliper gauge will merely record distinctions as falling within a range of variability. I will not dispute the possibility that foxes from Kent differ in appearance from Hampshire foxes, even if they have similar dimensions. There is also a firmly held belief that coat colour varies with habitat, the colour becoming lighter with elevation. In Breconshire it is claimed that dark foxes are forest-bred and the 'light' forms hill-bred. Again, there is no strong evidence to support these beliefs, and the known origins of tagged foxes recovered by hunters have often confounded expectation, as has been the case with the estimated age of tagged foxes. One fox 'without a tooth in his head', reckoned to be very old by the successful hunter, was tagged as a cub nineteen months earlier! ('Stump-bred' is a term applied in the older hunting literature to cubs born on the surface of the ground, under roots, in tree stumps, among gorse, and so forth. These were considered to be strong, healthy foxes and fleet of foot.)

Table 5 shows the monthly mean body weights of male foxes. Although the weights of foxes in smaples from south-east England and Wales are identical, there may be local differences in weight from north to south Kent, as there are between the Welsh counties mentioned earlier. Huson and Page (1979) found differences in skull dimensions between foxes from Wales and south-east England. Weights increase with age, as indicated in Table 6.

A large Scottish fox weighing 8.6kg, examined by Dr L. Harrison Matthews in 1951, confirmed his opinion that Tetley's views (1941) of the sub-specific status of the Scottish fox was correct. However, many heavier foxes have been found in England which could have been the progeny of Scottish foxes translocated for hunting, although heavy foxes have also been recorded in Wales, where it is unlikely that Scottish or any other foxes were introduced. For example, among a total of 463 male foxes from Wales, seven weighed over 9.1kg, the largest being 10.1kg.

Birger Jensen of the Game Biology Station, Denmark, found in a sample of 252 male foxes with an average weight of 7.6kg that twenty-eight weighed 9kg and over, eight weighed 9.5kg and over and the heaviest was 10.6kg. He also showed that the weights of adult foxes increased with age, at least up to two years of age (see Table 7).

In 1971 Ian Gray (personal communication) examined a sample of foxes from Cumberland, weighed them carefully on accurate balances and found the mean weights of a sample smaller than that examined for Scotland by Kolb and Hewson (1974) to be higher than those of Scottish foxes (see Table 2). The Cumberland sample may be representative of fell foxes killed by foot packs — in this case, the Bewcastle Hunt.

Sporting literature and journals record foxes weighing up to 14.9kg, but since one cannot be sure of the accuracy of the scales used and of the distinction between fact and fiction, the reports are not perpetuated here.

Weight is the criterion of size most frequently adopted, but it should be related to linear measurements in order to establish a factor representing the conformation or condition of the sample, in much the same way as is done for salmon. The factor derived by dividing the metric weight by the head and body length suggests that in addition to being the heaviest, the Scottish fox has a higher weight/length factor than other foxes in Britain (see Table 8), whereas the Irish fox, in spite of its heavy weight, seems to be leaner than foxes from the other regions.

**The coat**
There is much individual variation in coat colour in the red fox, even between litter mates. The general impression of the coat colour of foxes can vary from yellow to a rather rare, fiery henna red, and the underparts from white to black flecked with white or grey. The commonest colour impression, however, is yellowish-brown with grey-white underparts. Despite individual differences in colour, most foxes conform to a pattern of coat variation on different parts of the body.

The dense underfur, fibres of which are about 35mm long on the back and sides, is grey in colour throughout the pelage, but the terminal quarter of each fibre is reddish-brown. The overfur, or guard hair coat, which conceals the underfur and imparts coat colour to mammals, consists of hair fibres of different colour conformations on different parts of the body. Although of different lengths, guard hairs from the muzzle, over the head and neck to the loins are basically similar in colour pattern but vary in tone. The basal half of these hairs is grey or black, sometimes with pure white bases near the skin, and the terminal part is brown. Fibres from the mid-dorsal line from the nape to the loins, in a band about 76mm wide, and in a transverse band about 50mm wide across the shoulders, are darker in colour at the tips; these impart the characteristic darker red cross seen in prepared skins of red foxes. The guard hairs of the loins, rump and upper thighs are light or dark grey for three-quarters of their length; the terminal quarter is clear white, tipped with a short length of brown, sometimes running to black. The inclusion of the band of white in those hairs imparts the grizzled appearance of the coat in these regions – and the degree of difference between this and other regions of the coat depends upon the length of the white band in relation to the brownish terminal portion. These guard hairs also differ in shape from the others, the white portion being flattened in section, while the grey and brown portions are cylindrical, as in other guard hairs, and their set is such that the broad aspect of the flattened white band lies flat against the fur and thus exposes the most white. The fur of the flanks is lighter in colour than that of the back. The softer fur of the under parts is a mixture of all-grey fibres and those which are white-tipped. The inner aspects of the legs are white. The feet and the backs of the ears are black, and in most foxes a stripe of black fur extends on either side of the muzzle from in front of the eyes downwards towards the whiskers of the upper lip. A band of white extends from the nose along the upper lip to the throat, and the lower jaw is also white, or grey in dark forms. The most emphatic markings of the fox are on the head, face and neck.

The tail is a thick, quiver-shaped brush up to about 130mm in diameter when the dense fur is erect, and it is about two-fifths of the total length of the animal. The tip of the tail of either sex usually contains some white fibres. The remainder of the tail fur is a mixture of grey, brown and black and tends to vary greatly in colour from one individual to another. A spiral of light and dark bands is often seen in mounted fox tails; this is an artefact, brought about by the accidental twisting of the tail during mounting and is not found on the living animal. The guard hairs of the tail are longer than those on any other part of the body. On the upper surface of the tail, about 50mm from its root, lies the supra-caudal gland beneath the surface of the skin. The lozenge-shaped glandular area is devoid of underfur, and the guard hairs have thick white shanks for about a third of their length, running to black at their tips. The white tail tag is seldom longer than 100mm in British foxes, and few are without some white fibres at the tail tip. Both sexes can have large white tips. Although it is a variable feature, several writers have suggested that a distinctly marked tail tip may assist the young to follow their parents in the dark or in long grass. Others have suggested, since the tail is used in social signalling, that a tag is advantageous. If it is an advantage, it is clearly not essential, as many foxes have insignificant white tips.

In the breeding season the fur of the belly of most vixens assumes a pinkish-brown colour before and after parturition. In lactating females the underfur of the belly is lost and the naked skin becomes reddish-brown in colour. (The belly fur of some males also assumes a reddish hue at this time.) The belly fur of vixens is not plucked to line a nest, as is the case with rabbits, but falls out and is removed by grooming.

The intensity of black at the backs of the ears and feet varies, though the common black ankle socks are sometimes very pronounced and may extend on the forward edges of the legs up to the elbow.

Variations in the basic fur colour pattern are considerable. At one extreme, colours are diluted in light sandy-coloured foxes. Black hairs may be present, but the normally dark brown portions of the hair fibres are pale yellow throughout. The grizzled fur of the loins and rump varies according to the extent of the white band of the guard hairs. All-white foxes occasionally occur in Britain, but none of the descriptions recorded mentions the pigmentation of the eye; doubtless true albinos occur from time to time. (Talbot, 1906, records the killing of a pure white fox by the Garth Hounds near Virginia Water in the late nineteenth century.) White flashes on the forelimbs are not uncommon; occasionally a flash may extend up and over one or both of the forequarters. White stars on the forehead and on the point of the chest, present in some cubs, only rarely persist in adults. At the other extreme, exceedingly dark foxes, with scarcely a white fibre, have more black than usual in the terminal part of the guard hairs and a greater number of all-black hairs throughout the coat, especially in the tail.

Dark-coloured foxes occur in Britain, but truly black ones have not been recorded. Melanistic (black) variants of the red fox do occur naturally, however, in some parts of North America, Russia and, where the progeny of imported North American foxes have been released, in Scandinavia. Depending on the degree of blackness, these colour forms are known as black, silver or cross foxes. (Silver and black foxes were bred extensively in captivity when these furs were fashionable, but today no silver fox farms exist in Britain.) The black fox has a very high proportion of black in the guard-hair fibres, and those of the silver fox, in addition to a great deal of black, have white tips which impart a silvery appearance to the pelt. The white tail tip and any white on the belly remains in the melanistic forms, while the red, brown or yellow parts of the fibres are replaced by black. The pelts vary in quality according to the uniformity of the fibre colour types throughout the pelt. The silveriness extends from the rump forwards; a so-called quarter silver fox would have this condition on the rump only. A cross fox is a partial melanistic form of an otherwise red fox, in which the guard hairs over the shoulder and in the mid-dorsal line are much darker, as in the black fox, sometimes with white tips to the fibres. This form has a well-defined cross of black fur about 50—75mm wide over the shoulders. These variants are unknown in Britain, but a cross of darker, richer fibres over the shoulders is usual in British and European foxes.

The colour phases are determined by two genes, which combine in a two-factor type of inheritance (Warwick and Hanson, 1937), as shown below:

| Red | Cross | Silver |
|---|---|---|
| *Red* | *Cross* | *Silver* |
| AA BB red | Aa BB | AA bb aa BB |
| AA Bb smoky red | Aa Bb | Aa bb aa Bb |
| | | aabb |

The extent of silveriness is determined by the five genotypes, aa bb being the form selectively bred on fur farms to give maximum silver in the pelt. See Robinson (1975) for a review of fox genetics.

The occurrences of melanistic variants in the wild in North America is well documented in the records of the Hudson's Bay Company. In Labrador, for example, the proportion of silver foxes fell steadily from 16 per cent in the period 1834–1923 to just over 5 per cent in 1924–33 (Elton, 1942). Butler (1945) has shown that the decline continued in Alberta, from 7 per cent in 1916 to 3 per cent in 1944 – a mean reduction in the proportion of silver foxes of 0.23 per cent each year. The decline in melanistic forms is due to changes in natural selection operating through differential fertility, but Calhoun (1950) found no differences in the fertility (mean litter sizes) of the three maternal colour forms. Calhoun suggests that there is a mutual antagonism between genes a and b and that this may be manifested in differential survival of the genotypes *in utero*. Haldane's (1942) suggestion that selective shooting of the more valuable silver forms may be the cause of the decline does not appear to be an acceptable explanation of the change in proportion of the colour forms. Calhoun's alternative hypothesis is based on the post-glacial dilution of a predominantly melanistic northern form through the spread of southern red foxes, and on intra-uterine competition between the three genotypes. A comprehensive account of the genetics of colour forms and other features is given by Robinson (1975).

There is seasonal variation in the coat colour of foxes, the pelts being richer in autumn and winter and paler in late spring and summer. In summer the texture of the coat is coarser to the touch. There is also some variation in texture between individuals. The winter coats of some foxes are of a smooth, silky texture, which is associated with longer guard hairs, while others have short hairs which tend to be rougher and coarser. In cold climates guard hairs grow to a greater length and are smoother in texture than the hairs found in pelts of foxes living in warmer, wetter climates.

The coat colour of a fox may also change as it ages. Some writers allege that old foxes are lighter in colour, others that the black parts of the fibres assume a dark red tinge. Light and dark grey spots, or flecks, however, are found in both juvenile and older animals. Some have suggested that small white spots may be caused by ticks, but this has not been established. Coat colour cannot be used as a criterion of age, since there is so much individual variation even among juvenile and prime animals.

The whiskers, or vibrissae, of the fox are black. Those on the muzzle, the mystaciae vibrissae, are 100—110mm long, which gives a total span, including the snout, of about 255–280mm (greater than the width of the body). Other vibrissae on the head are shorter. A small number of vibrissae (carpal vibrissae) also occur on the forelimbs, slightly higher than the first digit. They point backwards and downwards and are up to 40mm long. Hildebrand (1952) has shown that the length of the muzzle vibrissae and the carpal vibrissae in different species of North American canids (kit fox, grey fox, red fox, coyote and wolf) are in inverse proportion to the size of the body – the longest being found in the kit fox and the shortest in the wolf – which suggests that these vibrissae are of greater importance to the way of life of the smaller canids than to that of the larger coyotes and wolves.

The set, or the slope, of the fur conforms to a pattern liable only to slight variation, in the position of the whorl, or cross, formed by converging slopes at the point of the chest, between the forelimbs, Figure 4. In newborn cubs each fur fibre emerges from a single simple follicle, and most of these fibres become the underfur of the older juvenile. In addition, a sparse covering of longer, slightly stiffer fibres is found, but I have not been able to follow the subsequent fate of these. At this time the fur has a woolly appearance and has no set to it. At about eight weeks of age additional fibres emerge from the follicles, and in the older juvenile and adult the guard hairs and the underfur fibres emerge from compound follicles, up to twenty underfur fibres being associated with each guard hair. The skin of the young fox soon develops creases and the set of the hair fibres, which emerge from the follicles located in the folds of the skin (crypts), is determined by the direction of the folding of the skin. Each hair bundle of the compound follicles is elevated by minute arrector pili muscles, which in cold conditions contract, causing the fur to stand up, thus increasing the thermal insulation.

MOULT    The fox moults only once a year. The coat is at its best in winter from November to February, for colour, lustre, density and insulation. In April and May the old coat begins to shed, first at the feet, then at the fore- and hindlegs. As the moult progresses from the hindlimbs over the rump to the abdomen and along the back, the underfur is shed in advance of the guard hairs and, particularly on the belly, it is shed freely. A sparse covering of the old guard hairs remains until

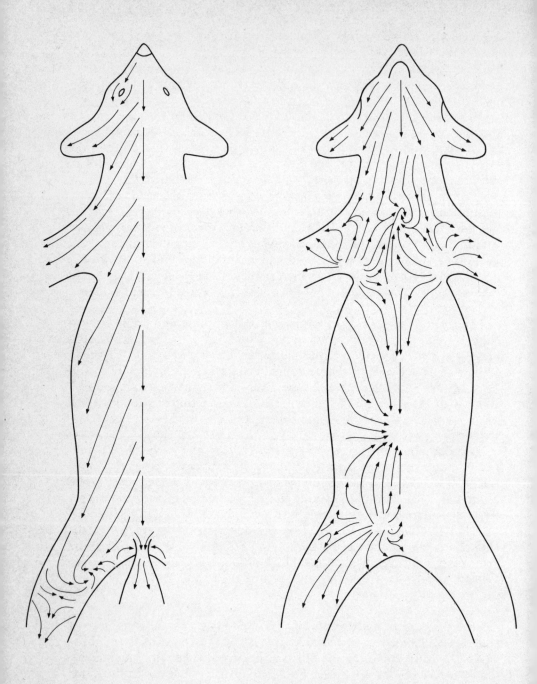

**4** Hair slope of the fox modelled on a diagram by Hildebrand (1952)

August, when both new and old guard hairs are present. The moult reaches the head and face just after the tail underfur has been lost. In July the animal is slender, with a thin, incipient covering of underfur and a sparse covering of old guard hairs which are replaced rapidly by new growth. By the end of September all old hairs have been lost and the new coat rapidly lengthens and thickens until mid-October when the coat is approaching prime condition. From April or early May the inner layers of the skin begin to show the dark blue coloration in the regions where moult is progressing (not visible externally), but by mid-October the skin begins to assume a creamy-white colour characteristic of animals whose hair has ceased to grow.

Moult is controlled by the endocrine glands, which are dominated in turn by external factors related to the time of year. Thus artificially increased day length from 3 May for thirty days will speed up moult and produce prime silver fox pelts one month earlier (in the autumn) than is usual in the wild (Bassett, 1946). If day length is increased from 1–16 May and decreased thereafter, prime pelt condition may be reached some two months earlier, since an increase in day length hastens the shedding of the old coat and a decrease in day length hastens the growth of the new. With cubs, the artificially accelerated shortening of day length from the summer solstice has been found to accelerate the growth of new fur.

### Heat conservation

The conservation and dissipation of heat present anatomical and physiological problems for mammals living in climatic extremes and for those subject to sudden changes in activity and to short-term changes in the temperature of the environment.

The red fox in northern latitudes is subjected to intense cold in the winter months but it is so well protected by its fur that it runs the risk of suffering from over-heating (by intense exertion, for example) rather than from the cold. According to Scholander *et al.* (1950), the arctic fox does not even need to shiver when the temperature is about minus 40°C; the insulation of its winter coat is so good that above this temperature it needs to pant to prevent over-heating.

The Fennec fox of the north African desert has avoided the problem of living in the open in the heat of the midday sun – unlike one metaphorical race of canids – by adopting an entirely nocturnal habit. In the cold of the desert nights its fur protects it, whilst in the heat of the day it withdraws to the shelter of burrows or rocks. It is unlikely that the red fox has the same physiological adaptation to arid environments as the Fennec. One of the water conservation adaptations of the latter is its ability to achieve a high concentration of urea in its urine, leaving a favourable balance of water to be used for thermo-regulation by panting.

The fundamental property of fur is to hold a layer of inert air close to the skin; the volume and stillness of air held – a property of the density of the fur – will determine the degree of insulation. Compressed porous material has poorer insulating properties than expanded material. Scholander and his colleagues, while examining the heat-conservation properties of mammalian fur, showed that the relationship between the thickness of the fur layer and thermal insulation is approximately linear. There are exceptions to this, for example in the seal, polar and grizzly bear, whose fur has greater insulation properties than are warranted by its thickness. The superior thermal insulation of these animals is emulated, in descending order, by arctic fox, caribou, red fox, beaver, rabbit (species not defined), marten, lemming and squirrel, weasel and shrew.

Thermal insulation properties depend upon the season of the year and the geographical origin of the mammals, however – particularly the fur-bearing ones – since, as has been mentioned elsewhere, the fur of the red fox in winter in northern Sweden is thicker than that of foxes in the Mediterranean countries. In addition, fat, skin and muscle also provide insulation, in the ratio of 3:2:1.

Shivering in resting furred animals warms the skin and protective layer of inert air and so helps to keep the animal warm. Air trapped in the fur is held within the layer of dense underfur, the guard hairs lying closely over the underfur to reduce heat loss by restricting the movement of the trapped air. The mechanics of this appears to be the attraction of the guard hairs to the lower fur layers by static electrical charges. The arrector pili muscles which elevate the hair of the compound follicles – thus increasing the volume of air that can be held in the fur – will only influence the lower portion of the guard hairs over most of the body of foxes, the upper portion of the guard hairs being closely applied to the underfur. In addition, heat loss can be regulated by readjusting the peripheral blood flow to less well insulated parts of the body, such as the legs and the ears. In a resting fox the tail may be curled over the feet and muzzle to provide some protection to these extremities which are not well endowed with thick fur.

The area of the heat conducting surface, the skin, is relatively smaller the larger the animal; Bergmann's rule, which applies especially well to birds, states that within species or between closely related species individuals in the colder regions have a greater body size than those in warmer areas. In central Europe the fox, roe deer and wolf increase in size towards the north-east and decrease to the south-west. But there are exceptions to this, as for example, between Britain and Norway (British foxes tending to be larger) and within Sweden, where the northern foxes are smaller. In keeping with Bergmann's rule it is interesting to note that mammals of cold climates show a decrease in the area of their heat-radiating extremities – the ears and tail; this is known as Allen's rule. The ears of brown bears, for example, become shorter towards the north. In the three species of foxes, arctic, red and Fennec, there is an enormous difference in size of ears and tails – those of the first being the smallest, and those of the Fennec the largest.

## The glands of the skin

The sebaceous and apocrine glands associated with the hair bundles serve to keep the skin and hair pliable and to protect them from both desiccation and saturation. These glands are not homologous with the sweat glands of man. Those of the fox are classed as apocrine because of their fatty secretion, which is formed partly through the breakdown of the gland cells. In man the secretion is watery and is produced by merocrine-type glands which secrete without concomitant cell breakdown. It assists in the thermo-regulation of the body, whereas in foxes the secretion functions only as a lubricant. (It may also impart a scent peculiar to each individual fox, but there is no evidence to suggest that this is so.)

The sebaceous glands secrete a lipid mixture rich in cholesterol, a precursor of vitamin D. Whether or not this is of importance to the fox as a source of this vitamin is not known. The fox probably gets as much as it needs from the skin and fur of its prey.

The heavily cornified skin of the foot pads of the fox contains true merocrine sweat glands, but I do not know if these serve any purpose associated with scent. Many biologists refer to scent glands located in the pit which lies in front of the large central foot pads. Some assert that these are found on the hindfeet only, but Peter Flood (pers. comm.), who has found well defined sebaceous glands in the inter-digital region of both fore and hind pads could not, on purely histological grounds, decide whether or not these glands function as scent glands.

Circumoral glands on the lips are apocrine and sebaceous and are probably of use for lubrication only.

THE TAIL GLAND   This gland, also known as the dorsal tail gland and supracaudal gland, lies about 75mm from the root of the tail, on its upper surface and in the region of the fifth caudal vertebra. Its position is not conspicuous, but it can usually be located by the small patch of black hair fibres which overlie it. This dark patch is almost always quite distinct in juveniles up to six or seven months old but becomes less marked in many older animals. The gland, oval in shape and about 25mm long by 13mm wide, lies within the dermis and subcutaneous tissue, and it comes away with the skin when the tail is skinned. The surface layer over it is devoid of underfur, and the coarse guard hairs, which emerge singly from simple but very large hair follicles, have thickened, whitish bases running to grey or black at their tips. Follicles without hairs are common in this region. A yellowish, waxy substance, which fluoresces strongly in ultra-violet light, is visible on the skin in the region without underfur and is derived from the gland secretions (Albone and Flood, 1976). (Subcutaneous and other fatty tissues also fluoresce with a pale to bright yellow colour in the fox.) One of the earliest references to this gland was made by Hartig (*c.* 1830), who called it *Der Voile*, or violet gland, on account of the smell of violets it allegedly gives off. Retzius (1848) later described the gland in detail and, in passing, likened its smell more to *Byssus iolithus* (a lichen) than to the violet.

Retzius considered the gland to be larger in males, but Toldt (1907–8), although finding individual variations in size, identified no seasonal or sexual differences. Tembrock (1968), however, has noted cyclical changes in the gland associated with rut, when the secretory activity increases. Peter Flood (pers. comm.) examined supracaudal glands from nine male and eleven female foxes taken in Wales in the months of January and February. He described the glands as tubular apocrine sweat glands lying deep in the dermis, their ducts passing through the sebaceous gland to open within the follicles. The sebaceous glands were massive and multi-lobular and showed two main forms, both different from the classical form associated with hair follicles. At this time of year the mean weight of the glands was 247mg in the males and 126mg in females. (See also Albone and Flood, 1976.)

The tail gland seems to occur in all canids, with the exception of most domestic breeds of dogs. It is very large and conspicuous in the grey fox (*Urocyon*), being up to 200mm long and about 12.5mm wide. Overlying the gland is a long mane of fur. The gland is relatively large in the kit fox (*Macrotis*), smaller in the arctic fox, coyote and wolf, and smallest (among these species) in the red fox.

Although I have investigated the region of this gland in dead foxes with my nose, I have been unable to detect anything unusual, but colleagues persuaded to investigate likewise have described the smell as not unpleasant, without being more specific. Retzius described the smell of the gland area in the arctic fox as similar to that of the red fox, but claimed that there was no smell in the case of the wolf. Dr Michael Fox of Washington University, who is investigating the behavioural significance of the gland, tells me that the smell of the gland is strongest in the arctic and grey foxes, less pungent in the red fox, milder in the jackal and coyote and faintest in the wolf. There seems to be an inverse relationship between the intensity of the smell and the sociability of the species.

During encounters between individuals of the same species, foxes and other canids sniff each other's tail gland areas, but there is little available information on the behavioural significance of the secretion. Dr Fox has observed that the gland weeps when arctic foxes have been playing excitedly. The stiff hairs covering the gland show piloerection in some situations and must help in the dissemination of the odour. Retzius and others have suggested that the gland aids identification (of individuals?); others suggest that the gland may be used to communicate information in dens or earths, or when passing through confined places where traces of the secretion can be deposited on an overhanging surface. Someone, I forget whom, presumably referring to violets, suggested that the secretion served to mask the scent of the fox's less agreeable secretions!

Albone and Flood (1976) have found the chemical composition of the secretions of the tail gland to be highly complex. It is apparently made up of four main constituents, one of which is identical to a plant product known to have attractant properties for some carnivores.

### The stomach and intestines
The stomach of the fox can hold approximately 1,000g of flesh and can stretch to a capacity of about 900ml. As the fox is a carnivore, its gut is short. The small intestine is about 1.1m long and the large intestine about 0.5m long. The caecum is almost vestigial. The characteristic odour of fox faeces seems to originate in the region of the caecum.

### Sexual characteristics
The vixen has four pairs of teats, each of which has eight to twenty lactiferous ducts. They are pale in colour in virgin females but larger and darker in parous vixens.

In the male the scrotum is smaller than that of the dog and is held close to the body. It is covered with cream- to white-coloured fur, in contrast to the surrounding coat. Once descended, the testes always remain in the scrotum. Unlike that of the dog, the penis is close to the abdominal wall and cannot be seen except on close examination. It includes a baculum, or os penis.

### The head
The eyes of foxes over three months old are a bright yellow-brown in colour, with short black eyelashes on the upper lids only. The hair on the inside of the ear trumpets is pale brown to white in colour, those on the forward margin being plentiful, stiff and long. The nose is dark brown to black. There are no glands in the skin of the nose (the planum nasale), and it is usually dry.

## Dentition

The dental formula $\frac{3.1.4.2}{3.1.4.3}$ of the fox shows a loss of one molar tooth from the full complement of the placental mammal. The tooth row is long, more than half the length of the skull, whereas in cats, which are exclusively flesh eaters and hunters, the tooth row is relatively short. With one exception the pre-molar teeth in foxes are simple and pointed. The exception, the fourth pre-molar in the upper jaw, is larger, heavier and longer in the tooth row and, with its opposite number in the lower jaw (the first molar tooth), forms the flesh-shearing carnassial teeth. This pair of teeth is more characteristic of carnivores than the canine teeth which can be well developed in other orders of mammals. The other molar teeth are adapted for crushing rather than grinding: indeed, the fox has very restricted sideways movement of its jaws, and the molar teeth have prominent cones on their surfaces. Since they are set far back in the tooth row, near to the fulcrum of the jaw, they can exert consider-able crushing power, especially at the tips of the cones. The third lower molar tooth is almost vestigial. The carnassial teeth are able to perform this shearing action because the pairs lie alongside and overlap when the jaw is closed. The pre-molar teeth do not meet point for point, those of the upper jaw lying slightly ahead of their opposite numbers (see Figure 5). The canine teeth are sharp and long but, being situated well forward,

**5**   Teeth of the fox

C = Canine teeth
P = Premolars
M = Molars

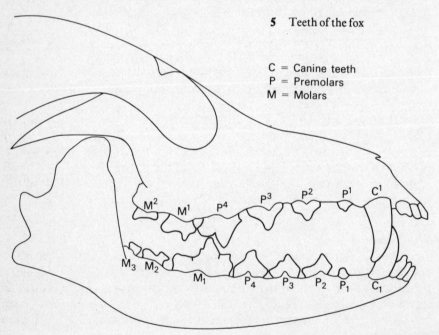

cannot exert much pressure, though those who have handled a struggling fox may have reason to disagree with this. Their function is to catch and hold prey until, by readjustment, it can be held by the premolar teeth; the canines then provide a clamp from which the animal cannot escape. Mutilated lamb carcases, when skinned, often show clearly this sequence of events – initial grasp, often in the chest region (small puncture marks visible), readjustment and crushing of the neck by the massive carnassial teeth.

The first teeth begin to appear in cubs of about three weeks of age. These milk teeth are replaced by permanent teeth, the complete set having erupted by between twenty-two and twenty-four weeks after birth. The diagrammatic representation of time of eruption and succession in Figure 6 is an amalgam of data from several sources, but much of it is derived from Swiss workers (Lups *et al.*, 1972) and from several cubs kept at my home. There is variation in time of eruption and sequence of permanent teeth, but Lups and his colleagues showed the following sequence.

| Upper jaw | $P^1I^1C$ | $I^2I^3$ | | $M^1$ | | $P^2M^2$ | | $P^4P^3$ |
|---|---|---|---|---|---|---|---|---|
| Lower jaw | $P_1$ | $I_1$ | $M_1I_2$ | | $CM_2I_3P_2$ | | $M_3$ | | $P_3P_4$ |

The sequence of eruption is from left to right — the first tooth to erupt being the lower first pre-molar ($P_1$) the second, the upper pre-molar ($P^1$) and the last two the third and four lower pre-molars, ($P_3$ and $P_4$).

Milk teeth may not be shed immediately the permanent tooth begins to erupt. Often the milk teeth may lie to one side or may cap the erupting tooth beneath them until their roots have been eroded or the tooth pushed aside. The two generations of canine teeth overlap for longer periods than other teeth.

### The feet and gait
The pads of the feet are naked, but the skin between is well covered with brown or dark red fur which protrudes between the pads: this can be clearly seen in soft mud prints and can serve to distinguish fox prints from those of dogs. There are five claws on the forelimb and four on the hind. The first digits (the dew claws) of the forelimbs are rudimentary but clawed and, as in dogs, do not make contact with the ground. They are probably only of advantage for grooming or scratching. Dew claws on the hindlimbs have not been described in foxes, but I have seen one male fox with a small fleshy lobe in the position where the dew claw is normally located in dogs. The forefoot has a small carpal pad, as in dogs.

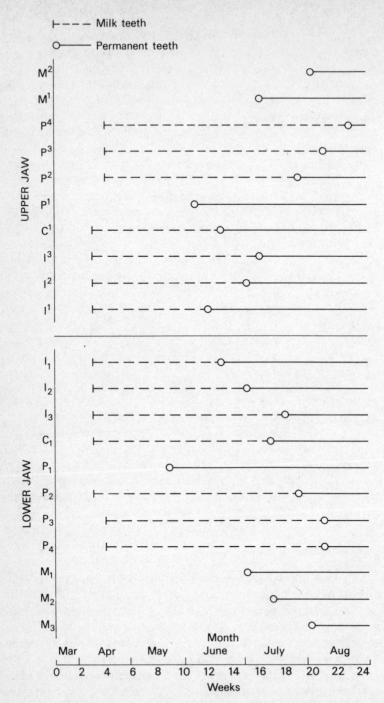

**6** Onset of eruption of milk and permanent teeth. (Week 0 = March 21 ± 7 days, for England and Wales.)

The claws, dark in colour and lighter towards the tips, are much longer on the forefeet than on the hind. The foot pads contain much fat to absorb shock, and in northern latitudes the sole fur between the pads is very long and thick, especially in winter. The forefeet are larger than the hindfeet.

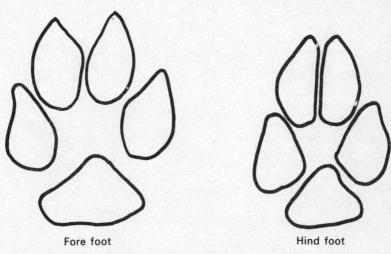

Fore foot                                    Hind foot

About natural size

7    Fox footprints. (In soft mud, prints of the claws can also be seen.)

It is necessary to consider the gait of the fox before describing the tracks revealed in snow or on sand and grass on frosty or dewy mornings. Whilst the fox spends much of its time walking when in investigative mood, it readily breaks into a slow trot of about 6–13km per hour, which is the gait most frequently observed when a fox is moving unhurriedly. When it needs to move more quickly it breaks into a lope or canter, a very easy, seemingly effortless pace. When speed is called for the lope extends to a gallop. I am uncertain of the top speed of a fox. I have followed one along a road at just over 48km per hour, but it is commonly held that the fox is capable of over 65km per hour.

In any gait the fox, unlike the soldier, may lead with either forefoot, but the sequence is always the same. While the fox is walking three of its feet remain in contact with the ground during much of the movement. The left foreleg moves first, followed by the right hindleg. As this moves forward, the right foreleg lifts just before the right hindleg completes its movement, and it is followed by the left hindleg. In the walk the prints

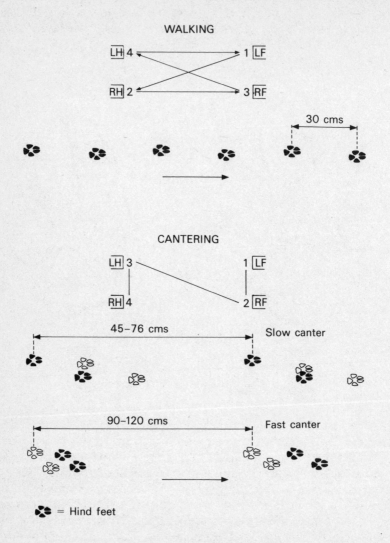

WALKING

CANTERING

30 cms

45–76 cms    Slow canter

90–120 cms    Fast canter

= Hind feet

**8** Fox tracks and sequence of leg movements at the four different gaits. While walking and trotting the prints seen are those of the hind feet which tend to overprint those of the fore feet. On firm ground this is less prevalent than in soft snow.

**TROTTING**

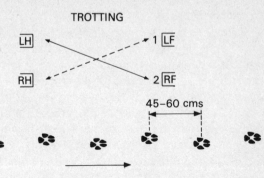

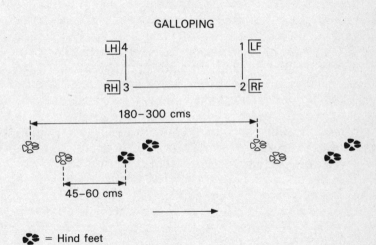

**GALLOPING**

= Hind feet

of the forefeet are usually overlaid by those of the hindfeet. The prints are close together, spaced regularly about 300mm apart.

When trotting the fox has two feet on the ground during most of the movement. Since the hindfeet often overlay the prints of the forefeet, the fox is airborne for a very short interlude during the cycle of foot movements. The gait involves concurrent and parallel movements of a foreleg and a hindleg on opposite sides of the body. The forefoot supporting the fox whilst trotting is lifted fractionally before the hindfoot on the same side is placed on the ground on the print of the forefoot. Since the trot is a more purposeful movement than the walk, the prints make a straighter line than that made whilst the fox is walking. Others with more experience of fox tracks in different snow conditions than myself suggest that the overlaying of the forefeet prints by the hindfeet is more pronounced in deep and soft snow than on hard surfaces.

The canter involves a completely different type of movement, the diagonal pattern of leg movements changing to one in which the body is supported alternately by the forelegs and the hindlegs. Assuming for explanatory purposes that the movement begins with the left foreleg, this is followed by the advance of the right foreleg. The body is supported by these legs until the right hindleg, followed slightly later by the left, is brought forward under the body. The animal is airborne for only a short space of time but it is a longer period than when trotting. According to pace, the hindleg prints may fall behind those of the forelegs, may partly overlie them or, when proceeding to a gallop, may be in front of them. They are usually, however, in distinct groups of four, and the intervals between the groups vary from 0.5m to 1m.

The gallop is an extension of the canter. It involves the same basic pattern, but with a change in the sequence of hindleg movements. In the gallop the hindfeet land ahead of the place where the forefeet have supported the body. Depending upon the speed of the fox, the hindfeet prints can lie from about 450mm to 900mm ahead of the forefeet prints, and the distance between the print groups can be as much as 2.5m (see Figure 8).

## The Senses
HEARING   As it is principally a predator of small mammals, especially those hidden beneath surface vegetation, the fox needs to be able to detect and locate faint sounds accurately. It needs to be able to discriminate between sounds that are likely to be profitable to it and those that are not. Possibly it has an inherited tendency to investigate certain kinds of sound – high pitched squeals and shrieks, perhaps – but being an opportunist and living in diverse habitats, an investigative nature and an ability to learn quickly are advantageous to it.

Acute hearing may be less important to the fox as an aid in detecting danger than for feeding and for intra-specific communication, such as when making or maintaining contact with other foxes. Whilst the fox is not endowed with the sophisticated auditory apparatus of night-hunting owls, its ability to thrive in a wide range of habitats must be partly attributable to its successful location of elusive prey. It has only two chances of capturing unseen voles moving under matted vegetation or snow; first by pinning the prey down with its forefeet, and if that is off-target, it can use its mouth at the second attempt. There is not much room for error if the fox is to subsist on voles.

Since sounds are registered at both ears, intermittent sounds originating from a point to one side of the head will be registered in one ear a very short time before the other. The difference in time will depend upon the distance separating the ears (tympanic membranes) and on the position of the head relative to the source of sound. Even if the sound is a continuous one, it will still register differently in the two ears since, especially at low frequencies, the sound will be out of phase in each. In addition, depending on the position of the head relative to the sound source, a sound may reach the two ears at different intensities. The animal has to learn to compare these differences and, by experience, to pinpoint their source. If the position of the head were not moved, the source of a sound would not appear to be coming from a single point, but from anywhere along a curved line on a plane defined by the relative distance between the origin of the sound and the right and left ears. Thus, a sound which has its origin directly in front of the animal would – because the sound is equidistant from both ears – appear to be located on a plane lying vertically over the animal, beginning at the true origin and ending directly behind the animal. As the position of the head is changed, the plane of possible origin also shifts but the true origin does not; thus, with experience, the fox learns that the sound can be located either by movement of the head or by movement of the ears.

Sound can, however, be located without moving the head. Since most sounds are a mixture of frequencies, the ear trumpets and the orientation of each relative to the sound source may cause the different components of the sound to reach the perceptive part of each ear differently; thus, all the information received corresponds only at the source. The possession of highly mobile ears enhances the fox's ability to locate sound by correlating differences in intensity. The fox, and other mammals that live mainly in a two-dimensional environment (horses, for example, which ancestrally lived in flat plains and were unconcerned with events overhead), has learned to disregard apparent overhead sound. Having located the approximate direction of the sound source at a distance, the fox moves in and finally pinpoints the origin at close quarters, with slight rotatory head movements to determine its position in three dimensions.

Investigations by Osterholm (1964) in Finland on the senses of sight, hearing and smell in foxes in relation to their feeding behaviour has thrown light on the versatility and significance of their senses in normal behaviour. He showed that captive foxes were able to locate sources of low-frequency sound more accurately than those of high frequencies. Greatest accuracy, to within 1° of the sound source was achieved in a high proportion (63–68 per cent) of tests at 700–3000 cycles per second (c/s). At higher frequencies the foxes were unable to locate the sound with the same accuracy, and at 18,000 c/s they were able to locate to within 5° in only a low proportion of cases. Osterholm considered that sound at this high frequency could only be located with an accuracy of 90 per cent. Isley and Gysel (1975) have also investigated the accuracy of sound location by foxes, with slightly different results – possibly because the sounds they used were pure-toned, whereas those used by Osterholm may have contained a small proportion of spurious frequencies, which perhaps enhanced the fox's ability to locate sound of which the major components were at the lower frequencies. Isley and Gysel found that foxes were able to locate sounds correctly in more than 90 per cent of cases from 900 c/s to 14,000 c/s, with best performances at 3500 c/s. Even at 34,000 c/s – the highest frequency used – foxes were able to locate the sound source accurately in 71 per cent of cases. However, even if the high-frequency calls of voles provide the fox with little more than an indication of approximate direction of sound source, the exact location might be pinpointed by sounds of lower frequency, such as the rustling sounds created by voles passing through vegetation or when scratching and eating. Osterholm observed that the fox, in common with man, could not locate stridulating grasshoppers with any accuracy. Many bird calls uttered in vulnerable situations are pure-toned and may have evolved to minimize the probability of detection by predators. Isley and Gysel consider that the fox may have evolved sound-locating mechanisms to override this.

There is very little information available on the auditory sensitivity of foxes to sound intensities.

SIGHT   An animal's sight is commensurate with its requirements for its mode of life and with its mental ability to make use of the information. A highly sophisticated visual apparatus relaying detailed visual patterns to the brain is wasted if the animal cannot understand and use the image to advantage. The eye does, however, offer to the brain more than it can comprehend – for example, a poacher's dog may approach to within a metre of a crouching rabbit but only sees it when it moves; the outline of the rabbit is perceived but not recognized. Similarly, a fox will approach to within very short distances of a completely stationary man, providing its other senses, smell and hearing, do not alert it to danger. The man has certainly been seen but not comprehended.

The visual apparatus of the fox is, however, well adapted for its particular way of life. Being primarily but not exclusively nocturnal, one of the main requirements of the fox's eye is sensitivity to light. It has a large, round pupil in poor light conditions, which is reduced to a vertical slit in bright light. (The Fennec fox is entirely nocturnal and has round pupils at all times.) Greater occlusion can be achieved with slit pupils than round ones, and verticality has the added advantage of permitting further occlusion when the eyes are partly closed. Thus the fox controls with great efficiency the amount of light passing through its lenses.

Light passing through the lens impinges on the retina, but much of it passes between the light-sensitive cells of the retina and would be entirely wasted but for the presence of the tapetum lucidum, a layer of cells which reflects this light back to the retina where some of it can add further stimulus to the light-sensitive cells. The efficiency of the eye is thus enhanced, but not all the light reflected is saved, since the eye-shine (the cat's eyes effect) seen when a torch is shone at a fox is startlingly bright and represents the reflected light passing back through the retina and the lens at the observer. The area not covered by the tapetum reflects a pinkish light of lower intensity, and when this is seen by an observer the eye is not orientated directly back towards the light source.

The visual requirements of an animal active both in daylight and darkness are more sophisticated than those of purely diurnal or nocturnal habit, and although various adaptations for night and day vision are provided, the whole visual system becomes a set of compromises. In a twenty-four-hour species, night vision demands sensitivity and daylight visual acuity; the former is analogous to the speed of a photographic film and the latter to its grain or definition, and the variation in size of the pupil is analogous to the aperture of a camera lens. Greater acuity is provided when the lens is stopped down in conditions of bright light and poorer acuity when the pupil is dilated.

Unlike a black-and-white photographic film, the retina is composed of two types of light-sensitive cells – rods and cones. Rods are more sensitive to light than cones, most of which are connected as groups to a single nerve cell, and when the total stimulation of light on groups of rods reaches a certain threshold, the nerve cell is stimulated; the result is a coarse-grain image. Cone cells are also grouped but fewer are connected to each nerve cell; although they are less sensitive to light than rods, they yield sharper images. The central area of the retina has a higher proportion of cones than rods in the fox, and the periphery contains more rods. In conditions of poor light the rods and cones adapt to the lower level of light stimulation. The cones adapt quickly, but their increase in sensitivity is slight. Rods adapt more slowly (rods in a rabbit in darkness, for example, may require two hours for maximum sensitivity) but their sensitivity is much greater; in some mammals whose retina is composed almost exclusively of rods the increase in sensitivity can be a million-fold (Tansley, 1965).

What does the fox see in daylight? It has good visual acuity at short ranges. It is able to run swiftly and safely through scrub, woodland, hedges and fences and over rocks and boulders, and it often exhibits remarkable co-ordination of limbs and eyes, so it must be able to judge short distances accurately. It will, however, ignore an immobile beetle or a crouching rabbit, and its visual ability in daylight is directed towards detection of movement rather than recognition of shapes. Cones, which permit a change of image over small areas of the retina, provide better perception of movement than rods. Consequently, at night rather larger movements of objects will be required before they are perceived by the fox. Dark-adapted vision will provide the nocturnal fox with the means to move freely but with a reduced ability to perceive and detect movement.

Predators have eyes positioned frontally, whereas prey species have ever watchful all-round vision of varying degrees. The optic axis of the eye relative to the axis running through the length of the animal lies at 80–85° in hares and rabbits, whereas it is only 15° in the red fox (Smythe, 1961) (see Figure 9). Not only does the rabbit eye command an arc of 360° in the horizontal plane, but its field of vision overlaps in front of and behind the head. The fox has some binocular vision, but its eyes cannot converge on a near object as well as those of primates and cats. Binocular vision also depends on the proportion of nerve fibres that cross over at the optic chiasma; however, I know of no information relating to this in foxes. The nictitating membrane – the third eyelid – is present in the fox, but it only moves when the eye is closed.

Osterholm, investigating vision in foxes, concluded that vision plays an important role in food finding in daylight and that in twilight vision is subordinate to sound stimuli; in darkness vision seems to play very little part. This contention, however, needs to be qualified, since a successful attack on a fast-moving prey may be the result of keen sight only after distance-perception by hearing. Tcmbrock (1957) considered that foxes have a capacity for colour discrimination, whereas Osterholm does not share this view. Most authorities on the physiology of the eye seem to agree that, except for primates, mammals are colour-blind.

THE SENSE OF SMELL   Of the three senses adapted for the detection of distant stimuli the sense of smell is least understood and, unlike the study of the anatomy of the fox's optic and auditory apparatus, coupled with a knowledge of physics of light and sound, little can be learned of the significance to the way of life of the fox of the olfactory organs by similar analyses. Furthermore, sight and sound are well appreciated by

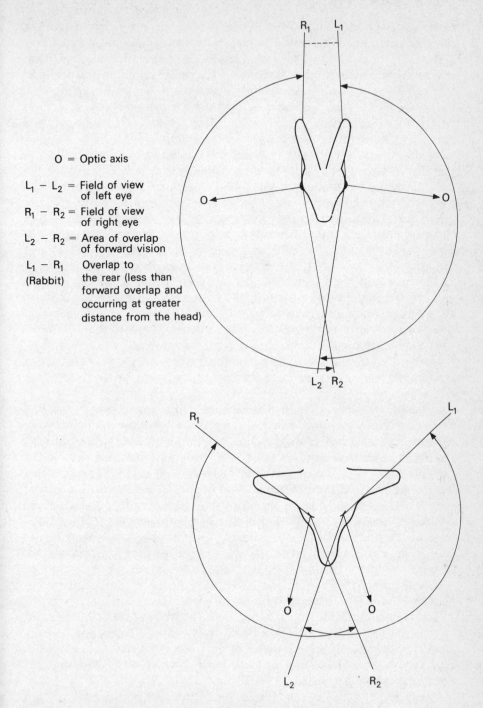

O = Optic axis

$L_1 - L_2$ = Field of view of left eye

$R_1 - R_2$ = Field of view of right eye

$L_2 - R_2$ = Area of overlap of forward vision

$L_1 - R_1$ (Rabbit) Overlap to the rear (less than forward overlap and occurring at greater distance from the head)

**9**  Optic axis and field of view of the European wild rabbit and red fox man, but our sense of smell appears to be less perceptive than that of the dog, for example. Whereas our olfactory sense is something of a luxury, and our survival would not be greatly threatened by its loss, wild mammals lacking a sense of smell would suffer a severe handicap which, in general terms, would considerably lessen their chances of survival. To many the sense of smell is essential, adding a further dimension to their environment for feeding purposes, for intraspecific communication, as a protective mechanism and even for reproduction.

In the case of the fox the sense of smell is important in hunting and plays a dominant role in scavenging. Since vision is impaired in darkness, hearing and smell assume greater importance in twilight and darkness, though even in daylight these two senses are invoked in all cases other than when hunting involves active visual pursuit of the animal.

Osterholm tested the olfactory perception of captive foxes and concluded that the fox could not detect pieces of meat lying on the surface of the ground at distances greater than 2m, and with meat buried at a depth of 10cm it could not detect it at a distance greater than 0.5m. Such a test, valid for fresh pieces of meat, might not be valid for the fox's ability to detect living animals or putrifying flesh, and field evidence suggests that these observations by Osterholm are an underestimate of the usefulness of the sense of smell in detecting potential food in the wild. Nevertheless, there is general agreement that for feeding purposes hearing is of paramount importance to foxes for both distant and close-up detection of living prey.

Foxes do, however, spend a considerable time scavenging, seasonally or regularly, and without visual clues provided by scavenging birds or foraging beetles, they probably detect carrion entirely by their sense of smell. As an example, in November 1971 seventy-two baits composed of frozen rabbit (one-fifth of a rabbit per bait) were buried beneath a turf layer 70m apart on the perimeter of an area of 340 hectares. Baits were renewed at alternate-day inspections as they were taken, and after ten days 82 per cent of the baits had been taken by foxes. Without a knowledge of the number of foxes in the area (seventy-six were subsequently caught in eight weeks), it is not possible to give an estimate of the chances of foxes finding baits laid in a non-random but haphazard manner, but in these particular circumstances there was a 40 per cent chance of any bait being found on the first day.

There is no available information about the size and function of Jacobson's organ in the fox. This small sac, composed of tissue similar to that lining the chemically sensitive part of the nose, is present in many mammals. It opens into the roof of the mouth, so whatever function it has may be highly specialized.

The sense of smell as a means of communication between individuals will be discussed later (pp. 164–8).

THE TACTILE SENSE   The tactile sense is highly developed on the muzzle, where the stiff vibrissae transmit touch stimuli to the sensory region at their bases. Small tactile hairs are present in the carpal region of the forelimb. The footpads are highly sensitive, but the region of greatest sensitivity I have observed in dogs is the hair which lies in front of the large foot pad. The lightest stimulus to these hairs will cause even a sleeping dog or one of my young foxes lying in front of the fire to withdraw the foot forcibly and repeatedly, whereas they will react less strongly to a light touch on the muzzle vibrissae.

The sensitivity of the feet, the sense of balance and extraordinary coordination of eyes and limbs whilst running enable the fox to negotiate the roughest ground at speed and to leave its pursuers stumbling to keep their balance. I have seen a fox running along the top of a garden fence with the assurance of a squirrel, and there are many reports of foxes being found high up in large trees, usually where a broken or trailing branch provides access. They have often been found on the crowns of pollarded trees.

## Voice

Having kept foxes in captivity and listened to the calls of wild foxes at night, I have probably heard much of their repertoire, but as I have a poor memory for music my notebook descriptions tell me very little. Were it not for the detailed researches of Dr G. Tembrock of Germany into acoustic behaviour (of foxes, especially), I would be unable to enumerate and describe not only some of the calls but also the behavioural situations in which the calls are made. Many of us are familiar with the calls of foxes, but most of us are denied an understanding of their behavioural significance because this can only be gained by observing the fox when the calls are being made, as Dr Tembrock has done with captive foxes. But even with captive animals it is possible that certain situations which occur in the wild may not be simulated in captivity, and a call made by a captive fox may have an additional behavioural significance when the animal is living free.

Burrows, in his studies of wild foxes (1968), was intrigued by the calls they made, and he approached the problem of interpretation differently. In his Gloucestershire study area he kept careful records of the kind of calls that he heard at different times of the year and at different periods of the fox's nocturnal activity. By reference to his knowledge of the seasonal life history of the fox – breeding, weaning and independence of cubs, for example – he inferred the behavioural significance of certain calls. In spite of errors which are likely to occur with this method of interpretation, Burrows's observations are very useful and reveal seasonal vocal activities which have not been documented elsewhere (they should be referred to by those interested in this aspect of fox natural history).

Tembrock (1963) describes twenty-eight groups of sounds made by the red fox, based upon forty basic forms of sound production. He credits the fox with a sound range of over five octaves, from about 100 to 5,000 cycles per second. Calls are made in greeting and in excitement, as a threat, in defence, while fighting, as an acknowledgement of inferiority or submission, as a warning or alarm, in social contact (including mating contact) and perhaps in defence of territory or as an advertisement. Infantile calls are basically of the 'I need attention' kind, and calls from adults to offspring signify 'Come here' or 'Look out!'.

Through calls, visual display during social contact and chemical communication – of which little is known – the fox has a considerable communicative vocabulary. Some sounds made by foxes may appear to the human ear to be very similar or even identical, but an analysis by a sound spectrograph may reveal differences; for example, the whining of male cubs even a day or two old is different in form from that of vixen cubs.

Fox cubs, like puppies, are noisy animals. Their whining in the immediate post-birth period is described by Tembrock as a 'care-call'. At low temperatures and in high humidity the cubs will call more frequently than when they are warm and dry. After about twenty days they are able to maintain a constant body temperature and the frequency of the calls then decreases. Hunger also increases the frequency of care-calls, and the vixen responds to the stimulus of these calls to attend to the comfort of her young. The male also responds; tape-recorded cub care-calls played by Tembrock to a male of a mated pair stimulated it to collect and carry food to its mate, even before the birth of cubs, and in investigations conducted in North America it was observed that male coyotes responded to the infantile behaviour of cubs and other species by regurgitating food for them (Robinson, 1952). Klenk (1971) also observed adult red foxes adopting and caring for alien parentless cubs. The whining of cubs gradually acquires a rhythmic character, which develops after about nineteen days into a series of distinct infantile barks or yelps, in stanzas of three, four or five, the last yelp often being more prolonged. The care-call which develops from the whining of the newborn, through the rhythmic yelps to the three- or four-call stanza becomes the contact call of the juvenile when it moves freely and independently of the parent vixen in the vicinity of the den. At this time a rhythmic growling also develops. Young cubs from about a month old develop an open-mouthed, explosive, spitting call, which is threatening or defensive and can be directed at other cubs or human intruders. In the adult this call becomes the characteristic open-mouthed combative call, frequently heard when two foxes are engaged in an upright pushing contest.

When digging or bolting cubs from earths the only sound I have heard uttered by adults is a low growl, but I am uncertain whether this was directed towards the intruders or to warn the cubs.

Adult foxes call their cubs to instruct them to come and feed or to summon them out of their dens with the same low growl. This call may also be used when cubs are led from their old den to a new one and as a contact sound between a pair at about the time of mating, but then it occurs as a stanza of four sounds. This low growling may also be superimposed on a whining sound to produce a whimpering growl of greeting. A whimpering yap is frequently heard when cubs greet their parents, or their owners in the case of pet foxes. This seems to be a signal of submission, too. The individual making the greeting flattens its ears in a downward direction; the head and shoulders are lowered; sometimes the tail is flagged, low, sideways, and in the case of the cub (if not in the adult) this is sometimes accompanied by urination. The teeth are bared in an open-mouthed grin, with the angle of the mouth drawn back, but the upper lip is not drawn up to expose the incisor and canine teeth. I have seen this greeting only once in the wild between adults, when contact was being made between dog and vixen at dusk. The dog adopted the submissive attitude, while the vixen, with a blackbird in her mouth, stopped momentarily, flagged her tail sideways and moved on in the direction of her den to feed her cubs. This is the kind of greeting pet or captive foxes give their keepers, usually after long absences or at feeding time. Adults sometimes greet cubs, and cubs each other, with a panting sound.

A threatening sound made by adults is a very strong whine, which rises to a prolonged, threatening yelp. In defence the yelp may be repeated rapidly. It is then more explosive in effect and best described as a series of cackles. The upper lips are drawn up to expose the canine and incisor teeth and at the same time the hackles may be raised.

The warning sound is usually a single bark. If it is made near the den, as Tembrock has observed, it is a faint, sharp sound made with the mouth closed. When the fox is distant from the den the bark is open-mouthed and loud, so that its location and the danger it indicates can be pinpointed by those receiving the warning. I have heard the loud bark many times, but only on one occasion in the wild have I heard the quiet bark, which is perhaps best described as a cough. It happened at Mill Bay in Pembrokeshire, when I approached a high field bank to observe a vixen and her cubs which were in the field beyond. The dog fox was disturbed by my approach and it uttered a single loud bark as it rose to flee. Surprisingly, the vixen was standing outside the earth looking in my direction when I peered over the bank. She watched the bank as she moved about uneasily outside the earth, which was on the edge of a well used National Park coastal path, where walkers have been startled to find cubs asleep in their path in the heat of the sun. The vixen and cubs were well used to the presence of man, but she was clearly disturbed by the warning cry. After a few minutes I blew on a blade of grass and, without hesitation, the vixen raced in my direction. She jumped on the bank and stood still about two metres away. Something alarmed her and she uttered the loud bark as she leaped off the bank. She reappeared on the cliff slope and stood by the earth, uttering the quiet cough described by Tembrock. Night was falling and it was time to leave. From my concealed position I shouted at the vixen. She responded by coughing again, and each time I shouted she responded. She continued to reply to my shouts even when I stood on the top of the bank, in full view of her as she stood some forty metres away. She was agitated as she watched me but did not move further than about ten metres from the den.

A strange encounter, which I hoped might be repeated for the benefit of my wife on the following night – but the foxes had moved elsewhere.

Tembrock describes a yelp directed at other species – referred to as the 'push yelp', from the forward, pushing posture of the body. A loud, open-mouthed, explosive yelp is uttered, similar to that provoked by an intra-specific threat, but it is repeated at longer intervals. Defensive, threatening or combative calls are harsh and explosive in character, whereas non-aggressive social calls begin softly and gently, increasing in volume gradually.

Contact between foxes is maintained or established by barking. The barks occur in groups of three or four during the period before the rut, but gradually the number of barks in a stanza is reduced and the barks finally cease after the birth of the young. Single, longer, harsh barks may also be uttered at these and other times of the year. These contact sounds serve also as pairing calls, uttered over a distance. Barking usually occurs early in the night. According to Tembrock, individuals can be distinguished by the mean duration of the barking stanza, or by the groups of barks and by differences in sound quality. I do not know whether or not the human ear can distinguish the difference between the bark of a dog fox and that of a vixen. The duration and length of the barking stanza of the individual fox at the onset of the rut remains characteristic of it throughout its life. Tembrock does not consider that foxes howl, but Burrows describes a howl as a slurred triple bark, the pitch and volume rising rapidly to end in a high, hollow-sounding, terror-inducing note. The call is familiar to many countrymen and is usually referred to as the 'scream' of a vixen – and so it might be, but Tembrock does not suggest that this call is exclusive to one sex. Talbot (1906) descriptively refers to this call as a 'squall'. It can be heard from early in the year to midsummer, but in the early months the call seems to be hoarser and does not rise to the high pitch of spring.

The calls of foxes clearly have individuality; a monogamous captive male fox reacted only to Tembrock's tape-recordings of its vixen. In some areas, notably where foxes are not abundant and where their home ranges are large, the death of a fox in the early months of the year may be followed by abnormally vociferous barking by one fox or several for one or two subsequent nights – presumably an attempt to establish contact with the missing fox.

I have used Tembrock's descriptions of fox calls almost exclusively here because he understood their behavioural significance. I have heard most of the calls described, particularly with captive foxes, but one call not described by Tembrock is a gentle hiss which is made occasionally at night by one of my captive foxes, probably the male, which elicits a quiet aggressive cackle from the other. Its significance I do not know.

Another call which I cannot identify from the descriptions of Tembrock and Burrows is the long-drawn-out scream without the preliminary double or triple bark. I have heard it frequently in captive foxes and in wild foxes, which always appear to make it whilst moving within their range. At close quarters on a still night the call can be frighteningly disturbing. Whilst recording fox calls in Surrey, not long after dark, I was able roughly to pinpoint the position of a barking fox as it moved about the valley. It came closer and passed by at a slow trot about 10 metres distant. To my surprise, about 20 metres behind it another fox followed at the same pace, uttering a quiet whine which I had not heard before, nor since.

The dog fox of the pair that I currently have makes an uninhibited, loud, explosive growl when a local sheepdog visits to growl and bark at him. He responds to each bark of the dog, each animal being nose to nose on either side of the cage wire. The vixen, on the other hand, exhibits the characteristic ears-down, open-mouthed, yelping, submissive posture on such occasions, even lying on her side to greet the sheepdog.

On some calm nights the captive vixen is irrepressibly vocal, uttering the four-stanza throaty bark described earlier as the scream. This can occur at any time of year. Often we are forewarned of this by a few subdued practice stanzas in day time and it can only be suppressed by bringing the vixen into the house for a while or spending some time playing with her before dusk. We interpret this call of the vixen as 'I am being neglected'.

Whilst captive foxes reared from a few days old and imprinted to some extent upon the person who has reared them may in many respects behave differently from wild foxes, some aspects of their behaviour can be very revealing.

It is difficult to reconcile their exhibition of rapacity (and aggression towards each other) when a dead squirrel, rabbit or lamb is given to them with their gentleness and show of affection towards their handlers

– that is, to all the family except me. They preen my wife's eyebrows and ears with their teeth and vie with each other for the favoured position – my wife's lap – where each will quickly curl up before the other can pull it away and then pretend to be asleep. If my wife is not alert, the vixen will sprinkle a drop or two of urine on her leg or skirt, as if staking a claim before seeking her couch. The dog fox, a more modest fellow, never bestows such favours.

Perhaps because these animals – now three years old – are imprinted to some extent on their handlers, some of the calls, especially those of the vixen are still recognizably juvenile in nature.

# 2

# Food

'The silver fox lives mainly on small mammals, birds and insects and seldom attacks domestic stock, but suffers severely from the stigma attached to virtually any "fox" or "jackal" in Southern Africa as killers of farm animals. Thus many farmers destroy the silver fox whenever they encounter it.'

Thus wrote Bothma in 1966 in his introduction to a study of the food of the silver fox, *Vulpes chama*. How right he is; not only in South Africa, but perhaps anywhere where a fox of whatever species impinges however slightly upon man's interests, its quest for food inevitably brings it into disrepute.

## Diet

Whilst some generalizations can be made about fox diets (the major items being voles, rabbits, hares, birds, fruits and carrion according to the season), the items taken by foxes will depend on the availability of particular foods wherever the fox lives. Being a predator and a scavenger, the fox is presented with an enormous variety of prospective foods, and its opportunist character enables it to live in all kinds of habitat in Britain. The main factor determining fox numbers in any place is food — but availability and variety of cover, dens, earths and sanctuary from man all play an important part in determining the number of foxes that any area supports.

The diet of the fox is enormously varied. The dustbin fox of suburbia, the sand dune dwelling fox, the heather moor fox, the fox of arable farming areas, of mixed farming areas, of grass covered hill sheep walks, of Scottish deer forests and of coniferous woodlands: the choice of foods of these foxes differs widely according to season and availability. In order to gain some understanding of the diet of foxes, their preferences and their efficiency as predators, the availability of foods must first be known in any area under study.

Much of the habitat in Britain is fragmentary and the availability of different food items may vary over distances which are small by comparison with the sizes of the home ranges of foxes. Except in fairly uniform habitats, such as extensive conifer plantations or large expanses of hill land where foods appropriate to the habitat are more evenly dispersed, it is difficult to determine exactly which food items are available to an individual fox at any season of the year, and in what quantity. The collection of a large number of faeces, or the examination of a large sample of foxes killed in an area for detailed information about possible food items, could provide useful data that are at present lacking. Burrows (1968), for example, noted that whilst the wood mouse (*Apodemus sylvaticus*) and the brown rat (*Rattus norvegicus*) were common in his Gloucestershire study area, they were not taken very frequently by foxes. Since rats sometimes figure largely in the diet of foxes elsewhere, it is not clear in this instance whether the foxes in Burrows' study area chose other food because of its abundance, because it was more readily available than the wood mouse and brown rat, or merely because it was preferred.

The diet of a fox in a particular area may not be determined simply by the relative abundance of different foods or its preferences; it may perhaps be related to which food satisfies the individual's hunting instincts or its nutritional requirements best, or which food it has been used to, especially during the period when it was reared as a cub, or when the juvenile fox developed its hunting skills.

Animals that feed on plants and small items of food spend much of their time eating. Other animals, essentially predators or scavengers, that feed on larger items which offer more nourishment in a given volume may spend less time actually feeding, but may need to spend much time searching for food. Although a predator, the fox falls into neither of these categories because it is not a specialized feeder and can survive equally well both on small items of food widely dispersed and on fewer, larger items. It could make a living, for example, on earthworms, voles, rabbits or carrion, but it hardly ever does so exclusively. Being ever alert, it will take what it can, even a beetle on a bellyful of rabbit, and in situations where prey abounds it may kill in excess of its immediate needs.

One possible reason for the fox's success in diverse habitats is its ability to hunt without developing dependency on any specific food image, whether this image is perceived by sight, sound or smell. Murton (1971), for example, has shown that wood-pigeons feeding on wheat fix their search on objects the size and shape of a wheat grain and, by so doing, are able to feed more effectively than would be the case if a variety of foods of different shape, colour and size were being taken.

The wood-pigeon is feeding by sight alone, however, whereas the fox uses all three senses, jointly or consecutively according to circumstances. By experience, the fox learns that having scented some small mammal, it should then take steps to catch sight of its invisible prey, perhaps by following the sounds it makes when moving through grass or when eating. Food-searching images may be of greater importance to the inexperienced juvenile fox, which will have to learn the significance of visual images, sounds and smells in terms of food (and perhaps danger). Having learned, the fox will become a more efficient food gatherer, if the search image can be modified or switched quickly as the fox proceeds from an overgrown hedge, through a kale field to farm buildings, for example. If foxes find an ample supply of lamb carrion on several successive nights, they may tend to search for such large items exclusively while the supply lasts, but the foods available to foxes are so enormously varied that an inflexible searching image would be more of a hindrance than a help to them in food gathering. Some individuals may 'perfect' predatory techniques for certain species of prey, but in general terms the fox is not a highly specialized hunter, and it owes much of its success to this.

Early in the development of juvenile foxes the characteristic 'mousing' pounce appears at about six weeks of age. There is little doubt that small rodents are the most common foods of foxes throughout their range, but they show no specialized physical adaptation to the hunting of small mammals.

The seasonal differences in diet revealed by faecal or stomach analyses may be a reflection of the changing exploitability of prey, perhaps because of some change in the habitat, or because of differences in numbers, behaviour or age structure in the prey population. Rabbits, crepuscular mammals in much of Britain, may be more vulnerable to foxes during the long winter nights – but young animals abound in the spring and summer, and these may be far easier to capture than adults are in winter. Most often, unless indigestible portions of bone or teeth are present in fox faeces or stomachs, prey is identified by fur or feather; thus, there is usually little indication of the age of the animal that has been eaten.

Many difficulties are associated with the interpretation of results of stomach and faecal analyses. One would be on safe ground in describing remains of horses in the stomachs of foxes as carrion, (as found in samples of foxes I examined from the New Forest in 1969), but what about sheep remains? Since food studies are mostly dependent upon the identification of fur or feathers, and since there are difficulties in distinguishing the wool of adult sheep from that of lambs, there is no means of knowing, in most cases, whether the sheep eaten was adult or lamb; whether it was killed or eaten as carrion; or even whether the fox may have eaten wool fibres deliberately or accidentally whilst seeking beetles lying beneath the wool of carcases picked clean by other scavengers. In any analysis concerned with the frequency of occurrence of food items a few wool fibres found in a stomach has equal rating with a stomach full of mutton. The problem of whether or not the contents of the stomach or faeces represent predation or scavenging is not confined to sheep; there are many known instances where turkey and chicken farms, and even abattoirs, have in the past dumped their offal on waste ground, and foxes have waxed fat and become numerous. Many items may be picked up by foxes at rubbish dumps, and dead animals are found on farm middens and on roadways. In the shooting season an unknown proportion of game birds are shot and wounded, and these, like rabbits impaired by an active infection of myxomatosis, may be particularly vulnerable to predation. Afterbirths of farm livestock are readily eaten by foxes, but these cannot be identified in faecal samples; indeed, such membranes (which are quickly digested) would be difficult to identify, since the fox has to chew and pick at them for some time in order to be able to swallow them in pieces.

Differences in the digestibility of different foods in the stomachs of foxes may bias investigations; more easily digested food items may apparently occur less frequently than less readily digested items. If, however, we are concerned only with the various items of foods that foxes eat and not with how they are obtained, then much can be learned, though difficulties of interpretation are encountered. For example, a dung beetle may be found in a stomach along with remains of rabbit meat; both have equal status as items of diet if regard is paid only to the frequency of occurrence of food items and not to their quantity or quality as food. Alternatively, ten beetles may be found and a few rabbit hairs, which may represent a meal of rabbit taken some hours, or perhaps even days, previously. Do those hairs represent the eating of a whole rabbit, a shared one or some remnant or portion cached after a previous meal? Sometimes the number of voles represented by stomach contents can be counted – in one exceptional case reported by 'Berwin' (1965) 302 small, presumably nestling, rodents were found in one fox's stomach. For that one night we learn something about that fox's feeding behaviour, but rarely is one so fortunate. The problem of assigning the real contribution of the remnants of various food items (found by analyses) to the nutrition of foxes is one which many biologists have attempted to resolve without real success.

Several workers have mistakenly reported or implied that the adult fox selects hares to feed to cubs, this inference being based on the observation that hare remains occur in stomachs or faeces of cubs more frequently than in adults. If a small food item such as a vole is carried to a den, there is a reasonable probability that it will be eaten by only one cub. If a hare, rabbit or lamb is presented to a litter, the cubs, depending upon their size, may devour it within a day or two, but the remnants, the skin, skull and extremities, may be available for cubs to play with and chew for many more days. Thus on the evidence of even a few hair fibres found in stomach or faecal analysis, one single large item might be identified as a food over a considerable period of time, though in reality it will have provided a significant contribution to the diet of the cubs for one or two days only. If an adult fox catches a hare, it may consume it over a period of up to three days, say, until none is left. Thus, for behavioural reasons and because cubs outnumber adults, a large food item would be recorded more frequently in cubs than adults.

Lockie (1959), however, following a lead given by Scott (1941b), attempted with some success to equate faecal analysis with quantity of food eaten. Quantities of different foods which the fox was known to eat in the wild were offered to captive foxes. The weights of the undigested matter in faeces derived from the different foods offered were measured and correction factors calculated. By applying these factors to faecal material, the mass of food eaten can be calculated with acceptable accuracy, as confirmed by Goszczynski (1974). Thus, a collection of faecal material from the field could be used to estimate the total volume of food that the faecal material represents. The method is imperfect technically; also, since it is unlikely that all faeces in any area can be collected regularly, one could not, for example, estimate the total effect of the predator upon natural prey. Much can be learned by this method, however, and its application to the contents of the lower intestine in a large sample of foxes would probably be more useful than the more usual analysis of stomach contents, because a high proportion of foxes examined have empty stomachs (especially those killed in daytime) and because the contents of the intestines represent feeding activity over a longer period of time.

Table 9 shows the major food items identified in fox stomachs by research workers in England, Wales, Ireland and southern Sweden, all areas where rabbits occur. Since the advent of myxomatosis in Europe in the 1950s – a significant ecological phenomenon which many feared would prompt foxes to seek other foods of economic significance – the diets of foxes have been investigated by several workers, notably Lever in England and Wales (1959), Fairley in Northern Ireland (1965, 1970a) and Englund on the island of Gotland, Sweden (1965a; 1965b). The data in the table show foods identified in samples of foxes collected before and after the first outbreaks of myxomatosis in the areas concerned. Since the method of identification of mammalian remains is sometimes dependent upon microscopic identification of fur, hares and rabbits must be grouped together because their hairs are difficult to differentiate. Some of the samples shown in the table were not collected over a twelve-month period, whilst others were; thus the seasonal changes in food intake are not equated in each case. Nevertheless, it is clear that lagomorphs (hares and rabbits) feature prominently in the list of foods eaten by foxes as measured by frequency of occurrence; furthermore, with the exception of the Northern Ireland samples, the frequency of occurrence of lagomorphs was less in the low-population-density, post-myxomatosis samples. The frequency of occurrence of rabbits and hares in the diet is, however, disproportionately high in the post-myxomatosis samples, when allowance is made for the relative numbers of lago-morphs in pre- and post-myxomatosis populations.

Evidence from Britain suggests that foxes did not increase their intake of hares to make up for the scarcity of rabbits during the post-myxomatosis period. Although hare populations increased dramatically later, their numbers were low (in areas of former abundance of rabbits) in the immediate post-myxomatosis period when the relevant studies were made. Thus the relatively high intake of lagomorphs during the period when rabbits were very scarce suggests that foxes were exploiting rabbits with greater efficiency than formerly, when rabbits were wide-spread and numerous. Englund, in Sweden, observed a similar dispro-portion in the intake of rabbits in pre- and post-myxomatosis fox populations than would have been expected if intake was linearly related to abundance.

It is difficult to explain the diet of the fox in Northern Ireland in re-lation to the other samples. Whilst I do not know if the numbers or biomass of small rodents in different habitats in Northern Ireland is equivalent to that in Britain, foxes in Northern Ireland have access to fewer species, since only the wood mouse (*Apodemus sylvaticus*), house mouse and the rat are available, whilst in Britain the bank and field voles are also present. The intake of small rodents is clearly different in Nor-thern Ireland (Fairley, 1970a) and it is possible that rats, hares and rabbits (not separately distinguished by Fairley) are of greater import-ance to foxes in Ireland because of the restricted variety of mammalian prey. The low intake of *Apodemus* in Northern Ireland is not uncharac-teristic of other areas where fox diets have been examined. In North America *Peromyscus*, the white-footed mouse, or deer mouse, which occupies a niche very similar to *Apodemus*, is also taken less frequently than would be expected if abundance were the only criterion determin-ing its exploitation. Goszczynski's study in Poland showed that 65 per cent of the diet of the fox was small mammals, and that of this 93 per cent was *Microtus arvalis*. In the Ukraine, where 91 per cent of fox diet was small rodents, 62 to 75 per cent of the diet was also *Microtus arvalis*. In Europe and North America voles of the genus *Microtus* figure more prominently in fox diets than another vole, *Clethrionomys*, and both of them seem to be preferred to *Apodemus* and *Peromyscus*.

But are they preferred, or does this order of apparent preference merely reflect relative abundance and susceptibility to predation by foxes? Although many workers have demonstrated this rather constant discrepancy in intake of small rodents by examination of stomachs and faeces, and have considered the problems associated with abundance, availability and preference, only Lund (1962) has conducted cage tests of preferences. He used three animals only, all colour variants of ranch breeds, and found a strong suggestion that *Microtus* was preferred. Whilst captive foxes may display idiosyncratic tendencies, Lund's observations are not at variance with field observations on wild foxes.

The proportion of birds in the different samples in Table 9 reflects the type of habitat and the time of year of sampling. The smaller species of birds, such as blackbirds, are taken mainly in the spring and summer and probably most of these are juveniles. Colonial nesting birds are frequently taken at nesting time.

Surprisingly, rats do not seem to be taken frequently by foxes. This is possibly a reflection of the lower number of hedgebank rats since the decline in the use of corn ricks and the advent of the combine harvester and of the reduction in acreage of root crops. Nevertheless, Southern and Watson's (1941) data (obtained before these changes in agricultural practice took place) show very infrequent occurrences of rats in fox diet. Carrion and other scavenged material are omitted from Table 9 as well as less important food items.

The table does not indicate the seasonal importance of fruits and berries to fox diet, especially in the early autumn. Blackberrying is a very common occupation of foxes. They gather them with the delicate poise of someone fearful of falling into the thorns. Standing on their hindlegs and balancing with their front legs against the bushes, they sometimes spend many hours picking at bunches of ripe berries. My colleague Bernard Williams, examining fox gut contents for parasites, found one stuffed full from end to end with nothing but blackberries. Apart from blackberries, foxes will take raspberries, bilberries, yew and sloe berries, cherries, hawthorn berries and where they are able to, strawberries in quantity in summer. Another colleague, Kim Taylor, has frequently seen foxes picking ripe (and to him, stinking) berries one to two metres above ground from wayfaring trees. Horticultural fruits are eaten – pears, apples and plums (preferably, it seems, at the over-ripe stage); on the Continent the grape has been a favourite food of foxes since historical times.

Of the insects, ground and dor beetles are seemingly eaten more frequently than any others, and whilst these and other insects may be taken commonly, their contribution to the bulk of food taken does not appear to be of any importance, except seasonally in some localities. Lever has cited the insects found in his studies on fox diet, but it is very likely that the species and volume of insects and other invertebrates taken will vary considerably according to habitat.

Earthworms, slugs and snails were identified in stomachs by Lever, who considered that they provided only a small proportion of the food of the fox. Slugs would be overwhelmingly vulnerable to predation by foxes, and the fact that they are not eaten in large numbers is probably connected with their relative unpalatability. At some times of the year, especially in late spring, the earthworm *Lumbricus terrestris* is found in large numbers on pastures at night. As the badger eats earthworms rather commonly, it would be surprising if foxes did not make some use of the opportunities provided for taking this readily available food. Earthworms may be rather difficult to identify, especially if, as is usually the case, stomachs are examined many hours after death. The chaetae are easily overlooked, but careful observation will reveal them, sometimes by the thousand. The total biomass of animal matter living in the soil can be as high as the biomass of animals feeding on the grass above the soil, and it is surprising that the fox does not exploit this soil fauna to a greater extent. Perhaps it does; but because of the worm's rapid disintegration in stomachs it is not readily evident and past studies may have overlooked it. Even if the earthworm is not a preferred food, it may provide a very useful buffer in times of food shortage.

Shrews are rarely found in foxes' stomachs; they are, however, frequently found outside cubbing earths, although they do not seem to be favoured as a food. Crowcroft (1957) considered that they may be unpalatable on account of their scent. In this respect the fox, the cat and the weasel seem to share a common aversion. Philippe (1950) observed that though shrews were available, they were not eaten by the American red fox on Montreal Island. They may be taken more frequently if times are hard, however, as might have been the case when Forbes and Lance (1976) found shrews in 15 per cent of fox faeces from Eire.

Moles are also not commonly eaten by foxes (Lever found only two examples in over 500 stomachs) but, as with shrews, they are frequently found at cubbing earths. Four captive fox cubs kept at my laboratory were each presented with a mole when they were about three months old. Three of the cubs promptly buried the moles and the fourth one ate one foreleg and shoulder, which it vomited a few minutes later.

Ducks – especially mallard – are vulnerable to attack by foxes, both on farms and in the wild at nesting time. Farm ducks often wander great distances from the buildings to forage and become vulnerable even in daytime. The loss of Muscovy ducks is not uncommon, but these ducks, capable of flight, often merely fly away rather than fall prey to the fox.

One prospective food item that has never been described in fox stomachs and which I believe is eaten in quantity seasonally is lamb faeces. The behaviour of foxes in lambing paddocks has frequently been observed, and one feature common to these observations is the time spent by foxes picking some objects with the incisor teeth or even licking the ground. The soft, creamy faeces of unweaned lambs and the fresh faeces of newly weaned lambs may be palatable to foxes, though there may be other explanations for this behaviour.

Grass and other growing vegetable matter occurs very frequently in fox stomachs, but not in quantity, and much of this may be taken in accidentally whilst hunting. As Lever pointed out, however, couch grass (*Agropyron repens*) is known to be a diuretic and an emetic for dogs, so possibly foxes need to eat grass at times. Murie (1944) observed wolf droppings consisting almost entirely of grass blades and roundworms, which suggests that the grass acted as a scouring agent.

It is possible that whilst foxes eat many different foods, they show a preference for certain items in order to obtain a balanced diet. However, experiments by Bezeau and Gallant (1950) in ranch foxes showed that, given a wide choice of foods, fresh meat was selected preferentially and made up 99 per cent of the diet. Rickets did occur in these immature experimental animals, and it was concluded that foxes are unable to select food vital to their wellbeing. Even when given a smaller choice of only seven different foods, the results were the same.

Bizarre items are often found in fox stomachs and faeces. One fox examined in my laboratory had nearly 1kg of fat in its stomach; silver paper, branded sausage wrappers, contraceptives – in fact, almost anything edible is likely to be taken from gardens, dustbins, rubbish tips, sewage beds, picnic sites and sea-shore strand lines. In sheep-rearing areas thick rubber bands are sometimes found in fox faeces; they are used to castrate ram lambs and are consumed when foxes eat sloughed scrota. A recent report from Melbourne, Australia, cited foxes as 'marauders' of cabbage plants! Complaints by a farmer that foxes were eating his cabbages were confirmed by stomach analysis. In Britain, silage is occasionally eaten by foxes, but in some areas, Anglesey and Pembrokeshire, for example, it occurs frequently and in some quantity in fox diet. They also eat potatoes in clamps and those left on the field after harvesting.

There is very little evidence that snakes or toads are eaten by foxes, but frogs are occasionally reported in stomach analyses. A frog's skeleton is soft and cartilaginous and it is likely to leave little trace in fox faeces, though frog bones have been found. Frogs may be extremely vulnerable to predation, especially just prior to and at spawning time. In Australia, where snakes and lizards are abundant in some areas, it was concluded by Coman (1973b), McIntosh (1963a) and Ryan and Croft (1974) that snakes and lizards were not a preferred food of the fox.

Of other vertebrates, the list of species likely to be taken by foxes is considerable. Hamish Murray, whilst game-keeping in Scotland, often found evidence of foxes having taken salmon, especially cock fish, from the shallow spawning streams of the Tilt near Blair Atholl and in the head waters of the Tummel in days gone by. He also had evidence to indicate that foxes eat adders occasionally.

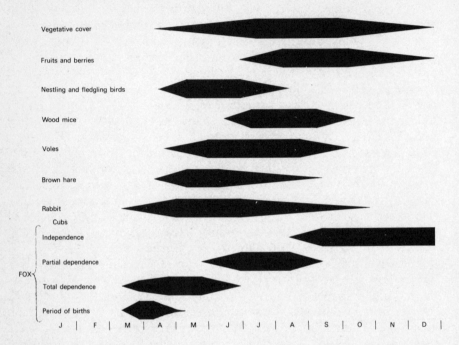

**10** Availability of prospective food of foxes and stages in the development of cubs. The periods of the year when young of mice, voles, hares and rabbits become available and are most vulnerable to predation are shown. The months of June and July seem to offer the best availability of prey.

John Cuthbert also found evidence of foxes eating salmon carcases in the Tweed, but this appears to be a seasonal practice; for example, one December, on a one-kilometre stretch of the Wye and Irfon, thirty-nine freshly dead salmon were counted on one bank. Collectively the dead fish represented at least 180kg of food, but none was apparently eaten by foxes. At Newgale, Pembrokeshire, weir nets erected at low tide to intercept fish at the ebb have to be visited promptly at the next low tide (if it occurs in darkness or the early daylight hours), otherwise foxes will have taken some of the fish; and in Ireland Nairn (1977) watched a fox digging up and eating sand eels (*Ammodylis* sp.), during their spawning period, in the exposed sand at the low-water mark.

In suburbia some householders consider the fox responsible for the sudden disappearance of cats, and remnants of cats found at fox dens is often regarded as proof that the fox is guilty. I know of no eye-witness accounts of a fox catching and killing a cat, though reports of encounters between the two abound. In such situations both species show a studied disregard for each other. It is more than likely that cats, victims of road accidents, are taken as carrion.

Dog remains have also been found at fox dens in suburbia, and Peter Swire (1978) identified dog foetuses in one fox he examined.

The results of stomach analyses on small samples of foxes from two different areas of Britain are shown in Table 10; for comparison, diets of foxes from an arid area of Australia, from a bush area in Missouri, USA, and from Finland and Bulgaria are shown in Tables 11–14.

## Feeding Behaviour

The fox, like most mammals, is endowed with three effective distant sensory perceptors – ears, eyes and nose. Each is of importance in food gathering, and whilst hunting the fox uses all three differentially in different situations. Osterholm (1964) in Finland examined the ability of foxes to find food sources by each of the three senses, and the experiments he reported, which were conducted with captive red foxes in small enclosures, are enlightening (see the section on senses in Chapter 1). He found that vision was of greater importance than the sense of smell in food gathering in daylight, but as daylight receded into darkness, the sense of smell assumed greater importance, until it was clearly dominant. Hearing is important to the fox both by day and by night – but especially at night – in alerting the fox to the presence of a source of food. Hearing is also the dominant sense for the location of distant stimuli, and the fox is able to pinpoint the source of sounds fairly accurately.

In general terms, Osterholm's observations confirm field observations of the fox's hunting methods. A fox can often be seen walking along a hedgerow, stopping, turning its head and then readjusting the position of the head, which suggests auditory location, probably of the rustling movements or the gnawing noises made by rodents in their pathways deep in or under the vegetation. In a small, newly planted forest in Wales which was suffering from a vole 'plague', foxes were seen to hunt in daylight apparently entirely by sight. A fox walking slowly through the plantation was seen to dash several yards to the right or left in pursuit of a vole which was exposed on the surface of the ground and which was undoubtedly detected visually. During the period of about forty-five minutes when this fox was visible, it made seventeen apparently successful captures, most of which it seemed to eat on the spot. When voles are breeding, from late spring to autumn, foxes may detect their nests by smell. They may also be able to use the pads of their feet to detect and perhaps even locate voles and other small mammals by the small vibrations that these animals make when they move unseen beneath dense vegetation.

Foxes have a better chance of detecting potential prey by smell and sound when travelling upwind, and they certainly do move in this fashion when seeking prey, such as rabbits, surreptitiously. But they also hunt at angles to the direction of the wind, especially if small mammals are the quarry.

Apfelbach (1973) studied the manner in which young polecats in captivity identify prey. He found that smell is important in prey-catching behaviour. Young polecats learn to recognize the smell of particular prey species from the food that is fed to them by their mother, so that by four months of age they tend, when given a chance, to select those prey species that are familiar to them. The smell of prey not previously encountered does not elicit a searching or hunting response. When offered familiar and unfamiliar meat, they continue to select the familiar, even when the other food has been offered to them for weeks. In the polecat the smell of prey has to be learned.

There is no information available on the mechanism of prey selection in foxes, but my own observation of captive fox cubs reveals that they have a distinct partiality for food that they are most used to eating (I have remarked that those fed on quail would apparently rather starve for twenty-four hours than eat rabbit or tinned dog food if quail were not available). It is possible that individual foxes or families of foxes in the wild are, in fact, specialists in particular kinds of foods, though not to the exclusion of the usual fox fare. It would be hard to infer this from stomach analyses, however, since all the information derived from each fox in a single area would refer to one feeding period only. It would also be difficult to deduce specialist feeders from faeces collected regularly in any area without knowing something about the individual foxes residing there.

Cubs are weaned at about six weeks of age. Their first solid food is regurgitated food matter provided by the vixen (and the dog?), and gradually, over a period of about a fortnight, fox cubs are weaned to feed upon solid foods exclusively.

There is good evidence from faecal analysis to suggest that small mammals are prominent among foods eaten by cubs, but almost any prey foods may be in evidence at cubbing earths. In sheep-rearing areas an enormous quantity of carrion, partly devoured or untouched, may be found. If the litter is of average size, the parents are kept very busy seeking food for their offspring. The excessive quantities of uneaten food often found at cubbing earths, however, suggest that the parents pay no regard to the amount of food already available there; conversely, evidence gathered during cub-tagging indicates that litters of seven cubs or more leave little surplus food. Since the fox is an opportunist feeder, it is probably of advantage to it to gather as much food as possible at any one time, as scavenging or hunting forays may not always be equally successful.

Little is known of the development of hunting and prey-eating techniques in young foxes. Dr Michael Fox (1971), using captive animals, observed that it is the movement of prey that prompts pursuit among young wolves, coyotes and grey and red fox cubs. On the other hand, I have noticed that almost any squeaking or squealing noise will attract foxes from considerable distances, even in daylight, and once the fox has shown interest in the sound, all caution seems to be abandoned in an endeavour to find the source of the sound. Squeals suggest an animal in distress, and no doubt in the ancestry of the fox the investigation of such sounds was of survival value, perhaps because they indicated the killing of prey by animals larger than the fox itself which would provide carrion for the fox once the larger predator had had its fill.

Once the prey has been sighted, the fox pursues it assiduously. A greyhound coursing rabbits through hayfields in which the sward is high or in ripening cornfields will, if a rabbit has escaped beyond its field of vision, make very exaggerated leaps as it tries to follow its prey. This leaping action is undoubtedly a measure designed to increase the dog's range of vision. So with the fox perhaps. If the fox has located prey by sound alone, a high leap may give it a good view of the prey; if the prey is not visible, the fox may be able to pinpoint the sound the animal is making more accurately as it descends from the leap and, if necessary, adjust the position of its forelegs accordingly. A high leap may permit two senses to come into play simultaneously. Co-ordination of 'hand' and eye is probably more readily acquired than that between 'hand' and ear, which may require a great deal of practice. The arctic fox performs the same leaps as the red fox but not so high, and the grey fox of North America performs a markedly lower leap. These differences in prey-catching technique may be associated with the habitats of the three species of fox. The arctic fox lives in the short vegetation of the tundra and in snow-covered regions, the red fox generally in areas of lusher vegetation, and the grey fox primarily in woodland, which is generally more open at ground level, perhaps, than the habitat of the red fox.

Dr Fox observed that a feature common to the hunting behaviour of all four of the species he was investigating was the habit of playing with prey animals both while they were still alive and after they had been killed. In the red fox initial investigation of the prey took the form of pawing it and pushing it with the nose. This was followed by a high leap – once the prey was motionless – resulting, usually, in the pinning down of the prey by its body and tail (very accurately, according to Dr Fox). If the prey remained alive, play might continue for another half an hour. When more than one prey animal was presented to the foxes, their attention was focused on the one that was most vocal; if none cried, the foxes concentrated on the ones that were most mobile.

Dr Fox considered that the prey-killing pattern and play behaviour of his experimental animals, present from early life, may also be incorporated in intraspecific play. Some prey-attack behaviour is similar to certain displays of aggression towards other individuals, and the prey-killing behaviour may facilitate the development of these aggressive displays.

Observations of my own captive fox cubs have shown that there is clearly much individuality in the manner in which foxes eat prey animals. Young foxes up to four months of age find difficulty in dealing with large, whole carcases of rabbits and lambs, but a paunched rabbit is easily dealt with even by cubs of eight weeks of age. They attack the exposed abdominal wall with their shearing molar and pre-molar teeth until much of the flesh of the body is exposed. Once this has been done, flesh can be picked off with the incisor teeth or chewed with the hindmost teeth.

An intact rabbit or lamb presents more of a problem, since young foxes have some trouble breaking through the skin to the flesh. Some of my cubs have achieved this by chewing and eating the head, after which they were able to chew their way into the body from the neck. Others would chew at the neck until the head was either severed (and usually buried) or until it was connected to the body by skin only. Once a cub had developed one of these two techniques, it adhered to it at least until about five months of age, the age at which the cubs were released. Occasionally a fox would chew at a hind- or foreleg until access to the flesh of the legs was gained, but this was less common.

Whilst single cubs may have difficulty in dealing with large prey, several cubs attacking one carcase can make short work of it. The inevitable squabbling and tug-of-war results in the carcase being torn, though it does not necessarily disintegrate. Often the strongest or most dominant cub claims it and, retreating to some corner, is able to repel attacks and protect the food by presenting his rear quarters to the other cubs while continuing to feed. It is only a matter of time, however, before another cub gains hold of the carcase and continues the tussle.

Cubs, even at eight weeks of age, will bury surplus food, providing it is not too large. The buried food is rarely completely concealed; the head of a rabbit, for example, or its legs, may often be visible above ground.

When a cub is presented with excess food the caching of it may be more of a ritual than good practice. Without exception, the many cubs that I have kept have 'buried' surplus food in some corner of the kitchen, perhaps, going through the motions of pushing the object lightly under the ground, then covering it with litter with pushing movements of its nose. All this on bare linoleum. Having gone through the ritual, the cub then considers the food buried and out of sight. Even adult foxes are liable to make a poor job of concealing cached food. Another captive family of cubs between eight and sixteen weeks old would often bury quail which were given to them rather than eat them there and then, preferring instead to frolic with their attendant. Sometimes, but not invariably, a cub would sprinkle some urine on the partially covered quail. The burying habit extends into adulthood, but it is not known how frequently a fox buries food that is surplus to its requirements. Foxes will often remove the head – sometimes the tail as well – of a dead or killed lamb and bury it, but lamb carcases found at cubbing earths, where the various parts belonging to particular lambs can be identified, are usually complete, which suggests that the fox removes and buries heads and tails or other portions of its prey if it is eaten at the place where it is found but not when the prey is carried to cubs. Sometimes the buried carcase may be very obvious – it is stuffed against a farm gate-post or a large boulder, no real effort having apparently been made to dig a hole or to cover it. A freshly dead ewe carcase found in a Surrey woodland was progressively 'buried' by a fox or foxes over a period of about a week. More and more soil and leaf litter was pushed over it each day until it was almost entirely covered except for the hindlegs and head. For a period of a week none of the carcase was eaten; unfortunately no information was obtained of its subsequent fate.

The burying of surplus food clearly must be advantageous (though I have not seen a fox remove cached food in the wild). It provides the fox with short-term insurance against shortage; it prevents scavengers (birds, in particular) from finding the food; and it might even provide rations not only for the fox that buried it, but for others in the area as well. Perhaps items found cached represent a surplus of preferred food, or the storage of a non-preferred food as an insurance against shortage of preferred food.

The burying habit of foxes once caused considerable consternation and perplexity to my research team when we had tracked down a radio-tagged vixen to a square yard of open moorland. The vixen lay, so we thought, below ground on the very spot where we stood. As we were in an area of peat beds, we assumed that the fox was in some underground watercourse, but our stamping on the turf did not cause the fox to shift its position, nor could an entrance to a watercourse be found within 200 metres. We returned time and time again to the place where the fox was

located, and after about two hours when we were on the point of returning home, my sharp-eyed colleague noticed a slight indication of soil
having been disturbed, bent down, pulled up a loose piece of *Molinia*
turf and found the transmitter – minus the fox – neatly buried there.
The vixen had somehow shed its ill-fitting transmitter, and it, its cubs,
or another fox had buried the treasure.

An elucidating investigation by David Macdonald (1976) into food
caching by foxes, using captive animals on leads and observation of wild
foxes, revealed much that must cast doubt on the content of the foregoing paragraphs. He found, for example, that foxes will cache food even
when they are hungry, and that only those foxes that bury the food (the
location of which they remember) make use of it later. He also found
that adults and cubs defend the cache and will move it to another place if
it has been found by another fox. He concluded that the question of
whether or not a food item is eaten or cached and later utilized depends
upon the fox's preference for that food item. These observations, whilst
clearly significant, may be more or less valid according to home-range
size, population density and size of the foraging area, distribution of
food and utilization of the same food source or feeding area by other
foxes. Macdonald's foxes did not scent-mark the cache or food items.
The few caches my colleagues and I have found, however – usually
lambs' heads or portions of rabbit – smelled strongly of fox, but whether
this was done before or deliberately after caching I do not know.

Henry (1977) has conducted investigations into the urine-marking of
food remnants. He observed that when wild foxes ate food placed for
them on the ground urine was deposited on any scraps that remained
after the meal. Henry also found that a fox would dig up food buried
beneath a scent-mark if the quantity was large (30g) but not if only a
small amount (3g) had been buried. He concluded that foxes deposit
urine at places where unexploitable remnants of scavenged food remain
as an indication that they should not dig at those spots the next time they
are in the area, in spite of the smell of food, because the effort will be
unrewarded; he noticed too that other foxes scavenging in the same area
pay due regard to each other's urine marks as 'no food here' signals.

Cached food was only marked in two out of the 225 caches observed
by Henry, but the site of cached food was usually marked after the food
was retrieved. Studies in Wales and in urban areas – along railway
tracks, for example – have revealed that buried flesh bait (perhaps rabbit
or chicken heads) is readily found by foxes and continues to be taken
from the same cache for as long as it is offered (a maximum of twenty
days). Henry's conclusions help to explain this, but my own observations of the urine-marking of cached food appear to be at variance with
both Henry's and Macdonald's findings. However, the different observations may not be irreconcilable, since in the situations where I have

observed the behaviour, the cache has been made in the presence of other foxes as a very short-term measure. Henry quotes Karyten and Solomin (1969) – work I have not seen – who suggest that foxes mark places where food has been obtained as a cue to future investigations of that area.

Arctic foxes habitually cache food, especially in winter. Some of their caches contain many items of food apparently placed there at different times; the cold climate ensures that the food remains edible. So far as is known, red foxes do not build up similar accumulative food stores in Britain, although buried animals or foods are readily found and eaten by foxes. In a winter series of field trials to investigate this habit, portions of rabbits were buried about 90m apart, on bait lines approximately 5km long; between 70 and 80 per cent of baits buried beneath turf at a depth of 75–100mm were taken daily by foxes over a period of ten days. By the tenth day some of the baits were badly decomposed but were still acceptable to foxes. Sheep carcases found on hills may provide a source of food for several weeks, so presumably foxes are unconcerned about the state of putrefaction of sheep carrion. Dead piglets are sometimes buried by farmers in dung heaps; in some cases they may be taken by foxes within twenty-four hours of burial, which suggests that they are found readily in spite of the olfactory camouflage of the midden. Sometimes carcases remain in a midden for several weeks before being exposed when the manure is moved. In spite of the conditions accelerating putrefaction in the dung heaps, even these carcases are acceptable to foxes. I do not know whether foxes in general prefer fresh food to carrion, or whether this may be an individual preference. In Scottish deer forests the gralloch may be a significant food item at certain times of year, and in some areas red deer calf remains may be found in profusion at cubbing earths (Lockie, 1964).

The adult fox requires 350–550g of food per day, and its stomach can hold up to 1kg of flesh. Small mammals are quickly crushed and bolted whole. The whole carcase of rabbits and squirrels is usually eaten, though at cubbing earths much of the skin may be discarded and, as with lambs, the head and sometimes the feet. In addition to providing roughage in the diet – if this is indeed of importance – the skin of its prey may be a vital source of vitamin D to the fox. When foxes eat birds the larger feathers, such as the primary flight feathers, are usually removed even from small birds before the bird is eaten; when dealing with birds from the size of a blackbird upwards, the flight feathers are removed by shearing them close to the bone – a feature that is frequently used by gamekeepers and others to identify the predator involved. The extremities of the legs and the feet of large birds are usually discarded by foxes, though they do sometimes occur in stomach contents. Whilst foxes are not apparently averse to eating small feathers, wood-pigeons

seem to have much of their covering removed by the fox, either accidentally or deliberately, before the bird is devoured.

The length of time that food remains in the stomach of a fox varies
according to the type of food and whether or not the stomach was empty
when a particular food item was eaten. Szuman and Skrzydlewski
(1962), showed that some of the food eaten will occur in the faeces
between five and ten hours after feeding, but remnants were still to be
found in the alimentary canal even after twenty-four hours. The
stomach begins to pass food into the intestine about two hours after in-
gestion and may continue for several hours before the stomach is empty.
Lever (1959) and others have shown that about 25 per cent of all stomachs examined were empty – this may be due merely to the time of day
the fox was killed and does not necessarily indicate that one fox in four is
unsuccessful in finding food each day.

Foxes mostly feed at night, but they emerge earlier in summer than in
winter and remain active for many hours after sunrise; in this respect
their behaviour varies seasonally. It also varies according to habitat. In
the solitude of the hills, commons and woodlands, and other places
where foxes are left in peace, they may be active throughout much of the
day in spring, summer and autumn, and from observation much of this
activity is apparently a search for food. The kind of daytime feeding activity reported more commonly than any other is 'mousing', which cul-
minates in the characteristic high pounce intended to pin the prey down
in its concealed run through grass or other vegetation or under snow.

Foxes will take rabbits in daylight, but their methods of hunting vary.
Some foxes have been observed to dash wildly about in a rabbit warren,
chasing rabbits quite unsuccessfully, until all the rabbits retreat to their
burrows. After a while the fox abandons this behaviour, but it still continues to move haphazardly throughout the warren, perhaps in the expectation that some of the rabbits will begin to graze again at the burrow
entrance. Indeed, they often do this, and it is then that the fox succeeds
in snatching one of the least wary rabbits. Foxes have also been seen to
stalk rabbits in daytime, but this method is not very successful when
rabbits are numerous, since rabbits have their own warning devices to
alert other members of their group to potential danger. Nestling rabbits
are easier prey. Foxes dig out nestlings from breeding stops separate
from the main warren. They usually dig from the entrance of the stop,
working towards the nest chamber. Juvenile rabbits are highly vulnerable to fox predation, and in the rabbit-breeding season most of the
rabbit remains found in cubbing earths are those of young animals.

At night the fox is more likely to catch a rabbit at the first attempt,
especially on dark, windy nights when rabbits move further from their
burrows to graze up to 275 metres away. However, hunting foxes have
been observed by the light of St Anne's Lighthouse, Pembrokeshire, to

run headlong into a group of grazing rabbits at night, as a whippet would, and meet with little success. The fox has the edge on the rabbit in speed, but I do not know whether it relies on stealth, patience or speed when preying on rabbits at night.

One feature of fox feeding behaviour often discussed by countrymen is how the fox carries the products of a hunting expedition back to its cubs. If it is a large item of food such as a rabbit, the problem does not arise, but when small items such as voles are caught, does the fox make separate trips to its den with each item? Clearly it could not generally afford to do this (though it may when it is hunting close by the den), so in this situation it appears to have three options: to hide the food and pick it up later; to eat it and regurgitate it later; or to carry it in its mouth as it continues to hunt. I do not know if the first option is ever exercised; certainly the second one is when cubs are very small, and by all accounts the third one is exercised very frequently. Some verbal and written accounts report foxes carrying small prey in bundles – either in a bundle of grass or between the body and the wings of a bird being carried. It is easy to understand how this could arise. Grass may be taken by accident, especially if a bundle of voles is put down from time to time, as might happen each time one is caught; and with a mixed bag of prey voles may indeed be successfully cradled in the wings of a bird.

Most medieval illustrations, carvings or otherwise, depicting foxes carrying plundered geese show the fox with the goose over its shoulder. This is almost certainly apocryphal – but an object as cumbersome and heavy as a goose would certainly present a vixen of 5kg or less with something of a removal problem, especially when the den is a long way off.

Foxes, even family groups, seem to have regular feeding habits; they often appear in suburban gardens to take food left for them, or to pillage bird tables at regular hours each night. A fox in Kent, I am told by a colleague, daily appeared at a farm at about 4 p.m. to collect milk strainers discarded from the milking machine; and there are many instances of foxes visiting night watchmen or guards to receive a morsel of food at very regular hours each night. A radio-tagged nine-month-old fox of mine, whose daytime lair was at one end of its range, used to perform much the same pattern of movement each night for the first three hours or so after leaving its lair. What it was actually doing I do not know, since the transmitter merely revealed the animal's position. Experimental work on the uptake of chicken heads offered as bait for foxes revealed that some baits were taken regularly, with a latitude of approximately a quarter of an hour, at any hour of the night, but more often in the first two or three hours after dark.

In addition to acquiring regular feeding habits in certain situations, foxes can also anticipate the supply of certain food items. Stock farmers in Pembrokeshire have often observed that groups of three or more foxes frequent fields in which cows are shortly to give birth, occasionally even as much as twenty-four hours before the cows calve. The only explanation for this behaviour seems to be the ability of foxes to recognize a cow that is about to calve and to associate the signs with an imminent supply of food, in this case the afterbirth. Perhaps foxes have learned to associate the smell of the embryonic fluids released when the membranes rupture – often many hours before the birth of the calf – with a prospective source of food. There are instances of foxes licking new-born calves, chewing the umbilicus and even attempting to eat the afterbirth before it has been shed by the cow.

Three instances are known in Pembrokeshire of foxes attacking and damaging calves during prolonged and difficult births – in each case the cow concerned was a young heifer. It is likely that the afterbirth, not the calf, was the object of attention and that the calf was damaged accidentally. Enquiries in other parts of Britain, however, have not revealed similar examples of foxes anticipating afterbirths; if these observations are correct the behaviour of Pembrokeshire foxes in this respect may have been recently adopted by family groups of foxes.

Cattle afterbirths may be of much greater significance in the diet of foxes than the various surveys reported here suggest. Remnants of afterbirths would not be evident in faeces and, except for freshly ingested membranes, there would be difficulty in recognizing them in stomachs. The foetal membranes of cattle weigh from 2.75–5kg according to breed and would provide a considerable supply of food for one fox or for a family. In Pembrokeshire in 1973 there were 78,000 cows and heifers. At a mean weight of 3.6kg each, the total volume of afterbirths in the county would be the equivalent of 3kg of afterbirth per hectare per annum. Most of this would be available to foxes, even when the calves were born under cover, since the afterbirths are never buried and are usually thrown on the midden where foxes may regularly scavenge (though this may be changing with modern husbandry methods). The availability of afterbirths from cattle calving outdoors tends now to be evenly divided between spring and autumn. The density of foxes in parts of Pembrokeshire is high – probably equivalent to one fox per 30–40 hectares in places. At 3kg per hectare, the mean weight of afterbirths available to foxes in twelve months would be 90–120kg each per annum at these two densities. With a food requirement of about 0.5kg per day, this source would go a long way in a fox's yearly housekeeping. In addition, there is the equivalent of about 0.3kg per hectare of sheep afterbirths shed in Pembrokeshire annually; this, however, is much more seasonal in occurrence and tends to be concentrated in hill land and adjoining areas. Scavenging birds also eat afterbirths, but they are not able to deal with them as effectively as the fox.

## Predation

Many countrymen consider the fox to be a useful predator, in that it helps to preserve the balance of nature – as is the case with the fox's predation of voles in coniferous woodlands, for example. In a stable predator/prey situation neither the predator nor the prey has a clear advantage: the predator must not be able to reduce the numbers of prey species beyond the threshold of recovery, otherwise it would eat itself out of existence; the prey, on the other hand, must not be so secure that it provides nothing for the predator – except perhaps carrion. Within limits determined in part by habitat, a predator/prey relationship reaches stability when it is within the capacity of both to maintain their numbers at some optimum level in the long run. A change in the environment may, however, enhance the success of the predator or the survival of the prey.

One environmental change of considerable significance to the rabbit is the presence of the myxoma virus in Britain. At the first occurrence of this epizootic in 1954–6, some 99 per cent of the nationwide rabbit population died. Survivors bred, and the populations increased in numbers slowly until some threshold of population density was reached when myxomatosis recurred. Over the past ten years the disease has recurred at decreasing intervals; in many local populations of rabbits it now occurs every year, in others at two-, three- or four-year intervals.

In the presence of myxomatosis the predators have suddenly gained an advantage, but this may not, however, be the whole story. Nearly twenty-five years after the first epizootic, the rabbit population in Britain is probably numerically still no more than 10 per cent of its former size, in spite of a higher reproductive productivity than formerly. In 1942 each doe produced a mean of between ten and eleven live offspring per year (Brambell, 1942) – a potential fivefold recruitment rate if all young born survived to breed. In 1957 the reproductive productivity of rabbits was much higher, probably a mean of over thirty live young per doe per season – a potential fifteenfold recruitment rate (Lloyd 1963). Examination of large numbers of rabbits in November and December over several years has shown that the ratios of adults to juveniles at that time of year is about 1:1.5 compared with the potential rate of 1:11 (based on the estimate of reproductive productivity in 1975). Even if it were assumed that all adults had survived, this would suggest a mortality of 85 per cent of rabbits from birth to the end of the calendar year in which they were born. As a general rule the reproductive rate and the survival rate of young show an inverse relationship to population density, such that these decrease as the population density increases. Since 1953 the reproductive rate of the rabbit has conformed to this pattern, but the survival rate of rabbits has not. Vaughan and Vaughan (1968) have indicated that recurrent outbreaks of myxomatosis mostly affect juvenile rabbits; this may be the main reason why rabbits are not achieving even a moderate proportion of their potential for increase. However, many of the samples of rabbits examined in my laboratory in November and December came from areas where myxomatosis had apparently not occurred in the preceding twelve months (one cannot always rely on negative evidence), which suggests that factors other than disease might be operating. It cannot at present be shown conclusively that predation, whether by a single predator or a whole range of predators, is producing this effect, but there is much supporting evidence to suggest that this is the case.

What has happened to foxes since the decline of rabbits? There is no documentation of the effects of the reduction of this large reservoir of food on the reproduction of foxes, but there is ample evidence to show that foxes have not declined in numbers. Indeed, in north Pembrokeshire the converse has happened in a very dramatic and interesting way. In this county the commercial rabbit-trapping industry flourished from 1914 onwards. Gin traps were used, often in the open on rabbit runs or outside the overhang of rabbit burrows, and this had the effect of accidentally catching animals other than rabbits; but, in addition, traps were deliberately set to catch buzzards and, in particular, foxes. Had this not been done, according to the trappers, a large proportion of rabbits held in traps would have been removed or killed and mutilated by buzzards and foxes. This widespread action reduced the fox population considerably – there was probably not more than a pair of foxes per parish. In south Pembrokeshire, where the trapping industry was not so extensive, foxes were more common.

After myxomatosis in 1954–5 the gin-trapping practice became defunct. Traps were no longer used, and the use of the gin trap became illegal after July 1958. By 1960 many farmers in Pembrokeshire were remarking upon the large numbers of foxes to be seen, and by 1962 there was much concern about the losses of lambs and of poultry, which hitherto had hardly needed to be shut in at night. The situation was aggravated because there was no tradition of fox control in the county and few knew how to go about it. In the context of this chapter, however, the significant feature of the Pembrokeshire example is that foxes increased very dramatically in a situation where rabbits had declined by over 99 per cent; even ten years later the rabbit population was numerically probably no more than 2 per cent of its former size.

In Australia too, some four years before the advent of myxomatosis in Britain, myxomatosis spread from an experimental site in the Murray Valley and effected a considerable reduction in the numbers of wild rabbits. Contrary to expectations foxes seemed, if anything, to be even more numerous in some parts of Australia after rabbits declined than they were formerly (Ratcliffe, 1956).

Clearly, rabbits are not necessary for fox survival, nor for the maintenance of high numbers of foxes, and in the Pembrokeshire example we have an indication of the capacity of foxes to survive by virtue of their ability to feed on a wide variety of foods.

Whether or not predators depress prey numbers will depend on the species of predator and prey involved, and upon the habitat. Whereas a limit may be imposed on the increase of a prey population by predation, this limitation may be the result of the combined efforts of several species of predators, not just of one species (see Figure 11).

How does the fox fit into the predator—prey pattern in Britain? Does it, in fact, have any effect on numbers of free-living wild prey? Most biologists believe that in general it does not. Among small rodents, voles in particular are prominent in the diet of foxes, as they are in the diets of weasels, owls, kestrels, buzzards and, to a lesser extent, stoats. Where voles exist they are sought by one or other of these species, each of which is adapted to prey on voles in different situations or habitats, and direct competition for the same food between all of them is unlikely to occur. For example, kestrels take voles in open country, but tawny owls hunt in woodland; stoats and weasels hunt in hedgerows, whilst foxes, it seems, can take voles in any type of habitat. Where two species are taking the same prey in the same habitat, each predator may be adapted to take a different fraction or component of the prey population. Perhaps the weasel is adapted to take young, healthy and active voles in their runs, whereas stoats may exploit older (perhaps ailing) animals; this is conjecture, but it is unlikely that they are both competing for the same food item in exactly the same way. Thus voles are important to the maintenance of many predators, but as direct competition for food between the different species is unlikely, the absence of one or two of these predatory species would probably not create conditions which would support a higher population of the other predators in the area. A regular reduction in numbers of foxes, for example, would not necessarily increase the food supply of other predators.

Various estimates of the effects of fox predation on vole numbers have been given. For example, Polish biologists estimated that foxes removed 39 per cent of voles (mainly *Microtus arvalis*) in populations of low density and only 3.2 per cent of the total number of voles in years of peak abundance (Ryszkowski *et al.*, 1973). How can a prey population predated by several species maintain its size when only one of those species can take as much as 39 per cent of its numbers?

In the first place, field and bank voles have a short life span; they usually survive only one winter. An equivalent of the total biomass of voles alive over winter could be taken (at the end of their life span) each

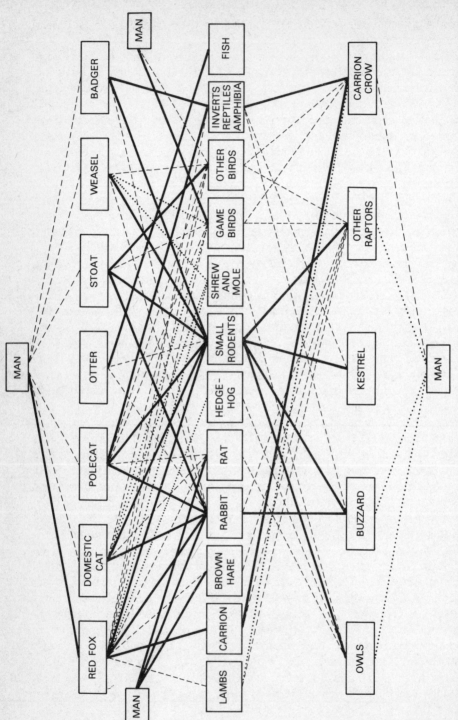

**11** Generalized pattern of some predator–prey relationships involving the more common predators and prey. (After Dr Sam Erlinge, with his kind permission.)

year, therefore, without having any effect whatsoever upon the population size. In addition, the number of voles produced during the breeding season generally greatly exceeds the numbers that can be supported during the winter. Thus predation could (without adversely affecting the prey population) remove annually the equivalent of the total number of animals that are surplus to the winter population size. There are no data on the proportions of the different components of a vole population that are predated, but it is highly likely that foxes are able to prey most successfully on young animals and ailing animals nearing their physiological life span. The removal of surplus animals, young or old, will have little effect on the size of the population that survives the winter.

Vole numbers vary temporally and spatially. In suitable habitats bank voles (*Clethrionomys glareolus*) not uncommonly attain densities of fifty adults per hectare, and short-tailed voles (*Microtus agrestis*) can vary in number from twelve to 500 or more per hectare – an equivalent of 1kg, and between 0.25kg and 10kg respectively per hectare. Population densities of voles of these orders occur in the mid-Wales study area, where the range of movements of a pair of foxes in the spring and summer is commonly five square kilometres in extent. Thus, foxes with a range lying entirely within a newly forested area would have available to them, in peak vole years, about 550kg of bank voles, and from 150kg to 5.75 tonnes of short-tailed voles. (Population densities of foxes in such places in peak vole years can, however, be at higher densities than this; also, home ranges are not necessarily exclusive to individuals or pairs.) These values would represent the biomass of voles that reach the limits of their life span each year, but they are minimum values, since many juvenile and nestling mice do not survive to an age when they can be included in any calculation of population density.

The reproductive productivity of voles is, of course, variable. In non-peak populations each adult female produces about four litters of four offspring in a season, or sixteen young per year. Surviving offspring of the first two litters may also breed in the year of their birth – adding, perhaps, in all, another eight juveniles to the population. The potential rate of increase represented is twelvefold or, taking account of adult mortality, tenfold. If the population is to remain steady from year to year, 92 per cent of the offspring must be lost, since only two of the offspring are required to replace the parents.

If foxes and other predators exploit the juvenile and ageing components of the population more readily than prime prey animals – and there is good reason to believe that this might be so – their effect on the prey population is probably insignificant, providing that the number of juveniles taken does not affect replacement of breeding adults and that old animals are not taken before they cease to breed. However, it is possible that selective hunting by predators has an important depressive effect on numbers of prey as prey populations begin to increase to former numbers after a period of absence or scarcity. Pearson (1966), for example, showed that carnivores at 'normal' densities can depress the rate of growth of a rodent population which has been reduced to low numbers, and in Poland Ryszkowski *et al.* (1971) indicated that in an area of about 135 hectares of woodland and fields, 70 per cent of the estimated total population of 1,800 small rodents were taken by predators.

Generally, what evidence there is indicates that the fox's predatory role is of little significance in limiting the numbers of its main prey foods. It may, however, have an important effect on certain prey species in some circumstances.

Some species are highly vulnerable to seasonal predation. Kruuk (1964) has described the havoc that can be wrought by foxes in black-headed gull colonies on Ravenglas. The food taken from large gull colonies to meet the needs of foxes, whether it be eggs, chicks or adults, may not have a significant effect on the size of the colony nor on its breeding success (unless many foxes happen to visit the colony), but often the fox will indulge itself in killing more animals than it can eat.

There is also evidence that breeding colonies of terns may be attacked by foxes, though the tern's characteristic abandonment of breeding places in some years may not necessarily be connected with this. Naturalists have implicated the fox as an important predator of little terns at Gibraltar Point; however, the build-up of foxes occurred there from 1960 to 1967 perhaps because of the increase in area of buckthorn scrub and the increased leavings of edible litter by visitors.

Bergman (1966) observed the influence of foxes on bird populations of Finnish islands to which the foxes would swim or on which they had become marooned after the melting of the winter ice. He considered their influence under these conditions to be considerable; on one island where twenty-four pairs of gulls and twelve pairs of eider ducks nested, all failed to rear young, and on another island the breeding success of herring gulls and lesser black-backed gulls fell from between 1.9 and 2.2 per pair to only 0.4. Eiders will apparently desert an island if the earliest nests are plundered by foxes. Since most gulls and eider ducks in Finland do not reside on fox-infested islands, the influence of foxes on the total population size is probably, of course, of little significance. On the other hand, the recent occurrence of foxes at the Newburgh eider colony in Scotland is causing some concern.

In North America, Kadlec (1971) introduced red foxes and racoons on to islands containing breeding colonies of herring gulls. As a consequence, the gulls failed to rear their young and after a time left the islands; moreover, repopulation of these islands by gulls was slow after the predators had been removed. On each island the predators released were all of the same sex, and it was found to be difficult to maintain their numbers without very frequent reintroductions.

Norman (1971), examining the possible effects of foxes on shearwater populations in Australia, concluded that on the islands studied, the fox did not have an important effect on shearwater numbers, even though one species, the 'mutton bird', formed a large part of fox diet during the birds' breeding season. Even where alternative vertebrate prey was not abundant, on one island the effects of predation were minimal. Whether or not foxes were present on this island outside the shearwater-breeding season (May—September) is not known – it seems rather unlikely, since the islands in question were only eight hectares in extent and were only a short distance from the mainland. Rabbits were present on other islands and probably provided a stable food source for foxes throughout the year; they also acted as a buffer against exclusive predation on shearwaters. As with the black-headed gulls at Ravenglas, Norman considered that, but for rabbits, foxes might not occur on these Australian islands.

Nyholm (1971) observed that in Finland island populations of alpine hares may be seriously depleted by foxes. Interestingly, he also remarked that foxes eating fresh hare meat would seldom touch any other prey.

Small-island populations are, however, atypical, in as much as the foxes may reside there for only a short period of the year; a broad variety of foods may not be available and the number of foxes may be exceptionally high relative to the area of the island, since they may be there by accident and at the time when birds, for example, are especially vulnerable. In more typical situations a wide variety of food provides a buffer against decreased availability of any one food resource, such that predatory pressure may be switched from one species to another according to availability.

Pheasant preserves may be regarded as islands in this context, but rarely does the fox have an opportunity to pursue its predatory activities in such areas without hindrance. One can only surmise that if the pheasants were not shot and did not disperse, hunting by foxes would affect the pheasant population drastically, since the number of birds is artificially maintained, initially at least, at a high level.

Island situations are atypical throughout most of the range of the fox, but whilst situations similar to those described for Finland may not occur widely in Britain, the effect of foxes on one island, Anglesey, should be carefully watched. On at least two occasions in the 1960s foxes were unwisely introduced there, and whilst efforts have been made to contain them, their numbers are now clearly increasing dramatically. Apart from domestic stock, wild species may also be adversely affected, especially colonial nesting birds, and curlews, oystercatchers, lapwings and mallard.

What is the effect of predation by the fox in more typical mainland situations? Generally, the numbers and distribution of predatory species are determined by the size of prey populations, but the fox is not exclusively predatory, and the alternative food resources on which it can fall back in many instances – albeit seasonally – may allow it to survive when its preferred prey becomes scarce. It would, therefore, have a greater impact upon a prey population if no alternative foods were available – as might be the case with more specialized prey-specific predators than the fox. (The absence of alternative foods and reduction in prey numbers sometimes even precipitates emigration, as happens with Arctic foxes in poor vole years; Kaikusalo, 1971.) For example, when the numbers of rabbits (a major prey species) were drastically reduced by myxomatosis (probably by 99 per cent and more) the numbers of stoats also declined, until by 1960 they were very scarce indeed as judged, for example, by the low numbers captured by gamekeepers in tunnel traps. The decline in stoat numbers may have been due to other things than the scarcity of rabbits, but it is very likely that it was the direct result of the reduction of one main food resource. For comparison with the diet of foxes, food identified in stoat and weasel stomachs separately by Day, Moors and Tapper is shown in Table 15. These studies were undertaken at a time when rabbits were more abundant than in the immediate post-myxomatosis period but were still relatively scarce (except in Sweden). Nevertheless, hares and rabbits frequently feature in the diet of stoats and weasels, and since the rabbit is physically large, its importance in the diet of the stoat must be considerable. How was it then that stoats declined and foxes did not in the post-myxomatosis period? Clearly, the fox is the more adaptable, and the stoat, which could not prey effectively on other species, declined, perhaps not so much from starvation as from an inability to breed.

Does the fox prey upon other mammalian predators? Studies of fox diet in Britain have not revealed such tendencies, but in Pennsylvania Latham (1952), who examined the relationship between fox bounties and weasel bounties, concluded that the fox undoubtedly killed but did not eat weasels (three species), and that where foxes were common they could effectively reduce the local weasel population. And in a sand-dune area in northern Holland J. L. Mulder (pers. comm.) has collected circumstantial evidence that suggests that foxes take stoats and polecats. He tells me that the settlement of foxes in his rabbit study area around 1968 is considered by gamekeepers to have played a role in the subsequent increase in rabbit numbers because fox predation has reduced the numbers of stoats and polecats in the area.

There is no information available on the predatory effect of the European red fox which was introduced into the eastern United States in the early settlement days, but there is some information on the effects of red foxes of British origin on the Australian native fauna. According to Troughton (1957), the fox hastened the disappearance of several species of marsupials. Among the eleven species that Troughton considered had suffered severely from the. predations of foxes, he particularly mentioned the bush-tailed rock wallaby and the black-footed rock wallaby. Marlow (1958) attributed the higher density of small marsupials in Tasmania than on mainland Australia to the absence of the fox.

The egg-eating habit of the fox has brought it into disrepute among naturalists in Australia. Mallee-fowl eggs, which are laid in large mounds of leaves and debris constructed for their incubation, are subject on occasion to heavy predation, and the fox may be responsible at least for hastening the disappearance of mallee-fowl in parts of Australia.

# 3

# Breeding and the Development of Cubs

The fox is a monoestrus species, the vixen coming on heat only once during the breeding season. Both sexes are usually capable of breeding in the season following that of their birth, at about ten months of age.

## Anatomy and Physiology

### The female
The female has the primitive, bicornuate type of uterus, the left and right horns being directly continuous with each other. The ovaries are enclosed in a thin-walled capsule, or bursa, which has a small, slit-like opening (ostium) to the abdominal cavity. Part of this capsule wall comprises a funnel leading to the fallopian tube, which describes a loop round the ovarian bursa, descending to join the uterus slightly to one side of its end. Since the ovary is enclosed within the bursa and the ostium is small, ova shed from the ovary are readily funnelled into the fallopian tube where fertilization takes place.

The vixen is on heat for one to six days; thus, the reproductive cycle is twelve months long. In the female the non-breeding season, the period of sexual quiescence, is known as the anoestrous period. About ten days prior to ovulation the ova mature and the Graafian follicles in which they are contained increase in size and become distended with fluid. Other changes in the sexual organs take place in this preparatory phase which lasts about a week and is called the proestrus period; oestrus follows. At some time during oestrus the ova are shed into the fallopian tube, but though the vixen permits mating during this period (perhaps several times), the period when fertilization is possible may be shorter than the oestrus period. The next phase of the cycle is more variable. If mating has been successful, the vixen becomes pregnant, and if the pregnancy is successful, lactation has to be completed before the vixen returns to the anoestrus condition. If the ova are not fertilized or if mating does not occur, the vixen reverts to anoestrus after a period of pseudo pregnancy, as is common in the domestic dog.

In anoestrus the uterus is thin-walled and flaccid. In a sample of 191 vixens in this condition from mid-Wales the mean length of each horn of the uterus was 10.9cm and mean weight 1.9g. In proestrus the uterus thickens; at oestrus it is firmer and more rounded in cross-section and can be up to 15cm long, with a mean length of 12cm. The cervix also shows considerable changes in size and turgidity at this time. The following measurements of the largest diameter of the cervical region represent the mean of those taken from a large sample: anoestrus, 0.77cm; proestrus, 1.09cm; oestrus, 1.01cm; pregnant, with developing ova in the fallopian tube, 0.85cm; pregnant, with blastocysts in uterus, 0.77cm. During proestrus and oestrus the cervix is very firm and round.

Between the sixth and tenth day after oestrus each uterine horn can be as much as 20cm long and is characterized at this stage by its roundness, turgidity and twisted shape, as if the uterus had grown at a faster rate than the uterine ligament by which it is suspended. At this time, when it may measure 6–10mm in diameter, implantation of the blastocysts in the uterus begins to take place and soon swellings, each representing a developing embryo and incipient placenta, will become obvious.

During the time from anoestrus to pregnancy visible changes take place in the ovary, which in anoestrus vixens measures about 7mm by 9mm and is somewhat flattened. In proestrus, follicles begin to increase in size until they are about 6mm in diameter; they can be seen near the surface of the ovary and are a slate-blue colour. When a follicle ruptures at oestrus, liberating the follicular fluid and the ovum (or ova) its appearance changes over about two or three days to that of an opaque, darker body, slightly reddish in colour, often with the sealed pimple-shaped rupture point visible on its surface. From this time it grows rapidly until it reaches its maximum size, maybe as large as a 12mm diameter sphere or, if ovoid in shape, up to 20mm in the long axis. The growth is due to a rapid increase in the size and number of cells within the former follicle, which becomes changed and functions as an endocrine gland of pregnancy known as the corpus luteum. It is whitish in colour.

At proestrus, the vulva shows some swelling, which continues into oestrus. In autopsied wild foxes, however, this swelling is not as apparent as in the living animal. Breeders of the silver fox use this feature to detect the onset of oestrus and, if the sexes are kept separately, the optimum time for the introduction of a male. There is no bleeding in proestrus in foxes as sometimes occurs in bitches. Microscopic examination of smears of the contents of the vagina can also be used to diagnose the onset of oestrus (Basset and Leekley 1942). In a live fox, between twenty and thirty days before oestrus, vaginal smears are slight in quantity; they show a few leucocytes, a few small nucleated and cornified cells and a little viscous mucus. From six days before the onset of oestrus the number of nucleated and cornified cells increase, but leucocytes remain few in number. The smear is less viscous than at anoestrus and, in addition to the change in composition of the smear, the total number of cells is much greater. Immediately after oestrus there is a decrease in the number of cornified epithelial cells and a very great increase in leucocytes. The smear is usually more copious and whitish in colour at this stage.

The ova are shed spontaneously at oestrus in foxes, unlike in some animals such as the cat, rabbit and weasel, which require the stimulus of copulation to promote ovulation in the oestrous animal. In both dogs and foxes the eggs are ovulated as primary oocytes. In the dog, sperm in the fallopian tube can penetrate the egg at this stage (before the formation of the first polar body), but in the fox sperm penetration cannot take place until the secondary oocyte spindle stage has been reached, a condition that may be unique to the red fox (Pearson and Enders, 1943). In most mammals each follicle at ovulation normally contains only one ovum (oocyte), but sometimes, in mammals which usually shed only one oocyte from each follicle, two or more may occur. Such multi-ovular follicles appear to be common among farmed silver foxes (Johansson, 1941), when as many as six oocytes may be found in one follicle. In the wild fox there is evidence from discrepancies in the number of corpora lutea and ova or embryos (when the latter exceed the number of corpora lutea) that some follicles must occasionally shed more than one ovum (polyovuly), as I observed in a sample of 682 pregnant foxes from Wales, and by Fairley (1970a) in Northern Ireland. The presence of multi-ovular follicles was not clearly demonstrated, however, until Creed (1972) studied this aspect in detail. He found, through microscopic section of the ovary, that multi-ovular follicles were not uncommon in the wild British fox. They occurred most frequently in the developing follicles of cubs, were less in evidence in pre-pubertal vixens and only rarely occurred in vixens near to oestrus. This suggests, as Creed indicated, that degeneration and disappearance of multi-ovular follicles occurs at an early stage in the life of developing females, or that supernumerary oocytes disappear from multi-ovular follicles. A deficiency in the number of follicular cells round the supernumerary oocytes suggested to Creed that these were non-viable and that functional polyovuly may be uncommon in wild foxes.

The production and loss of oocytes or follicles represents a negligible energy waste to a vixen, and the question that the reproductive physiologist must ask is whether or not this phenomenon is positively advantageous to the species and, if so, in what way. Behavioural and physiological phenomena of individual species must in general have some value for the survival of that species, or must at least not be harmful to its survival. A particular phenomenon may be adaptive, and the apparent losses of multi-ovular follicles described by Creed may vary according to external factors. It is certain, however, that the wild fox cannot successfully nurse a litter of more than about ten cubs unaided; consequently, it would seem that if multi-ovular follicles serve any useful function, it must be physiological rather than ecological.

**The male**
The anatomy of the male sexual organs is similar to that of the domestic dog. The prostate gland is small, and there are no seminal vesicles or Cowpers glands. There is a small glandular vesicle associated with the vas deferens where it joins the urethra, but its significance in reproduction is not known.

In the male fox, unlike the dog, there is a yearly cycle of fecundity. Changes occur in young and old animals between the summer, when the testes are inactive, and the period of full spermatogenesis from November to March. Most males are capable of fertile matings from December to early March (Bishop, 1942; Creed, 1960a), after which the testes soon become inactive until the following autumn. According to Starkov (1937), the average volume of semen ejaculated at mating is 6ml in adult males and 2.5ml in young animals, but it can be as much as 22ml. The total number of spermatozoa per ejaculate has been estimated to be, on average, in excess of 300 million.

## The Onset of Fecundity

Ognev (1931) mentions that the onset of the fox-breeding season in the USSR is variable and contends that the further north the locality, the later the oestrus. This hypothesis has been examined, using data from Britain, Switzerland and Sweden.

Dr Jan Englund (1970) of Stockholm collected data from an area extending from southern Sweden to Lapland and was thus able to cast light on the reproduction of the fox over a large range of latitude, even in regions approaching the northern limits of the range of the European red fox. Figure 12 shows the time of the onset of fecundity in male and female foxes, fecundity being defined as ovulation and the production of spermatozoa. Since foxes are not synchronous in their onset of fecundity in any locality, the time of year when 50 per cent of vixens had ovulated, and the time when spermatozoa were present in 50 per cent of male foxes were taken to be the times of onset of fecundity. These times do not coincide in the two sexes, since the male comes into breeding condition much earlier than the female; also, in the vixen onset or occurrence of fecundity is a sudden, unambiguous event, denoting the capacity to breed, but in the male the change from the inactive sexual condition to full spermatogenesis takes several weeks; thus the mere identification of a few spermatozoa does not signify that the male is capable of breeding at that time. Figure 12 shows that onset of fecundity in both sexes is retarded in the higher latitudes; for example, in the male fox it occurs in early October in Switzerland, whereas in Swedish Lapland it occurs in late January, and in the vixen it occurs in late January in Kent and in mid-March in northern Sweden. Figure 12 also shows that onset for the two sexes at the different latitudes falls upon two lines approximately parallel to each other, and that females reach fecundity on average seventy-seven days later than males. If the times when high densities of spermatozoa are present in the epididymides are noted, the interval between the time when 50 per cent of males are in full functional reproductive condition and the onset in females is reduced to approximately forty days.

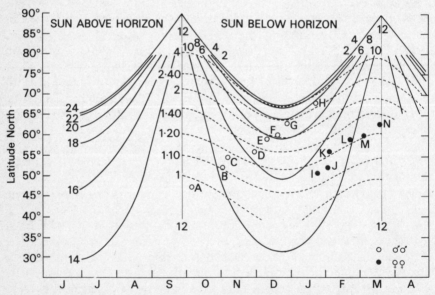

**12**  Onset of fecundity of the fox related to latitude, length of daylight and twilight.
————number of hours of daylight, – – –number of hours and minutes of twilight.
A = Switzerland; B, England and Wales; C, Ireland; D and K, Skane, Sweden;
E and L, Uppland, Sweden; F and M, Varmland, Sweden; G and N, Jamtland, Sweden;
H, Lappland; I, S.E. England; J, Wales. (Lloyd and Englund, 1973.)

So Ognev's statements are confirmed. But why should breeding not be more or less synchronous throughout the range of the fox, and why does the onset of fecundity follow such an apparently orderly pattern as that of latitude? In general terms the answer to the first question is that cubs must be born at a time which is optimal for their survival into maturity. This is especially important in species which produce but one litter a year. The period of birth is clearly important, but it is the availability of food at the period when the parents have to fend for the cubs, and when the cubs have to fend for themselves, that is crucial. In northern Sweden, for example, 50 per cent of the vixens have given birth to cubs by the first week in May — seven weeks later than in Kent. It is highly likely that it is some feature in the first three or four months of life that is of importance to survival and to the timing of breeding, not the time when cubs are approaching adult size at six to seven months (at the onset of the early northern winter): otherwise it would be of advantage to survival if the northern foxes bred earlier.

The true reason for the latitude-related timing of breeding is almost certainly not one single factor, but an amalgam of factors, each of which operates at different times of the season, ensuring the greatest chance of survival for all the offspring of litters in the different climatic regions.

Total annual daylight is the same at all latitudes, but as latitude increases there is less sunlight between September and March and more from March to September. For example, at 65°N in mid-Sweden there is 10 per cent more sunlight between the spring and autumn equinoxes than at 52°N in Kent. The amount of sunlight *per se* is probably of no advantage to a fox rearing a litter, but if the total volume and availability of prey is related to plant growth (which is determined by light and warmth), it would seem more likely that fox reproduction is geared to the availability of principal prey species. Figure 10 shows the time of breeding and availability of young of prey species in England and Wales, and suggests that the crucial periods are the time of total dependence of cubs on the mother and the early period of partial dependence when cubs are learning to fend for themselves.

Although Englund had data for the onset of fecundity of vixens at 68°N, the sample was too small for analysis. It would be most interesting to know when most vixens give birth to litters at latitudes near to or beyond the Arctic Circle. The apparent orderliness of the pattern of onset may be regulated by some physical factor such as light or ambient temperature. The monthly mean temperature at any given latitude and location may not vary widely from year to year, but if temperature triggers breeding, foxes must be required to respond to different temperature stimuli from place to place (at the onset of fecundity in males the temperature in Switzerland in September is very different from that in Lapland in late January). Similarly, total daylight at the time of onset is

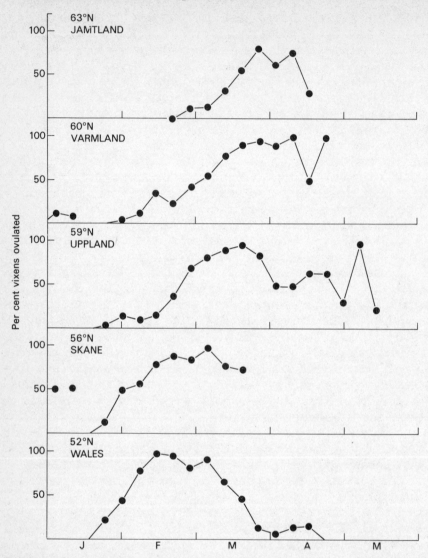

**13** Proportions of ovulated vixens in samples from Sweden and of pregnant vixens in samples from Wales

very different in these two locations, so if light is involved, it is not simply the total amount of daylight immediately prior to onset which determines its timing, nor, in the case of the male, is onset associated exclusively with decreasing day length, since Lapland foxes become fecund at a time of increasing daylight.

It is very likely that onset is determined by sensitivity and response to light at some phase in the endogenous rhythm of foxes, but this cannot be determined except by experimentation. Also, it is probable that northern foxes may respond differently in this respect from southern foxes, and this differential response may be inherited. One curious feature of the time of onset of fecundity is that it bears an approximate arithmetical relationship to day length some months earlier. If the total amount of daylight and twilight in the preceding sixteen-hour day (that is, the period from sunset to sunrise plus the time when the sun rises from or falls to 6° below the horizon) is calculated for each location shown in Figure 12, onset in males occurs at a mean total of 1,439 hours (the range is from 1,335 to 1,495 hours) and in females a mean total of 2,198 hours (the range is from 2,097 to 2,254) from the sixteen-hour day. Although this arithmetical relationship is an artefact, it may permit the onset of fecundity to be roughly predicted at locations at different latitudes.

In Australia onset of fecundity in 50 per cent of the dog fox population at 30.5°S is in May (November in the northern hemisphere), seasonally much the same time as in Britain (McIntosh, 1963b).

## Mating and the Span of the Breeding Season

Fox ranchers seem to be unanimous in their belief that the silver fox, a colour variant of the red fox, is fundamentally monogamous. In captivity, if sufficient males are available, monogamous matings seem to be preferred by breeders. It used to be the practice to introduce the vixen to the male by placing them in adjoining cages when proestrus was anticipated. This seemed to ensure a better chance of successful matings – or any matings – than if the male were put to the female without an introductory period. The monogamous tendency is a feature of the behaviour of the dog fox, and in the early days of fox farming, when the stock was only a few generations removed from the wild, this tendency was maintained. With selective breeding, or through training and husbandry, however, the polygamous male is now more common, though a normally polygamous male, if left with an individual female too long, may refuse to mate with other females.

After copulation the mated pair are locked, as with dogs, facing opposite directions (embarrassed by their predicament, as someone once suggested!). The whole act is usually accomplished in between fifteen and thirty minutes. In wild foxes it can occur by day or by night and is often accompanied by considerable vocal clamour prior to mating. Ognev mentions that mating foxes are able to uncouple easily at the least sign of danger, but three colleagues who came across such a pair on a steep-sided valley disagree. This pair showed considerable consternation and, being unable to move positively in any direction, they eventually tumbled down a steep slope and emerged separately before the rolling ball of fox fur, feet and tails reached the bottom some 100 metres below.

Whilst active participation in mating by the vixen is characteristic of oestrus, about 8 per cent of anoestrus vixens examined from Wales and south-east England had spermatozoa in their vaginae or uteri from six weeks before the onset of the mating season. The density of sperm in smears taken from the genital tracts was sparse by comparison with oestrus matings, which suggests that the full oestrus mating sequence had not occurred. Nevertheless, the vixens had clearly tolerated the males' attention to a certain degree. (If at autopsy sperm became unrecognizable to the observer a few hours after insemination, the incidence of such vixens in the field samples would be very low indeed, but it seems likely that such spermatozoa are identifiable for some days.) Possibly such behaviour may be of significance in accelerating the onset of proestrus and oestrus. Foxes in most situations are a solitary species, inasmuch as they do not live in packs like wolves, and if, indeed, they are monogamous in the wild, there would be some risk of unpaired vixens coming into oestrus, if oestrus was determined by abiotic, purely physical external factors such as daylight duration. If onset is influenced by biotic factors such as the sight, smell and behaviour of attentive males (perhaps including attempted matings by the male) the monogamous habits of the dog fox would then ensure a greater probability of a dog being available at oestrus. Oestrus in unattended vixens may occur later in the season when the ultimate physical stimuli alone produce the reproductive response.

Premature matings at anoestrus have been shown to occur in silver foxes, but they are rare (Szuman, 1960). German biologists have observed the mating behaviour of wild red foxes (Schmook, 1960; Rieck, 1965). Apparently, several dog foxes will attend a vixen and the dominant male of the group will mate with it. The other males remain in attendance and later may also mate with the vixen. Whilst this observation is beyond dispute, there is no real indication that the vixen is in oestrus when this occurs. Possibly the sperm identified in the reproductive tracts of anoestrus vixens may be the result of such matings. If one of the males then stayed with the vixen (there is no evidence for this), a monogamous union might later be established at and after oestrus. It is suggested by Tembrock (1957) that even among captive red foxes living in a group long-term monogamous unions are formed, which may only be terminated when a dominant male usurps the vixen.

The proportion of vixens pregnant throughout the breeding season are shown in Figures 13 and 14. Onset of pregnancies in Wales occurs between seven and ten days later than in south-east England. Occasionally some vixens become pregnant out of season; of 610 Welsh vixens examined, for example, four were pregnant before 17 January. Calculation of the dates of conception of these four sets of embryos showed that in two cases oestrus and mating occurred in early November, and in the others in late November and early December. Another pregnant vixen killed on Boxing Day, 1962, at Llandudno was near full term. All but this latter vixen had mated at a time when at least half of the males would have been fecund, though many of these males would not have been sufficiently developed sexually to achieve fertile matings. The Llandudno vixen had mated sometime during early to mid-October, a time of year when very few male foxes would have been capable of fertile matings.

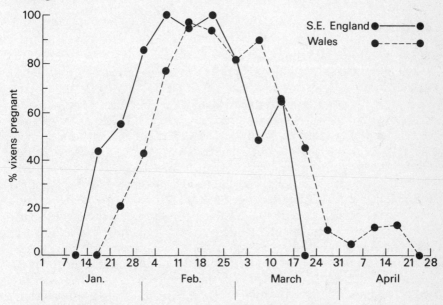

**14** The breeding season of vixens in south-east England and Wales

Pregnant vixens have been reported in July, August and September (verbally, from several sources). Such pregnancies must be of uncommon occurrence, since from May to September the dog fox is sexually inactive, spermatogenesis being in abeyance. Even in April, when a small proportion of dog foxes are fecund, most of the spermatozoa found in the epididymides are degenerate; thus mid-summer breeding is highly unlikely to be encountered often, since both sexes are normally sexually inactive at that time, and it would be a rare occurrence for a pair of sexually active foxes to be found out of season in one locality. Szuman has shown, however, that in ranch foxes a small proportion of vixens – less than 1 per cent – will come into oestrus twice in one season. In the cases cited here nothing is known of the reproduction history of the vixens and delayed implantation has not been described in the red fox.

Males reach their peak of fecundity in January in England, Wales and

Ireland, and most vixens are pregnant from the first week of February to the first week in March inclusive. An often-quoted account of the breeding season of the red fox by Bernard (1959) indicated that in Luxembourg pregnant vixens can be found throughout the year except in the months of August, September and October. (This evidence is based on foxes killed by bounty hunters from 1954—6 inclusive, when pregnant vixens qualified for a higher rate of bounty. The reward could be claimed without production of the carcase, which suggests the possibility that more pregnant vixens were claimed than were actually killed.)

## Gestation

The gestation period in most foxes is fifty-two to fifty-three days. Pseudo pregnancy in unmated or sterile vixens lasts for about forty days; corpora lutea develop and uterine changes follow, with the uterus remaining in a condition similar to that which obtains at implantation for the remainder of the pseudo pregnancy period. None of the pseudo pregnant vixens examined at my laboratory contained macroscopically visible milk in the glands, but Rowlands and Parkes (1935) identified milk in the ducts of such vixens microscopically.

It is not known how long the fertilized ova remain in the fallopian tubes before reaching the uterus as morulae. Examination of the relative frequency of occurrences of the different gestational stages suggests that the ova may not reach the uterus until about the sixth day. According to Creed (unpublished work), the eggs, as late morulae or early blastocysts, are first transported to the cervical neck of the uterus and are then redistributed numerically and spatially in a fairly even order throughout the two horns of the uterus. Some phenomenon of this kind must occur, since the blastocysts, embryos and scars frequently show this orderliness, even in unilateral ovulations.

The precise time of implantation is not known, but from the frequency distribution of the different stages of gestation in large field samples it seems likely to be between ten and fourteen days. Implantation is central. The zonary, endotheliochorial type of placenta is soon formed, and there is only slow development in the size of the embryo until the placenta reaches a dimension of about 15mm across the zonary band. At the two borders of the placental band a blood-filled sinus appears. The blood within it is stagnant; the haemoglobin breaks down and yields a brown, watery fluid. The sites of the placentae persist in anoestrus vixens as dark, pigmented areas known as placental scars; sometimes the scars of two or more pregnancies can be seen with the naked eye (McEwen and Scott, 1957, describe this in arctic foxes), the pigmentation being determined as a combination of haemosiderin and a lipid.

The mammary glands begin to increase in size visibly when embryos are about forty days old, but milk can only rarely be expressed from the nipples before the birth of the cubs. The fox usually has four pairs of teats. Many countrymen claim, by examining the mammary glands, to

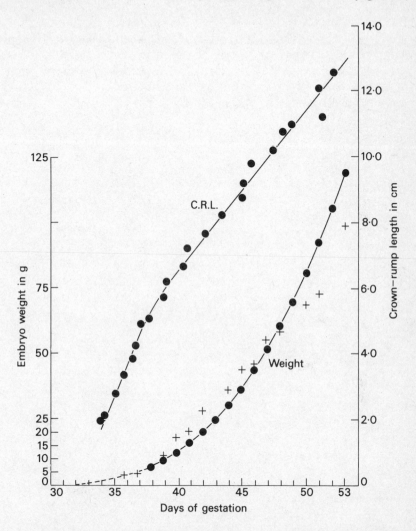

**15** Fox embryo weights and lengths related to embryo age. From the plot of the cube of embryo weight against age shown in Figure 17, the weights of embryos at daily intervals can be plotted. Layne and McKeon (1956b) derived growth rates from Smith's (1939) data (shown +). This follows the curve based on the Hugget and Widdas formula (1951) ± 1–1.5 days. From the relationship of weight to crown-rump length of fox embryos shown in Figure 16, the crown-rump length can, as shown here, also be plotted against stages of gestation. The ages of embryos post-34 days can be estimated to within one day by comparison with these growth curves.

be able to tell how many young are being suckled by a vixen. Whether or not cubs have a tendency always to suckle the same teat as implied, is not known, but in litters of four or less the posterior inguinally situated glands show evidence of having had most attention and the pectorally situated ones least.

The daily development of embryos is best known from about thirty-two days after conception until birth. At between twenty and twenty-three days the incipient embryo is first seen as a delicate streak of cells within the foetal membranes, which are surrounded by the encircling band of the placenta. From this stage the embryo develops rapidly, and by between the twenty-seventh and thirtieth days it is 7–10mm long. At

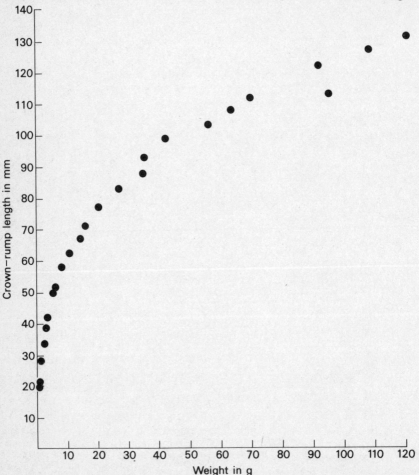

**16** Crown–rump length of fox embryos plotted against their weight. 394 embryos are divided into 24 groups of increasing weight and the means of each group are plotted against the mean C.R.L. of the group.

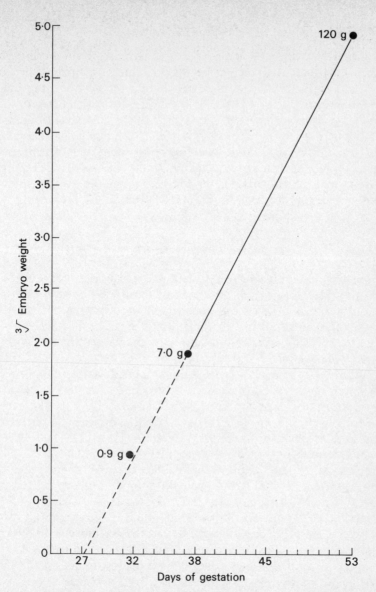

**17**    Regression of cube root of embryo weight on age. Hugget and Widdas (1951) derived
a formula describing the growth of embryos for a substantial part of the latter two-thirds of
gestation, from about the time when the definitive embryo is beginning to develop. The
formula is based upon a relationship between the cube root of embryo weight and embryo
age. If $t$ is the total gestation time, and $to$ the period from conception to the stage of
development at which the relationship begins, then a is the growth velocity which is
peculiar to the mammal concerned. Smith, in 1939, determined the weights of fox embryos
at 32, 38 and 53 days. The 53 day weights of the North American fox (at parturition) are
rather low at a mean of 85g compared with those of British foxes so the mean weight of the
largest embryos observed in samples of foxes from Wales (ie 120g), is regarded as the mean
birth weight and only the weights of the 32 and 38 day embryos observed by Smith are used
to derive Hugget and Widdas growth velocity constant, a. The plot cuts the axis at 27 days.

about thirty-two days the limbs, eyes and mouth are developing rapidly and two days later the embryo is about 20mm long. From this time to about thirty-nine days the embryo lengthens rapidly, at a faster rate than that of its weight gain, but from forty days onwards the rate of gain in weight exceeds that of length. The stages of development of cubs from about thirty days onwards has been well described and depicted by Layne and McKeon (1956b) (see Figures 14 and 15). The frequency distribution of the stages of development of embryos in all pregnant foxes sampled suggests that the period from ovulation to the time when the embryo begins to develop rapidly may be only a few days short of half the total gestation period.

## Pre-natal Loss and Barrenness among Vixens

If Figure 14 is examined – taking Wales as an example – very nearly 100 per cent of pregnancies are observed at about 15 February; since the gestation period is 52–53 days, the proportion of vixens pregnant from then until the cessation of breeding should be as indicated by E–F in Figure 18. This figure is derived simply by drawing a line following that for percentage pregnancy from 17 January to 15 February (D–C, 52 days after the first pregnancy) and inverting it from 10 March, the time when births would be expected to occur. The line in Figure 18 for the calculated proportion of vixens pregnant from 10 March (E–F) is not very different from that for the observed proportion pregnant from about 3 March. It does not coincide for two possible reasons: first, the samples were not representative of the population throughout the period; second, assuming the sample was not biased, some of the pregnancies recorded in the line of the graph from onset on 17 January to the peak at 15 February were unsuccessful and terminated earlier than normal pregnancies. There is no means of knowing whether either or both of these factors were operative. I would guess that the former was highly probable and, that being so, the unsuccessful pregnancies indicated might have an equal chance of being under- and overestimated in the figure.

This being so, Figure 18 suggests that 7–10 per cent of pregnancies did not survive to parturition. This possible loss of pregnancies can be examined in another way, by direct observation of the condition of the embryos at autopsy. Of the 114 vixens at stages of gestation at which the deaths of embryos could be ascertained, seven entire sets of embryos were dead, i.e. about 6 per cent; in addition, another four sets showed a loss of not less than 80 per cent of embryos each. None of these occurred in the last twelve days of gestation; thus it seems highly likely that these were also destined to be lost *in toto*. Combined, these losses amount to 9 per cent total loss of pregnancies in a sample comprising vixens in the last twenty-eight days of gestation. In these two ways a loss of at least

7–10 per cent of pregnancies is suggested. But these data refer to three breeding seasons, two of which provided adequate samples, whereas the third yielded fewer animals. In one season, 1968, pre-natal losses of entire uterine litters estimated in these ways was 22 per cent and in another, 1969, losses were negligible.

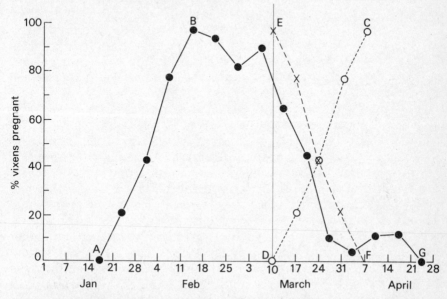

**18**　The breeding season of vixens in Wales (1959) showing possible extent of loss of entire sets of embryos – see text.

Higher losses and non-productivity are indicated, however, if non-pregnant, ovulated vixens are examined and included in the sample. Many (but not all) pseudo-pregnant vixens can be identified positively (by macroscopic techniques) from about fifteen days after ovulation, and vixens which have not ovulated can be identified as barren vixens if they are taken in samples collected after the peak in pregnancies has occurred. In all, five such vixens were identified. Vixens showing these two conditions represented 9.4 per cent of the total examined (Table 16). The proportion of uteri in which all embryos were dead was 6.6 per cent in the Welsh samples. In addition, thirteen vixens examined in April had, to judge by the state of their uteri, clearly given birth to live or dead young near or at full term up to about two weeks before the carcases were examined, but none had milk in its mammary glands, nor was there evidence that they had nursed cubs. These vixens had either aborted their litters or given birth to live young which had died accidentally, or as a result of some violation (by man or predators), or of natural causes soon after birth. Though these vixens without living offspring were not necessarily all physiologically barren, they must be taken into account in any estimation of the total productivity of the vixen population. By inference, therefore, they had lost their entire sets of embryos or young before, at or soon after birth, and they contributed another 4.5 per cent of non-productive vixens to the total. The total proportion of non-productive, barren vixens in the samples examined was 20.5 per cent.

As Englund (1970) has shown, the proportion of non-productive vixens varies from place to place, and between years and age groups; thus the productivity of vixens is likely to be determined by such external factors as, perhaps, population density, size of home ranges, social encounters and food availability. The proportion is unlikely to be constant in all populations of foxes, even in the habitats of Britain which are hospitable compared with the harsh areas of parts of Sweden.

Englund also examined pregnancy rates and pre-natal losses. In Sweden, as elsewhere, the fox feeds to a large extent on small mammals, but in the middle and northern parts of Sweden the vole population shows widespread, dramatic cycles of numbers; in some years they are extremely abundant and in others very scarce. In the years of scarcity the fox does not have a great reservoir of alternative prey in the winter and early spring in these parts of Sweden, and in such years Englund found evidence of a preponderance of scavenged food of low nutritional quality in stomachs and faeces. Rabbits occur in southern Sweden, but these do not show the periodic cycles of abundance characteristic of voles, and Englund was able to compare the reproductive performance of foxes obtained from areas where rabbits were present and absent and found that breeding proficiency was not as liable to fluctuate where rabbits were present.

In addition to the examination of the uteri of foxes obtained during the breeding season, Englund also used evidence given by placental scars (since these persist) to determine whether or not a vixen had bred, and if so, how successfully. The evidence provided by the placental scar is perhaps a little subjective and is based on the unconfirmed hypothesis that the degree of blackness of the scars varies according to the fate of the embryos *in utero*; that is, that black scars indicate successful births and grey scars indicate death and reabsorption or abortion. This has not been examined experimentally, but if large differences in reproduction occur between one year and another, Englund's technique might reveal this.

Using this evidence of placental scars in anoestrous vixens, and combining it with evidence from vixens examined in the breeding season, Englund estimated the proportion of barren, non-productive vixens to range from 23–67 per cent in older vixens, in samples taken from areas north of the limit of distribution of rabbits (59°–63°N). In 1968, when rodents were scarce in the winter preceding the breeding season, the proportion of barren females was high by comparison with other years, but even in good food years the extent of barrenness was high by comparison with Britain, except in the area where rabbits were present, where it was lower. In all but two samples out of twelve, Englund found that many more yearling vixens than older females were barren. Yearlings also tended to produce smaller litters, and their productivity, taking barrenness into account, was usually far lower than that of adult vixens.

There was little information on the density of the fox populations sampled. Although red foxes are generally a solitary species, much social contact between individual foxes occurs outside the breeding season, and in poor food years there may be much greater social contact, through competition for food and space, than in other years. If this occurs prior to and during the breeding season, its effect on reproduction may vary seasonally according to the degree of social contact that is forced upon the foxes. In poor food years, when scavenging at rubbish dumps is more prevalent, the availability of natural food is low and the intake of food per fox will be dependent partly upon population density and partly upon social factors which will almost certainly favour the older animals when in direct competition with younger ones. Thus it seems that in most years in Sweden a significant proportion of the fox population is barren, and in some years this proportion can be very high indeed. This is probably an indication that the habitat is marginally less suitable for foxes than areas where productivity is higher. On the other hand, the survival rates of cubs in Sweden might possibly be greater than those in areas of high productivity, which might redress the balance. Unfortunately, insufficient information is available on this aspect of productivity.

Thirty years earlier than Englund, Chirkova (1941) observed that food availability played an important part in reproductive success. She noted that in poor food years females would not come on heat, or that ova would not be fertilized and that sporadic losses of embryos would occur – even the reabsorption of entire sets of embryos less than 3cm long (less than thirty-five days' gestation) and the abortion of older foetuses. She also noted that some vixens could not feed their young as a consequence of poor nutrition or failure to lactate. Reproductive success was directly related to the abundance of voles, and under poor food conditions up to 47 per cent of vixens were found to be barren.

Chirkova (1941 and 1955a) observed that the fox population showed fluctuations in relation to vole abundance, but twelve months out of phase with the vole fluctuations, which have a periodicity of about four years. In years of high vole and fox numbers the reproductive success of foxes was very high, large litter sizes – up to thirteen cubs per litter – being not uncommon, with a mean litter size of 5.9. There was a reduction in fox numbers of about 50 per cent from peak to trough years, but in some years a three- or a fourfold increase was noted from trough to peak. (Such large litter sizes are unusual in Britain, but they are not uncommon in North America or in the USSR. David Johnston of the Ministry of Natural Resources, Canada, tells me that litters of ten and above are common in Ontario.)

David Macdonald, working at Oxford on a fascinating study (as yet unreported) of foxes living in what seems to be a very rich habitat at Boars Hill, has observed a remarkably low reproductive productivity of vixens living in the midst of apparent plenty. Here, it seems, population density or, rather, some function of it has a depressing effect upon reproduction.

The collection of a large sample of urban foxes from London has provided Harris (1979) with opportunities to describe the reproductive contributions of vixens according to their age. In the high-density population studied he observed that about 50 per cent of yearling animals (that is, those twelve months old) failed to breed. The productivity of older animals was high.

One sometimes hears from countrymen that unusually high proportions of vixens are barren in certain years. Usually the observations are based on the numbers of vixens killed at fox drives in March or April, when most should be heavy in young or nursing a litter, and the small proportion of vixens in these conditions in the shot sample is taken as evidence of extensive breeding failure. Samples of foxes taken by shooting at this time of year may, however, be heavily biased in favour of barren vixens, so that the samples may be quite unrepresentative of the entire population. A few days prior to parturition, and for two to three weeks afterwards, vixens will lie below ground in the daytime; barren vixens, on the other hand, have no cubs to nurse and will be in surface cover. Consequently, for about four to six weeks after the first litters of the season have been born, shot samples of foxes may contain a preponderance of barren vixens. This was the case in several samples I obtained from Kent in 1966, when the proportion of barren vixens was as high as 61 per cent in one sample. (There is no simple solution to the problems of the detection and avoidance of biased samples, except care in designing the sampling method. It is usually better to collect by a variety of methods than to rely upon one. In this way comparisons of data obtained by different methods can be made, even if collectively they may still not be representative. It is not often the case that definite bias can be detected in a well planned survey, let alone measured.)

## The Reproductive Capacity of the Fox

### Litter size
Adequate field evidence of mean litter sizes at birth is not easily

obtained, since it is difficult to secure large samples; also, not all the cubs in any one den may be found and mortality may occur among cubs between birth and the time that the litter is examined. Consequently, many biologists and interested countrymen regard the number of visible embryos found in dead pregnant vixens as representing the litter size at birth or simply the unqualified litter size. Data obtained from pregnant vixens yield a great deal of information about the reproductive success of foxes, but often it is impossible to make comparisons of data obtained by different workers because different criteria may have been used. Added to this difficulty is the probability that some samples will not be representative of the fox population from which they were taken, and comparisons of the reproductive capacity of vixens taken from different habitats, or in different seasons, cannot be made confidently, since these can be invalidated by so many biological factors. One worker may count all embryos and use this number to estimate the mean birth litter size; another may count embryos at different stages throughout gestation and estimate the mean litter size from the stages near to the time of birth. By statistical means it might be shown that a mean litter size of 4.5 is significantly different from a mean of 5.0, but such a comparison will not be justified if the samples are not biologically comparable. The following mean litter sizes, based on embryo counts, have been recorded in North America and Europe: 4.3, 4.7, 5.1, 5.3, 5.4 and 6.5. In some studies placental scars have been taken as evidence of litter sizes, yielding means of 4.4, 4.7 and 6.5, for example; and in others, embryo counts and placental scar data have been pooled, giving, for example, 4.5, 5.3 and 6.4 as the mean litter size. Though these data provide an indication of the possible range of mean litter sizes, nothing definite can be inferred by comparing these sets of data.

Data on numbers of embryos per pregnancy at different periods of gestation of foxes in Wales and Kent are shown in Table 17.

**Reproductive productivity**
It will be seen from Table 18 that the fertility of vixens and the mean number of offspring born seem to vary from one season to another and from place to place. As indicated earlier, these variations may be due directly or indirectly to such features as the proportion of yearlings in the female breeding population, to population density, to the richness of the habitat and possibly, in some circumstances, to direct interference by man; there may be other features of significance in this context, but there is no information whatsoever on the interaction between such factors as have been mentioned and the effects they have, jointly, and in some cases singly, upon breeding success in the fox.

Since the mean number of embryos per pregnancy observed in the last ten days of gestation varies between the different samples, it would require very large samples, collected over many seasons and in different locations, for highly reliable estimates of mean birth litter sizes and the range of the variation to be derived.

The best that can be done with limited data is to take the mean for the total sample of Welsh vixens examined (4.7; see Table 17), recognizing that this may be subject to much spatial and temporal variation.

The mean birth litter size refers only to those vixens which produce living young and, as shown by Englund for Sweden (1970), a considerable proportion of vixens may not be productive in some circumstances. Thus in order to estimate the capacity of the fox to reproduce and replace adult foxes which die from whatever cause, the mean birth litter sizes must be related to all the vixens in the population. The proportion of unsuccessful breeders may also be subject to considerable variation in place and time, but to provide a basis for calculation for the Welsh sample, the mean proportion of non-productive vixens over the four-year period (i.e. 20.5 per cent) is incorporated. Using these data (mean birth litter size of 4.7, and 79.5 per cent of successful pregnancies), the mean number of cubs born alive per vixen in the population is 3.7. (The range of litter sizes at birth is shown in Table 18.) If the data for southeast England are treated similarly, the corresponding figure is 4.5. These estimates provide no more than a general guide to the productivity of fox populations, and in view of the various estimates of litter sizes reported by other workers, it seems likely that they are not outrageously unrepresentative. They will be used in Chapter 4 as the basis for an examination of the population dynamics of the fox.

## Cub Sex Ratios and Weights at Birth

The ages of embryos from thirty-three days to birth can be determined by weight and examination of the embryos (see Table 20).

Fox embryos can be sexed by external characters from the thirty-sixth or thirty-seventh day of gestation, when they weigh about 3.5g. The sex ratio of 333 embryos from sixty-eight litters was 50.45 per cent male. Dividing these into embryos younger and older than forty-five days, the sex ratio from thirty-six to forty-five days was 48.9 per cent male and from forty-five days to birth 51.5 per cent male, an indication – but no more than that, in view of the small sample – that the male embryos may have a better uterine survival rate. Male embryos also seem to have a faster rate of growth than female embryos. In a sample of forty-four litters, containing embryos of both sexes, male embryos were on average 11.35 per cent heavier than female embryos. This was consistent throughout the period that the sex of embryos could be determined. In nine of the forty-four litters the mean weights of the females were greater, but in four of these the females were represented by a singleton in one uterine horn, the other horn containing from three to five male embryos.

It is difficult to obtain adequate data on birth weights of foxes without breeding them in captivity. In North America Smith (1939) indicated the range of birth weights of ranched foxes to be 70–100g, with exceptional individuals up to 160g in weight, and Tembrock (1957) recorded weights of 80–100g in Europe. I have no information for captive foxes, but much can be learned from records of the weights of embryos and young cubs (often accompanied by *post-mortem* estimated dates of parturition, as judged by the state of the uterus of the mother). I have not found embryos heavier than 126g. The smallest cub I have found alive weighed 84g, but this was one of a litter of six, the mean weight of the remaining five cubs being 143g. In another litter of five, about two days old, the cubs weighed a mean of 134g. Additional information suggests that in Wales, if not elsewhere in Britain, the birth weights of most cubs lie in the range 100–130g. The weight will depend to some extent upon the number of foetuses in the uterus, smaller uterine litters tending to contain heavier embryos at late stages of gestation.

## The Early Life of Cubs

In Britain most cubs are born between mid-March and mid-April. The vixen gives birth in a dry hole, sometimes a den with only a single entrance, sometimes a large earth. In coniferous forests cubs may be born in dry, overgrown drainage channels; they are sometimes found in the hollow beneath the buttress roots of large trees and in long grass. In rocky areas they may be born in the fastness of scree and boulder, and in dry years on hill land, in underground water channels in peat turbaries. Suburban foxes may have their litters in a variety of places which afford shelter and cover – beneath garden sheds or electricity transformers, under fallen tombstones or in excavated holes in quiet gardens and railway embankments. In suburbia, partly because of the large numbers of foxes and partly because of a lack of suitable birth places, two or more litters may be found within a few yards of one another, but in rural areas there is a more even spatial distribution of litters, though clumping does occur in certain areas.

The vixen does not make a nest or have any form of bedding for her offspring, which may be found in an enlarged chamber in the den as often as in a small blind end of a burrow system. Although the vixen spends the first fourteen days or more below ground with her cubs, only occasionally are adult dog foxes found with the vixen and her very young cubs (it is not known whether the dogs are there from choice, or have sought refuge after being flushed from cover).

At birth cubs are covered with short, dark grey fur, which gradually changes to a dark chocolate colour by two weeks of age. Even at birth there is a suggestion of red on the dome of the head and in front of the ears. The tail is usually tipped with white and the ears are almost black. The tongue of suckling cubs is large in relation to the mouth. It is wide, thick and flaccid, and at its margins lie a row of webbed, finger-like serrations, an adaptation to enable effective suckling. The margins fit into a groove on either side of the palate – anterior to the area where the molars will appear – to provide a tight seal.

The eyes and ears open between eleven and fourteen days. The eyes are slate-blue in colour when they open, and at about this time the fur of the feet begins to darken. The erect, sparse, juvenile guard hairs protrude about 13mm beyond the underfur. These are very fine and variable in colour and give the cub a slightly fuzzy outline, like wild oat in a field of wheat. At three weeks of age the black streaks from the eyes to the muzzle begin to show. The muzzle is white in month-old cubs, and there is much red on the face. The ears, which have been lying on the side of the skull, become pricked and erect and now lie in a position higher on the head, with their leading edge on the dome. Also at this age the muzzle, hitherto short and insignificant, begins to elongate, with the development of teeth, into the long, slender muzzle of the adult; a process not to be completed for some months. A few splashes of brown may appear in the grey pupil of the eye at this age.

By six weeks the brown nose has become almost black, the dark fur has faded, especially on the underparts, and the pelt now has a woolly appearance, the long juvenile guard hairs persisting at this age. The ears are pointed and pricked. The eye stripe is well defined, more so even than in many adults, and the feet, ears and legs are now very black. White patches on the upper lips become distinct and the site of the tail gland is well indicated by the light-coloured fur covering it. At this age the fur of the face in many entire litters of cubs has developed a fox-like red colour, and I have often wondered whether such cubs have emerged earlier than other litters and have had their facial hairs bleached by the sun. The full complement of milk teeth has erupted by six to seven weeks. At eight weeks the woolly coat begins to be covered by shiny guard hairs, the woolly coat remaining as the underfur beneath the new growth. The earlier, apparently functionless, sparse juvenile guard hairs now disappear. The new guard hairs indicate the incipient yellow-brown coat of the adult, but the fur of the underparts tends to remain dark grey until the autumn, though some distinctively marked cubs may have much white fur from a very early age.

Occasionally almost all the fur of a cub may be white or cream in colour, although black is present in the ears, feet and muzzle. This persists until the final guard hair coat begins to appear at about two months;

such cubs are later indistinguishable from those which have had normal coat colour from birth.

The rate of growth and development of cubs depends upon their nutrition. An interesting illustration of this is provided by the growth pattern of a litter of four cubs reared by a captive vixen kept by Jane Burton. The first time it bred the vixen seemed to have only two or three functional teats. A few days after birth the cubs appeared to be all of the same size, but a month later, when I first saw the litter, two were large and plump, showing normal development, and two were small and weak. The small cubs showed intermediate stages of fur growth and colour, and the shape of their muzzles and ears was characteristic of much younger cubs. Had this litter been found in the wild, it would probably have been regarded as evidence of the pooling of two small litters, the appearance of the two larger and two smaller cubs being so dissimilar. Removal of the two large cubs from the mother for several hours each day promoted a rapid change towards normal development in the weaker ones.

The male cubs continue to maintain their superior weight gain. In ninety-two mixed-sex post-natal litters containing 386 cubs weighing from 83g to 2.7kg each, the mean weight of males was 14.3 per cent greater than that of females. Some of these were collected in the field and released alive (sixty litters), and it is possible that they did not truly represent the litters, since the more active members, perhaps the heavier ones, may have escaped capture. In thirty-two of the ninety-two litters the mean weight of the females was greater than that of the males, but only in eight cases was a vixen cub the heaviest of the whole litter. The largest litter found in one earth, a single hole two metres long in a hedge bank, was twelve cubs. Nine of these weighed between 900g and 1.13kg and the remaining three up to 1.36kg. They were in good condition, but there was no means of telling whether or not they were smaller than cubs of similar age in smaller litters.

While the vixen occupies the earth in daytime the cubs derive warmth from their mother, and in order to conserve heat in her absence they form a pyramid, one lying on top of another. According to Tembrock (1957), thermo-regulation in cubs begins at about three weeks, at the time of their first meat meals. At this time the vixen (and dog fox?) offers regurgitated food to her cubs, which marks the beginning of weaning. Foxes and dogs have the capacity to regurgitate voluntarily, since the oesophagus, unlike that of man, contains striped muscle which is under the animal's control. In captivity orphaned cubs will take small quantities of rabbit embryos and minced liver offered in the period shortly after their eyes have opened, but the eating of solid food by such young cubs may not be usual in the wild, though the observation could add some weight to the widely held belief among countrymen that a dog fox can somehow rear cubs whose mother has been lost early in their lives.

The mean daily rate of growth from birth to about thirty days, when solid food begins to be taken, is 15–20g. There is a considerable overlap – in time and in body weight – between the first intake of solid food among the cubs of a litter and the termination of suckling. Growth rates from twenty-eight to eighty-two days are shown in Table 21.

Fox cubs in captivity rapidly develop a faintly peppery smell not observed in the wild. This is due to fouling of their bedding with urine. Stimulation of the genital area and abdomen of cubs will promote urination; possibly the vixen keeps the cubs clean by licking them, which also stimulates urination. Faeces are not found in dens containing young cubs, and the whining and wagging of the tail which follows defecation, often after a feed, may be a signal to the mother to clean up the mess. Cleanliness is of advantage in the maintenance of body temperature, since matted fur provides poorer insulation.

Partly digested whole food items become more prominent in the diet of cubs at four weeks of age. Bank voles, field voles and wood mice usually predominate. Cubs from four to six weeks old eat small items of food, and there is not much evidence of uneaten food in the earths, but as they get older, bigger items, often with larger indigestible parts – such as rabbits, lambs or, as in one example in the New Forest, the hind leg of a foal – are brought to the den. Once this stage is reached the dens often show considerable evidence of occupation by cubs, as food remnants are littered about and within the den.

Figure 10 shows the period of production of young of the more common prey species of foxes and the period when juveniles of these species are present in the population. The period of total and partial dependence of cubs upon the parents is also shown. Fruits and berries, although not eaten exclusively when they become available, contribute much to the seasonal diet of foxes in areas where they are available to them, and are also included in the diagram. The period of maximum ground cover is also shown, since cover enables foxes to approach some species of prey more easily when hunting by stealth (young rabbits, especially in daylight, do not move far from cover).

The abundance of prey is at its lowest ebb at the onset of the breeding season of the particular prey species, and in the case of the bank and field vole, which are the mainstay of foxes (though the fox shows a preference for the field vole), this occurs in April. During the latter half of March and April vixens are subjected to the heavy demands of lactation. The prey may perhaps become especially vulnerable at this time – alternatively, the vixen may need to spend more time hunting in order to cope with her increased food requirements – but whatever the situation, there must be some reason why this period has been selected in the evolution of the breeding pattern of the species as the optimum period for lactation, when a delay of six weeks or so would have coincided with greater abundance of young susceptible prey. The timing of breeding in the fox may be a compromise between the requirements of the vixen when the cubs are wholly dependent upon her and the requirements of cubs when they become independent. Or perhaps these two periods may be less important than the period of rapid growth of the cubs (between eight and sixteen weeks of age), when each cub requires 225–340g of food per day. A litter of five cubs partly dependent for food on the vixen in July would require about 1.8kg of food daily, the equivalent of seventy or eighty voles, or between ten and twelve newly weaned rabbits, or one and a third adult rabbits, or four young pheasants, or a third to a half of the afterbirth of a cow. Analysis of the contents of fox stomachs does not, however, often show such homogeneity of food intake, except when carrion is eaten or during the fruit season, and the suggested equivalents merely give an indication of the housekeeping problems of family groups at that time of year. For a family group of eight cubs and two adults, double the quantities would be required. In Russia, Chirkova (1941) considered that good nourishment was essential for female cubs during their first three months of life, and for six months for dog foxes.

At about six weeks of age the cubs begin to emerge from the dens. At first they merely explore the area around the entrance to one hole, but soon they investigate another hole, and then go from one hole to another, until by eight weeks old their activities above ground take them several metres away from the earth. Much will depend upon weather conditions, however. In sunny localities, especially where there is little disturbance, the cubs emerge in daylight, sunning themselves and playing in the open. In other areas they may emerge only at dusk, usually at about the time when the vixen appears from her daytime couch. She may have food for the cubs, but even when the cubs are large, they will attempt to suckle the vixen when she appears. Weaned cubs will be shrugged off by a kick of the back legs or by a snap, but unweaned cubs will be tolerated – and while the vixen stands or sits to suckle the cubs, she surveys the scene for any sign of disturbance. Should there be any cause for alarm, a single sharp bark and a sudden move away from the earth towards cover will send the cubs hastily back to their den. On other occasions a vixen returning to her cubs in the evening is able to call the cubs out of the den even from a few metres away, by some signal that I have not been able to detect. Cubs can sometimes be lured to the entrance of their dens in daytime, if the den is approached quietly and panting sounds are made at the entrance. Even gentle patting of the ground at the entrance may bring them forth, but they will rarely venture beyond the overhang of the burrow. There is much about the mother–cub relationship that is not known.

## Translocation and Dispersal of the Litter

Apart from providing warmth, the vixen probably spends the first four-teen days or so with the cubs to protect them from predatory intruders and to prevent them from crawling away from each other and perhaps out into the open. Whether or not cubs from two to four weeks old wander about much in the earth is not known, nor what restrains them from wandering far from the entrance to the den in the absence of the vixen. Perhaps there is an inherent tendency to avoid bright light at this stage in their development. Some cubs spend their time from birth to eight to ten weeks of age in the same burrow, while others of the same age may have had several homes. Disturbance of the dens by man or dogs (even a man merely standing at the entrance to the den) usually pro-vokes vixens to move their litters to another den, which may be only a few metres away or, as in the case of some litters observed on hill land in mid-Wales, up to one and a half kilometres away. The new dens of trans-located cubs are often very difficult to find. Spontaneous evacuation also probably occurs, but it is difficult to be sure of this because one does not know what events took place at the den prior to its abandonment. In a few cases, however, there is evidence of successive occupations of a series of dens close to each other, especially on hill land, and a common feature of these is the unwholesome nature of the vacated dens, in which large quantities of unconsumed carrion may be evident.

Single-hole birth dens are rarely occupied for long after the cubs' eyes have opened, and on hill land in mid-Wales cubs from this type of den are often moved into rocks. Turbaries usually only become occupied at dry spells from May to July, on land lacking adequate surface cover. Sometimes occupied holes in turbaries have water flowing through the entrance, but somewhere inside dry places must occur. These water-formed channels may extend for scores, even hundreds, of metres, and huntsmen have frequently observed that a perfectly dry fox will break its way to the surface from a watercourse in the turbary, followed by a very wet, black and peaty terrier. Such refuges seem rather dank and inhos-pitable, but they are well used by foxes.

In other areas, notably suburbia and (in my experience) occasionally in such places as the New Forest, where old badger sets may frequently be used, foxes will stand fast in their earths even after considerable dis-turbance. The vixen may be disinclined to move its litter in such situa-tions not because it has learned to live in close proximity to man, but because it simply does not have anywhere else to go – a situation quite contrary to that which obtains in my mid-Wales study area, where in the cubbing season on average only one earth in about eighty visited contains cubs (this excludes cairns, screes and boulder fields, but includes turbaries).

In addition to very young cubs, those older than six weeks are often moved, the evacuation being accompanied by much noise from the cubs. I have no idea how the move is accomplished – whether the cubs are escorted, herded or partly carried at this age – but judging by the vocal clamour, it would seem that the cubs do not follow their mother quietly, in Indian-file. Very young cubs must be carried by the mother.

The mean number of cubs in litters examined in mid-Wales diminishes from 5.2 in April to 2.6 in June. Many experienced fox-hunters believe that litters are split at six to eight weeks of age, the parted cubs being situated not far distant from each other. Others assert that they are not only parted but are also segregated according to sex, and whilst the latter claim is not upheld by observation, there may be some truth in the former. Even if decrease in litter size is not due to mortality (I have little information on this at present), it may not follow that the litters are deliberately divided by one or both parents. Such separation could be explained by adventuresome cubs wandering too far away from their original home, or by the vixens being unable to take or lead all her cubs when moving from one den to another.

At eight to ten weeks of age, from late May to early June, cubs usually abandon dens and live on the surface. Coniferous plantations on hill land are attractive to the family group from June onwards; elsewhere they tend to find cover in scrub and bracken, and later in cereal crops. Cubs hunt successfully for small mammals from twelve weeks old (captive cubs walked on a lead at four months of age will indulge in mousing in their characteristic manner).

Cubs begin to gain independence in July and August, and most are completely independent by September, though they may still be found as family groups. It is known from recaptures of cubs that some dispersal of litters may begin at six months of age, in October.

The gaining of independence is probably not simultaneous in all cubs in a litter, but there is little evidence to shed light on this. Some cubs, especially males, seem to disperse earlier than others, but whilst the dispersed cubs are clearly independent of their mother, so also may be those male and female cubs that have not yet moved away. The time at which cubs become independent is almost certainly determined to some extent by individual traits, but the behaviour and attitude of the vixen and possibly the dog fox to their offspring may also have some influence. Harassment by man or hounds in August may also precipitate complete independence in the young of the year if they are driven away from the range of their family group.

## The Relationship between Cubs and their Parents

There is very little sound factual information on the relationship between dog and vixen and between dog and cubs. Whether or not all dog foxes participate in the rearing of litters is not known to me; certainly some dog foxes carry food to the maternal dens, but I have also witnessed antagonism between vixens and dog foxes at the dens, though I have no means of knowing if the dog in question was a stranger. My impression is that the dog attached to a vixen remains in the vicinity of the den, even visits it regularly, but does not participate to any great extent in the rearing of the litter. (Indeed, on one occasion in mid-Wales a dog fox was seen to steal the remnants of a lamb carcase from cubs to eat it itself.) However, this is contrary to the beliefs of countrymen, and there is evidence from past use of gin traps that a dog fox can be trapped at the den shortly after the vixen has been killed, or, in the case of rocky outcrops or cairns in Scotland, the dog can be shot as he returns to the maternal den in the mornings.

Information on captive foxes seems to bear out countrymen's observations on the behaviour of the dog fox when cubs are born. The dog fox of a pair kept by my friend and colleague, Kim Taylor, was normally a very greedy fellow. It made sure that it got most of the food for itself, but immediately after cubs were born its behaviour changed and instead of bolting its dinner as usual, it carried the food back to the maternal den — presumably for the vixen. It is frequently asserted that the dog fox will carry food to the vixen at this time, and often a dead vole, mouse, shrew or even mole found at the entrance to a den signified recently born cubs. However, whether the dog regurgitates food for very young cubs, as does the vixen, and continues to supply food for weaned cubs regularly is another matter.

When the vixen leaves the cubs to lie above ground she usually, but not invariably, stays within a short distance of them. Evidence gained by radio-tracking of nursing vixens both on hill and low land has shown that there is much variation in this behaviour from day to day. On some occasions a vixen may be within a few metres of the earth and on others as much as 1,000 metres away. Sometimes vixens flushed in the vicinity of the den may bolt into it for cover, but usually they keep well clear of it. Some vixens lying close by will bark if there is any interference from man at the cubbing earths; when I was digging out cubs in the gloomy forests of Sweden with Jan Englund, a squeak produced by the sucking of the back of my hand stimulated the vixen to emerge from the surrounding trees and run to within thirty metres of the den and us – suicidal behaviour, had we been hunters. In Wales vixens on hill land usually do not show themselves when maternal dens are being investigated, but they are more inclined to bark or reveal themselves in forest. One startling exception to this occurred in 1971, when my colleagues, Desmond Isaacson and Bernard Price, were taking cubs for tagging from an earth on a quiet, bracken-covered slope. After the cubs had been bagged prior to tagging, a vixen approached and viciously attacked the terriers, which were no strangers to foxes. The dogs attempted to retaliate but, in spite of superior numbers, were no match for the agile fox, which bit them again and again in the hindlegs. She finally retreated to a nearby rock – a valiant vixen who would have met a sad end in other circumstances – whilst the somewhat subdued dogs sought refuge near their masters. This vixen (or possibly one of her offspring), distinguished by having an unusually bright yellow coat colour, attacked the same dogs in the same circumstances during the following cubbing season in a nearby forest.

Whilst tagging cubs for study purposes on common land in mid- and west-Wales, it is common practice to put the cubs into another earth nearby, or to excavate a hole for the cubs after tagging. However remote one may feel on the Elyneth plateau – the so-called Welsh Desert, a large area of mountain grassland, peat and forest – little, it seems, can be done unobserved, and consequently the cubs are hidden in the hope that bounty hunters will not visit the scene of activity to investigate with their terriers. Cubs have also been brought to me by hunters for tagging and have been released twenty-four hours later in the maternal den. In nearly all cases some member of these litters has been recovered many months later, indicating that the vixens probably not only sought their cubs, but continued to do so for at least twenty-four hours. Orphaned cubs which have been added to parented litters have also been recovered as adults, which suggests that the vixens have either accepted the aliens or were unable to distinguish them from their own brood.

## The Pooling of Litters

Undeniable evidence for pooling is difficult to obtain, but there is some evidence, such as Eric Ashby's ciné film of a litter of foxes in the New Forest, that two vixens may feed one group of cubs. In this case only one vixen nursed the litter; the other brought solid food for the cubs. Also, Hans Kruuk (1964) had evidence of two litters being pooled and cared for by two vixens.

There are several possible explanations for pooling. One of the vixens, having lost its own litter, may be able to suckle another litter if its own cubs lived long enough to be suckled for a while. On the other hand, one of the vixens may be barren, in which case it would not be able to help suckle the litter. In each case the implication is that the vixens were not hostile towards each other, which would suggest behaviour rather at variance with the generally accepted belief that foxes are non-gregarious, though the behaviour of foxes may change as a response to particular circumstances. High population densities precipitate situations in which the young of the year show a diminished tendency to disperse, and the integrity of the family group may be loosely maintained in the following season. This could lead to some sort of rapport between vixens of an erstwhile family group, possibly leading to litter pooling. It would be rather difficult to establish whether or not this speculation is near the mark, even with captive animals, since they would have no choice but to respond to a situation not of their choosing, which might never be encountered in the wild. Apart from the very slender chance of an observer in the field being presented with a particular sequence of circumstances leading to unequivocal conclusions, evidence of the pooling of litters would best be obtained by a blood- or muscle-protein analysis of the entire litter. This would, however, only indicate whether or not pooling occurs; it would give no indication of the frequency of occurrence, nor the circumstances which might lead to it.

In North America Hoffman and Kirkpatrick (1954) found one vixen with thirteen foetuses, including two pairs of twins. They report it as the greatest number of foetuses recorded in North America, but litter sizes in excess of ten are not infrequent. Seventeen seems to be the greatest number recorded. The fox has only four pairs of nipples, and it is highly unlikely that a vixen could successfully suckle more than ten cubs.

# 4

# Population Dynamics

This chapter is concerned with the balance sheet of profit and loss, of ingoings and outgoings of numbers of animals in fox groups or populations. To understand the dynamics of any population in its simplest form, it is necessary to know the number of animals of the species concerned in the area under consideration, the number born, the number that survive to breed, the number immigrating into and emigrating out of the area and the life span of adults.

## Loss and Replacement among Fox Populations

Naturally, one would like to know what factors influence the various entries in the balance sheet – why, for example, the balance in hand in the different accounts varies from year to year. Unfortunately, unless a very detailed study of an area is undertaken and unless the species can be studied with ease, the total number of animals and the number that may be lost or gained through dispersal may be difficult to derive. Moreover, though the cause of a change in population density might be identified for one area, a similar trend in another year or locality may be due to entirely different causes. We may be able to recognize that a mixed habitat offering much variety of prospective foods, cover, shelter, agriculture and afforestation is more suited to the maintenance of a high density of foxes than predominantly arable land affording little cover and shelter, but we have no means of defining fragmentary or uniform habitats quantitatively in terms of the precise requirements of foxes. Consequently, assessment of the suitability of a habitat is largely subjective and may not take account of many unknown aspects of the environment which are of importance to the population density, birth rate and survival rate of foxes.

Though the total number of foxes in any area cannot easily be estimated accurately, the profit and loss account can still be instructive if a population is assumed to be 100 and entries are made in terms of percentage. If a shepherd maintains his flock at the same number in the winter of each year, the number of sheep and lambs that are sold or die each year will be equal to the total number of lambs born. He may buy in some ewes or rams; if the number of the flock is still maintained at the same size, it can then be said that the number of new animals added to his flock – through births and purchase – is equal to the number that have left the flock in one way or another. So it is with fox populations. If numbers are steady from year to year at the breeding season, the number of cubs born is equivalent to the number of foxes of all ages that die each year. If a fox population over a small area of, say, sixty-five square kilometres were being considered, the number of foxes moving into the area and settling there, and the number of juveniles dispersing from the area, would have to be taken into account, since the number of incoming and outgoing animals may not be equal. Over a large area, however, this aspect would not be significant, since foxes do not generally disperse very far.

Fox populations are not maintained at a level as steady as that of the shepherd's flock, but unless there is some overriding influence tending to promote a steady increase or decline in numbers, a fox population will fluctuate annually around some mean population size and will tend to remain steady about this mean over a period of years. If over a large area replacement through reproductive productivity is less or greater than the number of foxes of all ages lost through deaths, the population will decline or increase respectively. With such imperfect data as are presented here, it will be assumed that the population remains steady over the periods for which data are available.

The reproductive productivity of vixens for a period of four years is known, albeit imperfectly (see p. 113), from samples obtained from widely scattered areas of mid-Wales. The mean number of cubs born annually per vixen is 3.7; thus 100 vixens would produce 370 cubs. Since the number of male cubs outnumbers the number of vixen cubs at birth – 51.5 per cent are male – the number of vixen cubs produced by 100 vixens is 179; thus, in such a steady population the number of vixens of all ages that die each year between breeding seasons, whether they be cubs, juveniles or adults, will be 179. The total annual loss of vixens, cubs and adults is 179 out of 279, i.e. 64 per cent. In order to determine how many adult vixens die each year, it is necessary to know how many of the cubs survive to become adults. Examination of foxes killed in Wales from January to March reveals that for each adult vixen during this period there are 1.35 vixens between nine and twelve months of age. For every 100 adult vixens, therefore, there are 135 young animals about to breed for the first time; these young animals replace adults lost since the corresponding period of the previous year. The total annual loss of adult vixens is 135 out of 235, or 57 per cent. Since 64 per cent of all vixens and 57 per cent of adult vixens die annually, the mortality of juvenile vixens is 67 per cent.

$$\frac{\text{mortality of all vixens} - \text{mortality of adult vixens}}{\text{mortality of all vixens}}$$

$$= \frac{179-57}{179} = \frac{122}{179} = 68\%$$

We now know the increase and loss of the female component of the population in terms of percentage. So far as is possible to determine, males broadly follow the same pattern.

The productivity rate of 3.7 cubs per vixen in the population (not the mean birth litter size, which is 4.7) may seem to be low to countrymen who may have encountered many litters of 6 cubs and over. But if, for example, the productivity were a mean of 5 cubs instead of 3.7, the annual mortality of vixens of all ages would then need to be 71 per cent of the population if the population were to remain steady and, since juvenile mortality is higher than that of adults, their mortality would need to be over 80 per cent annually. In such places as Anglesey, where foxes have been introduced to a favourable environment and have not yet reached peak numbers, it is possible that a mean productivity of 5 cubs or more per vixen might obtain, and the survival rate of juveniles might also be higher in such an expanding population than in steady, old-established populations. (In New York State, Layne and McKeon (1956a) estimated that red fox populations could be reduced by 68 per cent annually and would still be able to effect a full recovery in numbers following the breeding season.)

The next questions to be asked are: how long do adult foxes live, and is the mortality rate constant from year to year after the cubs reach adulthood? My colleague, R. J. Page, has been able to determine the ages of individuals comprising the samples obtained from Wales by examining the cementum layers of their teeth. The degree of accuracy of the technique is uncertain, but for the sample as a whole there was a strong indication that the determined age was correct in over 80 per cent of cases. (Although the methods used to obtain the samples varied, the samples were almost certainly not entirely representative of the populations, but they were probably as good as any that could be obtained short of examining the entire population.) In a sample of 154 foxes obtained from Pembrokeshire between January and March in 1971 and 1972, over a small area of about 1,400 hectares, it was found by tooth examination that the mean annual mortality rate of foxes between one and seven years of age was 38 per cent. The ratio of adults to sub-adults (pre-breeding juveniles) in the sample was 1:0.75; expressed differently, 43 per cent of the sample were sub-adults born in the previous breeding season (see Table 22). The ratio is very different from that for mid-Wales, where it is 1:1.35 (see Table 23). In the Pembrokeshire sample the total annual loss of adult vixens calculated by data for replacement was 43 per cent, which was not very different from the mean annual loss of 38 per cent calculated from tooth examination; thus, it seems likely that in this sample the mortality rate is much the same for adults of any age – their chances of surviving another year in Pembrokeshire then being about 57 per cent.

In 1969 and 1970 the jawbones of many of the foxes killed by professional fox catchers on the Isle of Skye were examined and aged by R. J. Page, and the proportion of adults to sub-adults in January and February was found to be 1:2.03 (see Table 23). Foxes were then under heavy pressure in parts of the Isle of Skye, and their numbers were fewer than some ten years earlier. The trappers maintained the population at a much lower level than those parts of the island could have supported, and the reproductive productivity of vixens was likely to be greater in a population which had room to expand, yet the population size seemed to be fairly steady in those parts of the island where foxes were controlled by trappers. The available data indicate a proportion of 67 per cent of sub-adult replacement animals and consequently an annual mortality rate of adults of 67 per cent. The three regions considered, Pembrokeshire, mid-Wales and Skye, represented areas where the intensity of control by man varied. In the Pembrokeshire area the population level was high and control minimal; in mid-Wales the population density was lower (empirically estimated at perhaps four or five times lower than in Pembrokeshire in the period 1970–3), with some degree of control exercised by man; on the Isle of Skye the population density was lowest and control activity more intense than in the two other areas. The data suggest that where the population density is greatest, the proportion of sub-adults in the population is lowest, and where the population density is lowest, in an area which could support more foxes, the proportion of sub-adults is highest. There is confirmation of these conclusions from America. Phillips (1970) calculated a ratio of adults to sub-adults of 1:2.56 in an area of little control activity, and in an area of intensive control, 1:5.59. These are much higher ratios than those observed in Britain and are partly explained, perhaps, by the fact that the samples were taken in November and December, rather than in January to March as they were in Britain (see Table 23).

These data give some indication of the age structures of different populations of foxes, but without data on the reproductive productivity in the year when samples were taken (as is available for mid-Wales), mortality rates from birth to adulthood cannot be derived for Pembrokeshire and Skye. Table 24 shows the number of adult foxes in different age groups per 100 sub-adults between January and March. Calculations based on these data and those in Table 25 show that in Pembrokeshire the mean expected survival span of adults – that is, when 50 per cent of the original 100 sub-adults are still alive – is a further fourteen months in Pembrokeshire, ten months and two weeks in mid-Wales and nine months on Skye. The mid-Wales data accord with the data (as yet incomplete) for the survival of foxes tagged and released as cubs in that area. The oldest fox aged by tooth section was ten years old. The oldest tagged fox recovered so far is six years old. A comparison of data on the age structure of fox populations reported by several workers is given in Table 25.

One feature of the biology of many mammals is that the reproductive productivity of adults and survival rates of offspring are higher when the population is reduced (for whatever reason) to a level well below that which can be supported by the habitat. Rabbits provide an example. As has already been mentioned (see Chapter 2), before the first occurrences of myxomatosis their mean reproductive productivity was ten to eleven rabbits per doe per season. Following the dramatic reduction in numbers after the epizootic, the reproductive productivity in very low-density populations was about thirty per doe per season – a very significant increase. There is evidence to suggest that the fox has similar reproductive resilience, but the kind of opportunity to study reproductive change as was presented by the effects of myxomatosis is not readily available. However, the expanding population of foxes on Anglesey may provide the right circumstances for detailed study.

Since the fox breeds only once a year and is not adapted to rear more than eight cubs – though, exceptionally, higher litter sizes may have survived – it has a severely limited reproductive capacity for increase compared with other mammals such as rabbits and rats, which produce many litters throughout an extended breeding season. The longevity of adults and the numbers of young which survive to adulthood is greater in foxes, however. The ecological mechanisms which ensure the maintenance of a steady population size are not understood, but the results can be described in terms of numbers of cubs born, their survival rate and the mortality of adults. This is shown in Figure 19.

## Methods of Estimating Population Densities

Estimates of population densities are derived in different ways by different workers according to differing topographical circumstances, study requirements and the availability of time and labour, but many fundamental difficulties are encountered in the search for precise data on the numbers of foxes in any area.

Although the fox is a very common animal, its numbers are low and its ranges large by comparison with those of voles, rabbits or hares, for example. Inevitably, therefore, the counting of foxes involves a great deal of effort and manpower. If, however, one were concerned only with foxes living in a small area, perhaps their numbers could be estimated with some accuracy, given suitable topography, simply by watching at dawn and dusk during the long days of spring, summer and early autumn, or after dark (if one were fortunate enough to have the equipment) by using night-viewing optics. This is a different problem, however, from that of estimating numbers over large tracts of land, say, areas in excess of ten square kilometres.

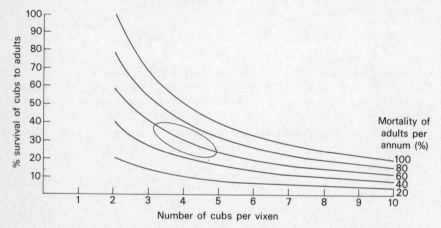

**19**   Relationships between mean numbers of cubs per vixen, survival of cubs and adult mortality rates in populations of steady size. The figure shows the relationships between the mean number of cubs born to all adult vixens in the population (whether they successfully produce cubs or not), the survival of cubs to adulthood and the annual mortality of adults. If, for example, the mean number of cubs per vixen is 4, then at 60% loss of adults per annum 30% of cubs would need to survive to maintain a steady population size; if, when the mortality rate of adults is 60%, the mean number of cubs that survive falls to 20%, the population will decline; if it decreases to 40% the population will increase. This relationship would not hold in the figure however, because the 3 parameters are related to produce a steady population size. The 100% annual loss of adults shown is unrealistic because it would imply that adult foxes survive to breed only once.

In England and Wales the most frequently encountered mean numbers of cubs per vixen in the population lie in the range 3 to 5, survival rates of cubs 30 to 40% and adult mortality 50 to 65%. This is shown in the figure by the oval area; the physiological, ecological and behavioural adaptations of the fox are such that there would be no great departure from this in steady populations.

Basically, four methods can be used to estimate numbers. The first, a direct census, involves a full count of numbers over the entire area under study. The second, an indirect census, involves the use of some indicator of the total number. A third method is to estimate the population size for a sample area by direct or indirect methods, and then to extrapolate for the whole area under study. The fourth method is to derive an index of population size for comparisons of relative abundance. All these methods have been tried by various workers, but no one technique lends itself to universal application.

Direct census methods which have been used involve the capture and removal of foxes (the method adopted by Lord, 1961), or capture, tagging and release (Wood, 1959). Cage traps are not effective everywhere, and certain trapping methods are illegal. In North America the use of leg-hold traps (modified gin traps) is permissible, for example, but in most European countries the gin and the snare are not permitted for the trapping of foxes. Anyway, snares and leg-hold traps have severe practical limitations in some situations. Direct census by visual counts over large areas of land is rarely possible, though both dens and foxes have been counted from aircraft in North America (Sargeant, 1975). Clearly the North Dakota habitat surveyed in this study and fox behaviour in the area must be very different from those in Britain.

Indirect census methods are those most commonly employed. Capture-tag-release and recapture techniques, for example, have been employed for grey foxes by Lord. This method – known as the Lincoln Index method – must be used at a time when foxes are sedentary. It should not be used during the period from August to December inclusive, since many of the tagged animals, especially the males, may have emigrated from the area under study and others may have moved in. The area studied should be large. Lord used an area of fifty-two square kilometres, and his trapping effort involved about 4,000 trap days, extended over a period of four months. He also used a technique known as the age-reduction census method, which involves the capture and sterilization of females by hysterectomy and the noting of subsequent changes in adult-to-juvenile ratios in the population twelve months later. Besides the fact that this method is rather drastic and of academic interest only, I doubt whether 52 square kilometres would be a large enough area in all habitats to avoid the possible bias which could be introduced by the emigration and immigration of red foxes. Another method investigated by Lord was based on the decreasing numbers of hitherto untrapped animals captured (and released) in his leg-hold traps; the data were extrapolated beyond the trapping period to extinction point. His various methods gave estimates ranging from 52 to 101 foxes in the same study area.

Another indirect method suggested by Pearson (1966) might be called the calorific censusing method. He estimated the calorific value of prey as represented by their identifiable remains in predators' faeces collected in his study area. The predators involved were grey foxes, striped and spotted skunks and cats, and he estimated their mean weight as 3kg per individual. He calculated the calorific requirements of these predators and by a diligent search and collection of faeces and a calculation of the numbers of prey represented, he estimated the number of predators. This method, if at all reliable, could only be used for estimating numbers of foxes in small areas because of the time required to search the area.

A further indirect method, and one which is widely used, involves a count of dens containing cubs. In the case of the red fox this has to be done very quickly, with the minimum of disturbance, preferably by scrutinizing the entrance to dens with binoculars from a few metres' distance. (This step is necessary because in many situations foxes will move their litters to other holes at the slightest provocation and such litters could well be counted twice or more, as could litters moved spontaneously by vixens to other earths; an additional difficulty is the splitting of litters into two or more earths.) All the prospective cubbing earths or dens should be known beforehand to permit the observer to get round them expeditiously. The number of cubs involved would not be known, but if it were assumed that each litter represented one pair of adults, a satisfactory result might be obtained. This method could certainly be used in open agricultural land, but I have not used it in mid-Wales because the study area contains an enormous area of turbary, dense forest and too many derelict rabbit holes and rocky outcrops to enable all the earths to be discovered. In addition, there is considerable disturbance by those out to kill foxes. In this area a mean of 80 earths needs to be examined before an occupied one is found. (In north-west Pembrokeshire in 1970–1, however, one in fifteen known fox earths contained a litter.) The method is used in some places on the Continent to estimate numbers of foxes before and after rabies outbreaks, and has been used by R. J. Page in an urban area in north-west London and by Insley (1977) in the New Forest. Chirkova (1941) was probably the first to use this method; the data obtained were combined with counts of the numbers of cubs which enabled forecasts of numbers to be made for the next trapping season.

Population density indices have been derived by several workers. Richards and Hine (1953) used fox tracks at scent stations (using castor lure) to obtain indices of fox abundance. Scott (1941a) proposed that sample plots should be used for this purpose, noting all visible fox signs. Road deaths have been used by McKeon (1952), and Wood (1959) used standardized trap lines and leg-hold traps. Wood and Odum (1964) have used the standardized trap-line technique for long-term studies of fluctuations over 900 square kilometres. Allen and Sargeant (1975) used road sightings by postmen to provide an index of numbers!

The standardized trap-line technique is not dissimilar to the use of hunting statistics to obtain indices of population numbers. The main difference is that hunting effort may not be constant from year to year. The method is used in Germany and Denmark, for example, to estimate the effectiveness of control methods and the reduction of fox numbers by rabies. The number of bounties paid for dead foxes in parts of Britain could be used in this way, but cautiously, since it is known that the effort put into fox control can vary from year to year. Huntsmen who have a long and intimate knowledge of their area can make good but unverifiable estimates of the relative number of foxes from year to year by sightings, field signs and hunting success.

None of the trapping methods described is suitable for general application in Britain because the live trapping methods involved are either illegal or unsuitable, or require too much effort in some areas, or interfere with the population under study.

Visual counts with the aid of spotlights will provide a good index in certain situations. The eye-shine of foxes is considerable and can be detected with a 60-watt spotlight from about 400 metres under clear conditions. I have used this method effectively in areas well intersected by roads. In such places foxes in fields adjoining roads are not disturbed by passing cars and sightings can be made at fixed intervals along the roadside. (For many reasons, the agreement of landowners should be sought before lights are shone in their fields.) In open country it is a different matter, because movements of the observer on foot tend to disturb foxes and produce dubious results. If spotlight counts are made in a particular study area at a large number of points, and at the same points on each occasion, in such a way that the observer can get from one point to another without disturbing the movement of foxes, a fairly reliable index can be obtained. In open country such as hill land, where spotlights are not so useful, foxes can be lured to within eye-shine range (and often much nearer) by vocal lures or calls. This method has been investigated, but not yet in sufficient detail for the usefulness of the results to be ascertained. An infra-red light source is not perceived by the fox, the eye-shine in near-infra-red light is considerable and easily detected with suitable viewers.

As an index of population density, the take of bait buried beneath turf can provide some information, especially during the November to May period, when baits are more readily taken than at other times of the year. But the method only provides comparable data for a single site in different years, and comparisons between different habitats are unlikely to be valid. Some preliminary work – ancillary to anti-rabies control investigations – has been done on this method in Pembrokeshire, where 102 baits were laid for periods of three weeks from December to March on an area of 325 hectares. Baits were visited on alternate days and those removed by foxes were replenished. Eighty per cent of the baits were being taken ten days after baiting began; subsequently fifty-one foxes were captured and removed. Baits were relaid and 42 per cent of the baits were being taken after ten days. Twenty-four foxes were subsequently captured. Bait was again relaid and 28 per cent of the bait was being taken ten days later, but no further trapping could be done because by that time some vixens would have had dependent cubs.

Tracks in snow could perhaps provide a useful index of fox density if it were possible to quantify the signs. I have been unable to investigate this method because of the obliteration of fox tracks by sheep and because of a succession of mild winters, but where domestic stock are not present tracks should provide some information on the relative abundance of foxes from year to year and from place to place.

Few of the methods mentioned above would be of value in suburban or urban areas. Counts of cubbing earths and visual sightings on roadways at night in urban areas may provide a means of estimating absolute numbers or an index of abundance respectively. With the co-operation of householders and others, a useful and voluntary army of observers might be available. This pinpoints one of the main problems of counting foxes, that of the availability of assistance which most techniques require.

## Variations in Population Density

If we take the bank balance analogy a little further, the incomes and outgoings of the fox population may vary from year to year. Salary-earners whose incomes are largely derived from one source will not show much change in income from year to year. Not so business men, however, whose incomes are influenced by variable factors from time to time and may consequently be subject to fluctuation. Similarly, outgoings, though they may not show much change, are liable to be incurred by different sets of circumstances continually, and the salary-earner, even in his stable environment, might be faced with unexpectedly high outgoings following some minor disaster or extravagance. In all such cases, it is not only the amounts credited and debited that are of interest, but the circumstances that lead to the various entries, whether the balance be steady or unsteady.

Features which influence entries in the balance sheet are very difficult to define in natural communities of mammals and could be due, singly or in combination, to factors associated with social behaviour, numbers, climate, food availability and quality, disease or other changes in the environment.

As far as the fox is concerned, little is known of the way such features influence rises and falls in the population, except in certain circumstances such as when disease affects a population or when food is in very short supply. Many observations on the population dynamics of foxes and factors influencing it are highly speculative – as the reader is doubtless by now aware – and may in the course of time be shown to be mistaken.

Variations in population density within or between areas, even if they are clearly detected, may be due to a variety of causes, none of which may be immediately obvious, or if apparently obvious, may not be the only factor operating. Even in a population which appears to be steady in numbers, it is possible that the credits and debits are derived in a different way each year. In one year the total number of cubs born may be high but their survival rate low; in another year the converse could obtain, but the population level could remain the same. Because these influences are difficult to define, the yearly balance of the number of animals in the population is usually calculated at the time of the year when numbers of adults are lowest and the situation is uncomplicated by the presence of mobile young, that is, from January to April, just prior to or during the period when vixens are pregnant or when young are still dependent upon their parents.

Actual population densities vary widely. They may range from as high as one fox per 30 hectares in rich habitats to one pair per 4,000 hectares (Lockie, 1964) in poor habitats such as the higher Scottish hills. One sometimes hears of large numbers of foxes being caught over comparatively small areas – such as in the immediate vicinity of a rubbish tip; over 100 foxes were snared by a trapper during the winter months near a municipal rubbish tip in west Wales in 1969. Clearly this, and the case of forty-two foxes which were killed at a series of fox drives over about 280 hectares of woodland in one afternoon in Kent, cannot represent actual population densities, since no information is available about the areas over which those foxes disperse during their nocturnal activities and, furthermore, some of the foxes killed may have been itinerant at the time.

In the example mentioned earlier, when seventy-six foxes were captured over 325 hectares, centred on Dowrog Common, St Davids, the apparently high density of foxes killed in the area – one fox per 4.27 hectares – is unreal because many of the foxes would have ranged partly or mainly outside the trapped area. From information which has been gathered about the movements of foxes in Pembrokeshire, it is known that most ranges are less than one kilometre in diameter in late winter, and that dispersal distances of young are also very small – a mean of 4.6 kilometres for males and 1.9 kilometres for females. If we assume that the seventy-six foxes killed all resided in a roughly rectangular area extending to 325 hectares plus a zone one kilometre deep all round, the density represented would be one fox per 19.6 hectares. If the zone were increased to 1.5 kilometres the density would be one fox per 33.9 hectares. Taking other features into account, it seems probable that the real density lay nearer to one fox per 19.6 hectares.Foxes were then (1969–70) thicker on the ground in that part of Pembrokeshire than in any other place I had visited. Numbers have since declined in Pembrokeshire, as judged subsequently by field signs, though foxes are still numerous.

Counts of litters of foxes in a suburban area of about 700 hectares by R. J. Page have yielded a density of about one fox per forty hectares. In two areas of Pembrokeshire higher densities were estimated by the number of foxes killed over 1,200 hectares, and by the number of litters found in a smaller area where a large number of foxes had been trapped and fitted with radio transmitters. Estimates of population densities encountered by different workers are shown in Table 26.

Field observations suggest that in fragmentary habitats offering wide varieties of food, surface cover and denning places, the most frequently encounted densities of adult foxes lie in the range of one per 40–120 hectares. This represents the range of densities which actually obtain and not those which could occur in some areas if foxes were not pursued for sport or for control purposes.

It is tantalizing to attempt to estimate numbers of foxes at large by numbers known to have been killed, whether as adults or as cubs dug out from dens. Unfortunately, too many assumptions usually have to be made which not only tend to invalidate the results but lead to widely divergent estimates according to how the same sets of figures are treated. An example, which reads like a schoolboy's arithmetic problem, concerns a fox destruction society concerned with an area of 18,600 hectares which kills on average 450 foxes a year, comprising 178 sub-adult or adults and 247 cubs (any fox killed after September in any year is regarded as an adult for bounty purposes). How many foxes are present in the area? Calculations based on these figures yield widely different estimates of numbers, all of which are inaccurate. All that I can be sure of is that each year at least one sub-adult or adult fox is killed per 104 hectares and one cub per seventy-five hectares. The number of breeding foxes and the total number of cubs born remain unsolved.

# 5

# Movement Behaviour

Foxes are solitary animals. They do not form packs, as do wolves; nor do they live in communal dens, as the badger does; nor are they nomadic – once settled, they delimit quite rigidiy the area in which they will spend all or part of their life, the area known as the fox's home range. The home range of the parent fox, however, is not necessarily that of its cubs, which tend to move away to settle elsewhere. The dispersal of the fox and its home range are attracting a great deal of attention at the present time, both for their fundamental, biological interest and for their applied value in the study of wildlife rabies epidemiology.

It is not an easy matter to study the movements of the fox. Many observers assert that in some esoteric way they understand its movements, but evidence can be misleading. The journey of a hunted fox which heads the hounds for twenty kilometres from point to point may be taken to indicate that a fox regularly travels over such distances; or the loss of lambs on the fringe of hill land and the discovery of lamb carrion at a cubbing earth some ten kilometres away may be assumed to be evidence that foxes will travel considerable distances to feed. (The old saw 'A fox will not kill (lambs) in its own parish' is presumably a reflection on the cunning of the fox and its acknowledgement that to prey on lambs is a punishable offence, the consequences of which it evades by perpetrating indiscretions only at some distance from its home!)

In fact, while some foxes may be distinguishable by an obvious distinctive feature – a white blaze over the shoulders or a bob tail – it is not possible to recognize an individual fox with any certainty unless one has had an opportunity to study particular foxes closely, observing minor distinguishing features. Without some knowledge of the origin of a fox, it would be no more than conjecture to deduce that two places fifteen kilometres apart were within a fox's area of regular activity simply because the same clearly marked animal was seen in both places.

Such a fox could be in the act of dispersing on one or both occasions. And a hunted fox which appears to know the area through which it is being hunted may be familiar with the territory not because the area constitutes its own home range but because it passed through the area when dispersing from its original home.

The only way to identify a fox with certainty is to mark it in some way. The simplest method is to apply some temporary or permanent marker which can be identified in the hand or at a distance in the field. However, if the animal can only be identified in the hand, the information it can yield will be limited to data ascertainable on recapture. It is more useful to the observer to be able to follow the fox's movements at all times, and for this purpose radio transmitters have been fitted to animals. Under favourable circumstances this technique presents observers with opportunities to record detailed observations of the movements of individual foxes and should produce a wealth of information in due course both in North America, where the technique was developed, and in Europe, where its widespread use is only just emerging. Field study of mammals in Britain, for example, has long been the Cinderella of biology and the financial and technical resources needed to develop high-quality radio-tracking equipment were lacking until the Radio and Space Research Laboratory at Slough (now the Appleton Laboratory) undertook to develop equipment which has been in use in mid-Wales and elsewhere for seven years.

The technique, in its simplest form, involves the attachment of a collar incorporating a small radio transmitter to the neck of a fox, the location of which, after the fox has been released, is pinpointed simultaneously by two radio receivers employing directional aerials. Under ideal conditions – when the transmitter is in line of sight of the receivers – adequate minimum-error signals can be received at distances of up to fifteen kilometres (sometimes even further); under other conditions, however, even at close range, large errors in pinpointing the fox can occur, and one of the problems with the use of such equipment is the recognition of errors of unacceptable magnitude. In optimum conditions simple equipment will enable the position of the transmitter to be located to within $\pm 1.0°$, but in practice $\pm 2.0°$ is acceptable for most purposes. As far as possible, the mobile receivers are sited so that the fox is approximately three kilometres distant. Radio signals from the transmitter can be received when the fox is in earth and rock dens, and the pulsed signals vary in pitch and intensity when the fox is active (thus some information can be gathered even if the fox is apparently stationary).

The method is extremely useful, but it has many limitations. All that is known is the position of the fox; nothing is known of its behaviour except by inference. Although a fox may spend much of its time in a particular field, it is not possible to tell why it is there or what it is doing; nor – even if other foxes in the same area are radio-tagged – can much be learned about its social behaviour. Conclusions based on slender evidence are very liable to be mistaken, but data obtained from many foxes in different habitats will permit more conclusions to be drawn than is possible through the study of the movements of a few animals.

## Dispersal

Many studies of dispersal are referred to as 'migration' studies, but unless there is good evidence that a fox has taken a return ticket, so to speak, its movements are better defined as dispersal. To distinguish genuine dispersal from a fox's movements within the home range of its parents, some knowledge of local home-range sizes is required. This poses problems, since mean home-range sizes vary from place to place, and the recapture of a cub three kilometres from its birth den may indeed represent dispersal in one locality, while a cub found five kilometres from its den elsewhere might not.

Dispersal generally occurs when cubs are between six and nine months old, during the period September to January/early February, but it is known that even among litter mates some animals disperse as much as two months earlier than others, and that males often move away first.

The tagging and radio-tracking of animals has assisted in studies of fox dispersal. In Wales 409 cubs, eighty-six adults and eight foxes of uncertain age (either sub-adults or adults) were tagged over a five-year period up to 1971, and others subsequently in the course of radio-tracking studies (see Figures 20 and 21). Elsewhere, in several areas of England, 362 foxes have been tagged since 1977, but insufficient time has elapsed for the recapture of all tagged animals to cease. Urban foxes have also been tagged by my colleague R. J. Page in north London, but in this case, too, results are not yet complete.

Even in Wales some of the tagged animals are still at large, though 43 per cent have been recovered. The total sample seems adequate, but analysis of the recapture data often permits only tentative conclusions to be drawn about some aspects of dispersal. For example, in common with the research of other workers in Europe, few animals over three years of age have been recovered, and in Wales 91 per cent of the recaptured animals were under fifteen months old. In the USSR, where similar studies were carried out, 21 per cent of 126 tagged cubs were recovered, but only one of these was recovered as an adult eighteen months old (Chirkova, 1955b). In an extensive study in Illinois and Iowa, where commercial fox trapping and shooting is common, Storm and his colleagues (1976) tagged 1,987 cubs and found that 82 per cent of recovered

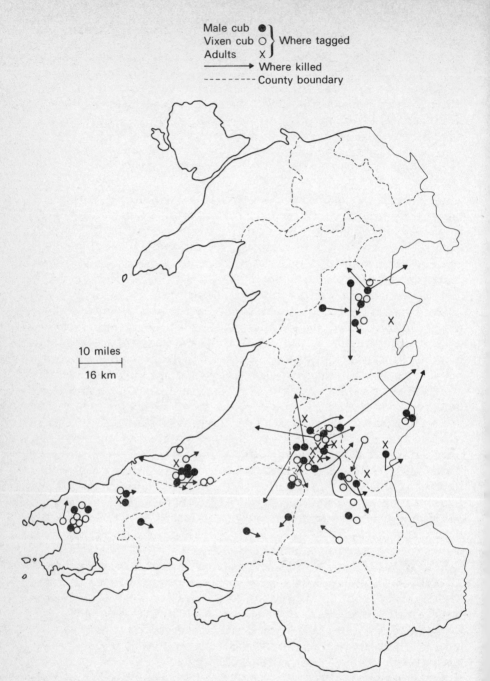

**20** Movements of tagged foxes, Wales 1966–72. Locations where recovered or recaptured foxes were tagged and (arrow) where they were recovered alive or killed are shown. Animals with less than 6 months between tagging and recovery are omitted and, for clarity, some other foxes recovered are not included. A symbol without an arrow indicates that the fox was killed within 2·5 km of the place of tagging. Of the four adults recovered at distances greater than this the single vixen had moved the furthest (9·5 km).

foxes were killed in their first year, 15 per cent in their second year and the remaining 3 per cent as older animals.

The mean ages of animals recaptured, according to data obtained from the two main areas of Wales where foxes are being studied, were 8.5 months in mid-Wales and 18.6 in west Wales. Since dispersal of juveniles occurs during the period September to February, and the mean date of the recaptures is mid-November in mid-Wales but later in Pembrokeshire, it is very likely that the data for mid-Wales includes more animals that had not dispersed by the time they were killed than is the case in the Pembrokeshire sample. From 1966 to 1971 only 46 per cent of the cubs killed in west Wales were under twelve months of age, as compared with 91 per cent in mid-Wales. The information contained in Table 27 shows some of the features which might affect dispersal in these two areas. There are many environmental differences between them, but it is impossible to determine which, if any, of the features indicated influence dispersal or its timing and extent.

Such data indicate a very high mortality rate among juveniles. In addition to being more numerous, young animals may also be more vulnerable than settled adult foxes because of their inexperience and their unfamiliarity with the terrain.

It seems that juvenile foxes disperse quite randomly. For example, five cubs out of a litter of six, all killed within eighteen months of birth, were widely scattered. One male was killed by a train 9.5km east of its birth place, another by a gamekeeper 52km to the north-east, another by a Forestry Commission warrener 24km to the north; two vixens were snared 24km and 2km away to the south-west. The remaining cub, a vixen fitted with a transmitter, was last located 16km north of its original den. A scatter diagram of the direction of dispersal of all tagged foxes recovered reveals no positive trend.

Information about distances travelled by young tagged dispersing foxes derived from the recovery of dead foxes is somewhat biased. A comparison of the movements of young animals under twelve months old with those of foxes recovered at two years of age and upwards reveals that the older animals have travelled further. Since foxes tagged as adults are usually recovered near the place where they were captured initially, even years later (a mean distance of 2km for males and 2.5km for females), it is clear that many of the cubs recaptured under twelve months old had not even begun to disperse when they were killed. Others were probably killed whilst dispersing.

In areas of moderate to low population density, on predominantly sheep-rearing hill land or upland areas of mid-Wales, the mean linear distances travelled by cubs from their rearing dens to the places where they were killed are 13.7km for males and 2.3km for females. In areas of higher population density, on enclosed farmland in Cardiganshire and

Pembrokeshire, the corresponding distances are 4.7km and 1.9km respectively. In mid-Wales 69 per cent of females had moved less than 1.6km and in Pembrokeshire, 66 per cent. In mid-Wales 39 per cent of male cubs had travelled more than 10km and in Pembrokeshire 11 per cent. Thus, over half of the vixens tagged and recovered in both areas had moved less than the diameter of most home ranges in the two areas (as was later revealed by radio-tracking). The dispersal movements of foxes was generally much greater in mid-Wales, and many of the recaptured male cubs in west Wales were within 1.6km of their birth place. The longest distance travelled by a dispersing fox, a male, in mid-Wales was 52km, and only 10 per cent of foxes have travelled distances greater than 19km.

Rather greater dispersal distances were revealed in a thorough study by Jensen (1973) in Denmark, where three juvenile males out of a total of 202 foxes recovered had moved between 50 and 110km. His studies showed that of 167 foxes recovered after September, 49 per cent had travelled less than 5km, 26 per cent 5–14km, 19 per cent 15–25km and 23 per cent over 25km. Slightly shorter distances were reported by van Haaften (1970) in Holland.

In Northern Ireland sixty-one cubs were tagged by Fairley (1969b), of which thirty-two were recaptured. Of the eight cubs recovered later than 100 days after tagging, one had travelled 58km and another 37km, the average being 16.5km. One vixen had moved 30.5km; all other vixens had moved less than 3.75km.

In North America variable (and also much greater) dispersal distances have been recorded (Errington and Berry, 1937; Sheldon, 1950 and 1953; Arnold and Schofield, 1956; Longley, 1962; Ables, 1965; Phillips, 1970; Phillips *et al.*, 1972 and Storm *et al.*, 1976). Ables recorded the greatest distance – a male fox which travelled 394km – but most studies in North America record individual distances exceeding 100km. As in Europe, juvenile dog foxes travel further than females; for example, in Michigan, Arnold and Schofield record a mean distance of 68km and 14km for males and females respectively. Sheldon observed that male juveniles tended to disperse from their family home ranges earlier than vixens, and Arnold and Schofield that they tended to disperse in a northward direction, an observation confirmed by Phillips *et al.* and by Storm and his colleagues. Clearly, the distance and direction of dispersal can be influenced by geographical and topographical features; in Denmark and Northern Ireland, for example, long-range northward movements could not be undertaken by dispersing foxes; even so, there may be fundamental biological differences between North American and European red foxes in respect of dispersal behaviour.

The monograph by Storm and his collaborators, which updates data on dispersal reported by Phillips *et al.*, provides a comprehensive and detailed account of dispersal and other aspects of the life history of the red fox in North America. Their tagging studies reveal that cubs recovered at 10–12 months old had not travelled as far as animals recaptured at between two and four years of age – a strong indication that dispersal also occurs among settled adults. (Their findings are different from results obtained in Denmark, Ireland and Wales, where there is little evidence of significant movement among settled adult foxes.) The initiation of dispersal among juveniles was examined by an experimental approach using castrated cubs and by radio-tracking, and Storm and his colleagues concluded that no single factor seems to initiate dispersal. It is apparent that dispersal among the North American fox population studied occurs without prelude, fairly quickly, over greater average and extreme distances and with a tendency towards northward orientation – features not observed in Europe (possibly because the dispersal of foxes has not yet been adequately examined in Europe).

Dispersal distances are so variable among local fox populations, among populations in different areas and different countries that it is probable that differences in population density and habitat are largely responsible for variations in dispersal movements, not only at the place of origin of the dispersing fox, but, more important, also in the area to which the fox moves after leaving the family group. Since, in any population of steady size, the foxes recruited into the adult population replace adults that are lost, foxes in high-density populations (over a large area) would not normally need to move so far to find a vacated space to live (see p. 159–160 for the composition of a breeding population). Any unusually long individual dispersal distances recorded may merely reflect a fox's inability readily to secure a place for itself.

The growth of the fox populations of Anglesey, the Lleyn Peninsula and areas of Pembrokeshire help to illustrate differences in local dispersal movements. It is likely that the Anglesey fox population, now numbering many hundreds, originated from the release of a small number of captive animals in 1965 or 1966. In 1968 numbers were still small, possibly under twenty, all in one restricted area. It was not until 1975 that foxes were found throughout the island (the area of which is 716 square kilometres), though there were no physical barriers to rapid dispersal. The recolonization of the Lleyn Peninsula and certain parts of Pembrokeshire, on the other hand, was accomplished much more quickly. In these two areas foxes, though few in number, were widely dispersed. Their reproduction, coupled perhaps with unimpeded immigration and settlement of foxes from adjacent counties with higher-density populations, enabled the establishment of high fox numbers within four years.

**Observations of dispersal movements**
Though tagging and radio-tracking do not furnish conclusive evidence

of the movements of the fox, as I have observed above, these techniques assist in sketching the outline of certain aspects of fox behaviour. Individual foxes may not be regarded as typical of all foxes; yet studies based on the movements of several foxes in an area can be revealing. Some observations are offered below. No apology is tendered for the parochial nature of these observations; I hope they will be regarded as examples which may help to elucidate some aspects of a general pattern of fox behaviour.

A male cub, recaptured in November fifty metres away from the earth where it was tagged six months earlier in May, was fitted with a radio transmitter and its movements observed for sixty days. Its range of nocturnal movements was very well defined at the westerly perimeter of its range, at the edge of a 320-hectare conifer plantation at Bwlchciliau where it spent most of its time resting on the surface in daylight. To the east and north its movements were very erratic and unpredictable, and great difficulty was sometimes experienced in keeping track of it when it moved quickly from one valley to another. At dusk the fox would leave its couch and travel swiftly through the woodland for about 600 metres, down a long steep bank to an unoccupied farmstead, Cwm Chwefru, where it would sometimes spend an hour but would often proceed directly over a small bridge spanning a stream four metres wide. If the water was low, it would apparently ford, jump or swim the stream at another place nearby. The remainder of its time, usually until about one hour before dawn, was spent on an open hill rising from 230 to 500 metres. On a few occasions in the early days of my study of this animal it would disappear for a short while over the ridge of a hill about three kilometres north of the river bridge towards the vicinity of Lluest Newydd. At first radio contact with it was lost for about an hour after it had passed over the ridge, but after about a month it would be missing for as much as six hours on some nights. It was believed to have passed over the ridge of Gamrhiw. At about this time there was reason to suspect failure of the transmitter battery, so an attempt was made to recapture the fox to replace the transmitter. The bridge and stream were manned against the fox after its night on the hill and it was prevented from returning to the conifer wood. It approached to about 400 metres of the stream and was later tracked almost continuously for seven hours in daylight on the hill, being kept on the move for almost the whole of this time. The aim was to force it to seek refuge in an earth, but it was reluctant to enter any on the hill, including the one where it was born and reared on Allt y Clych. Often the fox was no more than 200 metres ahead of the mobile radio receiver, and although clear views of the area were obtained from high vantage points, the fox was not seen on the several occasions that it had to move across clear sheep-grazed pastures. Since it would not go to ground, the attempt to recapture it was abandoned. On

23 December a mounted hunt pursued a fox into the conifer wood where the tagged fox lay. It responded by moving about 300 metres from its couch to a small dense stand of unbrashed conifer. Several hounds and hunters passed by (some 20—60 metres away) on several occasions, but the fox was not detected. The fox survived the day.

On Christmas Day the fox was missing from the woodland but was found two days later nine kilometres away in a heap of boulders near Talwrn, directly north of the river bridge. The hill ridge over which the fox used to disappear at night was directly in line with the place where it was found in the boulders, which might indicate that the disappearances of increasing duration may have been a prelude to the final movement away from the home area. While at its new location, the fox may have been disturbed by loose hounds in the vicinity of nearby hunt kennels, because two days later the fox moved northward across the river Elan in daytime, travelling about ten kilometres to reach the edge of a small lake (Gwyn Llyn) about seven kilometres away, where its arrival was advertised by much vocal alarm by mallard. It found refuge during the next six days in or near rocks in woodland close to the lakeside, but it disappeared again two days after another pack of hounds, hot on the scent of another fox, passed by its refuge in the rocks. Again, the fox moved slightly when the hounds approached to within 200 metres or so of its couch, but it lay low and was not detected. Two days later the fox was found in a conifer plantation thirteen kilometres due north of the lake at Pencloddiau, near Llangurig. A week later the conifer plantation was hunted by another pack, and the fox returned south to a *cwm* at Lloftyddgleision in the Wye valley, about 2.5 kilometres north of the lake; it returned to the plantation two days later. It encountered yet another pack of hounds at a fox drive six days later, and on this occasion it fled in daylight. As my colleagues listened to the transmitter, the repetition rate of the signals, normally steady, suddenly changed as the fox left the wood. Whether or not the fox had been shot at and the transmitter damaged is not known. It was impossible to keep track of it as it sped away, but it was located a day later at its former refuge north of the lake. Again, an effort was made to recapture it, but although it was known that the fox was moving in gorse and heather and was only 200 metres ahead on some occasions, it was not seen even from clear vantage points. What happened to the fox subsequently is not known, since the radio signals expired at nightfall. The adventures of this fox are recorded at length because it illustrates the hazards that beset foxes in these hill areas – hazards which may have some influence upon the behaviour and extent of dispersal by foxes. This young fox survived hunts on at least four occasions; it had been harassed on one other occasion whilst attempts were made to recapture it. Each of its four major movements occurred shortly after encounters with hounds, suggesting that disturb-

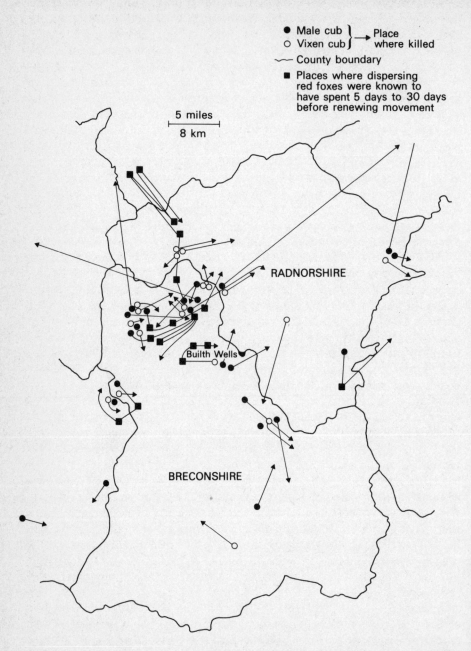

**21** Dispersal movements of some juvenile foxes; some of the movements were revealed by radio-tracking and the places where such animals spent more than 6 days are shown.

ance may have promoted emigration, but this might have taken place without such stimuli, and there is no means of knowing until the movements of several similarly placed foxes have been studied.

At no time did the fox seek refuge in a fox earth, though it used cover afforded by rocks on three occasions. Its lying-up places were always in scrub oak or conifer woodland, except on the last day, when it was found in heather and gorse. Prior to emigrating, the fox was inactive in daylight, but having made its first dispersal movement, it was usually active in daylight, sometimes over small areas but on a few occasions making movements of a kilometre or so in a short space of time. Apart from the presence of woodland, there was no other obvious feature common to all the places that the fox chose to stay.

Another tracking exercise involved a juvenile vixen, radio-tagged in a coniferous woodland in September, which showed little signs of dispersal activity in the following two months. It moved away about 1.5 kilometres from the place of capture and, having settled, ranged over an area of about a one-kilometre radius during the autumn months. Whether this short movement represented dispersal to an area new to the vixen and outside its existing home range or (more probably) that of its parents is not known; neither was its natal earth. This vixen was the first juvenile female to be radio-tagged. The many others tagged since then reveal that its behaviour – the short shift in range – is not uncharacteristic of juvenile vixens.

A juvenile male fox tracked for seven weeks during November–December spent most of its time in daylight in various coniferous woodlands near Builth Wells, east of the river Wye between Cefn Dyrys, Pencerrig and Newmead, but on most nights when it was tracked it crossed the river via a railway bridge (at Builth Road) two kilometres or so distant. For about three weeks, on those nights when it crossed the bridge, it went south about five kilometres – along the railway line for part of the way – crossed a stream and then (this is known only by inference because the river was high and swift) crossed the Irfon by a footbridge at Caer Beris. Sometimes it went two miles further on, to the watershed of the Duhonnw (as far as Pantypyllau, Cwmhinddu and Dollynwydd), but on other occasions it spent the remainder of the night in a field near a small piggery at Rhyd yr Arian before returning the way it came. On two occasions it spent the day in cover near Llys Buallt on the outskirts of the town. On those nights when it had ventured from and returned to its couch in the conifer woodlands east of the Wye, it had travelled at least twenty kilometres from point to point; the real distance it had covered as it wandered about would have exceeded this considerably. Later, the fox changed its direction of nocturnal activity, going north along the west side of the Wye, which it probably crossed below its confluence with the Ithon. Sometimes it spent the day in coniferous and deciduous woodland close by Llys Dinam, near Newbridge. A few days before Christmas the fox was active in a coniferous woodland alongside the Wye, opposite Brynwern, and after a few days of ominous inactivity it was found dead, curled up in a couch beneath a bush which it had clearly been using for some time before it died. Autopsy revealed that it had suffered massive bruising to the hindlimbs and back (though no bones were obviously broken) — possibly the result of a collision with car or train. Its range of movement for the time that it had been tracked covered an area of at least 36 square kilometres.

Two vixens radio-tagged in a small conifer woodland near to the Duhonnw at its junction with the Wye, two kilometres south of Builth, both showed that movements of vixens at this time of year can also be extensive. One vixen (Amey) crossed the Wye fairly regularly, but prolonged rainfall and bank-high water may at times have interfered with its intended movements across the river, since there are no bridges where it normally made the crossing. The fact that it swam the river with some apparent regularity – no small feat – suggests that this vixen was adult and knew its range well. During the month that it was tracked its movements encompassed at least 26 square kilometres. The other vixen (Daisy) had a more restricted range of about sixteen square kilometres for the first month that it was tracked, but at the time of year when most vixens are nearing oestrus (late January), when one would expect vixens to be settled, it moved to a conifer woodland seven kilometres from its previously known limits of movement. On several occasions Amey and Daisy moved close together over parts of their overlapping ranges, thirteen square kilometres of which were common to both. At least once during December both visited the outskirts of Builth on the same night, moving through house gardens and those of the hospital and the cricket pavilion. Both ran the gauntlet constantly: skinners and bounty hunters had set snares in many parts of their ranges. It is known that hounds killed at least seventeen foxes in December and January, within a three-kilometre radius of the woodland where the two vixens were usually located. Amey (adult by tooth examination) was killed by a car as she was making her way across a road from a local quarry towards the river. Daisy emigrated to settle in an area even more noted for its anti-fox activities, but it survived for a further twelve months.

Another vixen and dog fox fitted with transmitters at the same time as Daisy and Amey, and which had ranges partly overlapping theirs, both moved away in December. The dog, Albert, was intercepted by a snare and killed about fourteen kilometres away, on the fringe of Radnor Forest. Victoria shifted only two kilometres away, to a new centre of activity which included much of her old range — indeed, her shift was hardly a dispersal movement. She somehow survived all the efforts of the local shooters who were aware that a radio-tagged fox was in the area and even produced a litter. Victoria was shot two years later in daylight by a farmer's young son, as she was picking at windfall apples in an orchard adjacent to the farmhouse.

It is clear that some males and females disperse suddenly and settle quickly, whereas others precede dispersal by reconnaissance extending over periods of weeks before the final move away is made. It is not known what stimulus promotes dispersal, or whether it is the same for all foxes, or even for the two sexes. In addition to the apparent precipitation of dispersal by harassment, the considerable disruption of the social structure and of relationships between foxes resulting from the killing of foxes may influence dispersal motivation. This disruption of an unsettled and a partly settled population from October to January, and of a settled population thereafter, must have a traumatic influence on the behaviour of both sexes, but the radio observer is able to gather little information about this, especially in the case of those animals that are about to form, or have just formed, a relationship with non-family foxes. An important – if not the most important – feature of the environment of a fox is another fox. Even if its relationship with another were competitive, the sudden disappearance of one must affect the remaining fox, even if the least that happens is the forming of a new relationship with a newcomer to the vacancy. It will be very difficult to learn anything about this because man's activities cannot be controlled over large areas, but some area suitable for studies of undisturbed foxes may be found.

## Home Ranges

The home range of a settled fox is the area on which it depends for food, shelter and the other requirements of life. The range may partly or largely overlap those of other foxes at some or at all times of the year, but a part of it may be defended from encroachment by other foxes – in which case the defended area is more suitably described as a territory. The home range may be shared by a dog, vixen and cubs, comprising a family group as was described for the red fox in North America by Sargeant (1972), but other social groups of foxes have been described by Macdonald (1977b) and will be mentioned later.

Intruders upon family-group territories within the home range may be repelled more or less vigorously as the sense of territoriality waxes and wanes according to the season. This is speculative, however, since there is at present no good information on the territoriality of foxes throughout the year.

In North America Hamilton (1939) estimated individual ranges to be about 280 hectares and Schofield (1960), 800–1600 hectares; Scott (1943), studying three separate families, estimated their ranges to be about 400 hectares each, and Storm *et al*. (1976) report the range of two family groups to be 9.6 square kilometres each. Studies in Northern Ireland (Fairley, 1969b; 1970b), in Denmark (Jensen, 1973), in Holland (van Haaften, 1970, and Niewold, 1973), in Switzerland (Wandeler, pers. comm., and Behrendt, 1955) show that the estimated ranges of adult foxes varied from about 400–1600 hectares – much the same as in North America.

During the five years that radio telemetry has been used to study fox movements in different habitats in Wales, eighty-four foxes have been tracked; these comprise sixteen nursing vixens, thirteen adult dogs, twenty-six juvenile dogs, eighteen juvenile vixens, and six vixens and five dogs of unknown age. Much information about home ranges has been gathered but a great deal more remains to be done on this topic and on aspects of fox behaviour related to home ranges.

Some of the results obtained in Wales will be described, before other considerations, in order to illustrate the kinds of home-range movements observed.

The first two foxes to be tracked were nursing vixens captured on the same day in different earths a little less than a kilometre apart on hill land rising to 650 metres. The furthermost limits of their range boundaries were four kilometres from enclosed cultivable land in one case and 2.5 kilometres in the other, and their nearest recorded distances from such land were one kilometre and a few metres respectively. Only one vixen was close to conifer plantations, which later it was found to use. Since these vixens were the first to be fitted with transmitters, they were subjected to considerable interference during the initial period when the use of the equipment was being learned and its versatility investigated. Both were tagged on 15 April and both had cubs of about three weeks of age. Little was learned about their home ranges in darkness. One had five known resting or denning places – one in rocks, three in earths and several in conifer woodland. The two denning places furthest apart were separated by 3.5 kilometres. The other vixen had eight daytime refuges – four earths, one hole in a turbary, two dens in boulders and a couch in a patch of sedge. Neither was active in daytime, except when disturbed above ground, and they would move only when approached to about 400 metres. In both cases their few known night-time positions and their daytime resting places encompassed an area of about 6.5 square kilometres. Both vixens were intermittently located with their cubs until both moved from their rock and earth dens to reside above ground about thirty days after first capture. In mid-June their cubs were located at the edge of their known ranges at the higher elevations. Unfortunately, both vixens shed their transmitter collars at this time, within thirty-six hours of each other.

There were technical difficulties associated with locating an adult dog fox (George), fitted with a radio in early September, since its range included undulating enclosed land, steep-sided valleys and flat hill land, and its quick movements through its range necessitated frequent and frantic shifting of the receiving stations in order to keep track of it. It was very active both by day and by night for the entire two-month period that it was tracked. Its range, about 5.5 kilometres by 1.75 kilometres, included a variety of habitats, but it seemed to spend much of its night on open hill land, in young conifer or scrub-covered areas. It had four regular daytime denning places – a fox earth, a disused badger sett, a bracken area and a conifer woodland. It became active at dusk and remained so throughout the night, resting in the early mornings and resuming activity from about midday until the late afternoon, when it rested a while again.

The entire perimeter of George's range was never patrolled by the fox on a single night, and there was a tendency for the fox to stay in one part of its range for a few days before shifting to another; altogether three parts or sub-areas of activity within the range were apparent and there were others which it did not frequent. It was equally active under dry, frosty conditions and when the weather was wet and windy. Its choice of daytime denning places was not apparently influenced by weather conditions, nor did it, for example, confine its activities to the comparative protection of the lee slopes of hills when the weather was bad. The direction of movement at night was not correlated with wind direction. The only pattern of movement which was fairly consistent was the comparative inactivity of the fox, as measured by distance moved, during the first two to three hours after emerging or stirring at dusk. Its pattern of behaviour in daytime was often very bold, since it would move across agricultural land close to human habitations. It was last located in the small hours in late November at the extreme limit of its known range and has not been found since.

Since George was the only fox being tracked, nothing is known of the movement of other foxes in its area; but subsequent investigation of fox behaviour in the area suggests that it is highly likely that several other foxes used the same area. Though the limits of its range were not well defined, the fox could have patrolled its perimeter (a total distance of about fourteen kilometres) at a slow trot in less than two hours – but it never did so. George was the cause of some consternation and amusement, since its rapid movements kept my colleagues and me active throughout the night, moving from one receiving station to another; also, our activities with aerials and headphones on public highways by day and by night prompted a sudden increase of purchases – and renewals – of television licences in the area!

A juvenile vixen tagged in September in conifer woodland gradually shifted over a period of one week to another area 1.5 kilometres away. Its movements were monitored for three months, for varying periods each day, and its range was found to be very restricted – an area with a radius of about 0.5 kilometre. Three-quarters of its range was in woodland, where voles were plentiful; the remainder was enclosed sheep pasture. This vixen was active in daylight within the woodland, and its slow progress throughout its range clearly indicated some sort of activity other than merely the shifting of position from one place to another. It weighed about 3.8kg when tagged and 5.7kg when recovered three months later. The abundance of food in the woodland may have had an important bearing on the size of this vixen's range.

Another adult vixen which provides an example of home-range behaviour was tagged near Aberduhonnw, a kilometre south of Builth Wells. From October to February it occupied a range of about a one-kilometre radius, encompassing houses on the outskirts of the town, mixed farmland and open hill. During this time it used about thirty different areas for daytime refuge, five of which were used more often than the others. In mid-February it disappeared from the area overnight and was found a day later in a conifer woodland about nine kilometres west of the centre of its range, where it stayed. Its new range, with less than a 0.5-kilometre radius, was mainly in a coniferous woodland, a wet valley bottom and enclosed pasture. The date of birth of its cubs in early April indicated that it had moved from its first range after becoming pregnant. The new range remained small until about three weeks after the cubs had been born, when the vixen began to make nightly sorties in an eastward direction to a municipal rubbish tip four kilometres away. It later extended this movement, and eventually its range assumed the shape of a string of beads – the beads being foraging areas of different size (no greater than between three and four hectares) and the string merely travelling routes from one small foraging range to another. This arrangement continued until July, when the vixen gradually began to spend more time in the foraging areas, some of which were gradually extended to form a single foraging area with a radius of about 0.5 kilometre. In August it abandoned the second range completely and moved to the foraging area.

The movements of the vixen before it moved the second time crossed the ranges of two other radio-tagged foxes. In addition, several other foxes were known to reside in the area; thus, the vixen was clearly encroaching upon several other fox ranges, though not necessarily at the foraging areas. The opportunity to follow this fox through another twelve months was lost when it was accidentally killed.

Radio-tracking studies of home range sizes have been conducted elsewhere in Wales in a different habitat from that of hill and adjoining land in mid-Wales. In 1976–7 foxes were tracked in an area with a high-density fox population at Tre Marchog near Fishguard, Pembrokeshire, by a student, David Cowen, who was assigned to assist my colleague,

John Woods, as part of his training. Eleven foxes were tagged in November and December in a study area of 6.25 square kilometres. Most of this area was cultivable land under grass, barley or potatoes, but 18 per cent was scrub and rough land. The area, lying at about 100 metres' elevation, included parts or the whole of thirteen farm holdings and 113 kilometres of hedgerows (many overgrown and as much as three metres wide), and was bounded (but not intersected) by thirteen kilometres of roadways.

The aim was to catch as many foxes as possible in the area to study their utilization of the area. The seven dog foxes and four vixens tracked probably represented over 50 per cent of the foxes using the area. It was later found that six litters were reared in the central part of the area, where most of the observations were made, and two near the periphery, which none of the tracked foxes were known to have covered. It was assumed, hopefully, that the foxes caught and tagged in November and December would not move out of the area, since ear-tagging in Pembrokeshire had revealed only short dispersal distances. The assumption proved to be correct, in that only one male moved away permanently to a place four kilometres distant. Another male made a short excursion out of the area but returned (to stay) a few days later.

One of the main reasons for selecting this particular study site was the occurrence of two rocky elevations which enabled most of the land to be kept under radio surveillance from two vantage points. Daytime locations of the foxes were made throughout the study period, which ended in June, and night tracking was done at regular periods.

Considerable overlaps of home ranges were observed, especially from November to February inclusive, when range sizes were as large as 133 hectares. Overlaps of lesser extent still occurred from March to May, but range sizes were smaller, being no greater than seventy-two hectares. The mean range sizes for the two periods, winter and spring, were fifty-eight and thirty-four hectares respectively – very small compared with the lower-population-density areas of mid-Wales. Accompanying the decrease in range size in the spring was an apparent cessation of activity over some parts of cultivated land by all the foxes collectively.

In the spring period the observed ranges of two dog foxes and one vixen coincided almost exactly, but there was evidence of another untagged vixen in their range – consequently, the shared range could have included another vixen. Two litters of cubs were located in the shared range. Forty fox dens or small, mostly single hole badger setts were found in the area. Only one fox, Arnold, used an earth regularly. The other foxes made use of the abundant cover afforded by hedges and scrub. A fall of snow, which is unusual in the area, caused most foxes to seek cover below ground. On this occasion two radio-tagged male foxes were located in the same single-hole den. As in other areas where cover is dense and abundant, foxes preferred to lie up on the surface.

Food availability in this area of small home ranges was not overtly abundant. Faecal analyses showed that small rodents, calf carcases, beetles and earthworms featured prominently in the foxes' diet from November to May. Cattle afterbirths in this stock-rearing area may have supplemented the more usual diet, as well as silage. There were very few rabbits in the area. Indeed, they were probably outnumbered by foxes.

These preliminary radio-tracking investigations in the two areas of Wales permit but few generalizations because so few of the observations could be related to physical or biological features. However, the movements of many foxes studied had some degree of predictability after a few days of observation, since there are often certain areas within ranges which are visited more frequently than others. There was also an indication that utilization of different parts of their ranges varied seasonally.

Though a few patterns are beginning to emerge, there is as much difference in home-range behaviour between foxes in Pembrokeshire and mid-Wales as there is between individual foxes in mid-Wales. Contrary to the observations of other biologists, in my experience home ranges are not exclusive to individuals, nor to pairs of foxes, nor, it seems, to family groups consisting of a pair of adults and their offspring. Nevertheless, range boundaries often coincide with physical features such as roads, field boundaries, streams, sheep tracks, a hill ridge and so forth, and there must be some motivation for having fairly precise limits to ranges even though they encroach upon ranges of other foxes.

Paradoxically, the enlightening researches of David Macdonald in this field make the situation even more perplexing. He revealed, by the combined use of radio-tracking and visual observations of the movements and behaviour of foxes at night (using infra-red binoculars) that foxes can form social groups (Macdonald 1977b). He observed the organization of foxes into groups of up to five adults, comprising in each case one dog fox and several vixens. These animals occupied a group range, within which one vixen dominated the others; some of the others might be relegated to occupancy of only a part of the group range. (Such observations could only be made by the techniques used by Macdonald and serve to show that there is no substitute for patient visual observation – albeit with sophisticated equipment – in behavioural studies.)

His study population, in a rural area which includes a ribbon development of houses with large gardens, agricultural land and much deciduous woodland, occupies non-overlapping group ranges as small as thirty hectares, the boundaries of which are at times vigorously defended. The movement and home-range behaviour at Oxford is so different from that observed in mid-Wales that I am inclined to believe the Oxford population represents the largest number of foxes, untrammelled by man, that can be supported at a stable level in a diversified habitat throughout the year. The vital factor is probably the availability of food all year round. When I visited the area the Oxford habitat did not appear to me to contain a greater abundance of prospective fox foods than many low-lying areas of mid-Wales; in mid-Wales, however, the critical factor affecting the maintenance of the maximum number of foxes that the area can support is without doubt interference and mortality due directly to man. In Pembrokeshire, on the other hand, there is little interference by man. Perhaps the availability of natural foods was no greater in Oxford than in Pembrokeshire, but augmentation by other food resources not available to the West Wales foxes might enable the population to be maintained at a steady level throughout the year. Clearly, it is the period of minimum availability of food which maintains the base population level, not a seasonal superabundance of food. In this context Macdonald considers that the inclusion of dwellings, gardens and orchards within the group ranges may provide an important source of food, which might act as a buffer against seasonal shortages of other more natural foods.

Although the fox population density in Pembrokeshire is considered to be high (about four per kilometre square in the study area), it could be higher locally and seasonally because ranges shrink in the spring and tend to coalesce. Even so, density seems to be lower than observed at Oxford, if the social groups there are typical of larger areas. Furthermore, the sex ratios of adults in the two areas are very different, which suggests that there must be high rates of mortality or dispersal among males at Oxford.

Macdonald's observations raise many fundamental questions concerning the social organization of foxes and point the way to similarly rewarding studies in different environments. One such study of fox movement behaviour, by Freek Niewold (1973) at Arnhem, Holland, sheds further light on range movements. His adult radio-tagged foxes had well established ranges, but excursions were made, primarily for foraging, to places up to six kilometres beyond their residential ranges. Some of the food resources utilized were transient, and the question is: how did the vixens know that food was available well outside their residential range? Dr Niewold also tells me that independent cubs three to four months of age, of different litters, team up and wander about as a group in the woodlands of Arnhem.

In North America radio-tracking studies on home ranges of foxes have been conducted since the early 1960s. Though there is much information which can be compared with that obtained in Europe, it is difficult to assign causes to the differences observed because there is insufficient information on the factors which may have a causative effect, such as habitat, food availability and population density. Nevertheless, there are many features of the home-range behaviour of the North American red fox which strike a familiar note and in all probability are relevant to Britain.

Storm (1965), reporting radio-tracking studies of red foxes in Illinois, showed that adult foxes regularly returned to familiar places in daylight but seldom to a particular couch. The extent of the home range of one adult male over a six-month period was 3 by 2.3 kilometres; the average range size for two other adult foxes was 3.8 square kilometres. Storm's studies also suggested that foxes may have a series of pathways connecting high-use areas, an observation which tends to confirm impressions gained in Wales and which is not unlike Niewold's observations.

Ables (1969b) studied eight radio-tagged foxes in Wisconsin; he observed ranges of 56 to 160 hectares in a diversified habitat, compared with 5.8 square kilometres in a less diverse farming area. He, like Storm, postulated that the activity pattern indicated areas of regular high use within each home range. Neither of these two biologists detected much interaction between foxes, and it was Sargeant (1972) in Minnesota who, with the aid of very accurate radio-tracking equipment, first detected family groups of foxes occupying non-overlapping, well defined territorial ranges, as distinct from home ranges. He observed that the territorial boundaries were often contiguous with certain physical features such as roads, streams or lake shores, and that somehow the territories were maintained by non-aggressive behaviour. The boundaries were not regularly patrolled by foxes, yet occupants of adjacent territories maintained the integrity of these boundaries without physical contact. (However, he observed that a pair of foxes were quick to encroach on a neighbouring range when the male and cubs occupying that range were killed.) Nearly all the land area studied was occupied by foxes. The territories were occupied by the adult male, vixen and juveniles of the family, but the strong sense of territoriality observed may have been seasonal, since the observations refer only to the period from the breeding season to August. Sargeant suggested that the sizes of territories are a function of population density – as densities diminish, so territory sizes increase, and areas not occupied by foxes only became apparent when population densities fall dramatically. In Sargeant's study the territorial and range boundaries apparently coincided.

Comparisons of radio-tracking observations of home ranges suggest that there is no typical home-range behaviour or movement, except in relation to particular sets of circumstances, and that an understanding of such behaviour will only be achieved by very detailed examination of environmental influences upon the foxes under study and perhaps of their kinship. Although it is clear that home-range sizes are larger in mid-Wales than in Pembrokeshire (which could be due to the lower population density in mid-Wales, to instability because of the almost incessant disruption of the *status quo* by man, or to the less even distribution of food) it is not possible to account positively for the differences of behaviour within the two areas.

It seems, therefore, that radio-tracking alone will reveal little more without adopting Macdonald's approach or without a field experimental approach manipulating the situation by the removal of known animals, the introduction of aliens in specific situations, or the provision of food, for example. Coupled with this, the quantification of those features which have a bearing on home range behaviour would be essential.

## Homing and Migratory Movements

Although in nature foxes may not often need to be able to return home from distant places – and if they did, they could generally travel over familiar ground – investigations on homing movements have been carried out by transporting foxes to places well outside their home ranges and then releasing them.

Marcström (1968) undertook such a study in Sweden, where some juveniles and adults were translocated to distant release points while others were released at their point of capture. The thirty-five translocated foxes recaptured after release were distributed in a random manner in relation to their original home, but they were recovered at greater distances from their point of release than those which had not been translocated. Over 90 per cent of the translocated foxes were killed by hunters at a mean interval of seventy-five days after release (excluding two foxes that survived for over a year). Those released at their point of origin survived longer – a mean of 147 days (excluding two foxes that survived for two and a half years). Rather similar results were obtained in North America by Phillips and Mech (1970), who nevertheless observed the return of one adult vixen to its place of origin fifty-six kilometres away in twelve days, and Talbot (1906) recorded an example of homing by a vixen and its cubs which were transported to an area thirteen kilometres away from their den and returned in due course.

There is very little evidence of migratory movements among foxes. It is clear from radio-tracking evidence that there is a tendency for foxes to move their centres of activity to higher land in hilly areas in Wales in the summer, but this is merely an extension of existing home ranges to include land which is not habitually favoured in the winter months – though foxes are found at the higher elevations in the winter.

In the hard winters of 1947 and 1963 there were numerous reports of foxes moving to the valleys from hilly areas, but other reports contradict this and indicate that foxes survived very well on the hills, living on the carcases of sheep that had died in the severe weather. It is probable that foxes in the valleys did not fare as well as those on higher ground, and that they were seen frequently as they explored for food.

In Switzerland foxes move higher up the valleys of the Alps in the summer, often to breed in marmot burrows. It seems that there is a definite seasonal movement among foxes as snow advances and retreats, but again this may not be genuine migration so much as the extension of home ranges.

## Territoriality and Scent

### Dispersion and territorial behaviour

The pattern of dispersion (spatial distribution) of any species evolves in response to its environment and is adapted to enhance its survival. The advantages of particular kinds of dispersion may be very subtle, however, and as Tinbergen (1975) indicated, 'selection acts when situations are critical'; thus, the survival value of any feature (the result of selection) may not be readily apparent in non-adverse circumstances.

The pattern of dispersion of a species has ecological consequences not only for the species as a whole but differentially for all the individuals in a population. The consequences will vary with population density, food availability and social status for the component members – adult males, pregnant and nursing females, weaned and independent juveniles and so forth. Since habitats are not uniform throughout the distribution of a species, its behavioural patterns may be very different according to environmental circumstances, and the different patterns of dispersion, home-range behaviour and territoriality described for the fox are a response to extrinsic features which operate to optimize the survival of the greatest numbers.

The units of dispersion of foxes observed so far in Britain are of three kinds: that observed in mid-Wales, where the primary unit seems to be composed of one adult male and female; that observed in Pembrokeshire, where in one case two males and two females constitute the primary unit in any location; that observed by David Macdonald (1977) in Oxford, where the primary group consists of one male with more than one female. Doubtless other kinds of grouping occur which may be the consequence of, and may depend upon, the degree of non-natural mortality inflicted by man upon the population. Of the three kinds observed, that studied by Macdonald is influenced least by non-natural mortality. If, in the absence of interference by man, foxes dispersed over large areas all conformed to the third pattern outlined above and the sex ratio at birth was 50:50, there would be a differential survival of juveniles in favour of females, or many all-male groups would occur, or many unattached single male units would be formed (or become itinerants) to enable the female-predominant groups to prevail. Though the sex ratio of adult foxes killed in most fox populations favours males for example, 54 per cent (1:0.85) in mid-Wales over a fifteen-year period, locally very different sex ratios are sometimes observed, as in one part of Pembrokeshire – an area of about twenty square kilometres – where the population was 67 per cent female (1:2.03).

Such differences in grouping indicate differences in home-range and territorial behaviour, but only that observed in mid-Wales can be discussed in the light of my experience.

In many species vigorous defence of territory is seasonal and usually coincides with the mating, breeding and rearing period only. Man defines his territories by the erection of a physical boundary which can be readily perceived, defined and upheld by law. Lower animals which establish territories must continuously advertise their claim to them without construction of physical boundaries. Some mammals use existing physical features to define their boundaries; hedges, the edges of fields, forest rides, fences, railways, roads, lakes and rivers, even sheep paths often coincide with the perimeter of the ranges of foxes, though the use of such features is probably merely a convenience to enable a fox to define its range the more easily.

In the mid-Wales situation, where population densities are lower and ranges large and overlapping, there may be areas within the range of each pair of foxes which are exclusive and from which intruders are repelled. Unfortunately, the deficiencies of radio-tracking techniques have not enabled this to be determined yet, but evidence gathered from tracks and scent-marking in snow suggests that this does occur, in which case the smaller exclusive areas may be regarded as defended areas (or territories) rather than home ranges which may not be defended. Information is also scarce about territorial behaviour when foxes have settled home areas but make foraging forays to distant areas. In addition, little is known about the circumstances in which territoriality may not be maintained, and whether it is maintained more or less strongly at different times of the year. The probability is that it is weak from August/September to December, after the dispersal of juveniles and before pairing prior to mating.

Circumstantial evidence suggests that pairs remain together for as long as both members remain alive. Since the mortality rate of adults is high in the mid-Wales area, there must be a considerable change among the paired territory-holders from one year to another. The probability of change is shown below.

Assuming the fox population is 100 pairs (200 foxes) and that mortality is random, the possibilities are: (a) that both members of a pair will die; (b) that one member of a pair will die; (c) that both members will survive.

If adult mortality in mid-Wales is 57 per cent (as suggested in Chapter 4), the probability of any fox dying is 0.57. Therefore the probability of both members dying (a) is $0.57 \times 0.57 = 0.3249$. The probability of one member of a pair dying (b) is $0.57 \times 0.43 = 0.2451$, and for both sexes,

$= 2 \times 0.2451 = 0.49$. The probability of both members of a pair surviving (c) $= 0.43 \times 0.43 = 0.1849$.

Thus between the seasons there will be:

| | |
|---|---:|
| 32.5 pairs where both members die | 65 dead |
| 24.5 pairs where the male dies | 24.5 dead |
| 24.5 pairs where the vixen dies | 24.5 dead |
| leaving | 49.0 alive |
| 18.5 pairs where both members survive | 37.0 alive |
| | 200 foxes |

Of the 18.5 pairs that survive as a pair, the number that will survive as a pair to the next season will be $(18.5 \div 100) \times 18.5 = 3.5$ pairs.

In any breeding season 57 per cent of breeding foxes will be yearlings. Thus the composition of a population of 100 foxes, assuming a 50:50 sex ratio will be: 28.5 yearling males, 28.5 yearling vixens, 12.25 adult males, 12.25 adult vixens, 18.50 still paired (9.25 males, 9.25 females). A graphic representation of this is shown in Figure 22.

In such a situation, before the mating season, 28.5 juvenile males and 12.25 adult males will be competing for the corresponding number of juvenile and adult vixens. Thus, though the annual mortality rate of adults is 57 per cent, the proportion of the population seeking mates is much higher, at 81.5 per cent. Though this relates to situations where foxes remain paired throughout life (fox breeders suggest that the wild fox is monogamous), there must be a conflict for space or for a mate, whatever kind of social grouping exists. The extent of competition is determined not by the number of cubs born but by the mortality rate of adults.

The various observations on aggregations of foxes competing for vixens are consistent with the high proportion of unattached foxes in pre-breeding populations. It is possible that the intermittently itinerant foxes observed by radio–tracking in Wales are those that have lost mates since the previous breeding season – but against this is the evidence from ear-tagging that once settled, most adults do not move far thereafter. The large gaps in the territorial units (shown in Figure 22) might also partly explain the apparent ease that juveniles have to move freely during dispersal. A slackening of territorial awareness at this time could, of course, produce the same apparent effect, through greater tolerance among territory-holders and the non-observance by juveniles of territorial claims.

Adult mortality rates could also explain why dispersal occurs over shorter distances in high-density populations – assuming that the social units are strictly pairs and not groups. In such a situation, because the

**1**    The end of the hunt, and of a fox. Humanely killed with a pistol, it is thrown to the hounds. Though dramatic, the scene is tame by comparison with the more common and horrific ways in which foxes can die by other means.

**2**    In France, next to the fox, the cow is the animal most frequently infected with rabies. The inquisitive cow investigating a fox behaving peculiarly is usually bitten on the nose.

**3** Fox cub aged about 18 days. At this age the fur is dark chocolate in colour. Many who see a cub at this stage do not recognize it as a fox.

**4**   Adult male fox. Although dog-like in the photograph, the white on the muzzle and throat and the long hair on the leading edge of the ears give it away.

**5** Danish fox pelts. The fox on the right is not unlike those in Britain. The one on the left shows lighter fur on the neck and behind the shoulders; the spiral in the tail is caused by twisting whilst drying. The three centre foxes are unusual in the degree of blackness and spotting of the fur (not due to ticks). The cross of dark fibres over the shoulder is more apparent in these than in the more common forms (Photograph by kind permission of Helge Walhovd, Aarhus).

**6** *Right* Extreme example of a sampson fox (in Aarhus Museum, Denmark). The fox is full grown, in good nutritional condition and almost devoid of hair. Comparatively uncommon in Britain, sampson foxes in Finland tend to forage on human waste at rubbish dumps more persistently than normal foxes (Photograph by kind permission of Prof. H. N. Thandrup, Aarhus, Denmark).

**7** *Right, below* North American red fox with cottontail rabbit. Although smaller than British foxes, the American counterpart is more handsome with long, flowing fur, a thick pelt and an especially bushy tail.

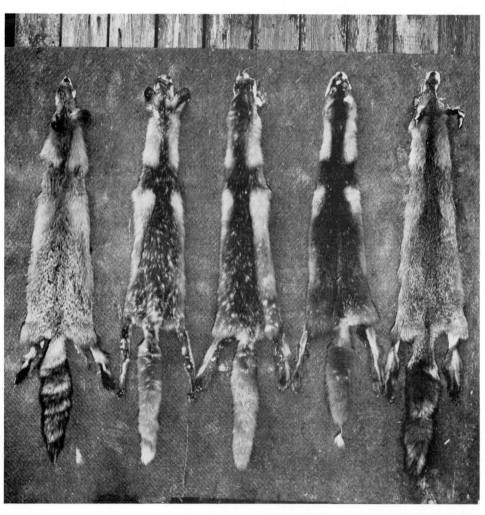

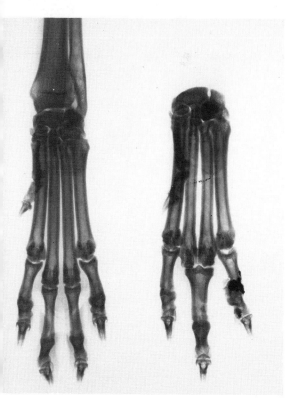

**8** The radiograph of a normal fore foot and a three-toed foot. This and other skeletal abnormalities of the feet are uncommon.

**9** Post-partum uterus showing placental scars about 14 days after partuition. Four embryos were present in each side of the V-shaped uterus.

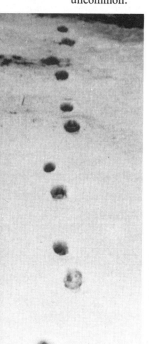

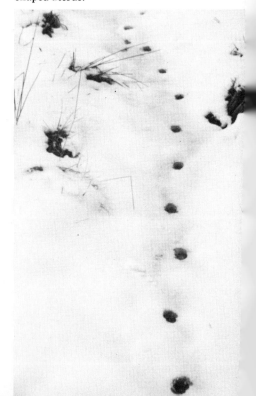

**10** *Left* The tracks of a slow, bounding, cantering fox, not commonly seen. The nearest print is that of a fore foot; that ahead of it a hind foot print (which is smaller). The next print is that of the other fore foot — and so on in that sequence.

**11** *Right* Tracks of a walking fox. The prints seen are those of the hind feet which, by overprinting those of the fore feet, have obliterated them.

**12**    Early morning fox in Sweden. In addition to the fluffing of its fur for insulation, these northern forms have more dense fur than British foxes. Note that the near fore foot is about to be lifted and the near hind foot placed in its print.

**13**   Domestic fox scene. The earth is in easily excavated sand, but its size suggests repeated use by foxes, or occupation at some time by rabbits. The broad dome of the distant fox suggests a male – the sex of the other is not known.

**14**   Entrance to a fox den in a turbary. This underground watercourse in peat, usually dry in the spring, extends for many hundreds of metres, two to three metres below ground level.

**15** Railways in urban areas afford 'quiet' denning places.

**16** A typical quiet piece of waste land where cubs can be reared without disturbance. There is a single hole fox den in the clump of gorse in the middle distance where cubs had just begun to emerge.

**18** *Right* The competitive pushing contest developing in young cubs. Note the flattening of the ears in the contesting cubs and the erect ears of the alarmed cubs in the background. Also the black spot on the tail of the left-hand cub which reveals the site of the tail gland.

**17** Cub outside its den caught with incriminating evidence. A single cub would have more difficulty in breaking into a carcass of a rabbit or large bird than several cubs competing and pulling at it.

**19** *Right, below* Caught in the act. The portliness of this urban fox is not characteristic, though a higher proportion of urban foxes than rural ones run to fat.

**20** *Left*   A contrived illustration of Aesop's fable, 'The Fox and the Grapes'. A reminder that the fox in pulling down the vines to reach the grapes in ancient times resulted in the development of smaller vines in Roman times. Though foxes still took grapes they did less damage to the plants.

**21** *Left, below*   The opportunistic fox, here taking food put out for birds.

**22** *Right*   Before fox pelts became valuable this scene was not uncommon.

**23**   Characteristic mousing behaviour.

**24** Receiving aerial in use in the mid-Wales hills. The ranges of transmitters at these elevations are considerably more than on flat ground.

**25** Transmitters for radio tracking can be mounted in different ways. Here a plastic rainwater downpipe attachment is used. The final construction with collar attached represents about 2 per cent of the total weight of an adult fox.

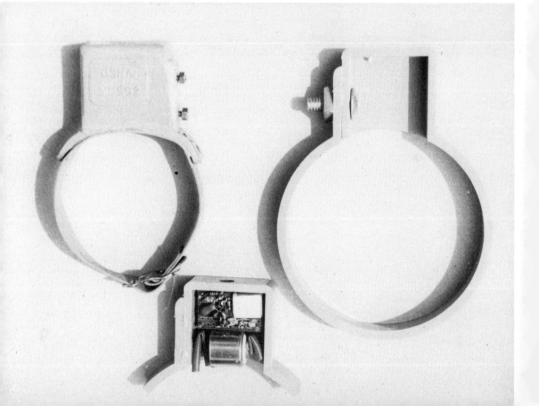

**26** Electronics in field studies. A transmitter is attached to a fox whose movements can then be followed for up to 12 months by the use of radio receivers. Firm handling is preferable to the use of anaesthetics.

**27** A dirty trick? Transmitters implanted in dead lambs are used to locate cubbing dens when adult foxes take the carcass to feed their offspring.

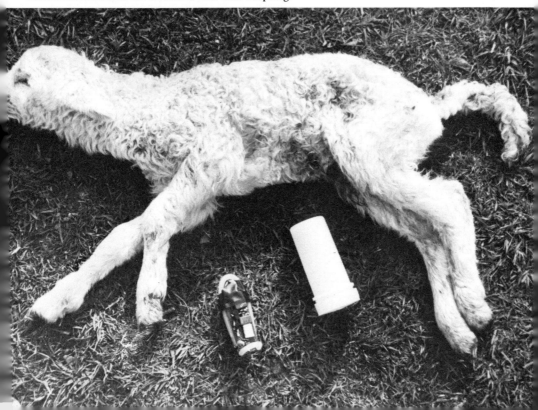

**28** Mother and young of about 8 days old. The vixen leaves her cubs for very short intervals only at this stage.

**29** The fox throughout most of its range in Britain is immune to predation. Potentially the introduced mink could kill cubs, as does the golden eagle represented here. The prey in the nest comprised another skinned fox cub, a leg of lamb and an entire grouse.

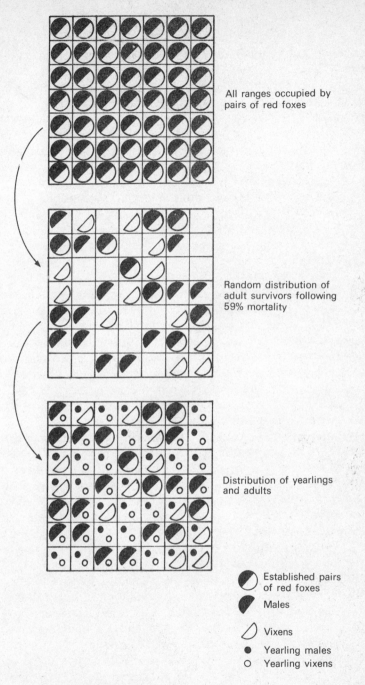

All ranges occupied by
pairs of red foxes

Random distribution of
adult survivors following
59% mortality

Distribution of yearlings
and adults

Established pairs
of red foxes

Males

Vixens

● Yearling males
○ Yearling vixens

**22** Schematic representation of vacancies occurring annually in home ranges occupied
by pairs of foxes when adult mortality is 59%

density is high (and adult mortality low), the dispersing animal would not need to move far to find a vacant place because even in a situation where the mortality rate of adults is low, at 33 per cent per annum, only 45 per cent of pairs will have remained intact since the previous season.

Radio-tracking observations by Sargeant (1972) and Ables (1969a; 1969b) and the field observations of Vincent (1958), Burrows (1968) and Macdonald (1977b) clearly show that territories do exist at least at some times of the year. Sargeant describes family territories for three families of foxes, and concludes from his observations of these, and from evidence of the movements of twenty-nine other radio-tagged foxes, that the red fox is a highly territorial species. He also suggests that the fox has an innate maximum and minimum spatial requirement, and that within these limits territory size is determined by population density, which will vary according to the richness of the environment. Territory size increases as population density decreases, but all areas within a large territory may not, of course, be visited with equal regularity.

This inverse relationship between territory size and population density – and the innate maximum spatial requirement postulated by Sargeant – may be accompanied by another feature; that is, that the higher the population density (and the smaller the territory), the greater the potential conflict between neighbouring territory-holders and consequently the greater the vigilance of territorial defence. The corollary, that these features would slacken with decreasing population density would, however, only refer to those populations, unaffected by man, whose numbers and dispersion are regulated or restricted by the availability of food in their habitat. In Wales such populations are few and the populations that are studied, at moderate to low densities, occur in areas which could support higher numbers of foxes. Thus, the apparent absence of well defined territorial behaviour in my study area may be related to a diminished territorial awareness in areas where there is no great conflict between individuals for space and food. The removal of a pair of foxes sometimes results in a shift of activity or range of surviving neighbouring foxes, and the degree of shift may indicate the relative richness of vacated and usurped ranges. Competition for the better habitats enhances the survival of the greatest number of foxes, since if all foxes had equal opportunities and were non-territorial, none would be obliged to live outside the more desirable areas and a greater number would be subjected to sub-standard conditions. Competition for the better habitats, even if territories become small, will enhance the survival and successful breeding of at least part of the population, and the remainder, whether they survive and breed successfully or not, will not have depressed the chances of survival of the others. Other advantages are conferred by territorial behaviour; especially important might be familiarity with an area to enable more efficient food-finding.

A hierarchical social structure has been observed by Vincent (1958) in Alaska, even in the autumn when it is presumed that territoriality is slack. His observations were made when wild foxes were offered domestic food scraps, which proved to be attractive to them throughout much of the year. The food was sited, by chance, at the junction of three fox territories. Snow tracks indicated that the territorial boundaries overlapped and were only loosely defined in the winter months, and the presence of alien foxes at the feeding sites suggested that they were able to trespass undeterred by the presence of the holders of the territories. Vincent observed the establishment of a social hierarchy twice each year, in November and in February. The first coincided with the onset of the harsh winter period and the second with the onset of mating. The hierarchy was established by aggressive contests. Sometimes a single contest established the dominance of one individual over another; sometimes, especially among the middle-ranking animals, several contests were needed to settle the issue. The establishment of the November hierarchy was not settled as readily as that in February. The top-ranking dog fox, however, appeared at the feeding sites only in February in the two years that Vincent was able to observe events. On both occasions this same fox confirmed its status very easily. Young animals were always low in the social order, and the first fox to visit or renew visits after the summer period had no advantage in establishing high status. Apart from itinerant animals that may have been seen only a few times, the number of resident animals varied from five to six over an eighteen-month period. A paired vixen acquired the status of the male of the pair.

The aggressive behaviour observed during the establishment of the social order was violent only when the top-ranking dog was involved in the conflict; otherwise the social order was settled by bloodless, highly vocal, ritualized combat. Initial aggressiveness was signified by the baring of teeth, snarling and the raising of the hackles of the neck. A decisive defeat was indicated when a fox slunk away with its head down and its tail between its legs. A less decisive victory was indicated when the winner retained its chosen location while the loser remained in the background. The more common method of combat (not an uncommon sight for countrymen in Britain), also accompanied by much clamour, is an upright stance; the contenders stand on their hindlegs with their forelegs placed on the chest or shoulders of the other and, as Vincent described, 'with hind feet widely spaced, tails curved out and downward, ears flattened, mouths wide open, whilst holding each other at approximately 45-degree angle, they attempt to push the opponent backwards'. With noses only a couple of centimetres apart, their jaws snap without grasping the opponent. The winner seems to be the one which pushes the opponent backwards. If one combatant turns away, the encounter ends. During the contest the animals scream at each other. When I witnessed a contest of this kind in Surrey the contenders uttered sharp, explosive noises at each other when they were standing upright; elsewhere another pair behaving similarly made no vocal noises whatsoever, but their jaws could be heard snapping shut with a sound like dry sticks being knocked together. The explosive noises made by the first pair were not unlike the alarm calls of a jay or of a cornered pole-cat.

Another form of combat observed by Vincent, usually between foxes of opposite sex, was more passive; contestants lay or sat face to face with their noses almost touching, screaming the while, until one contestant moved quietly and quickly away. Violent fighting sometimes involved the shedding of blood, but this was observed by Vincent only when the top-ranking dog fox was involved. Such fights were silent. One wonders if the availability of a superabundance of food (a sheep carcase, for example) when territoriality is strong evokes greater tolerance towards boundary trespass.

As indicated earlier, because of adult mortality there are many vacant territorial gaps annually, and dispersing juvenile animals may readily find spaces for themselves. The annual loss of adults may cause some shifting of range among survivors, but ear-tagging and radio-tracking evidence suggests that if this is so, it is confined to males. The dispersal distance of juvenile vixens is generally so small that it must frequently represent no more than a shift over the boundary of its former family range. The small shift suggests to me that it is likely to be the vixen that forges a new territory or range, which is subsequently acquired by an itinerant or mateless adult male which pairs with the vixen. The short distance of dispersal of vixens also suggests that females are tolerated more by resident foxes than are itinerant males, but whether or not this will be borne out in the high-density social groups described by Macdonald remains to be seen.

### Scent-marking

If scent-marking behaviour is associated with territoriality, then observation of my captive foxes suggests that the vixen plays the primary role in this aspect of behaviour. But before discussing this a description of the scent armoury of foxes is required.

The fox has two main scent secretions – urine and the product of the glands of the anal sac. Both contain volatile compounds which have some persistence and can serve to convey whatever the scent signifies for some days, if not longer, after marking.

The chemical components of urine are many. Because it contains the chemical breakdown products of hormonal secretions (those of the ovary, for example, or of the male organs, or of substances excreted by the target organs or tissues of these glands) urine can probably convey information about the animal's sex and sexual condition, but whether it can constitute an identity tag for an individual is not known.

The secretions of the paired anal sacs are released, under voluntary control, via short ducts to the anus, and in both sexes can be expelled directly onto whatever object is being scent-marked. Although much is known of the chemical composition of the secretions (Albone, 1977; Albone and Fox, 1971; Albone and Perry, 1976; Albone, Robins and Patel, 1976), very little is known of its significance in the behaviour of the fox. The composition of the secretion of the cells of the sacs is different, however, from that of the substance ultimately expelled because of microbial fermentation the primary secretion within the sacs (Gosden and Ware, 1976). The significance of this may be that close contact between member foxes of social groups (of whatever kind) allows cross-infection of the anal sacs, which might, through the action of the mixed microflora, produce an ultimate anal sac secretion characteristic of that group. Whether faeces or anal-gland scent-marking of objects are involved in group recognition or territorial marking is not known, but the location of faeces along urine-scent-marked tracks in snow suggests that it serves some such function. Unlike marking by urine and faeces, there is no field evidence of the ejection of anal-sac fluids for marking purposes – but there is among captive experimental animals. The fluid is extremely pungent and in small doses, to my nose, not unlike that of fox urine, the characteristic smell of which is due mainly to two components, isopentylmethylsulphide and phenylethylmethylsulphide (Jorgenson et al, 1978).

Urine clearly serves some territorial or advertisement function. Intermittent falls of snow will reveal that certain fox tracks, on forest rides, along fences, or across open moorland, for instance, are frequently patrolled, and urine is disposed often at the same place. Certain tracks are consistently marked; other tracks regularly used show no evidence of marking. Not only are prominent objects such as trees, molehills, stones and tufts of grass regularly marked, but the fox selects objects at prominent places – on the tops of open banks or along prominent hill ridges, for example. If a forest road traverses the side of a hill, the marking is almost always done on the outer edge of the road, though there may be many tracks along the inner edge.

Faeces are found singly or in clumps, indicating regular usage of tracks, but it is at present impossible to determine the special significance of places used regularly. Faeces are regularly found on sheep carcases or their remnants, or in their immediate vicinity, and whilst these presumably serve as advertisement of some sort, the message conveyed is not known.

Even less is known of the function of the tail gland (supracaudal gland) in scent-marking. Interestingly, one of its chemical constituents is a terpene (Albone, 1975), a compound related to the constituent of the catnip plant (*Nepeta cataria*) which evokes considerable interest and unusual behaviour in cats.

To revert to my tame vixen. At some time each day, even in a small cage, it spends at least one hour, but not more than two, marking its patch (shared by a dog fox) with urine. Whilst engaged in this activity, its tail is characteristically elevated and curved, and it wanders incessantly and apparently haphazardly across the ground and on the elevated walkways, marking the netting, posts, food trays and any other object that happens to be there. The quantity voided is small – certainly less than 10 millilitres at each marking. This marking behaviour, which can occur at any time in daylight, ceases as abruptly as it has begun, and up to 200 scent-marks can be made in the time. The dog fox, on the other hand, never performs in this way, and on the occasions that it has been seen to urinate, it is clearly done to empty its bladder. When loose in the garden the dog fox very occasionally marks a shrub or bush, but the vixen, which sticks to a much smaller range when free (about 200 square metres), spends much of its time during the first fifteen to thirty minutes in scent-marking. There are favoured places, such as the vegetable patch and the herbaceous border, and certain plants in all areas are marked each time the vixen is loose. One flattened plant in the herbaceous border is invariably marked more liberally than others, and on each occasion the vixen rolls on the plant as if to mark itself with its own urine. The dog fox also shows interest in this plant but never urinates on it. Sometimes, having rolled, the vixen makes its way to a recumbent juniper bush and sweeps her back and flanks along it, as if marking it with her urine-tainted fur. Often, when in her cage, the vixen's coat smells strongly of urine, but I am uncertain whether or not the dog fox is responsible for this.

Clearly, substantial conclusions cannot be drawn from such observations, nor can much be deduced about the significance of marking from the descriptions of the constituent components of the scent glands; investigations in this area are sadly lacking but could be very rewarding.

In addition to urine and anal-gland and tail-gland secretions, the sweat glands of the foot pads may also serve some communicatory function. Although all three undisputed scent glands can communicate information at the scent-marked place when the donor fox is remote from it, the persistence of the scent is not known. Indeed, the identification of highly volatile and less volatile substances in urine and anal-sac secretions may indicate that some constituents function for a short time only, while others may serve for the long term. The ability of the fox to detect minute traces of scent may be as acute as that of the dog, which, according to some reports, can distinguish a glass slide held by a man from a clean one for up to six weeks.

It is presumed, possibly mistakenly, that a fox marks the perimeter of its territory only. If this territory boundary is contiguous with others, do adjacent territory-holders mark the same boundaries? To my knowledge, there is as yet no clear indication of this. It cannot be tested effectively with urine (except perhaps on snow or sand), but attempts to observe overmarking have been made using faeces. All fox faeces found on sheep and deer tracks and on footpaths, forest rides and other pathways were removed and alien faeces from captive foxes substituted in their place. None was overmarked, but unfortunately this does not prove the point because, among many other imponderables, it is not known whether the faeces from the captive foxes were coated with anal-sac secretions. Drops of urine, likewise did not prompt overmarking with faeces. A thorough investigation of this kind, on scent tracks observed in snow, could be revealing. Visual observations on wild foxes would, however, be more convincing.

The frequency of urine-marking on boundary tracks may reflect the individual's intolerance of or preparedness to repel intruders. This may be related to the size of the range occupied by the fox, since it would be more difficult for it to make as many scent-marks around a range of 1,000 hectares as one of 100 hectares. The persistence of the mark would, of course, be very significant in this context.

Urine scent-tracks, with marks at short distances apart, may also lead intruders along the tracks to the other significant, but less frequented, faecal scent-posts – which themselves could be reinforced from time to time by ejection of anal-gland secretions. Speculation of this kind, with slender field evidence as a guide, does not clarify the issue; it does, however, serve to indicate the complexities of scent-marking and the need for subtle techniques to unravel them.

In addition to conveying information to other foxes, scent-marking may serve to reassure the donor fox new to an area, which may be more assertive or may feel more secure when its own familiar smell surrounds it. Certainly, a captive vixen, confined in a compound strange to it, will soon begin to mark objects within the compound if it is undisturbed by man. A male in a similar situation marks less frequently than a vixen. Captive red foxes observed by Devra Kleiman (1966) did not use faeces for marking or depositing scent.

Sargeant's observations (1972) of the maintenance of territorial boundaries from winter to early spring without regular patrolling of the boundaries suggest that their integrity can be maintained by long-lasting scent-marking or by reinforcement with other signals. The removal of a group or a pair of foxes from one territory is, according to Sargeant, quickly perceived by adjoining territory holders, which then tend to cross the boundary. This is a clear suggestion that territorial awareness is not maintained by olfactory clues only. Burrows (1968) described foxes barking as they moved near the perimeter of an area of about 3.2 square kilometres. This was the contact bark, which could also serve to alert territorial neighbours. Burrows regards the barking of foxes in the winter as an aggressive activity.

A pheromone is a substance secreted by one animal which evokes a response in another of the same species. Some of the scent secretions of foxes may be pheromones, for example, the urine of an oestrus vixen may evoke a search for it by a male, or the urine of one fox may prompt overmarking by that of another. Certainly, close physical contact between individual foxes involves olfactory clues, cues and responses. Tembrock (1957), for example, has shown that foxes making close-quarter social contact investigate each other by smell, particularly in the head and neck regions, in the ano-genital region and in the region of the tail gland. Such olfactory investigation between foxes is often associated with ritualized postures, especially during the period of initial contact and during the establishment of hierarchical status; in a pair of foxes the pre-mating display may serve as a psychological stimulus hastening oestrus, as well as stimulating sexual acceptance of the partner. Cutaneous glands in the region of the lips – the circumoral glands – are investigated by foxes, cats and wolves when making contact with other familiar members of their species (Tembrock, 1957), but the motivation for this is obscure. Often the male fox marks the female with tail and anal gland secretions during pre-mating displays. Frequently the male passes its tail over the shoulders of the vixen at such times. Both sexes are known to urinate on the partner during sexual displays, but this may be a physical display or stimulus in which scent as such plays no stimulatory role.

The behavioural, ecological and physiological implications of territoriality in foxes are by no means well understood. A more thorough investigation of this aspect of fox behaviour would help to explain much of the fox's way of life that is still a mystery.

Scent marking associated with the catching of food is mentioned at page 80.

# 6

# Relations with Man

The earliest references to foxes are censorious; the Bible refers to foxes spoiling the vines (*Song of Solomon*) and allegorically the fox is chosen to represent falsehood, as in 'Oh Israel, thy prophets are like the foxes of the desert' (*Ezekiel*, 13:4). Pliny refers to methods of preventing foxes from taking poultry – thus whether it be the red fox or another species (as perhaps in the Biblical references), the fox has a rascaly reputation that goes back into the mists of antiquity.

This chapter is primarily concerned with the fox's predatory indiscretions. However, not all countrymen regard the fox in an uncompromisingly bad light; the hunter, for instance, regards the fox's capacity to provide supremely good sport as its saving grace. Surprisingly, though most of the inhabitants of these islands have never seen a fox, it provokes considerable interest and well polarized opinions on many aspects of its relations with man. Argument is rife over the issues of whether or not it is a pest or a nuisance, whether it should be hunted or not, or outlawed as a potential reservoir of rabies and, latterly, whether it should be killed solely for its skin. Even naturalists tend to be somewhat ambivalent towards the fox. The most vehement anti-fox man has a considerable regard for its tenacity and ability to survive when all the odds are against it. No other animal in Britain evokes such universal interest and argument – not even the badger.

## The Fox as a Pest

### Poultry
Since the fox is an opportunist, it presumably first became a nuisance when man learned the arts of animal husbandry, though man the hunter must have had to cache the flesh of his quarry securely from pilfering foxes, other wild carnivores and his own dogs. Some species of domestic

stock would have been vulnerable to foxes only at certain times – sheep, pigs or goats, for example, when their young were born. Domesticated birds would have been vulnerable at all times, since it is unlikely that birds would have been tethered; nor would grain have been grown specifically for them, so they would have ranged widely for food. This seems to accord with the earliest references to the predatory behaviour of foxes, which refer mainly to the taking of poultry.

In Britain the wolf rather than the fox was of concern to the shepherd and goatherd, and it seems reasonable to suppose that only with the disappearance of the wolf did the farmer focus his attention on the fox, since the fox then became the largest four-footed predator of livestock in Britain.

The relative importance of the fox as a pest of economic significance must have varied from time to time according to the numbers of vulnerable prey and changes in animal-husbandry practices. Poultry, ducks and geese, though not as numerous as today, were widely distributed among the small cottages and homesteads, at a time when more people were closely connected with agriculture. Today most of the domestic poultry reared in Britain are secured under cover in factory farms and are no longer vulnerable to foxes. Geese still range freely in the traditional way on many farms. Although the goose – the farmer's sentinel – may not feature very largely in the diet of the fox, Charles James (a colloquialism used in England) is frequently blamed for losses of post-Christmas breeding stocks of geese (especially of the sole remaining gander), and whilst this loss is not of economic significance nationally, it can be extremely irritating to the farmer's wife for whom the goose often provides Christmas pin-money. Ducks tend to range very widely from farmsteads and are often taken in daylight when they are far from the farm buildings. Muscovy ducks readily take flight when disturbed by foxes, and there are many examples of this variety taking wing, never to return, after being frightened by foxes. On the other hand, a group of Muscovy ducks which I frequently used to see at night on a small pond at the edge of the village green at Shalford, Surrey, an area where foxes were numerous, appeared to survive for years without mishap, though they were apparently never shut up at night. The calls of guinea-fowl seem to attract foxes to their roosting places (frequently outdoors), and losses, though small, are an annoyance to their owners.

## Sheep
Nowadays lambs are more susceptible to losses than poultry, since they are very numerous and widely dispersed, and in some areas they suffer from poor husbandry and are exposed to severe climatic conditions. They have no defence and no means of fleeing from the fox. A lamb is entirely dependent upon its mother for protection.

As I have found in my study areas in upland and hill sheep-rearing areas, not all farmers or shepherds will agree that the fox is an inveterate killer of lambs. Disagreement on this exists even between neighbours, but the controversy is rarely aired – the men of action usually have their way. There is no doubt that the 'lambing percentage' (that is, the number of lambs reared related to ewes of breeding age) varies considerably from place to place, even in similar types of environment, but each flock is subjected to its owner's management regime, and there are so many variables – ranging from the extent of supplementary winter feeding to population density (stocking rate) – that one single factor, the predatory activities of foxes, should not wittingly or unwittingly be invoked to explain disappointing results everywhere. As an illustration of this point, one relative newcomer to hill farming in mid-Wales had in each of three consecutive years increased his stocking rate of breeding ewes on poor hill land by about one-third, and was dismayed to find that the number of lambs reared on that part of the hill did not increase – in fact, the lambing percentage decreased spectacularly. He was uneasy about the presence of foxes, but in this instance placed the blame for lack of lambs on two or three foxhounds which appeared to be living wild in the area after the close of the hunting season. The hounds may or may not have had some impact on the lamb crop, but their presence did at least divert attention from an injudiciously high stocking rate of sheep.

To understand the relationships between foxes and sheep some consideration must be given to the history and development of sheep farming in Britain.

The numbers and value of sheep have varied considerably in their long association with agriculture in Britain; in the Middle Ages much of the agricultural wealth was derived from the wool trade, but sheep numbers probably did not reach their peak until the early nineteenth century. Since then sheep management has changed. The old methods of folding sheep, especially the large wool-bearing breeds, and close supervision by the shepherd, especially at lambing time, would have given a measure of protection not afforded to breeds of small sheep grazing lonely and impoverished areas. There have also been changes in the distribution of sheep, but it was not until the late eighteenth century that a switch in the numerical distribution of sheep and their breeds came about. Formerly sheep were mainly reared in lowland areas, but increased stocking of upland areas started the trend towards the ultimate numerical domination of the sheep industry by the small upland breeds. Elfyn Hughes and his colleagues (1973) have documented the changes in sheep numbers on rough grazings in parts of Wales from 1300 to the present day: they have estimated that the non-winter population sizes may have increased twenty-fold from 1600 to 1900. In 1600 goats out-

numbered sheep on rough grazings but today only a few herds of feral
goats remain.

Sheep rearing dominates the agricultural scene in upland and hill
areas. Since it is in these areas that shepherds are most vociferous concerning the fox's predatory behaviour, the management of sheep on
rough and upland grazings warrants consideration. Management though
variable, tends to follow a pattern. Yearling ewes are brought down to
cultivable or improved land at six or seven months of age in order to
benefit from better nutrition, essential at this period of growth. If insufficient land is available, the yearling lambs are sent away to be reared on
grazings in milder lowland areas, an accommodation for which the
farmer pays. Breeding ewes, that is, those of two years of age and
upwards, are left on mountain or hill land until November to January,
those on mountain land being brought down earlier. They may be
brought down in one large group or gradually in small parties, with
younger ewes and those in poor condition being transferred to winter
land first. Whilst on enclosed land, ewes receive more attention, and
their nutrition may be supplemented by manufactured food or forage
crops, but stocking has to be controlled in order to preserve some
enclosed areas for lambing and summer grass production. Lambs are
born in April or early May.

There are two critical periods in the lives of ewes. The first, which
establishes the basis for future well-being, is the availability of good
pasture from six weeks of age to adulthood. If the growth rate of a lamb
is poor during the first six months of its life, it will remain small, with
little chance to build up reserves, however good the winter grazings.
The other critical period for breeding ewes is the latter half of the gestation period. In addition to the careful control of nutrition at oestrus –
known as flushing – a good plane of nutrition before and during early
pregnancy may increase the proportion of ewes that become pregnant
and may reduce losses of embryos at early stages of gestation, but whilst
nutrition at this period is clearly important in determining the reproductive potential of ewes, the period when discrepancies between available
natural feed and the nutritional requirements of pregnant ewes is
greatest is during the late gestational stages. It is during this period that
most attention is devoted to maintaining nutritional levels.

After lambing the ewe and lambs are returned to the hill. Ewes with
twin lambs are usually maintained on the lower land longer than those
with single lambs. Ewes are usually allowed to breed three or four times
on hill land and are then sold to lowland farmers.

Careful maintenance of pastures, the improvement of hill pastures,
balanced stocking densities, the provision of supplementary feed,
disease control, the rigorous culling of poor-performance animals, a
pride in the flock and the provision of suitably hardy rams all combine to

produce good results. Inadequacies in some or all of these features can result in poor reproductive performance, poor survival rates among lambs and adults and poor body condition. Some of these features are beyond the control of the shepherd; for example, many hill farms in mid-Wales have inadequate areas of enclosed land for the wintering of flocks. In some areas, as where reservoirs have flooded almost all the bottom land of holdings, the problem is exacerbated. In other areas, where common land predominates, the unenclosed hill pastures are not deliberately improved and many cultivable areas of enclosed hill land or areas which could be improved are planted with trees. In many instances hill farms are sold and planted (though possibly some fields are retained), but the grazing rights on common lands persist, which only increases the pressure on wintering land.

Where long-established traditions of sheep rearing are maintained, and where as much attention is given to flock performance as is given by dairy farmers to the breeding and performance of milking cows, there is every chance that all requirements for a high productive performance will be met. On such holdings complaints about lamb losses to foxes should be taken seriously, but where there is no great pride in the flock complaints against foxes should be regarded with some scepticism, since so many features associated with mismanagement can cloud the picture – which leads to one final point concerning sheep management: that of defence against predation. Observations by farmers and others suggest that the fox is easily deterred by aggressive behaviour in ewes, whether with lamb at foot or not. Alexander and his colleagues (1967) also observed this in an experimental situation in Australia. Aggressive behaviour in a ewe, its preparedness to stand and stamp at an intruder – dog, fox or man – is indicative of its physical condition and, if it has a lamb, of its ability to protect and nurture it. Flight is indicative of the reverse. One can get a good impression of the vigour of a flock by this aspect of maternal behaviour. The better maintained flocks show greater aggression, which suggests the possibility that some of the blame for lamb losses must be placed at the flockmaster's door.

In natural situations it is known that predation is beneficial to the prey population in evolutionary terms, since the predator–prey relationship is one aspect of the survival-of-the-fittest complex. In well maintained flocks the shepherd does much of the selection and removes or moves to better quarters those least likely to survive or most likely to produce non-viable offspring. In poorly maintained flocks the fox, if it preyed on a significant proportion of weak lambs, would be performing this same function, and in the long run, under the management regimen obtaining, perhaps not to the farmer's disadvantage, but I doubt if this argument (even if valid) would gain much credence among practical men.

Since the early nineteenth century the proportion of holdings rearing sheep has decreased, and in 1960 they were reared on only about 25 per cent of holdings in England and Wales. Allied to management, a more recent influence tending to create conditions suitable for fox predation has been the government subsidy offered as an incentive to maintain flocks of breeding ewes on hill and upland farms. The subsidy is paid for ewes only. Whereas up to 1939 most upland and hill flocks maintained a significant proportion (up to about 30 per cent) of wethers (castrated males a year of age and over), the introduction of the subsidy has promoted an increase in the proportion of breeding ewes in the hill flocks and a decrease in the number of wether sheep. In many areas the subsidy has to some extent defeated the object of increasing productivity by encouraging shepherds to maintain more ewes (and in some cases as many ewes as possible) in the subsidy-eligible areas, while wether sheep, hardy because unhampered by the physiological demands of breeding, could withstand better the rigours of the climate and the poor nutritional status. Though the full potential for increased productivity may not have been achieved by the subsidy, without it the resultant decline in sheep rearing in hill and upland areas would have far-reaching effects on rural depopulation, on the economic, social and even cultural way of life of rural communities, as well as on agriculture in lowland areas. The production of lambs for fattening on lowland farms is best done on the cheaper hill pastures, and to some extent even the flow of the older ewes no longer capable of surviving on hill land to the lowlands contributes to livestock production in Britain.

Ewes in poor physical condition at over-stock densities on upland and hill produce more non-viable lambs than lowland ewes (if not actually more, then relatively more per breeding ewe) and are less able to rear lambs than those at moderate or optimum stocking densities. The result is a greater apparent loss, if not a real loss, of lambs to foxes. As an example, one hill farm in my mid-Wales study area produces in most years a mean of one lamb (which survives to weaning) per two breeding ewes, that is, a lambing percentage of about 50 per cent. The productivity of this flock is exceptionally low and is not typical. The non-productive half of the breeding ewe flock either do not give birth to lambs, or give birth to stillborn lambs or lambs which die after birth because they were non-viable or, more usually, because the ewe could not rear them. Failure to rear lambs is a widespread feature of some breeding seasons. Prolonged wet weather prior to lambing debilitates ewes; the maternal instinct to care for the lambs is impaired and many are abandoned. In other cases, although the lamb is not abandoned, the ewe has insufficient milk to rear it. These features are also prevalent in poorly maintained flocks where the nutritional status is low or where the flock is of poor-quality stock. Such areas containing an ample supply of fresh carrion are, of course, ideal for foxes at that time of year, and in years of very heavy natural mortality among lambs one hears few complaints of damage by foxes.

Data for the number of sheep, holdings and workers, and extents of grass, rough grazing and woodland in two parishes in the mid-Wales hill area are shown in Table 28. The encroachment of coniferous plantations since 1949 is readily apparent, as is the reduction in the number of people (occupiers and workers) engaged in agriculture in the parishes; but the decline in the number of holdings has been accompanied since 1949 by an increase in the mean size of holdings and grazings – from 288 hectares to 421 hectares in 1970. The mean number of sheep per holding had decreased slightly by 1970, with a concurrent decline in sheep density from one sheep per 0.5 hectare in 1940 to one per 0.6 hectare in 1970. The lambing percentages for the four years shown are not constant, being high in 1949, when sheep density was much reduced after the severe winter of 1947, and lowest in 1970. But sheep are not the only agricultural enterprise in the two parishes, and a greater number of cattle have been reared since 1940, though sheep rearing is still dominant. The decreased stocking density of sheep may be entirely due to increases in cattle on the lower land, but another feature may be of importance in this area, where common hill grazings amount to over half the total area. Common grazings are not planted with trees; thus, afforestation is confined to rough grazings (and fields) in private ownership. Common hill grazings are not cultivated and improved (though they could be by cattle grazing), but hill land in private ownership often used to be managed (in one way or another), which improved its production; thus, encroachment of afforestation on to land which could be improved may have diminished the extent of hill land of better quality where sheep densities were higher than on common grazings.

One-third of the area in 1970 was woodland and the two parishes have lost about a quarter of the grazing of 1940 to afforestation, in spite of much ploughing and the cultivation of rough grazings in recent years. Agriculturally the parishes are probably the poorer for this, and the sheep, although at lower stocking densities overall, seem, to judge by their lambing performance, to be worse off.

Many sheep rearers complain that afforestation makes fox control problematic, and whilst this might be true (depending upon what control methods are adopted), the problem posed by afforestation in regions where common grazings form a significant proportion of the total area is the loss of grazings of marginally to significantly better quality than common land.

The data presented here are intended only as an outline of the sheep industry on hill and upland areas and are used liberally to illustrate the suitability of hill areas for foxes at lambing and cubbing time – two events which coincide. Detailed field studies would be required to enable the relationships of foxes and sheep to be defined more precisely.

On hill land, except where ewes are of good stock, well managed and given adequate supplementary winter and spring feed, a lambing percentage of 100 per cent is rarely achieved, and in the mid-Wales hills the percentage typically lies somewhere near 70 per cent. About 10 per cent of breeding ewes (that is, of two years of age and over) appear not to produce lambs; thus, for each 100 ewes between fifteen and twenty lambs (or foetuses) are available to foxes and other scavengers or are killed by them. The mid-Wales fox study area, which includes the whole or part of ten parishes, covers about 76,100 hectares (excluding woodlands), about a quarter of which is enclosed grassland, the remainder being rough and common grazings. The total number of sheep on this area, excluding lambs of the year, is 123,000, of which 78,000 are breeding ewes. In 1970 this number of ewes produced 66,000 lambs surviving to at least six weeks of age – a lambing percentage in round figures of 85 per cent. These figures do not distinguish between the lambing success of sheep brought down from the hills to winter on cultivable pastures and those which spend the winter on the barely improved enclosed areas between hill and fields (known as the Ffridd in Wales). Some holdings, either without or foregoing common grazing or hill sheep walks, stock sheep which are not put on the hill. About 25 per cent of sheep are in this category. These, however, are likely to show lambing performances in excess of 100 per cent, but, if taken as 100 per cent, the hill flock of 58,500 will produce 46,500 lambs, a lambing percentage of 79.5. If (from an amalgam of opinions) 10 per cent of hill sheep of breeding age do not produce lambs, the 52,650 hill ewes which produce lambs rear only 46,500. Thus at a conservative estimate, 6,150 still-born or live lambs are lost over the area of 76,000 hectares – a density of dead lambs overall of one per twelve hectares.

The population density of foxes at cubbing time in mid-Wales (Table 26) is about 1.23 foxes per square kilometre. Thus, over an area of 76,100 hectares there would be about 940 foxes. If both lambs and foxes were evenly distributed over the area, each fox would have access to 6.5 lambs, which, at an average weight (including still-born lambs) of about 1.8kg each, would represent about 12kg of food per fox. Depending on the behaviour of foxes, and on whether or not they are able to gain access to sheep afterbirths before the ewes eat them, afterbirths at 0.25kg each could constitute another not inconsiderable seasonal food supply.

This estimate of food availability from lamb deaths, from whatever cause – natural or predated – is already inaccurate without introducing further imponderable features, but it would be fair to state that the estimate probably represents the minimum of availability. The non-hill-breeding flocks (25 per cent of the total number of sheep in the area) show a better performance than the 100 per cent used for purposes of calculation; also the average weights of dead lambs has been underestimated. Counterbalancing these, perhaps, is the loss of carcases to other scavengers, notably birds of the crow group, but of course this would apply only to lambs which have died of natural causes, not to any viable lambs killed and eaten by foxes.

Whilst not strictly pertinent to this section on the fox as a pest (but relevant to the contribution to fox diet made by sheep farming), another supply of food is provided by deaths of adult sheep. Loss of ewes of breeding age is of variable extent and it is estimated by sheep-management specialists and shepherds that a 5 per cent annual loss among the better maintained upland and hill-fringe flocks is possible. It is difficult to derive an estimate of losses for hill sheep, except that it must be greater than 5 per cent and must be subject to greater or lesser variability according to management and the severity of winter weather.

Jack Sarl, writing in the *Farmer's Weekly* in 1971, reported a survey on Dartmoor from March to April 1970 which revealed a high loss of ewes related to the over-stocking of inadequate pastures. As Gunn and Robinson (1963) indicated, ewes can lose much weight from October to March, and Sarl suggested that the ewes lost on Dartmoor – which had been inadequately fed in the latter part of pregnancy – had either aborted and died in March, or had succumbed to the stress of lambing in the following months. Severe weather from February to April disguised the true situation. Sarl considered it possible that heavy tick burdens might be associated with these losses of ewes. Adult female ticks do not appear in large numbers on sheep until April or May; thus, the heavy parasitic burden in itself is perhaps not significant in the Dartmoor story. Some sheep diseases are tick-borne – louping ill and tick-borne fever – but these were not investigated.

If, for purposes of calculation, the 5 per cent mortality rate is extended to hill flocks, the 78,000 breeding ewes in the study area of 76,000 hectares would lose 3,900 ewes annually. Such ewes would be small or light, providing perhaps no more than 14kg each of edible carrion. Using this figure, 5,4600kg of carrion would be available to 940 foxes. If only half of this quantity were available, it would represent the equivalent of 28kg per fox. As with the calculation of the weight of lambs eaten by foxes, this figure could be wide of the mark. The actual number of sheep carrion is without doubt a considerable underestimate, but offsetting this is the scavenging of carrion by other feeders – and a seasonal increase in the number of foxes after the breeding season, before family groups have dispersed. However, between sheep and lambs, without any contribution to food by afterbirths, the minimum quantity of food available per fox is not less than 40kg per fox – a useful annual contribution towards the fox's yearly requirement of about 160kg.

Purser and Young (1959) studied lamb survival in hill flocks and related losses to the numbers of lambs born. They found, in Welsh mountain ewes, that 88 per cent of lambs born survived to weaning (there was no mention of the possible role of predators in this context). The chance of survival of lambs was closely related to their birth weight and to the age of the dam. Lambs born to two-year-old ewes had a survival rate of 83 per cent, whereas among lambs born to three-to four-year-old ewes, 91 per cent survived. (One of the study areas was at Rhydyclafdy, Merioneth, an area where complaints about foxes are persistent and frequent.) Losses of lambs (both live and still-born) were attributed to the condition of the ewe, to climate, exposure, lack of milk, poor vitality and accidents, but no mention was made of foxes.

Thomson and Thomson (1949), in a study of the effects of diet on lamb survival, observed, 'It is not unreasonable to suppose that the greater part of wastage in lambing of hill sheep . . . is due to impaired nutrition of the pregnant ewes.' Their observations suggest that lamb losses soon after birth may be due more to the inadequacy of the ewe (lack of milk, for example) than to the vitality of the lamb.

Dr John Doney (pers. comm.), of the Hill Farm Research Organization, is of the opinion that a lambing percentage (at six weeks of age) of 50–60 per cent is not untypical for some seasons in the western highlands of Scotland, though the number of ewes that give birth to lambs is not known. In eight years of observation at the Hill Farm Research Organization farm at Sowehope unusual losses of lambs occurred only once, when about ten lambs disappeared over a period of a few days. At other times unexplained losses did not appear to exceed more than two or three lambs for over 1,000 born.

Ministry of Agriculture Experimental Husbandry Farms play an important role, through experimentation, development and report, in investigating potentially beneficial animal- and plant-husbandry practices. The aim is the development of practical management techniques which will lead to greater productivity. Hill and mountain sheep have not escaped attention and detailed investigation; (see, for example, HMSO 1975, *Pwllpeiran Experimental Husbandry Farm Annual Review 1974–5*). Investigation has shown that productivity (as measured by the ultimate test of what is sold off the farm, whether as lambs, draught ewes or wether sheep) is closely related to stocking densities and to nutrition. These two factors are to some degree interdependent, but where hill-land improvement is undertaken it has been shown to be of immediate benefit to the health of the flock and to the production and survival of lambs. Other improvements in management increase the optimum stocking rate with further benefits to production. Practicable management improvements have resulted in clear demonstrations of increases in production of lambs on mountain and hill pastures which are the envy of many occupiers of potentially better land. Even Experimental Husbandry Farms, where detailed investigations on the fate of lambs are undertaken and missing lambs seldom attributed to foxes, do not discourage fox control in their immediate vicinity.

On upland farms – as distinct from hill farms – the Welsh ewe is often tupped with larger-breed rams in order to produce quick-growing lambs for slaughter. These lambs tend to suffer more from difficult births, and some may quickly become moribund and die from shock and exposure. Upland farmers are as vociferous in their complaints against foxes as hill shepherds but, as on hill land, one wonders whether their complaints are entirely justified.

It is very difficult to quantify the true effect of foxes on lambs in Britain. Since there is no uniformity of habitat and management, intensive study of sheep/fox relationships on one or even several holdings might not provide data of general applicability, though it would certainly provide clues. Many farmers and shepherds have doubts about the villainous role of the fox, but in the absence of sound evidence to the contrary, they are perhaps justified in taking measures which they hope may prevent or alleviate losses in general.

One feature of complaints against foxes that I find difficult to interpret is their comparative scarcity in poor lambing seasons, when many lambs die of natural causes. At such times foxes and other scavengers have an abundant supply of food, and my colleagues and I have observed a rapid clearance of such carcases by foxes (and perhaps dogs) concurrent with an increase in lamb carcases found at cubbing dens in the vicinity. At these times, perhaps, the farmer's attention is diverted from thoughts of fox predation to concern about saving his lambs from natural losses; alternatively, the abundance of carrion may alleviate predation of lambs, though how the shepherd would know this is another question. There is no doubt that foxes are well provided with carrion in hill areas in the cubbing seasons in any year and may not need to take viable lambs, but being a predator and an opportunist, the fox may pay no regard to the law of supply and demand and may kill or collect more food than is needed for its immediate purposes.

In 1967, a survey of the opinions of farmers on the extent of lamb losses to foxes was conducted in the three counties of Radnorshire, Breconshire and Montgomeryshire, the idea being to learn something about farmers' attitudes towards foxes and to gain information about the losses they considered they sustained through fox predation. Eight per cent of all holdings in the three counties were surveyed by questionnaire; although the holdings were selected in a random manner, they cannot be regarded as being entirely representative, since the numbers of hill farms surveyed, for example, were small by comparison with the proportion in which they occurred throughout the three counties. Much of the information sought was entirely factual, but some was subjectively based, such as the number of lambs considered to have been lost to foxes by individual occupiers in the year in question; this, one of the more important questions in the survey, was subject to several sources of error. In large flocks, especially those lambing on hills or remote from the farmsteads, the actual number of lambs born is not necessarily known, and the loss of a twin lamb may go undetected if it occurs in the first few hours after birth. Mutilated lamb carcases found in the lambing field may have been still-born or may have died of natural causes after surviving for a few hours only. The occupiers involved in the survey were more likely to have exaggerated their losses than to have minimized them. Of the 71 per cent of the holdings rearing sheep 21 per cent claimed losses from foxes. On holdings where lambs were reported to be lost, the mean number lost per flock was 4.6 lambs. The total number of lambs reared on all the holdings surveyed was 79,800; the number allegedly lost to foxes was added to this number and the numbers lost for the entire sample of holdings calculated as a proportion of this. This yielded an estimated total loss of 0.53 per cent. The estimates for the three counties were 0.49 per cent, 0.49 per cent and 0.54 per cent. Whilst this is based entirely upon the subjective opinions of occupiers, it is a surprisingly low estimate.

Presented with this as if it were an accurate estimate, the farmer would be perfectly justified in retorting that but for the control of foxes, losses would be far higher.

The sporadic losses of lambs to foxes is obviously of some concern to the shepherd, but his real worry is the possibility of heavy losses occurring on several nights or on one single night. Occasionally as many as twenty lambs may be killed in one field in one night. The lost lambs may range from new-born to fourteen days old, and the evidence in many cases clearly implicates foxes. Where many lambs are killed on one night, the carcases are usually left on the field. Some may be decapitated; others may have lost their tails and the removed portion may be found buried, though most often this occurs only when two or three lambs have been killed. (Characteristically the neck, or the neck and shoulders are severly crushed, with evidence of canine toothmarks or puncture marks clearly visible on the inside of the lamb skin: these are made when the lamb is first seized. When puncture marks are distinct the distance between the marks can give a clue to the size of the predator, as can the depth of the tooth puncture into the flesh. If a large dog is suspected, confirmation can be obtained in many cases by such examination. The fox has a very slender jaw and the distance separating the canine teeth (25–32mm) is considerably less than in most sheep dogs, for example (see Table 29). Toothmarks which may be seen in the region of the neck are made by the pre-molars mainly, and repeated crushing bites in this region make it difficult to distinguish the width of the tooth row of the predator.) However, the excessive killing of lambs is not common, perhaps because most lambs and cubs in Britain are born at the same period of the year; all other foxes at that time are adult and have passed through the learning stages of prey killing. Information about the age, sex and reproductive condition of the foxes responsible for lamb killing would be required to permit anything more than speculation on the motivation of the behaviour. The burying of lamb carcases usually occurs before the cubbing season is well under way, but when cubs need to be fed, the vixen, if not the dog fox, will carry surplus food rather than bury it. Some farmers suggest that excessive lamb killing is performed by vixens which have lost their cubs, but there is no real evidence for this. Others say that dogs or vixens which have lost their mates are responsible.

Large numbers of dead lambs may be found at some cubbing earths. The most I have found, in a recognizable condition, is twelve. Fifty-two were allegedly found in a rock den near Talisker on the Isle of Skye; the farmer reporting this regarded them all as having been killed by foxes. When such large numbers are found it is difficult for the shepherd to accept the possibility that some of the lambs, if not all, have been scavenged by foxes, and the uncertainty creates intense anti-fox feeling. Undeniably, foxes do kill lambs, and whilst excessive killing behaviour is comparatively uncommon and not of economic significance to the sheep-rearing industry as a whole, any lamb mortality is a disappointment, and fox predation can sometimes cause a significant financial loss to a small individual flock. The loss which may be of real significance to the industry is not the lamb found dead after attack, but the lamb which disappears with or without the knowledge of the farmer. If the disappearance is noted, there is no infalliable means of determining the cause, nor even whether it was killed or taken as carrion, but it is usual to blame foxes (though 60 per cent of the farmers in Breconshire approached in the questionnaire survey also implicated sheep dogs as important predators of lambs). If lambs disappear with some regularity efforts may be made to find and kill foxes in the area. If losses cease after the killing of one or several foxes, the predator responsible is considered to have been accounted for, but this is rather dubious evidence, since lamb loss will often cease as suddenly as it began without any foxes being known to have been killed locally. In some cases, however, there is clear evidence that a particular vixen or her mate has been responsible for killing lambs. Some farmers mark their lambs as soon as possible after birth and in this way it is sometimes possible to trace the origins of lambs found at cubbing earths.

In Australia, estimates of lamb predation by foxes are fairly firmly based, since it seems that the carcases of lambs can be found and examined even if the cause of death cannot always be determined; usually, however, a trained observer can assess whether a lamb has been killed by a predator or eaten by a predator after death. Rowley (1970), in an elegant description and discussion of lamb predation in Australia, describes the problems of assigning the causes of death and the various factors which may mask the real causes of death. One firm impression given by Rowley's account is the similarity of the behaviour of foxes in Australia and Britain, and many of his observations on fox control and sheep-rearing practices and problems are pertinent to the British situation.

Many Australian workers have ascribed the losses of lambs to predators – the number of predatory species in Australia is slightly higher than in Britain (and include the pig, for example). Curiously, one feature characteristic of pigs and foxes is that they both often decapitate lambs they have killed or eaten. In his summary of the affect of predators upon lambs in Australia, Rowley accounts for most deaths of lambs by starvation due to mis-mothering; that is, the death of healthy lambs is due to an inadequate milk supply in the ewe, a deficiency which may be due to several causes. Starvation in new-born lambs occurs frequently in some parts of Australia, and such animals are easily taken by predators. This boosts the estimates of predation by foxes, but such calculations are artifacts, since these lambs would have died anyway. Another study of lamb predation in Australia is that of McFarlane (1964), who, on examining 3,039 dead lambs, found that 46.1 per cent had been eaten by predators or scavengers, but that only 9.8 per cent of the sample had actually been killed by predators. This represents an estimated total predation loss of all lambs born of 2 per cent. McFarlane showed that 90 per cent of lambs killed by foxes were attacked soon after birth, and a third of these showed evidence of difficult births. Dennis (1965 a and b), also in Australia, showed that most lambs died from starvation, shock or disease in the first twelve-hour period after birth and between one and two days later. Perhaps of more significance to British conditions, the work of Alexander, Peterson and Watson (1959) showed that exposure of lambs to cold, wet and windy weather contributes to the death of a high proportion of the lambs that die within three days of birth. McHugh and Edwards (1958) observed that attacked lambs were often weak from want of food and Smith (1964) that Australian pigs and foxes usually attacked lambs which had depleted fat reserves.

One feature of fox behaviour which differs in Australia is that few lambs are carried intact from the place where the lamb is killed or found as carrion. One reason for this is that the lambing and cubbing season may not be as synchronous, as in those areas of Britain where sheep populations are most dense. Also, Ian Rowley informs me, the distances from lambing paddocks to fox dens may be greater in Australia than in Britain. The lambs are also larger, and with rabbit-proof fences to negotiate, foxes may be prevented from carrying whole lambs very far. Consequently, only portions of lambs may be taken away. Thus, the samples of lambs collected for autopsy examination in Australia are probably fairly representative of the true situation, whereas in Britain I believe that missing lambs are of greater significance than those found mutilated in a field or cached, and for this reason comparable studies on the lines conducted by Australian workers cannot be done in Britain.

Also in Australia, Alexander and his colleagues (1967) watched the behaviour of foxes in paddocks containing lambing flocks. Two features stand out: first, ewes, even when resting, were not disturbed by the presence of foxes at close quarters and, second, foxes approached ewes and lambs very cautiously. When they were in the paddocks foxes seemed to be attracted to birth sites, where they ate foetal membranes. On several occasions it was observed that foxes readily retreated when recently lambed ewes moved aggressively towards them. Sometimes this happened even when lambs, motivated by curiosity perhaps, moved towards the fox. When a stray sheepdog entered the paddock in daylight, however, considerable alarm was shown by the ewes. One example of a fox kill was observed; a lamb walked towards the fox, which seized it by the neck and, after killing it, fed on it for about an hour. Examination showed this lamb to be apparently normal and healthy. On the few occasions that I have seen foxes move among flocks of sheep no young lambs were present, and the sheep took more interest in me than in the fox; but on one occasion when a fox ran swiftly away after having detected me, its rapid movement alarmed the sheep. To most sheep in Britain the fox must be a familiar sight, a harmless part of the environmental scene. An alarmed fox, however, may transmit some of its alarm to the sheep, which then react not to the fox, but either to the stimulus which caused the fox to flee or to its unusual behaviour.

## Calves and pigs
Several cases of foxes killing calves have been investigated; all refer to new-born calves. In one instance a heifer gave birth to twin calves in a snow-covered field at Fareham. Both calves were dead when found, and their ears and a substantial part of their hindquarters had been eaten. It is not known whether these calves were born alive. Another case in Carmarthenshire and an identical one at Pinner, Middlesex, relates to calves being attacked while being born, with the heifer (in both cases) lying down. Both calves were dead, one having been attacked in the head. In the first case, three foxes were seen in the field, and in the second five foxes were seen attacking the calf. Reports of such behaviour are rare, but I am inclined to believe the three cases reported here and three others that have come to my notice. Even if the two singleton calves attacked were still-born, the behaviour seems to be uncharacteristically

bold for foxes and few would believe the fox capable of such bravura.

The fox has little opportunity to kill piglets, but free-ranging piglets at Elstead, Surrey, were allegedly frequently taken by foxes, even from sows farrowing in the open. In this instance nothing was known of the health or viability of the piglets taken.

## Game

In company with the stoat and domestic cat, the fox is a traditional enemy of the gamekeeper, but most gamekeepers regard the domestic cat as the more persistent predator, taking pride of place at the head of the gamekeeper's list of harmful animals.

Nowadays the pheasant is the most important game animal in Britain; the partridge is in decline but where it is abundant it is highly regarded and its status carefully preserved. In Scotland and parts of England the grouse, of course, is the more dominant game species. Gamekeepers mostly agree that, given the opportunity, the fox is a more significant predator on partridges than on pheasants. The partridge roosts on the ground, nests in hedges and, until comparatively recently, could only be reared in the wild. Though pheasants may sometimes roost on the ground, their nesting places are widely dispersed.

Middleton investigated the factors controlling partridge numbers in 1935 and implicated the fox as the most important predator of partridges and their nests. In many cases the species of predator responsible for pillaging nests of eggs in Middleton's studies could be identified; of 962 nests known to have been lost on a Hampshire estate from 1911–24, 347 were pillaged by foxes; farm work destroyed 344 clutches and corvids 86 nests. Sitting birds were usually taken by foxes during the first week of incubation after laying a full clutch. Excluding losses of sitting hens, Middleton quotes evidence that of 480 eggs laid, 302 were lost to predators, and of the 176 eggs that hatched, only 108 chicks survived until August. For practical reasons the loss of chicks to predators is difficult to estimate.

The available information on losses of game attributable to foxes refers to situations where fox numbers are not permitted to reach levels that would obtain naturally in the absence of control by gamekeepers. Under conditions where predator control is not practised, the effect of fox predation on game would indeed be much greater. The virtual absence of pheasants in areas where they are not preserved may not, however, be attributable solely to the effect of wild predators.

Predator control is only one of the steps taken by game conservationists – a modern name for gamekeepers – to maintain as high a population of game as is possible for sport. In itself it may produce little effect, if other considerations such as habitat, disease or farm management are not also manipulated to provide surplus game for shooting. If, however, game animals are not exploited to the full and there is a surplus of stock required for breeding, predator control might well be a waste of time. Jenkins and his colleagues (1964) showed, for example, that where the grouse surplus is not fully exploited, predator control would be of little use without concomitant improvements in the habitat where the unexploited part of the surplus could live and breed. Predator control is not, therefore, of unequivocal benefit in all game-rearing areas, but where every effort is taken to improve the management of game, predation may become a factor of importance in limiting the number of game available for shooting. If game were to be fully exploited in such areas, the time and effort required to maintain the predator population at a very low level would probably be justified on grounds of game conservation. On poorly managed pheasant shoots, especially if the area is under about 400 hectares and is isolated from other sporting preserves, the time spent at fox shoots is probably a complete waste of effort, since far more birds, wild or reared, would be lost by dispersal from an area of this size than would be taken by foxes.

Middleton (1966) has stated that no clear and detailed picture of the effects of predation on game is available, nor information about the results of reducing predator pressure. This general statement I think refers to the medium or large shoot areas extending to upwards of 1,200 hectares. In isolated shoots of 400—800 hectares sporadic fox control would, I think, produce only a minimal improvement in shootable stock. Time and money spent in attempting to limit fox numbers might more profitably be spent in creating conditions to encourage pheasants not to disperse from the shoot. Small shoots of a few hundred hectares tend to regard the low returns of tagged pheasants as evidence of predation, and attention is focused on foxes. Snares are set; foxes are killed and may continue to be killed throughout the winter. The return of tagged birds does not improve; more determined efforts are taken to kill foxes outside the game-shooting season and so it goes on, with the shooters being more and more convinced that the fox is responsible for their problems, since they cannot apparently eliminate them. Nor will they either, especially on small shoots. The dispersal of young foxes from October to January is reflected by the regular capture of foxes in snares, and even from March to June the vacuum created by the killing of a dog or a vixen may, if the habitat is rich, result in its being filled or partly filled by foxes occupying contiguous home ranges. An example from Pembrokeshire may illustrate this point. Seventy-six foxes were snared from January to March on 325 hectares of agricultural and common land in an area where practically no fox control was exercised for many miles around. At the end of this period the weekly catch decreased, since at the approach of the birth of cubs foxes were becoming more sedentary (snaring was discontinued when the first parous vixen was caught). After nine months' rest from fox control snares were again set from December to March, but this time over about 1,415 hectares, including the original area. This time the catch of 102 foxes was relatively smaller. The increase in the catch at the second snaring over the larger area probably represented an increase in the number of fox territories (or home ranges) that were intercepted or encompassed by the snare lines. Had the first survey area been only 150 hectares, or had the snares been set in a single line transecting the 325 hectares originally designated, it is very likely that the number of foxes killed would not have been much less than the seventy-six that were caught. In both years about 40 per cent of the captives were young animals.

Examples of surplus killing of game by foxes are not uncommon; the opportunity occurs when reared pheasants are released into large pens in woodland prior to their being released into the wild. If a fox gains access to these pens, considerable damage can be done (as in a poultry house), and this is an anxious time for gamekeepers. Foxes are not killed to protect winged game only, however; wherever game is preserved for shooting efforts are taken to reduce the number of foxes. In Sweden, for example, hunters consider that foxes are important predators on roe deer (juveniles) and blue hares (*Lepus timidus*) and bounties are paid for their destruction.

Increases in game bags of pheasants and hares have been recorded by many observers independently in Central Europe, following widespread outbreaks of rabies among foxes. There certainly seems to be an inverse relationship between fox and game numbers in these examples but it does not necessarily follow in every case that this is directly attributable to the predatory activities of foxes.

The red grouse must suffer some loss from fox predation but information is scanty (see Jenkins, Watson and Millar, 1964).

I know that my shooting friends will look askance at me for not painting as black a picture of the fox as possible because, as they will surely tell me, everyone knows that foxes kill pheasants, partridges, grouse, duck and lesser game. Certainly they do, but the impact of the fox cannot be measured by their numbers in an area, since so many other factors in game management can be involved. One of these friends will doubtless remind me of the winged partridge that was snatched by a fox from under my nose and that of my startled retriever – out of range, of course.

## Hunting

In the oldest English book on hunting, *The Master of Game* (*c.* 1420), a translation of Gaston de Foix's, *La Chasse*, by Edward, Second Duke of York, the fox was regarded as game, but one of a lowly order. Edward prized game in this descending order of merit: hare, hart (red deer), buck (fallow deer), roe, wild boar, wolf, fox, badger, wild cat, marten and otter. Hunting was a way of life for many of the aristocracy and churchmen, and they and their huntsmen knew their quarry well; Edward (or was it Gaston?) wrote that 'men know by the outer side of a hare's leg if she has not passed a year', a reference to the prominence at the distal epiphyses of the ulna in young hares, which today is used by some biologists to age hares and rabbits. Also, on the same topic, 'And so man should know of a hound, or a fox and of a wolf, by the little bone that they have which is next to the sinews, where there is a little pit' (I am not certain of the part mentioned, but I suspect it to be the proximal epiphysis of the tibia, which is also used by biologists to distinguish juvenile animals).

Edward regarded the fox as a common beast and not a particularly sporting animal, which 'will scarcely leave a covert, and will not take to open country for he trusteth not in his running, nor in his defence, for he is so feeble'. Reference is made to the stopping of earths on hunting days; Gaston in France advocated this, but Edward in England did not. Gaston gives directions for evicting foxes from earths using 'orpiment [arsenious sulphide] and sulphur and niter and salt petre'. Gaston and Edward both regarded the fox as vermin rather than a beast worthy of being hunted. Their attitude can be summed up in Edward's writing:

> The fox does not cry when men slay him. He liveth on all vermin, and all carrion, and on foul worms [earth worms?]. His best meat that he loveth are hens, capons, ducks and young geese, and other wild fowls, also butterflies and grasshoppers, milk and butter. They do great harm in warrens of conys [rabbits] and hares which they take cunningly with great malice and not by running. There are some that hunt like the wolf and some that go nowhere but to villages to seek the prey for their feeding. Foxes commonly dwell in great hedges or in great coverts, or in burrows near some town or village, for to ever more harm hens and other things.

According to Canute's laws, the fox was a Beast neither of Venery (that is, hunting) nor of the forest. Under Norman law the Forest Laws were quite separate from Common Law, and at one time the fox was protected by them. The Beasts of the Forest were the king's beasts – they were his property, and within a defined tract of land all were protected. The right to hunt them was exclusive to the king and to the owner of the forest. Outside these forests the Beasts of Venery were still protected by Forest Laws. When a king granted a forest to one of his subjects, his own rights passed to the grantee, and the game animals of the forest were then known as Beasts of the Chase. The Beasts of the Warren also belonged to the king but the grantee – usually the Lord of the Manor – had the right to hunt them in defined areas. The fox was a Beast of the Chase, regarded, as it was, less highly than hares, red deer, wolves and wild boar, which were Beasts of Venery. These laws related to the declared forests. Grants of warren enabled the beneficiaries to enclose areas for hunting, with the right, possibly, to hunt hare, cat, badger, fox, polecat and otter. According to Forest Law, the fox-hunting season opened on Christmas Day and ended on 25 March, but at some times it began on 8 September, at the 'nativity of our Lady'. Edward I's wardrobe accounts refer to 1 September as the opening day, but probably it varied according to the quality of the pelts in any year.

The English kings kept both foxhounds and otterhounds. In 1410 it was recorded that a William Melbourne was the king's Valet of Otterhounds, and in this capacity he was sent about the country to kill otters and foxes, partly for their pelts but also to prevent damage by foxes. Edward I's wardrobe accounts for 1299–1300 include wages for his Fox Hunter and payments for clothes and for his horse, which carried nets for the purpose of catching foxes.

Greyhounds were often used to course foxes both in France and England, but in the early days of hunting hounds were used against hare, fox, stag or wolf. (In 1591 Sir Thomas Cockraine gave expression to his preference for hunting foxes rather than hares in *A Short Treatise on Hunting*.) In Elizabethan times foxes and badgers were sometimes preserved for hunting. It was not until the end of the seventeenth century that hounds were being bred exclusively for fox hunting. One of the earliest packs of foxhounds, established in Dorsetshire in 1730, was purchased by Bowes of Yorkshire, and fox hunting as a sport really began.

According to Trevelyan (*English Social History*, 1944), an important stimulus to fox hunting was the destruction of deer parks and deer during the disorders of the Civil War, and the substitution of the fox as a sporting quarry. Packs of hounds were privately owned and were used, in the main, for hunting hares. As deer declined and woods were felled, the open-country fox chase became more and more common. The hounds were slow but dogged, and hunts usually ended at an earth from which the fox had to be dug out, often after dark. One consequence of the rise of fox hunting was that whereas hare hunting did not take the hunters far from home, the fox would run over greater distances, which conferred on fox hunters their traditional privilege of hunting over large areas of ground without explicit permission to do so. Since hunting was not then so effective with the slow hounds and almost always involved the use of the spade, the sport did not become universally popular and appealed mainly to those interested in the mysteries of scent and the working of dogs rather than horsemanship and the exhilaration of the fast chase. All this was changed by the breeding of fast-moving hounds, the first exponent of the new form of hunting being Hugo Meynell of Leicestershire, who hunted for fifty years, until 1800. According to one source (Peter Beckford, 1810), to kill three foxes in one day at those times was an exceptional occurrence; his own pack killed about fifty foxes a year and a neighbouring pack about twenty-four foxes – modest numbers by comparison with later days.

The enclosure of land by hedges and fences had not been a hindrance hitherto, but they became more than a nuisance to the followers of the faster packs when the horsemen were unable to keep up with the hounds. As with the breeding of the new type of hound, the modern fox hunter was bred for its speed, stamina and ability to jump over obstructions. This combination of fast horses and hounds and open hunting country led to a peak of finesse and expertise among huntsmen and an exhilaration never experienced before. Bovill, in *English Country Life 1780–1830*, gives a succinct but comprehensive account of the development of the sport at this time. He describes the antipathy of country people towards foxes for the damage they did, and illustrates this by an account of the pealing of church bells in Devonshire, summoning men with pick axe, gun and terrier to help Parson Jack Russell, whose hounds had run a fox to ground.

Foxes were becoming too few to sustain the popularity of fox hunting – mainly because of the destruction of foxes as pests. Often, apparently, a hunt was terminated when it seemed as if the fox would be killed by the hounds. This shortage led to the fostering and preservation of foxes, and their importation for hunting or breeding. A trade in foxes from the Continent thrived at Leadenhall Market, London; bagmen, as such foxes were called, were either turned out in the hunt area or kept at the kennels for hunting on specific occasions. (Some of these foxes sometimes turned out to be juvenile wolves!) Sometimes the kennel bagmen were recaptured by the huntsman when the hounds were getting close to the fox and were returned to the kennel to be hunted on another day – in one case as many as thirty times altogether. Bagmen were not considered to provide good sport – for one thing they allegedly always ran down wind! Since there was money to be had for foxes, they were dug from earths by poachers to be sold to hunts, and many a hunt, it seems, bought their own foxes! Foxes were imported from Wales and Scotland where there were few mounted hunts. Indeed, hill foxes from northern England and elsewhere were considered to provide the best sport, since they and their offspring were tireless and would provide long hunts. In order to preserve their sport, fox hunters were at one time paying blackmail or protection money to poaching gangs for immunity from fox-catching raids. They also paid money to farmers in recompense for poultry and lamb losses, to gamekeepers as rewards for rearing litters on their beats and to others for the purchase of foxes. All these measures led to an increase in huntable foxes in the latter half of the nineteenth century, and the experience of the hunts at this time is one of the reasons why huntsmen still maintain that if it were not for fox hunting, foxes would have been eliminated in many parts of Britain.

There is no evidence that fox hunting helped to promote an abundance of rabbits in the nineteenth century, but they were certainly encouraged in order that they should provide food for foxes and potential earths. In a different context, some gamekeepers today are glad to see rabbits widely distributed in their sporting area, since they believe that rabbits divert predatory attention from their game.

One clash of sporting interest that has been maintained to this day is that between the gamekeeper – who is employed to rear as much game as possible, and who reduces the number of foxes in order to achieve this – and the sporting proprietor, who, in addition to a good head of game, wishes to provide huntable foxes for the local hunt. Hunting still thrives, and is the object of considerable interest and controversy. Its future probably lies not in the hands of abolitionists but in the goodwill of farm owners and occupiers, who could put an end to it all by denying fox hunters access to their land.

## Fox Pelts

In Britain the pelt of the wild red fox is not as much in demand by furriers as those from the northern latitudes of Europe, Asia and America. (Silver-fox farming was not uncommon in Britain in the period between the two world wars but long-fibred furs became unfashionable, and silver-fox farming declined in consequence.) On the continent of Europe the demand for the natural red pelt is increasing, mainly for use in hats and coat trimmings, though red fox fur coats are now very popular in Europe. Blue foxes (a colour-phase of the arctic fox) are still farmed.

Since 1975 the demand for fox pelts in Britain has increased steadily, as reflected by the increase in value from about £4 per skin to £20 in 1978 for large, best-quality pelts. The market for finished pelts seems to have expanded even to Japan, but the supply from continental Europe may have diminished because of a reduction in the availability of pelts from rabies-endemic areas. Consequently, in order to satisfy the demand, pelts are now sought from areas such as Britain, where pelts of killed foxes have not traditionally been harvested. If the response in Wales and the West Country is any indication, fur dealers have found a responsive source. Many bounty hunters (see page 194) are now becoming pelt hunters, and because of the potentially high values there is much competition for killing foxes, and even a perceptible change in the *laissez-faire* attitudes of occupiers in sheep-rearing areas towards those who come on their land in pursuit of foxes for their own gain.

The prices paid for fox pelts in Britain are low by comparison with those of other countries in Europe. In Sweden and France, for example, good-quality pelts will fetch £40 (in 1977), and it is reported that at least one enterprising local dealer in Britain has found it profitable to by-pass British dealers by selling green uncured pelts in France. In some areas those who kill only a few foxes a year find it less troublesome to sell fox carcases to others who market the pelts. The skinners are very much in the hands of dealers, since there is no organized marketing system and they usually have to accept whatever price is offered.

If the skin on the back of a fox continues to carry a high premium and the demand is maintained, there could be a change in attitude towards foxes. The fox could be unofficially promoted to 'game' status, and as in Finland, its role as a pest overlooked and bounties abandoned. If the market remains steadily lucrative, numbers of foxes could fall dramatically – a sinister situation for the fox, and perhaps for the traditional fox-hunting fraternity as well. However, if the importation of furs of wild species were to be restricted by legislation, the fox could become a focus of debate, since British fox pelts are mostly exported. Like the swings of fashion, legislation may save the fox's skin.

# 7

# The Control of Foxes

A pest is an animal or plant in an environment where it is not wanted –
for whatever reason. It can be a pest in one situation and not in another
(for example, bindweed in a herbaceous border or a kingfisher at a trout
hatchery). Its effects can perhaps be counteracted by the provision of
adequate protective measures, but the cost and inconvenience of these
themselves constitute a nuisance.

Some tolerate pests for the delight of seeing them – even acquiescing
to roe deer browsing on rose bushes for the pleasure of having visiting
deer in their gardens, or welcoming bullfinches and turning a blind eye
to the damage to fruit buds. The commercial grower, however, might
soon be out of business if he tolerated a pest which was known to have a
significantly adverse effect on his crops. Ambivalent attitudes towards
animals that can be pests in some situations and not in others promote
considerable ill feeling from time to time, but in general if someone kills
or removes an animal claiming that it is a harmful pest (though not
necessarily to him), the argument is usually decided in his favour. If, for
example, a fox is shot and the action needs to be justified, the bald statement that foxes kill lambs would at most times go undisputed.

An animal can be relegated to pest status on slender evidence, but the
converse will require much argument and documentation to win the
day. In the last twenty years or so widely held beliefs concerning pests
have been questioned; there is a growing awareness of the hazards, accidental or deliberate, that beset all forms of wildlife and, little by little,
greater tolerance and even protection is being afforded to species capable
of inflicting damage of one sort or another. Generally speaking, an
animal comes to be regarded as a pest when it occurs in large numbers;
when it is unobtrusive little may be said or done against it. The more
numerous a pest and the more persistent it is, the more assured is its
status as a nuisance, but without economic assessment of the damage

caused, numbers alone do not provide a true perspective of pest status. In sheep- and game-rearing areas it is traditional to regard foxes as pests, but attempts to impose a limit on their numbers have become an unceasing seasonal commitment; this has happened with foxes since they first impinged upon man's interests.

In Britain organized control of foxes, coupled with the hunting of the animal for its pelt, probably began with the appointment of the royal Fox Hunters of Edward I (see page 188). Later an Act enabled the payment of bounties for the destruction of vermin to all and sundry from moneys obtained from landlords and lords of the manor (Act 24 Hen. VIII C. 10 1532–3). In Elizabeth's reign this Act was changed, enabling fund-raising by levy from landowners and others, the proceeds being administered by churchwardens for the same purposes; this Act (8 Eliz. C. 1556), renewed twice in Elizabeth's reign, was not repealed until 1863.

Bounties were primarily concerned with grain-eating bird pests – for example, a total of 135,000 sparrows were submitted for bounty in seven separate years in the parish of Willington, Bedfordshire – but the fund could be used in payment for the destruction of a long list of 'Noyfull Fowles and Vermyn'. Initially twelve pence was paid for the destruction of each fox or badger, one penny for polecats, weasels, stoats, martens and wildcats, and two pence for otters and hedgehogs. In some parishes the values of the fox bounties were higher; Sidbury, Devon, paid 5s. per adult fox in 1567, Hawkshead in Lancashire the same sum from 1731, and Eaton Socon, Bedfordshire, 6s. 8d. for a vixen. At Llanffestiniog, Merioneth, £1 per fox was paid in 1801. The latest recorded churchwarden payment for a fox was at Dean, Bedfordshire, in 1829, and in 1863, on the repeal of the Act enabling Church bounty payment, bounties were paid in Ffestiniog out of the receipts of rents from the market place (Hope Jones, 1974). As late as 1924 the parish council of Llanfachraeth in the same county were still managing a fund used to reward the killing of foxes, moneys for which were obtained from contributions by farmers and landowners.

The number of foxes killed in some areas was remarkably low, considering the value of the rewards. In the parish of North Hill, for example, ninety-five foxes were bountied from 1665 to 1813, and eighty-seven foxes at Ravensden from 1710 to 1796; rather few by comparison with the numbers often killed today. On the other hand, Charles Oldham (1931), in a detailed account of vermin payments in the *Transactions of the Hertford Natural History Society*, suggested that in certain places the payment of bounties sometimes ceased because of a marked increase in the number of rewards being claimed – as at Sandridge, Hertfordshire, in 1732 and at Welwyn in 1748, when in both cases foxes were mentioned in this context. Perhaps it was at this time in the chequered relationship of fox and man that the new vogue for fox hunting demanded that they be preserved.

Clubs or societies for the promotion of vermin destruction are not an innovation. Various rat and sparrow clubs existed until the 1930s; the Highland Squirrel Club, for example, in its first twenty-two years of operation up to 1925, killed 76,000 red squirrels. (Today there are still clubs in England devoted to the destruction of squirrels, but now of the alien species.) In some suburban areas of London pet clubs offer bounties for foxes killed in their neighbourhood, apparently because foxes disturb birds in aviaries or even gain access to the cages. In the past county courts have sometimes made orders that the Treasury should reward the killing of vermin on a standard scale, but Owen (1950) regarded such authorization as illegal. The fox destruction societies which operate in some parts of the country today are merely perpetuating a tradition which began in the sixteenth century.

## Fox Destruction Societies

In some parts of Britain fox destruction societies have been formed in non-hunting areas in response to complaints by farmers that fox control by individuals is ineffective or lacks incentive. During the war years fox destruction societies were formed primarily to operate on unenclosed land, and today approved societies can pay a bounty for foxes killed. (The government added an equal sum not exceeding 50p and 25p for adult foxes and cubs respectively to the bounty but its contribution was withdrawn as of August 1979.) The actual bounty, therefore, was usually £1 for adults and 50p for cubs (up to August), but latterly as much as £2.50 was paid by some societies for vixens. This is an unusual bounty scheme, in as much as the societies have defined areas and the farmers pay half the bounty reward, which is a slight safeguard against the submission of foxes killed elsewhere. Sometimes only society members are permitted to claim the bounty. In Scotland there is provision for societies to employ a full or part-time fox hunter, and the government contribution went towards his salary rather than bounty payments.

In England there were a few 'non-subsidized' fox destruction societies. It is curious that attitudes towards foxes in Britain should be so varied that at one end of the spectrum foxes are fostered for sport, and at the other a government-approved bounty was offered for their destruction; no other wild animal in Britain had the distinction of being the object of a government bounty.

There are 139 fox destruction societies in Wales (twelve with footpacks of hounds), forty-nine in England (eleven with footpacks) and thirty-three in Scotland. The distribution of these in England and Wales

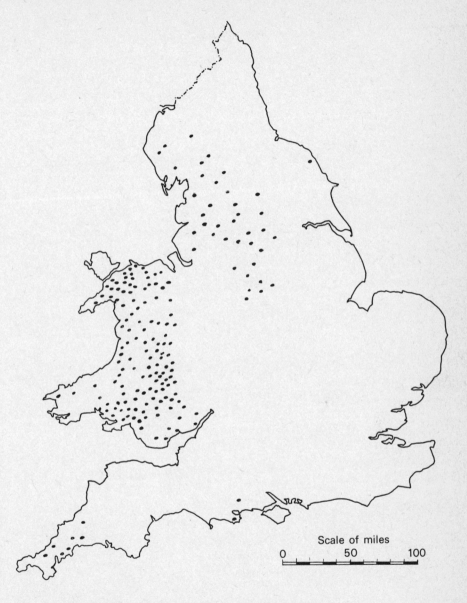

**23** Distribution of fox destruction societies in England and Wales

Scale of miles

0                50                100

Number of Hunts
England = 160
Wales   =  20

**24**   Distribution of hunts recognized by the Masters of Fox Hounds Association in England and Wales is shown in Figure 23, and the distribution of hunts affiliated to the Master of Foxhounds Association in Figure 23. The relationship between these four features needs no explanation. Fox destruction societies fulfil one undeniable function; they provide occupiers with contacts on whom they can call for help when it is necessary to kill foxes locally. The formation of such societies usually staunches complaints to official quarters about fox damage to lambs, though, in the opinion of members, damage may still occur.

The societies each have their own sets of rules. Some require a minimum membership fee, which may be sufficient to pay the cost of the society's portion of the bounty; others augment their income by raising funds in other ways, and the Forestry Commission usually provides financial support as well. Some allow non-members to submit foxes for bounty; others restrict bounty payment to members only, and although very little money is involved, I have known members of some societies to complain that some submit too many foxes for payment!

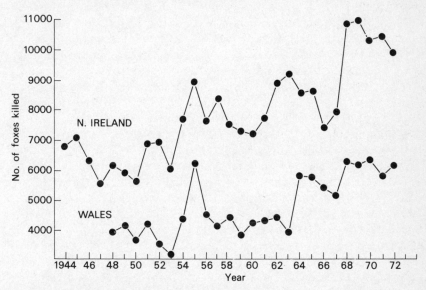

**25**  Numbers of foxes of all ages submitted for bounty by fox destruction societies; Northern Ireland and Wales, 1944–72

The number of foxes killed annually by individual societies has been fairly steady for a period of nearly thirty years (see Figure 25). It is clear that their impact on the fox population is much the same each year and that they are removing an exploitable proportion of the fox population at large. Unfortunately, data for numbers of foxes killed by societies since their inception during the period 1941–4 are not available for comparison with total kills in later years. The annual kill varies, but it is not possible to be certain of the causes of significant variations from year to year. It is also not known whether or not the variations reflect changes in the number of foxes at large since, in addition to changes in the biology of foxes, there are so many factors which could influence the activities of fox destruction societies – in particular, their vigilance and effectiveness in any year. However, it is clear from data for Northern Ireland (Figure 25) that significantly higher numbers of foxes were being killed in the 1970s than was the case in the 1940s; clearly, on this basis the fox destruction societies are not making significant inroads into the fox population.

The occurrence of myxomatosis in 1954–5 was one factor which, in those years at least, promoted greater activity against foxes. Investigations by my colleague, C. J. Armour, in Wales in June 1955 – some nine to twelve months after the first occurrences of myxomatosis – revealed that farmers and other countrymen had been and still were very concerned that the fox might turn its attention more to domestic stock in the absence of rabbits. Consequently, greater efforts were made to kill foxes in the winter and spring of 1954–5 than before. This apprehension had also promoted the formation of twenty-one new fox destruction societies in 1954 and 1955 – an increase of 20 per cent in total. Another product of Armour's enquiries was the frequently volunteered information that litter sizes of cubs in 1955 were much lower than in previous years. Whether or not the decline in numbers of foxes killed in 1956 reflects this is not known. However, increased hunting pressure may not have been the only reason for the increase in kills in 1955. Hewson and Kolb (1973) suggest that in north-east Scotland cubs born in 1954 may have had a superabundance of dead or dying rabbits as food, which may have resulted in higher survival rates among cubs born in that year. This could have led to higher numbers of foxes in the winter and spring of 1954–5, which could have resulted in a greater number of kills (see Figure 25) without any increase in hunting pressure. It is not possible to distinguish between the effects of greater hunting effort and a possible increase in the survival rate of cubs in accounting for the rise of 40 per cent among foxes killed in Wales in 1955. Since 1963 the number of foxes killed in Wales has again increased and has remained at a higher level. The reason for this is not known, but obviously either increased (or more effective) control, or increases in the number of foxes, or both, could produce this result, but why this should have been so in 1962–3 is a mystery.

In Australia, where foxes are considered to be a pest and are killed in large numbers, the number of foxes killed in the year following myxomatosis increased dramatically from 14,000 to 36,000 in Queensland. And in another smaller area the numbers killed increased fifteen-fold (Ratcliffe, 1956). It was also considered that lamb predation increased following myxomatosis.

Analyses of the number of individuals claiming fox bounties in forty-two of the 130 Welsh Fox Destruction Societies in 1962 show that 359 individuals claimed bounty on 1,577 foxes – a mean of 4.4 each. The number claimed by individuals in the forty-two societies ranged from one to sixty-two, and the average number of foxes bountied by these societies was 37.3 each.

Many older members of long-established societies have remarked that the numbers of foxes being killed in their areas are no higher than during the period before the societies were formed. Rural depopulation increased dramatically after 1946, and prior to the war many more people participated actively in fox control in rural areas. The small financial incentive has simply maintained the pressure on foxes.

The cost of killing foxes can be enormous. Calculations based on the time spent by different individuals operating in fox destruction society areas yield estimates of between £20 and £50 per fox in terms of time spent. Food, accommodation and transport for a footpack of hounds and a part-time huntsman's wages may cost well over £2,000 per annum (in 1978). With perhaps 100 foxes to their credit, the cost per fox killed would be at least £20, without any consideration of the time spent by individuals participating at shoots when hounds are used. One has to bear in mind, however, that time spent may not necessarily be time lost, since there is an element of sport involved.

Foxes are harmless to forestry interests but the Forestry Commission and private forestry groups are considerably embarrassed by their presence, since they are often very difficult to control in extensive thicket-stage conifer plantations, and shepherds and others complain that forest plantations provide secure harbourage for foxes, making their own efforts at control difficult. In the interests of public relations, the Forestry Commission attempts to deal effectively with foxes in its own woodlands. A bounty is offered to Commission employees, and foxes killed within about five kilometres of Forestry Commission woodlands qualify for an additional payment by the Commission to fox destruction societies. In Wales the Commission has an agreement that under certain circumstances foot packs may be paid about £10 per day for hunting its woodlands. The Forestry Commission estimates that its total annual expenditure on fox control in 1972 was close on £40,000 – a modest sum, perhaps, by comparison with the inflated economy of the late 1970s. Details of the number of foxes killed and expenditure for that year are shown in Table 30. The cost of killing each fox in 1971–2 was approximately £9, but in the North Wales Conservancy the cost of killing a fox by Conservancy staff only was just short of £15 – heavy expenditure, which offers no tangible reward to the Commission. In 1978 these costs would at least be double those of 1972.

## Methods of Controlling the Numbers of Foxes

Some bizarre methods of controlling fox populations, based upon inadequate knowledge of the animal, have been proposed from time to time – such as that which would involve the capture, sterilization and release of dog foxes as a means of reducing productivity to the point at which a high proportion of matings would be infertile. A variation of this is the suggested use of anti-fertility agents administered in bait – hypothetically a feasible and interesting proposition, which suffers, unfortunately, from four main disadvantages. It would be necessary to ensure that a high proportion of vixens over large areas did not breed and that non-target species were not similarly affected. Treatment would need to be repeated, probably annually, and accurate estimates of numbers of foxes would be required to enable the degree of population management achieved to be determined and to assist the assessment of further courses of action. The method appears to have some potential, but the logistics of such an undertaking could be formidable. Means of depressing the reproduction of mammals has been investigated, however, by Balser (1964), Linhart (1964), Linhart and Enders (1964) and Oleyar and McGinnis (1974), although no extensive field trials with foxes have yet been reported.

The discussion of control methods below is restricted to those commonly used in Britain and elsewhere today.

### Shooting

In Scotland, especially in hill land, foxes are shot with rifles at dens in cairns of boulders or screes where terriers may not safely be entered. (Even when the gin trap was permitted, its use was not always possible and shooting was often a last resort.) Often the hunter will lie in wait for the fox to return to its lair at dawn. Having taken such pains and walked many miles in the hope of killing a fox, an experienced rifleman is very likely to make the most of the opportunity to kill the fox cleanly. Most gamekeepers and many shepherds in hill areas of Scotland are used to handling rifles, and in their hands the method is humane, especially if high-velocity ammunition or large-calibre rifles are used. Not so, however, in the case of shotguns, in Scotland or elsewhere. These may be used at fox drives, when bolting foxes from earths with terriers, or opportunistically. The shot sizes most commonly used are 4, 5 or 6 (that is, medium-sized game pellets), and while these sizes are not generally recommended for fox shooting, they could not be condemned if foxes were shot at ranges not exceeding 25 metres. Many participants at fox drives have rarely, if ever, shot a fox, however, and organized drives with beaters can promote much anticipatory excitement and indiscipline. Shots are sometimes fired all too freely, with the result that many foxes are shot at from excessive distances and wounded. (The gunman who boasts that he knocked a fox over at 100 metres or killed it outright at seventy-five metres would deserve to have his gun licence withdrawn if that were possible.) Another cause of shooting at great distances is the often inadequate number of guns available to cover the perimeters of woodlands at organized drives. Foxes seem to have a knack of finding the weak points in the field of fire covered by the guns, and organizers of fox drives in Britain do not seem to have any means of overcoming this. In Finland flag lines, comprising long lengths of cord with small pieces of flag-like material attached at three-metre intervals, are strung in a long line about three metres above ground to dissuade foxes from breaking out at weak points or to funnel them towards the guns. (This is mentioned not so much to suggest how drives might be conducted more effectively but to indicate methods that will obviate the temptation to shoot at long ranges.)

It is commonly believed that a pricked fox will die of gangrene, and this belief may in some cases precipitate the risking of long shots in the hope that even if the animal is not killed, it will be hit by at least a few pellets. Whilst the fox with a heavy load of shot may die, especially if shot in the viscera, the assumption that gangrene will set in is fallacious. In Chapter 8 reference is made to infections probably caused by gunshot wounds, but my laboratory evidence of old rifle, air-rifle or shotgun damage suggests that the fox heals remarkably quickly. A veterinary colleague, on examining a dead fox for possible cause of death, found a shotgun pellet lodged in the heart muscle. This was not the cause of death, however, the pellet having been there for months, or perhaps years, with no sign of permanent injury. Many foxes examined in my laboratory had suffered broken limb bones, the results of old gunshot wounds; some had lost one or two feet (mowing machines?); some had accidentally been caught by the legs in rabbit snares and had lost the extremities of the limbs; one, a vixen, had a broken fox snare completely embedded beneath healed skin round its loins. Though impaired, all were healthy animals, but the vixen, which was pregnant, would not have been able to give birth to its cubs. Harris (1976), in a painstakingly detailed examination of over 300 fox skeletons collected from urban areas in London, found evidence of healed fractures in 27.5 per cent of his sample, but he considered that most of the fractures had been caused by vehicles. Dr Jan Englund (pers. comm.) has found much evidence of permanent injury among the foxes he has examined in Sweden. Forensic experts have advised him that the impact shock of a high-velocity bullet penetrating flesh could fracture a limb without actually hitting it. Fragments of shot and bullets have been found in many fractured limbs examined by X-ray, however.

Shooting is a humane method of killing foxes when used by careful and considerate gunmen; unfortunately the method is widely used by incompetent or unthinking gun handlers, and because of its widespread use shooting probably inflicts as much suffering on foxes as all the other methods of control combined. Clearly, even the best gunman will not always kill his quarry outright, but the damage inflicted by competent shooters is small by comparison with that which results from gross misuse of the gun.

Many shooters advocate the use of BB-size shot for foxes. This size of shot has great carrying power, impact and penetration and is rather hazardous if used at fox drives. At ranges up to 30 metres a broadside fox in the centre of the pattern would usually be killed instantly, but at greater ranges the pattern becomes too open to ensure a clean kill. This can be demonstrated simply by superimposing a broadside silhouette of a fox (with the brain, heart, large blood vessels and spinal cord illustrated) on the pattern of different shot sizes at different ranges. Whilst it is possible to show the probability of the animal's being hit in a vital place by moving the silhouette on the pattern, this does not take account of the effect of the impact force of different shot sizes. However, with twelve-bore shotguns and normal loads at ranges up to thirty metres, shot sizes from BB to number 4 shot will provide dense patterns, which will kill cleanly in nearly every case when at least two-thirds of the fox is in the shot pattern. At distances greater than this the chance of foxes being wounded increase steeply. Shot size 5 should not be used, since the fox would probably need to be less than 25 metres away to ensure consistently clean kills. Though not readily available, shot size 3 is preferable from all points of view.

Foxes can be attracted to within shooting distance by vocal lures in daylight (if the fox is active) or at night. At night a spotlight is used to identify the fox, which will often make little effort to avoid the light. The technique requires skill and practice, and one of the secrets of success is to be as quiet as possible and to be down wind of the foxes. Vocal lures can be purchased or made spontaneously by producing squeaking, squealing noises with the lips or against the back of one's hand. A few people are expert in this technique, which is more commonly used in North America than in Britain. One of my colleagues has noticed that foxes are attracted at dusk to electronically amplified starling distress calls, and at least one sporting estate has abandoned this method of starling dispersal from roosts because it allegedly attracts foxes into the area.

Night shooting of foxes or other species, whether done on foot or from vehicles, though not totally illegal is not freely permitted by law and participants should ensure that they are not transgressing.

# Hunting

Hunting, or the use of hounds for killing foxes, falls into three categories: mounted hunts, foot packs and the use of hounds to drive foxes from woodlands and other cover to waiting guns. The number of mounted packs exceeds the number of foot packs.

Mounted hunts pursue foxes mainly for sport, although it is possible that many participants hide their true motives behind the killing-foxes-for-control smokescreen. Those who support hunts, especially in sheep-rearing areas, do so because they feel that hunts help to control the numbers of foxes and alleviate damage; furthermore, most hunts will readily help a farmer who has a fox problem on his hands. The sporting aspect of fox hunting is, however, of paramount importance to those who have any real interest in it – the exhilaration of the chase, the behaviour of the fox, the vagaries of the weather and its effect on scent and on the working of the hounds and, above all (for some, especially children, this is the only reason for participation) the horsemanship involved. The success of a day's hunting is not necessarily measured by the number of foxes killed. To participants with a keen interest and knowledge of hunting, a blank day can often provide more interest and enjoyment than a series of kills, though a hunt may not receive much support if it has not secured a respectable tally of foxes by the end of a season.

The pros and cons of fox hunting arouse strong emotions. I hold no brief for it, and my upbringing in one Welsh environment, where most mounted followers were alien to the area, which to them was no more than a playground, has promoted in me an emotive anti-fox hunting attitude. Be that as it may, I do not propose to discuss whether or not it is morally proper to pursue and kill animals in the elaborate manner of hunting or even whether morality comes into question at all. Whilst I have been responsible for killing several hundred foxes, none was killed for sport; on the other hand, I have spent many hours on the river bank hoping that the next salmon may be so large and strong that it will take hours to exhaust it and bring it to the gaff. So my objectivity in this context must be suspect.

Hunts must have foxes to hunt – not too many, or the huntsmen in many cases will not be able to keep their pack to one fox, and in marginally less suitable fox habitats they must be sure not to kill so many foxes that sport is impaired in the following season. In such counties as Leicestershire, Northamptonshire or Wiltshire foxes could be eliminated or reduced to very small numbers fairly easily, since the various methods of control are adaptable to these areas where the habitat will not support large numbers of foxes, and the farm tenants and owners who meet the obligation of tolerating foxes for the hunt would be released from this in the absence of hunting. Whether they would need to control fox numbers or would be inclined to do so is another matter. In some hunt areas foxes are tolerated and fostered and their numbers augmented, even today, by foxes translocated to provide sport; but in most parts of Britain it is not necessary to augment the number of foxes, since the annual kill by hunting has little influence (by design or otherwise) upon the size of the fox population. The argument that but for hunting, foxes would be eliminated in Britain is in my opinion invalid, except perhaps (depending upon the attitude of the farming community) in a few middle-English counties.

The initial pursuit of the fox is comparatively slow if the hounds are following by scent, but if the fox comes into view of the hounds, then the pace changes and the fox must at this stage feel some alarm. In many areas foxes are not often killed in full flight, but after they have reached some cover where they feel more secure. This allows the hounds to get close, and if the fox is not then killed in cover, whether it be woodland or thicket, the hounds have at least gained ground and the conclusion is usually reached soon afterwards. At some stage of the hunt the fox which is pursued and killed must be distressed, but probably for a shorter period of time than with some methods of control. Although the actual kill is a savage affair, the fox is completely outmatched and is usually dead within seconds of being caught by the hounds. The result of a hunt is always positive and final, the fox either escaping completely unharmed, or being quickly killed. Since (I think) the fox is neither distressed nor greatly alarmed during most of the actual hunt, I would consider the killing of foxes with hounds to be relatively humane, albeit primitive and anachronistic. Furthermore, the hunts have a strict code of conduct and observe a close season when vixens have dependent offspring. The moral and humanitarian aspects of fox hunting as a sport, however, as with any other blood sport, is another matter.

Whilst I would consider hunting to be more humane than shooting in general, hunting with horse and hounds is not essential as a method of control. If it were necessary to control the numbers of foxes in the better hunting counties and the occupiers were so induced, it could be done more readily, more cheaply and with more permanent results by other methods — especially by the gassing of dens during the breeding season. Elsewhere hunting has little effect upon population size of foxes overall, so it would not be missed from this viewpoint, if it were abandoned. Hunting with hounds could, however, be a more effective method of reducing fox numbers if cubs were hunted from July to September, but for many reasons this is not done, though it used to be practised in the Oakley hunting country in the early 1800s from July onwards (Berkeley, 1854).

Foot packs of hounds generally fulfil a different function. These also are supported by hunting enthusiasts, but they operate over country where other methods of control are not easily applied. The Lake District is well known for its foot packs, and there are several in Wales which also operate over hill country or in and about areas of coniferous woodland. Their aim is to reduce fox numbers in order to prevent or lessen possible damage to lambs, and if indeed this is necessary, hunting with foot packs can be an important ancillary method of control.

Gassing of dens is not always feasible in hill country, especially if they are located in boulders and scree, and the method of trapping that used to be practised on hill land in Scotland (described below) was not favoured in England and Wales, except by Scottish gamekeepers. Terriers are used to bolt foxes driven to ground by hounds, and during the fox breeding season terrier handlers visit likely cubbing dens. But in late autumn and winter, when itinerant foxes which mostly live on the surface are about, hounds offer a more effective method of coming to grips with foxes than terriers. Foot packs are hunted regularly and the hunt often involves really hard work over rugged country.

Foot packs of hounds are not used in Scotland, nor are mounted hunts numerous there. In anticipation of control problems that would arise with the banning of the gin in 1973, a Cumberland pack of hounds was tried in a wooded area of Scotland. Whether or not this method will find widespread favour there remains to be seen.

Another method which is becoming more widely practised in some hill sheep-rearing areas is the use of hounds to drive foxes to waiting guns. Extensive areas of coniferous plantations cannot be successfully hunted with horses and hounds and other methods of control which may be applicable are time-consuming and are not usually accomplished through the co-operative efforts of groups or occupiers. Gunmen are usually available to participate in shoots, but because many plantations are so large, the impact of this method of control on the local fox population depends to a large extent upon the topography and the support of gunmen. The method can be successful, however, or can at least produce apparently successful results in blocks of woodland and overgrown dingles and valleys up to about 40 hectares in extent. In some areas hounds are also used to drive foxes on open hill land. In these cases marksmen – if this is the correct term for men with shotguns – are usually located near prominent sheep paths or tracks leading away from the areas to be driven or on the fringe of nearby woodland.

### Snares
Steel-wire snares for taking foxes in the open have been used by gamekeepers for many years, and the method is becoming increasingly popular in sheep-rearing areas. It is widely used in Scotland, Wales, Devon and Cornwall, but I have little information on its use elsewhere in England, except that it is still favoured by gamekeepers.

Snares are set mainly on fox runs in fences, hedges and forest rides or in overgrown dingles or thickets. Flexible multi-stranded cable is used; the sliding loop may be free-running or of a non-return, locking type. Rarely is a 'stopped' snare used. Foxes caught in snares may be strangled, but usually they are alive if the snares are not set against fences and are visited before noon daily. It is widely considered that the lock–type snare is more humane, but evidence is accumulating to indicate that foxes caught in these in the open, where they do not become tangled up in fences or branches, suffer more than those found alive in free-running snares. It used to be believed that the shorter the wire attaching the snare to the anchor peg, the less the damage inflicted on the fox, since its movements were more restricted. The optimum length of wire is now considered to be about two metres in any open area. This provides some freedom of movement, and less damage is done to the fox in its effort to escape. However, much will depend upon the location of the snare. Foxes snared on a fence line are often found dead, having been strangled after jumping over the fence; and in a forest or hedge the fox often strangles itself if it twists the snare wire round a tree or other obstruction. Sometimes snares are deliberately not anchored firmly to a hedge, fence, tree or peg but are attached to a small log or fallen branch, which the snared fox will drag sometimes hundreds of metres until it becomes tangled in hedge, fence or undergrowth. The steel wire is less likely to break when attached to some movable object.

In a series of field investigations by the Humane Traps Panel on the humanitarian aspects of snaring (comparing free-running with locking snares) clocks attached to snares permitted the time when the fox entered the snare to be determined. Veterinarians examined the snared foxes, most of which were alive (irrespective of the type of snare), and surprisingly found that bodily injury or mutilation was slight. Those held in locking snares were in a semi-moribund condition because their breathing was restricted. However, these snares were set in forest rides, where there was more freedom of movement for the snared fox and little chance of the sort of self-inflicted damage which occurs when foxes are caught in fences or hedges. It seems that careful siting of snares can reduce injury, but few people setting snares are aware of this aspect, their concern is to set snares in places where foxes are most likely to be caught.

In addition to the siting of snares, infrequent inspections of them can cause unjustifiable and prolonged suffering, and this is the major criticism of the method and its use. On a small property snares can be and usually are visited daily, but only too often in other situations snares are visited sporadically or at very infrequent intervals, for a variety of reasons. Daily visits to snares are a legal requirement. Flexible high-tensile stranded wire, such as Bowden Steel Cable, is the only type of steel wire suitable for snaring, but other types of wire are sometimes mistakenly used. Snares made of single-stranded fence wire, copper wire and multi-stranded electric wire break at the point of twisting and the fox escapes with a lethal, tightly twisted noose round its neck, shoulder or loins. Flexible high-tensile wire is essential, otherwise the snare may break when twisted and remain firmly attached around the fox's neck or other parts of the body. Snares fitted with swivels lose their advantage in this respect when set near fences or hedges.

In general terms, snaring is responsible for a considerable amount of suffering, partly because of the method but often because of the irresponsible attitudes of those setting snares. The use of knotted or stopped snares, which will prevent the noose from drawing tight on the animal's neck, or of snares with a strap or cushioning sleeve round the length which will come in contact with the neck should be investigated. Stopped snares offer a distinct advantage as far as the accidental capture of some other animals is concerned. Not infrequently, deer and sheep are accidentally caught by the foot in fox snares set in the open, but stopped snares will prevent the noose from drawing tight and the animal will not be held by its foot (cattle and horses will be held, however). If fox snares are set where deer are found, it is good practice to place a stick or branch across the run about half a metre away from the snare to encourage deer to jump over it. Neck sizes of adult foxes weighing between 4.5kg and 9kg range from 175mm to 280mm in circumference, and the stop should be fitted 280mm from the end.

Snaring, even with stopped snares, is also indiscriminate. Though care may be taken to avoid setting snares on obvious badger runs, badgers are frequently caught, and since wire cutters are not usually carried by the snarer and because there is some risk of being bitten, captive badgers are usually killed. The indiscriminate nature of snaring can be illustrated by two examples. In Breconshire, where thirty snares (visited twice daily) were set for forty-eight nights, four foxes, eleven badgers (alive) and one dog were captured; in addition, one fox and three badgers escaped with snares attached to them. In Pembrokeshire 270 snares were set for sixty days; 102 foxes and fourteen badgers were caught; four of these badgers were dead. In both cases the setting of snares on obvious badger runs was avoided and snares were not placed in the vicinity of known badger setts.

Snaring should not be undertaken lightly. It imposes the responsibility of visiting snares daily, even if they have not been successful for days or weeks. Though dogs are captured occasionally in fox snares, they usually come to little harm, since the dog tends to stay put without struggle.

More and more snares for foxes are being used each year, and it is only a matter of time before public awareness of the suffering that snares can cause will promote a clamour for their banishment. In turn this will direct critical attention towards alternative methods of control, towards the humanitarian aspects of fox control, the economics of fox damage and the protection of susceptible prey. Current high fox-pelt values, although they have caused more foxes to be snared, do to some extent alleviate suffering because the snarer, concerned with the quality of the pelt, will visit his snares frequently and regularly!

## Traps

Metal leg-hold traps are a comparatively recent innovation and are based on the principle of ancient spiked wooden gins, activated by torsion springs either of rope or sinew. The jaws of the old gins were kept apart by a small piece of wood delicately poised so that the trap would be sprung when it was dislodged by the foot of a passing animal. Olaus Magnus (1555) mentions a trap known as a *pedica*, which may have been similar to the spiked wooden gin traps. The traps mentioned in some of the versions of *Reynard the Fox* and those mentioned by Gaston Phoebus, a fourteenth-century French huntsman, fit this description. These may have been derived from the ancient but ingenious wooden valved traps which, depending on the method of setting, could be used for many mammal species, but probably would have been baited for foxes and wolves. Such a trap was found in an Irish peat bog in 1859 and was estimated to date from the late Bronze Age. However, there is evidence from a carved stone – the Clonmacnois cross, depicting a deer with its foot in such a trap – that this was in use in Ireland as late as AD 700–800 and, based on other evidence, in Poland and Hungary in the late Middle Ages (Berg, 1950–1).

Later a live-capture trap, constructed of stone, was used for foxes in at least two areas in Britain – in Yorkshire, where the trap was known as 'kist', and in Breconshire where it was referred to as a 'wych', (see Figure 26). If a fox were located in a hole in rock, all holes except one were blocked and the stone chest was constructed over it. The tunnel was about 300mm long internally; a third of the way along a heavy slate was so fastened that it could slide down and block the chest and cut off the retreat of the fox. This slate was held by a cord which was attached to a stick fitted to a ring at the window, and when this was dislodged by the fox the slate fell and imprisoned it. (Topsel describes a beehive trap designed for use against foxes, but I am not clear of the method of operation.)

The old vermin traps found in Dartmoor described by Cook (1964) were of such a size that they could have been intended to catch foxes as well as smaller predators. These traps, made of dressed stone (about 1m long by 255mm high by 130mm wide internally), were located near rabbit warrens and sited with funnelling approach walls as much as 3.5 metres long. As Cook suggested, they seem to have been designed for catching the smaller predators which shun open spaces, and probably went out of use before 1800.

Peter Beckford (1810) refers to catching cubs by 'tunning' them: this method simply consists of digging a deep trench outside the main entrance to the earth. The cubs fall in when they emerge and are unable to climb out. This was a fox poacher's method (cubs being poached from one hunt area to be sold to another) and also one which my biologist friend Birger Jensen has used in Denmark for capturing cubs for tagging.

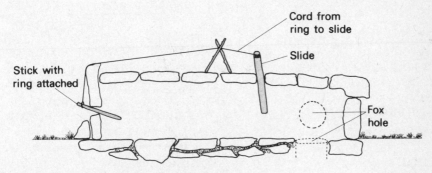

**26**  Diagrammatic section of a Kist or Wych fox trap

In North America Storm and Dauphin (1965) have used a 'wire ferret' for evicting foxes and skunks from their earths. This consists of a length of spring-steel wire 6.7m long, cranked at one end like a car starting handle and fitted at the other end with a tightly coiled 300mm-long spring with a wooden plug at its end. This is inserted into the hole and wound into it. Storm found that foxes were flushed quite easily by the use of this tool. Three out of thirty foxes captured were accidentally dragged out of their earths because the wire became entangled in the fox's fur — which reminds one of the briar or bramble sometimes employed by countrymen to extract foxes and rabbits from their holes.

CAGE TRAPS   As a general rule, cage traps are hopelessly ineffective as a method of reducing the fox population significantly. They may sometimes (but not usually) be of use in the vicinity of poultry houses or game-rearing enclosures, and they achieve most success in suburban gardens. This is not to say that foxes cannot be caught in cage traps, but the results are usually disappointing. The mechanical design and size of traps practicable for control purposes is relatively unimportant, as it has been shown in field trials that foxes will generally avoid entering baited open-ended wire cages (without any trapping mechanisms attached). In

Sweden a large wooden trap made from forest thinnings, four metres long by one metre square, is commonly used to take foxes in woodland areas. These traps are not portable, and although bait is sometimes used, it is the usual practice to encourage small rodents to live beneath the trap by providing hay and grain for them. The fox is attracted to these traps in winter, when up to a metre of snow covers the ground, and at this time they are fairly successful. Hunters must consider these traps to be useful, otherwise they would not be used.

Cage traps about 1m by 30mm by 300mm, with flap-type doors but without any spring mechanism, can sometimes be used successfully to catch cubs. The trap entrances are firmly pushed into the entrance burrow and cubs will enter them as they emerge in the evenings. Such traps, of slightly larger size and of stronger construction, are also effective for young and – occasionally – adult badgers. However, these traps are not likely to be of use as a method for controlling foxes in Britain.

GIN TRAPS   Gin traps were primarily a gamekeeper's tool when used for fox control. In hunting areas where the gamekeeper (whose primary function was to foster large numbers of birds for shooting), in accordance with the occupier's wish to preserve some foxes for hunting, intended not to capture foxes, gins were set for small vermin either without being concealed, or concealed but were reset every day. Cats, stoats and weasels would fall victim to such settings but rarely the fox, reputedly because human smell remains strong on traps handled daily or set without a cover of soil or vegetation. In Scotland the regular use of gin traps for foxes by hill shepherds was more common than elsewhere in Britain.

The gin was an extremely versatile instrument (the 12.5cm size was favoured). It could be set almost anywhere where one suspected that a fox would pass, and foxes could be attracted to it by lures or baits. The urine of a vixen was considered to be one of the most attractive lures, especially in January. Throughout most of England and Wales the gin was not used regularly for fox control (except by rabbit trappers), the method usually being reserved for occasions when an offending fox had to be caught.

In Scotland, where fox control over vast areas of hill land was considered necessary, the gin trap was used in a water set. Basically, the technique was to select a water-hole in a peat bog or to make a hole two or three metres in diameter and about half a metre deep in suitable wet ground. A pathway of turf was made, leading to a centrally situated island where bait was hidden from the view of winged scavengers. A gin trap was set on one of the stepping places to the island. Foxes attracted by the smell of the bait would use the stepping places to reach it; once caught in the trap, the fox would flounder in the water and if the hole was deep enough, apparently it would quickly drown. The method was developed in order to permit the trapper to maintain a long line of traps, perhaps as much as twenty kilometres long, which was visited at infrequent intervals. By all accounts it seems that few foxes, once caught, escaped from these traps. A water set is also commonly used in North America, where in winter months, when still water if frozen, traps are set in water flowing from springs. The gin is now a thing of the past, having been banned throughout England and Wales since 1958, and Scotland since 1973.

In North America padded gin traps are used by biologists to capture foxes for study purposes (Sheldon, 1949a). Sometimes a textile pad, which has been steeped in a tranquillizer or which contains tranquillizing substances, is attached to the jaws of the trap. Trapped foxes bite at this when caught, relax under the influence of the drug and consequently do not damage themselves in an effort to escape (Balser, 1965). This technique may be related to the Australian method of trapping dingoes, which was similar, except that strychnine was placed on the pad and the dingo poisoned itself after being caught by the trap.

In Britain designs have been sought for a humane fox trap which either holds the fox by the foot without injury or kills the animal outright. No traps in the latter category have been tested, but various leg-hold traps tested extensively in the field have failed to meet the standards of efficiency laid down by the Humane Traps Panel, although from a humanitarian point of view the designs were adequate. One trap – a foot snare – tested in many forms for many years, was based on the Verbail trap invented by Dr Bailey of the US Biological Survey in 1935. It met with little success, though it did not inflict any physical injury on dogs, cats and foxes captured. The leg-hold trap continues in use in North America, but there too alternative humane traps are being sought. A killer trap, known as the Conibear, holds out some promise of success for some of the smaller carnivores, but even if it were effective for the fox, its use would be a hazard to many wild and domestic animals and would hardly be suitable in Britain.

Scent lures have been and are still used in various ways for fox control. Vixen urine is the most common lure used in Britain, but rabbit or poultry offal dragged in a sack has been used to divert a fox towards whatever was laid in store for it. In North America putrid attractants concoted from a mixture of putrifying fish, glycerine and a small quantity of the secretion of the castor gland of beaver are widely used. Such putrid scents are sprinkled on the traps laid for foxes. Valerian and oil of rhodium has also been used as a scent lure.

## Gassing
The gassing of foxes with a cyanide generating powder is without except-

ion the most humane method of killing foxes in their dens. Hydrogen cyanide is a non-irritant, highly toxic gas which kills by blocking the transfer of oxygen from the lungs to the tissues and organs. Its action is so rapid that dogs must not accompany gassing teams because they may dig out a blocked gassed hole. Several dogs, with only their heads in the opened rabbit burrow, have been known to be killed in this way.

However, foxes do not spend much of their time in dens or earths, except when there is no surface cover to provide harbourage for them. The vixen will spend from ten days to three weeks with her cubs after they have been born, and occasionally an adult dog fox will be found as well. At other times of the year, where there is adequate ground cover, foxes will live on the surface in daytime, but prolonged heavy rainfall or long spells of wet weather during the months of October to February inclusive will precipitate a return to ground, and occasionally when foxes are disturbed or pursued they will seek the security of dens or earths. Cubs will live in dens for about ten weeks; thus, for only about ten weeks in the year is gassing possible as an effective method of control. In West Germany and Switzerland it is estimated that a population reduction of up to 50 per cent can be achieved, for purposes of rabies control, by the gassing of dens in areas where foxes breed predominantly in earths. A higher level of control could be achieved if more of the cubbing earths could be found. In an area of Pembrokeshire where foxes were studied in 1972 one earth in eleven contained cubs in April, but in the hill areas of mid-Wales from April to early June only one earth in 80 known or prospective earths contained cubs. The reason for the large discrepancy between the two areas is that in north Pembrokeshire fox earths are few in number, most being less than about fifteen years old (since foxes were scarce before 1958), whereas many of the numerous mid-Wales earths may be of considerable antiquity and more are being excavated every year. The mid-Wales data are also inflated by the occurrences of disused rabbit burrows which have been excavated by foxes at some time or other in recent years, though they may not necessarily have been occupied, and by prospective breeding places in boulders, which are used intermittently for cover. A further bias in the data for mid-Wales is the difficulty in locating earths in conifer plantations between fifteen and twenty years old, where it is known that many litters of cubs are born and reared. (It would be helpful for the purposes of fox control if the areas immediately around the earths in conifer plantations were left unplanted.)

Gassing is not widely practised because those concerned with fox control prefer to have visible evidence and a tally of the number of foxes that they have killed. Furthermore, in fox destruction society areas there is a bounty payment to be had on production of the brush of each fox killed. When the use of the gin trap was legal gassing was not practised because the participants – usually gamekeepers – preferred to have an open earth at which they could set traps regularly, outside or just within the overhang of the burrow, and in this way intercept any stray or immigrant foxes in the area. The tracking of foxes in snow, which has shown that foxes may visit earths often without entering them, suggests that this was probably sound practice.

## Bolting foxes from earths

Foxes will bolt from earths very readily if given a chance. Most terrier handlers are unable to call their terriers out of earths, and consequently the cornered fox may be unable to escape; in a very large number of cases the spade has to be used to reach the fox, or to encourage the terrier to retreat and enable the fox to bolt. If the terrier can be persuaded to come out without too much vocal interference by the handler, the fox will usually bolt within a minute or two; if there has been a great deal of disturbance, the fox may not bolt for some time. It can easily be caught in purse nets at the burrow entrance or shot as it flees from the den. Done quietly, with obedient terriers and two alert gunmen, the method is quick and humane. Unfortunately, tenacious killer terriers are favoured, and this often leads to much savagery below ground, where the fox is virtually baited by the terriers, which themselves often suffer injury.

Foxes will not bolt as readily in large earths or badger setts, and in many such cases it may be necessary to re-enter the terrier and to keep it below ground until the fox eventually bolts. Aerosol sprays, of almost any kind used around the house or garden, sprayed into some of the holes of the smaller dens will sometimes persuade foxes to bolt. The merest whiff of something alien to the den is enough. Vixens with cubs will also occasionally bolt after someone has walked heavily over the earth. Cubs of three to six weeks old can sometimes be enticed from their holes – usually shortly before dark – with panting sounds and gentle taps on the ground at the entrance to the earths. On some occasions cubs emerge from the earths when terriers investigate the entrances quietly before moving into them.

Artificial earths have been used by hunts to further sport and by gamekeepers and others to increase the effectiveness of their control efforts. There is no standard pattern to these earths. Some may be simple tunnels constructed of stone, sometimes 100 metres long and with a series of entrances at about ten-metre intervals. The more usual kind is much smaller – Y-shaped, with two entrances and a chamber at the blind end. Sometimes a chamber may have an inspection lid. They are usually constructed of stone, on a slight slope, but with an earth floor sloping gently downwards from the chamber to the entrances. Usually the construction is sunk into the ground and covered with soil. Some gamekeepers have taken considerable pains to provide inspection covers to natural earths. Terriers are introduced at the entrance of these earths, and, if they are occupied, the fox may retreat to the lidded area where it can be shot. Foxes have been known to bolt from rabbit warrens when a ferret has been introduced, but this behaviour may be a response not so much to the ferret as to human presence above ground.

Terriers are also used to evict foxes from heaps of boulders and scree and from rocky outcrops. Here it is often necessary to encourage the terriers to stay below ground, since the foxes may have plenty of room to manoeuvre; under these circumstances bolted foxes have to be shot, as it is not usually possible to set purse nets.

In some areas it has been the practice to use large lurchers or greyhounds to run down foxes bolted by terriers. Whilst the fox may often be brought down within fifty metres of the earth, unless the hounds are strong and fearless they are frequently unable to kill the fox quickly and the method is decidedly inhumane. Fortunately, it is not commonly used.

**Control of suburban foxes**
The methods described earlier are all suitable for rural situations, but the use of hounds, for example, with or without horsemen, would hardly be appropriate in suburbia. There is, it seems, a need to reduce the numbers of foxes in some suburban areas, if only to placate those residents who complain. Control is usually in the hands of the local authorities, which may or may not have an official fox catcher. Within urban areas it may be possible to drive foxes to guns – on railway embankments or other open spaces – but the method appropriate to most urban areas is to locate the vixen and cubs during the breeding season and to dig them out, or to bolt them to nets or guns, or to use cyanide gas. Snaring is not appropriate in suburbia but, as indicated earlier, cage traps can sometimes, and in the right hands, be effective.

At present the fox is only a nuisance in urban areas, but it could attract the attention of those concerned with public and animal health if it ever became significant in the transmission of disease to man or his pets.

## The Effect of Control on Fox Populations

How many foxes are killed annually in Britain for sport and for control purposes? Southern (1964) has indicated that the number is probably 50,000. This may well be an underestimate, as in most years since 1965 about 22,000 foxes are known to have been killed by fox destruction societies and by the Forestry Commission alone. In addition, mounted and foot-pack hunts kill several thousands and the number of foxes killed by other agencies, gamekeeprs and farmers and others is considerable. Increasing pelt values have also promoted a more determined pursuit of foxes in many areas of Britain – even, I understand, by private individuals in suburban areas — so that in 1978, 100,000 foxes killed is probably a more realistic minimum figure. The interpretation of data for foxes killed by fox destruction societies from about 1976 onwards will probably be of dubious reliability as a relative indicator of numbers of foxes at risk of being killed, because henceforth many more foxes killed in society areas will be pelted rather than submitted for bounty, and there is no means of knowing whether or not the proportion of the total treated in either way is steady from one year to another.

If this estimate of foxes killed is related to the total area of England, Scotland and Wales, it represents one fox (cubs, juvenile or adult) killed per 229.5 hectares. Since there is a considerable area of hill land in Scotland where fox population densities are very low, and fox disperal is not uniform elsewere in Britain, this figure is meaningless when applied to particular areas. If, however, for the purposes of estimating the likelihood of 100,000 killings annually it were assumed that no foxes were killed on half of the total area of England, Scotland and Wales, the figure would represent one fox killed per 114.5 hectares. In average to good fox habitats this annual take-off of foxes could easily be maintained, and I believe that even 100,000 foxes killed may be a lowish estimate at the present time.

Records or estimates of the numbers of foxes killed are available for other countries. In Western Australia the largest number killed for bounty in any year was 55,000 (Crawford and Veitch, 1959); in France, 95,000 in 1967 (Bougerol, 1968); and in Sweden some 80,000 foxes are killed annually (Englund, pers. comm.). The numbers of foxes known to have been killed in different parts of Europe and North America are shown in Table 31.

It is very difficult to estimate exactly what advantage is gained by the killing of foxes without being able to quantify the extent of damage before control began and after it has been under way for some years. In sheep-rearing areas the killing of foxes (except to relieve particular circumstances) may not materially alter the extent of lamb losses, and unless a large proportion of the population is removed over a large area, control will certainly not have any significant effect on the overall population size.

Some of the questions relevant to control that need to be answered are: are natural mortality and mortality resulting from control additive? Does fox control, carried out locally at different times of the year, have a lasting effect on the population size in each locality, or does immigration and an increase in the survival rates of young and old animals maintain an even distribution and a steady number of foxes? If control efforts significantly depress populations locally, does the fox population respond to artificially reduced population densities by compensatory increase in the level of reproduction, and do the offspring subsequently enjoy a higher natural survival rate? At what level of fox-population density would farmers cease to complain about lamb damage? Does the killing of foxes at cubbing time aggravate lamb losses? Most of these questions could be answered satisfactorily if it were possible to manipulate population densities for study purposes in different habitats, without pressure from occupiers and others to control fox numbers. Without such facilities, inferences have to be made from a knowledge of the biology of the fox.

One of the features of the life history of the fox which needs to be restated in any consideration of such problems is that populations of any species do not expand without limit. So far as the fox is concerned, the ultimate limiting factor is the availability of food, but this restraint may operate only in populations not subject to reduction in numbers by man, by epidemic disease or by other catastrophes. Even in populations undisturbed by man, however, food supply may not be critical throughout the year, and numbers may be limited by food availability in winter and early spring only.

A shortage of food, as such, is unlikely to limit numbers of adults directly through starvation, and in populations of high density its effect is likely to be experienced directly or indirectly through social stress, reduced levels of reproduction and lower survival rates of cubs and juveniles. In areas where foxes are few and represent the maximum the area can support the survival of cubs and their emigration – rather than reproductive success – may have greater effects on population levels. The number of foxes found in different environments does not necessarily represent the number that the habitat can support because the variable extent and the timing of interference by man can have a considerable influence upon numbers at different times of the year.

Competition for food between foxes begins at birth, the strongest or most adaptable cubs getting more than equal shares of food, be it milk or, later, solids. If food is abundant, the weaker or least adaptable might not suffer, as competition affects weak animals adversely only when food is short. Competition for space and food among old adult animals may leave sub-adults or yearlings less well off and unable to breed, as Englund (1970) observed in Sweden in poor food years, but whether or not social behaviour and a hierarchical structure among adult foxes are sufficient to impair breeding capacity among certain individuals under conditions of stress (as with populations of wild rabbits) is not known.

Compensatory reproduction and survival rates (inversely proportional to population densities) are common phenomena among animal species. If a species has room to expand in a favourable environment, it can respond – within limits – by increased reproductive output. The survival of juveniles (and perhaps of adults) is generally enhanced by favourable conditions, and accumulating evidence suggests that the fox is no exception in this respect. Consequently 'artificial' mortality by man's control activities will produce seasonal and localized reductions in fox numbers, which might not necessarily effect any lasting reduction in numbers at a given level of control, but the demonstration of clear evidence of this, as with the identification and interrelations of factors influencing the natural regulation of numbers is very difficult.

One of the most problematic aspects of the study of foxes over large areas is the estimation of numbers at different times of the year; consequently, the examination of the effects of control over wide areas becomes somewhat hypothetical, perhaps without relation to reality in many instances. For example, it is simple enough to take an arbitrary figure for population density just prior to the birth of cubs, and from this to estimate the potential population size after breeding. But in order to simulate reality, it is then necessary to know, in sheep-rearing areas, for instance, the number and proportion of all litters of cubs killed by man during the two months following the births of the first litters, the numbers and proportions of juveniles and adults killed thereafter, say from November to March, and the numbers of immigrant animals that have moved into the area.

Lack of knowledge about the effects of control exercised during the period of birth and during the autumn and winter precludes comparisons between one area and another. Different degrees of control at these two times of the year may greatly influence the overall number of foxes at different times of the year, even if the pre-breeding population size remains much the same each year. Figure 27 shows the hypothetical effect of control on a population which is of moderate density in March.

In (a) no cubs are killed and the mortality of cubs is entirely due to natural causes – a situation obtaining in many sporting hunt areas. In September and October there is an abundance of juveniles to be hunted, and the return for effort is very high initially, becoming progressively less rewarding in terms of numbers killed as the season progresses. In (b) 50 per cent of cubs are killed in the breeding season. There are fewer juveniles and adults in the autumn and the return for the same effort as in (a) is less. In (c) 75 per cent of cubs are killed and the return for the same effort as (a) in the autumn is low.

The success of control by available methods is density-dependent, that is, the numbers killed as a proportion of foxes at risk of being killed is greater at high population densities, and in (a), (b) and (c) it is 57 per cent, 45 per cent and 35 per cent respectively. If the return for effort were independent of density and the same proportion of foxes at risk were killed at all times, fox numbers could very easily be reduced to low

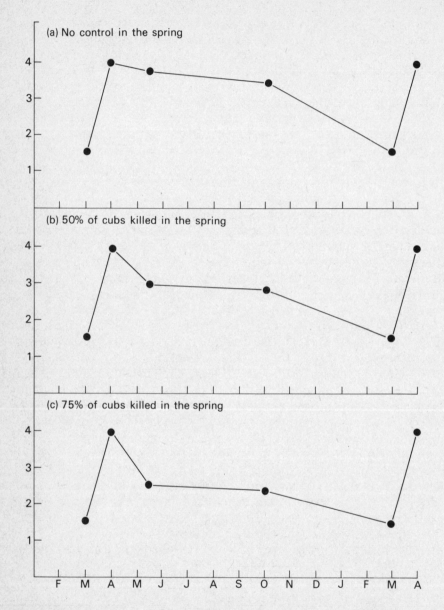

**27** Hypothetical patterns of fox numbers in populations of steady size in March. (a) No control in the spring; (b) 50% of cubs killed in the spring; (c) 75% of cubs killed in the spring.

numbers, simply by maintaining the same effort. In a density-dependent situation, however, the effort has to be increased as the numbers at risk dwindle, if the proportion killed is to be constant.

In each of the three situations demonstrated in the figure the results of control on the number of foxes alive in the following March/April period is the same but, depending upon the time when control is applied, there would be considerable differences in numbers of foxes at other times of the year. The situation represented by (a) is not atypical of hunt areas where foxes are mainly tolerated. If in such areas the numbers of foxes in the autumn are so high that sport is likely to be impaired, cubs can be and are killed in August and September, or if not killed, are persuaded to disperse. At the same time the hunting appetites of the hounds are whetted for the hunting season proper. Fox hunters with whom I have discussed the number of foxes optimum for sport are not all agreed that a large number of foxes is favourable.

So far as the sheep industry is concerned damage is seasonal, and if the extent of loss is related to numbers of foxes, the timing of control should be determined by the time of year when lambs are susceptible. In lowland areas where lambs may be born before cubs this should be prior to the fox breeding season, but in hill areas, where births of lambs and cubs tend to coincide, control at the time of birth of cubs might be more appropriate; however, the timing of fox control to coincide with the anticipated period of lamb damage may be misconceived. In sheep-rearing areas foxes have been killed at or about the lambing season perhaps for centuries, and the disruption of the family units of foxes at that time may exacerbate losses. The killing of one of a pair of foxes rearing a litter may cause the other to turn to more readily available food resources, such as lambs. If this, as many believe, is true, the killing of foxes should not be undertaken between the time of birth of the earliest litters and about ten weeks later. It is very difficult to disentangle the effects of control on lamb loss from the fox's inclination to take lambs under more natural conditions, and opportunities to study this aspect of fox behaviour by the experimental manipulation of field situations have not been available. The untimely killing of foxes over widespread areas in this context needs investigation.

In rabies-endemic areas the peak number of instances of rabies in foxes occurs in the winter/early spring pre-breeding and breeding population, with a reduction in prevalence from May to September. The disease is maintained by the summer population, of which as many as 70 per cent may be juveniles, and clearly the chain of rabies transmission would be less effective where a high proportion of cubs are killed than where efforts are concentrated against the autumn/winter population. Furthermore, if rabies kills between 20 per cent and 60 per cent of the population, as is usual, the hunters would find their return for effort diminishing at a much faster rate than could be attributed to their efforts — with a consequent slackening of hunting incentive and impetus at the very time when it should be increasing. Thus, the effort to kill cubs in continental Europe, as the main method of rabies control in foxes, seems to be well conceived, but it seems likely that an insufficient number of litters are destroyed.

Timing and the incentive to kill foxes determines patterns of abundance throughout the year and leads to all sorts of complexities. If, for example, in hill sheep-rearing areas the accent changes from the killing of foxes for bounty (which includes cubs and, in some areas, a special premium on breeding vixens) to the killing of foxes for pelts only, a situation approximating (a) in Figure 25, where many litters need to be fed, could result, but if the incentive is sufficiently strong to increase effort in the autumn, the population could fall below that at which full recovery to the usual post-breeding numbers could occur. Compensatory reproductive output might offset this, however, if the breeding population has not been drastically reduced. If a free-for-all situation exists, where foxes are exploited for pelts rather than cropped at the best time of year for pelting and cubs are also killed at the lambing period, a haphazard, indeterminate pattern could emerge. Whether or not a change in incentive, prevalent at the present time, will have any effect on the extent of lamb loss is another imponderable matter. (All the foregoing remarks refer to large areas where immigration would not influence results. As mentioned elsewhere, because of the dispersal of juveniles, the autumn/winter killing of foxes over small areas surrounded by areas where little is done can account for many more foxes than the area can support.)

Although there is a lack of information about the effects of control on fox numbers in particular cases, a persistently high degree of control annually would obviously have a permanent effect on the fox population in general, and the question is whether the present level of control and its timing is sufficient to achieve this. Although the fox shows considerable reproductive resilience in response to local situations, there is a comparatively low upper limit to the production of young; thus, though it may respond appropriately to artificially decreased densities, the fox population cannot increase beyond a certain threshold, whereas control effort can be increased enormously. In practice, control, or cropping, does not proceed at the same pace throughout the season of control and the degree of effort required to remove 50 per cent of autumn foxes in any particular situation will be considerably less than the effort required to reduce the remaining 50 per cent by half again by traditional or currently employed control methods. Those concerned about the number of foxes killed for pelts at present and in the future may be reassured by the fact that in good mixed habitat with abundant cover the fox is likely to be able to withstand considerable pressure before being relegated to the status of an uncommon mammal. The only worry is that unlawful means of killing foxes for pelts, used only on a small scale today, may become common if competition between skinners intensifies.

At the present time it is difficult to generalize about the effects of bounties upon fox numbers. In general I believe that well supported and well organized societies can maintain the winter/early spring numbers of foxes below that which would obtain in the absence of bounties, but there is no evidence firm enough to permit even an informed guess about the general (as opposed to local) effects upon the extent of lamb damage of such reductions as are apparently achieved. A patchy distribution of societies, or a patchy distribution of vigilant societies among a large block of less effective ones, may have little effect on numbers of foxes because annual dispersal from the least effective areas to the vacuum in the effective areas might simply top up the levels of breeding animals each year.

So far, this consideration of the effects of control has concerned itself with the motives and methods of individuals who stand to gain by the number of foxes killed. Persons employed specifically for pest control can maintain their effort whatever the level of population, and are consequently successful in reducing populations to lower levels than those whose efforts slacken with decreasing success.

## Control of Damage

Poultry losses can be prevented by adequate housing at night, but little short of killing the offending fox will stop daylight losses of free-range poultry, unless one is prepared to erect high protective fences.

Apart from better husbandry, with a view to producing stronger lambs and, more important, well nourished ewes at the lambing period, damage by foxes could be considerably reduced by keeping lambing ewes under cover, since most losses occur when lambs are under twenty-four hours of age. Lambing in pens close to buildings is a practice which is gaining in popularity, but neither this nor lambing under cover are primarily intended as anti-predator expedients.

A common practice is to rub a sheep-marking fluid (Jeyes Fluid or Stockholm tar) on new-born lambs. This is said to reduce losses, and so it may indirectly, since the shepherd has to visit his flock regularly, and by handling the lambs he can tell if they are weak or abandoned and can take appropriate action. Since close attention will increase survival rates among lambs, even if foxes are absent, the marking technique reflects good management rather than the usefulness of these fox 'repellents'. In other places flashing amber lamps, bird-scaring aluminium strips, white pillow cases or cloths on poles are sometimes used in lambing fields.

These devices, which are of uncertain efficacy when left in fields for a long while, seem to have the effect of deterring foxes for a few nights after they have been placed in position. (It might be better if the various devices were used alternately rather than concurrently.) Some farmers spray turpentine, diesel oil or paraffin round the headlands of lambing fields, but there is no evidence that this has any repellent effect upon foxes, and proprietary brands of repellents, which shall be nameless, are of doubtful efficacy.

Faeces of the cougar and the coyote were found to be effective localized repellents for black-tailed deer (Muller-Schwarz, 1972); the fox might be similarly deterred by a natural product which has some atavistic significance as a danger signal. The most hopeful developments in the field of repellents are investigations into the scent secretions of foxes and their function, if any, in the maintenance of territorial integrity. (Reports that fox faeces have a strong repellent effect on rats have not been confirmed.)

Where it is possible to bring ewes to lambing paddocks electric fences are an effective deterrent. An ordinary wire-netting fence 1.20m high, with a strand of electric fence situated 0.5m from it about 30cm high on the outer side, will deter most foxes. The wire-netting fence need not be fixed rigidly, and short-circuiting of the electric fence must be prevented by keeping grass short beneath it. Alternatively, a low wire-netting fence 60cm high with a single strand of electric wire 10cm from the top of the fence at an outward angle, but preferably with two strands 10cm apart, will deter foxes. Such a fence has been successfully used in north America to protect nests of ground-nesting birds (Sargeant *et al.*, 1974).

For pheasant poults a permanent enclosure should have wire netting about 2 m high, with an overhanging portion about 0.5m wide facing outwards at right angles to the top. Three strands of wire should be placed at an angle of about 60° to the ground, with the lower wire about 60cm from the fence. The middle strand of the three should be earthed and the upper (60cm from ground level) and lower ones should be live. Sometimes a single strand of electrified wire about 30cm above ground level and 0.5m from the wire enclosure is effective. An alternative method (which can also be used in sheep paddocks) is to erect a fence with a single strand of live wire about 15cm above it.

A last word on this topic: though many have complaints, real and imaginary, against the fox, and many pursue it in one way and another for one reason or another, I believe few would wish the fox to disappear from the country scene.

# 8

# Parasites and Diseases

Little is known of the diseases of foxes in Britain. Whilst there are many records of disease and parasites in individuals or in small samples of foxes, and a few instances of dramatic local outbreaks of disease, most information comes from a small sample of foxes examined by Blackmore (1964b) and a larger sample by Ross and Fairley (1969). These and other workers have recorded the pathological conditions found, but the prevalence and possible effects of disease upon the population dynamics of foxes in Britain are largely unknown.

Whilst parasites and diseases of wild foxes command the consistent interest of parasitologists, ecologists and others, only those parasites and diseases which are of importance to the health of man and his domestic animals receive special and detailed study from time to time. Consequently, there is considerable bias in the literature towards only a few diseases, some of which may be of little importance to the fox (for example, the tapeworm *Echinococcus*), while others, such as rabies, can have direct and indirect effects upon the abundance of foxes. This chapter will be concerned mainly with diseases of this nature, but will not be confined entirely to foxes in the British Isles.

The diseases of wild foxes were of more widespread interest when silver foxes were bred for their fur. Ranches were securely fenced to prevent wild foxes from making contact with, and possibly transmitting infection to, their caged brethren, especially at mating time, when the calls of vixens attracted neighbouring wild foxes. Whilst little effort was made to determine which diseases were likely to be transmitted by wild foxes, commercial interests paid considerable attention to ranched animals, with the result that a great deal is known of the diseases of foxes in captivity.

Doubtless many of the congenital and physiological disorders described for captive foxes occur in wild foxes also, but, the frequency of occurrence among farmed foxes is not relevant to wild populations. Selective breeding, inactivity and crowded conditions (by comparison with those of wild foxes) are all conducive to increased susceptibility to disease.

## Parasites

### Ectoparasites

MITES   Some external parasitic conditions were well known in ancient times. The Greeks knew of mange in foxes, and the condition alopecia, or fox-evil, in man is derived from the Greek *alopex*, a fox. This disease has been familiar to huntsmen since the middle of the eighteenth century, when fox hunting became popular. The earliest references to fox diseases in modern literature all refer to mange (Peter Beckford wrote of it in 1810, for example) and whilst large-scale outbreaks may not have been frequent, the disease apparently caused much concern because fox populations were sometimes severely reduced. Gerald Lascelles (1915) mentions a great epidemic of mange which began in 1895 and ranged over 'almost all of England' for three years. It spread to his area of special interest, the New Forest, where, according to him, even badgers were 'woefully affected'. But hunting of foxes continued until the supply of foxes began to fail, and it was feared that the 'great scarcity of foxes' which was earlier reported by the Lord Warden of the New Forest in 1789 was about to recur. Within ten years of the 1895 outbreak foxes were plentiful again. Mange may not always have been correctly diagnosed, however. The symptoms, as understood by the modern huntsman, implicate mange but there may have been other causes for losses of large patches of fur – the condition of so-called 'mangy' foxes.

Mange in foxes can be caused by two species of mite, *Sarcoptes scabiei* and *Notoedres notoedres*. Both species burrow into the superficial layers of skin and a scab of dried tissue-fluid exudate is formed, beneath which the mites multiply rapidly. Hair is lost in patches and the skin assumes a dark, encrusted appearance because of the presence of sloughed but unshed epithelial cells. At this stage the characteristic sweet, 'mangy' odour, which may be due to a secondary bacterial infection, becomes evident.

*Sarcoptes scabiei* is the more common causative agent but *Notoedres* sp. may occur more frequently than the literature suggests. (In 1969 several foxes in the suburban area of Cheam, Surrey, were severely affected by *Notoedres*.) Mange infection usually has its focus near or on the tail. It may appear on the rump and progress along the tail and the back to the ventral surface, shoulders and head. Animals with extensive scabious patches are usually underweight. Severely affected animals are listless and exhibit less fear of man – in some cases they can be chased on foot and run down.

Mellanby (1943) has shown that evidence of mite infection can remain for a considerable time after the infection has subsided. Ross and Fairley (1969) cite reports, and have observed themselves, that severely infected foxes tend to seek refuge in their earths rather than lie above ground. It is believed that foxes cannot recover from severe infections.

Fox mange may be confined for ecological reasons to foxes only, but there is circumstantial evidence to support the belief that it may be transmitted from foxes to dogs, and possibly vice versa. A border terrier in Camberley, which had little contact with other dogs, habitually used a fox run passing from a garden to a common. A fox (or foxes) seen several times in the garden was observed to have a bare back and tail, and the dog subsequently developed sarcoptic mange. Both the terrier and the fox used to make their way to the common by passing beneath a very low chestnut paling fence, and in pushing through both animals scraped their backs on the lower edges of the railings, which developed a dark, greasy appearance. Unfortunately, the palings were not examined by a parasitologist, so the evidence for cross-infection in this way remains circumstantial.

Some biologists consider mange to have a considerable adverse influence on fox population sizes, especially when foxes become numerous. Linhart (1960) cites an instance where mange effected an 80 per cent reduction in fox-population density. In Australia in the 1940–50 period foxes were estimated to have been reduced in number by 80 per cent by sarcoptic mange (Ratcliffe, 1956). Rolls (1969) records that there was little breeding during the time the disease was prevalent. When the disease was rife foxes hung around homesteads to glean whatever scraps they could, even where rabbits were numerous. Rolls suggests that towards the termination of the epizootic, foxes became infected but less severely, and they soon recovered their health and vigour. In Ireland Ross and Fairley examined 584 foxes, 10 per cent of which had marked patchy loss of hair. They were not able to determine the exact proportion suffering from active mange infections, but it was not less that 2.5 per cent and not more than 10 per cent. In Wales out of a sample of over 900 foxes taken from 1966 to 1973 none exhibited a condition resembling mange, but in some areas of Britain, notably the fringes of suburban London and along parts of the Surrey/Sussex border, it has become more prevalent since about 1968, and many infected foxes have been seen in these areas. It has been recorded as prevalent in parts of Glamorganshire in 1974. The sporadic nature of outbreaks of this condition suggest, since the mite could be transmitted readily throughout the fox population, that healthy foxes may be fairly resistant to infection and that the organism gains hold only when the fox population is debilitated by some other disease, by old age, perhaps, and lack of food, or simply by population stress in areas of high fox-population densities.

Stone and his colleagues in North America (1972) reported experiments on the transfer of mange from wild canids to wild and domestic mammals. Sarcoptic mange of red fox origin was successfully transmitted from free-living coyote/dog hybrids to captive red foxes, grey foxes and coyote/dog hybrids, but infection in the grey fox was not persistent. Infection could not be transmitted to raccoons, striped skunks, opossums, cats, rodents and a cotton-tail rabbit. Stone concluded that since sarcoptic mange mites from red foxes were freely interchangeable among red foxes, dogs and wild canid hybrids, the type was *Sarcoptes scabiei*, variety *canis*. The earliest recorded occurrence known to me of sarcoptic mange in wildlife in North America was in 1937 (LeDune), possibly, therefore, it is of very recent origin in North American wildlife. Even in 1898 M'Fadyean showed that sarcoptic mange in the fox was transmissible experimentally. The foxes he examined were obtained during the widespread outbreak at the end of the nineteenth century. Writing in the early years of this century, Millard (1906), who regarded foxes from the standpoint of the game preserver, considered mangy foxes to be more of a nuisance than healthy ones – presumably because in their debilitated condition they were attracted to easy pickings in the game preserves.

Another parasitic mite, *Linguatula serrata* (known as the 'tongue worm' of the dog), a degenerate mite which at first glance resembles a flatworm more than a mite, infects the nasal passages, pharynx, larynx and oesophagus of foxes. It has been found in Germany (Haltenorth, 1938) and twice in Britain, near Oswestry (Watkins and Harvey, 1942) and in Northern Ireland (Griffiths, in Lapage, 1956). It also occurs in the fox in Australia. The fox in Britain may not be the definitive host of this mite.

Beresford-Jones (1961), in a survey of the helminth parasites of British foxes, found mites of *Demodex* species in the faeces of foxes: such hair follicle mites can cause a form of mange, demodectic mange, in many species of mammals, but this form of follicular mange has not been recorded in foxes in Britian. Beresford-Jones also found *Psorergates simplex*, another skin mite, in fox faeces. Probably this and the *Demodex* mite were ingested with prey which were host to the mite.

The relatively harmless harvest mite, the nymph of *Trombicula autumnalis*, has frequently been observed on the ears and eyelids of foxes in September and October, and Watkins and Harvey (1942) have identified *Otodectes cynotis* in a wild fox.

FLEAS   Several species of fleas have been found on foxes, but there is no evidence that the fox has a flea exclusive to itself. Most fleas lay their

eggs in the nest or bedding of the host; the fact that there is no flea specific to foxes may be connected with fox denning behaviour and the
absence usually of a nest or bedding.

Dogs and foxes are recorded as the normal hosts to *Ctenocephalides
canis*, a flea commonly found on foxes. All other fleas found on foxes in
Britain occur as stragglers normally found on other species. Since the
fox is a predator, it is very likely to pick up fleas from a wide range of
prey species and a carefully conducted survey would probably reveal a
lengthy list of flea species acquired in this way. The following fleas have
been recorded on foxes in Britain by Smit (1957a):

|  | Normal host |
|---|---|
| *Pulex irritans* (Linnaeus) 1758 | Man, badger, pig |
| *Archaeopsylla erinacei erinacei* (Bouche) 1835 | Hedgehog |
| *Ctenocephalides canis* (Curtis) 1826 | Dog, fox |
| *Spilopsyllus cuniculi* (Dale) 1878 | Rabbit |
| *Paraceras melis melis* (Walker) 1856 | Badger |
| *Malaraeus penicilliger mustelae* (Dale) 1878 | Microtine rodents (voles) |
| *Monopsyllus sciurorum sciurorum* (Schrank) 1803 | Red squirrel |

In addition to the above, with the exception of *M.s. sciurorum* the following have been recorded from foxes examined by R. J. Page at the Pest
Infestation Control Laboratory, Worplesdon.

|  | Normal host |
|---|---|
| *Ctenocephalides felis felis* (Bouche) 1835 | Cat |
| *Orchopaeus howardi howardi* (Baker) 1895 | Grey squirrel |
| *Nosopsyllus fasciatus* (Bosc) 1800 | Black and brown rat |

Ross and Fairley, in addition to some of the above, recorded the following in Northern Ireland:

|  | Normal host |
|---|---|
| *Dasypsyllus gallinulae gallinulae* (Dale) 1878 | Ubiquitous on birds |
| *Ceratophyllus gallinae gallinae* (Schrank) 1803 | Ubiquitous on birds |

*Chaetopsylla globiceps* (Taschenberg) occurs on foxes on the European
continent, but has not been recorded from the British Isles. *Chaetopsylla
trichosa* (Kohaut) occurs on the badger on the continent and has been
recorded on this species in Scotland. Smit (1957b) has predicted that
both *C. trichosa* and *C. globiceps* will occur on foxes in the British Isles.

In north-east France, Aubert and Beaucournu (1976) found *Ceratophyllus fringillidae*, *Ceratophyllus columbae* and *Ctenophthalamus agyrtes
impavidus* in addition to those fleas found on foxes in Britain (except
*Dasypsyllus gallinulae gallinulae*). These were all regarded as stragglers

from their non-carnivore hosts. *Chaetopsylla globiceps* was abundant on the foxes examined.

TICKS    Arthur (1963) records the following species occurring on foxes:

|  | Normal host |
|---|---|
| *Ixodes ricinus* (Linnaeus) 1758; adults | Sheep |
| *Ixodes hexagonus* (Leach) 1815; adults, nymphs, larvae | Hedgehog |

In addition to these, adult females and nymphs of *Ixodes canisuga* (Johnson) 1849 have been recorded by R. J. Page from foxes from Wales. The fox is a host to *Dermacentor reticulatus* (Fabricius) 1794 in Europe. This tick has been recorded from dogs (Walton, 1918) and cattle (Evans, 1951), in south-west England and in Cardiganshire respectively. *D. reticulatus* was not recorded from any Welsh foxes examined by Page at Worplesdon. Not infrequently *Ixodes* may be found almost completely encapsulated within the dermal layers. These are usually dead. Presumably they have burrowed deep into the skin and been trapped by the swelling of their abdomen after becoming gorged with blood.

In addition to the fox ticks mentioned here, Aubert (1975) found *Ixodes negicallis* and *Ixodes icuminatus* on foxes in France. The occurrence of *I. icuminatus* was considered to be accidental.

LICE    *Trichodectes vulpis* (Denny), the normal host of which is the fox, has been found in Welsh foxes, and by Watkins and Harvey (1942) and Bagnall (1932). *Trichodectes melis* (Fabricius), normally found on badgers, was also found on Welsh foxes.

## Endoparasites

NEMATODES    Helminths found in surveys of the parasites of red foxes are shown in Table 32. (For a world-wide fox host/helminth list see Soulsby, 1965.) Since the practice of importing foxes for hunting from France and elsewhere was once commonplace, internal parasites of Continental foxes may have been introduced in this way. Nevertheless, four species of tapeworm commonly found in France have not yet been identified in British foxes. Of the nematodes listed in the table, *Trichinella spiralis* has probably been subject to more investigation internationally than other nematodes found in carnivores. In Britain, in spite of the many deliberate searches, it has been found in carnivores by three investigating teams only: Oldham and Beresford-Jones (1957) (one infected fox); Corridan and his colleagues (1969), who found three infected foxes out of seventy examined in Eire; and O'Rourke and Verling (1971), who found it in fox hounds. *Trichinella* is common in foxes in most European countries. Gould (1970) observed that its occurrence among foxes is more frequent in mountainous countries.

Trichinosis, the disease caused by this very small nematode, occurs widely in carnivores but is also seen in pigs and, occasionally, man. Ingested larvae hatch and develop into adults in animals consuming infected meat (man is infected usually by eating uncooked, infected pig meat). These adults produce larvae (by ovipary) which migrate into skeletal muscle, settle and produce cysts. The fate of the host depends upon the magnitude of the dose of larvae received on a single or multiple infection. It is a very common parasite of arctic carnivores but is less common in Western Europe; for example, Hörning (1965) found it in only 15 per cent of 228 red foxes examined in Switzerland. It is a serious disease in man, but none of the few outbreaks that have occurred in Britain have been shown to be connected with wild animals, directly or indirectly. In England living larvae of this parasite have been found in rats and pigs by Evans and Lennox (1953); Furnell (1957), Redahan (1967) and Verling (1972) found infected rats in Ireland. An interesting observation concerning *T. spiralis* by Rodonaya (1965) suggests an antagonism between this parasite and *Echinococcus multilocularis* in foxes, such that the presence of either prevents the other becoming established. Nemeseri (1962) suggests that the scavenging habit of the fox encompasses feeding on fox carcases skinned by hunters – a very likely route of infection among foxes.

Hookworms of the genus *Ancylostoma*, species of which are seriously debilitating parasites of dogs and cats but are happily rarely present in domestic animals in Britain, have been identified twice only in Britain, in a wild fox cub taken near Oban (Beresford-Jones 1961), and by Bernard Williams (1976), in a Pembrokeshire fox. Blackmore (1964b) identified eggs of *A. caninum* in wild foxes, but in reporting this mentioned uncertainty about the identification. *Uncinaria stenocephala*, another hookworm commonly found in dogs and cats in Britain, has been found by most workers in a high proportion of foxes examined. This nematode outnumbered all other helminth parasites. In view of its high prevalence, it must be assumed that foxes can tolerate the burden, though infection among ranch foxes is a serious problem, causing death and poor pelt quality if left untreated.

*Toxocara canis* and *Toxascaris leonina*, ascarid nematodes, are commonly found in both dogs and foxes. *Toxocara canis*, as is the case with many other nematode species, can infect offspring before birth. Heavy burdens of this nematode are sometimes found in cubs and may be very harmful. Such animals are usually in very poor condition, but the high number of parasites is possibly the result of other factors which create conditions suitable for *Toxocara*. Once established, however, high parasitic burdens may be a factor of some importance in determining survival rates of juveniles. Cook (1965) found 49 per cent of adult foxes to be infected, but of these only 13 per cent had more than four worms per fox. Not only does a heavy parasitic burden reduce vitality in young animals and lessen resistance to other disorders or infections, but it also renders juveniles less able to compete with litter mates for food collected by their parents.

*Toxocara mystax*, found in domestic and wild cats, has been found in ranched foxes only, in Britain. Cats were often used as foster-mothers on fur farms and undoubtedly this practice promoted such infections in foxes. Conversely, both *T. canis* and *T. mystax* sometimes occur in kittens reared with fox cubs (Watkins and Harvey, 1942). Cook found 12 per cent of foxes to be infected with *Toxascaris leonina*.

Lungworms have not been reported to be a serious infection in wild red foxes, but in North America *Capillaria aerophila* and *Crenosoma semiarmata* were very troublesome on fox fur farms. Watkins and Harvey suggested an inverse relationship between infections by the two lungworms *Capillaria aerophila* and *Crenosoma vulpes*. Heartworms have not been recorded in British foxes, but in North America foxes infected with *Dirofilaria immitis* were found in an area where domestic dogs were infected (Stuht and Youatt, 1972).

TREMATODES (FLUKES)　　The following trematodes are reported by Nicoll (1923) to have been found in wild foxes in Britain: *Alaria alata* (intestine), *Echinostomum melis* (intestine), *Opisthorchis conjunctus* *(bile duct), *Opisthorchis felineus** (gall-bladder), *Pseudamphistomum truncatum** (gall-bladder), *Metorchis albidus* (gall-bladder and liver), *Heterophyes heterophyes* (intestine).

Cook (1965) recorded four trematodes in his survey: *Microphallus similis* †, *Maritrema linguilla*†, *Alaria alata*, *Cryptocotyl lungua**.

Bernard Williams (pers. comm.) found *Echinochasmus perfoliatus* * in west Wales, and *Alaria alata* and *Maritrema linguilla*. The intermediate hosts of *Alaria alata* are snails and tadpoles. *Troglotema acutum*, found in the frontal sinuses of the fox, mink and polecat, occurs in Europe but has not been recorded (possibly not sought) in foxes in Britain, though it has been found in polecats. The final intermediate host is the frog. *Paragonimus kellicotti*, a lung fluke, has been found in foxes in North America (Stuht and Youatt) and dogs in Britain (Nicoll), but there are no records for British foxes.

CESTODES　Tapeworms occur in a high proportion of adult and subadult foxes. As the fox is a carnivore and feeds on a wide range of prey species, it has been exploited, in the evolutionary sense, by a great

---

* *Mollusc and fish intermediate host.*
† *Mollusc and crustacean intermediate host.*

number of endoparasites. It is characteristic of most tapeworms that intermediate or alternate hosts of a different species, sometimes two, are needed to enable the life cycle to be completed. A carnivore with a very restricted prey spectrum would present fewer species of parasites with a chance to exploit the food-chain route of infection, but an animal like the fox, which is opportunist in its feeding behaviour, becomes involved in the life cycle of a greater number of cestodes than a host-specific predatory species.

Though nematodes exploit the food chain, many species can complete their life within the same individual or species. Since so many foxes were once imported from France, it is surprising, as far as cestodes are concerned, that French foxes are apparently host to a greater number of species than British foxes. Weak links in the food chain in Britain may have prevented the life cycle of *Diphylobothrium latum*, for example, from being completed, but the nematode *Ancylostoma caninum* does not require an intermediate host. In evolutionary terms, parasites are as old as the host species, and in this context it is only a very short time ago (6,000 years) that Britain became separated from the Continent. The English Channel, however, would not necessarily be an absolute barrier to infection by parasites, since viable parasite eggs can be transmitted across water by house flies, for example.

The cestode most commonly found in British foxes is *Taenia serialis*. The larval form known as *Multiceps serialis* (formerly *Coenurus serialis*) is a large cyst which used to occur most frequently in rabbits when they were numerous, and sometimes also in hares and squirrels.

*Taenia pisiformis*, although not recorded by Beresford-Jones (1961), is also common in foxes. The larval form, *Cysticercus pisiformis*, is a small bladderworm about the size of a very small pea and is found in the peritoneum of rabbits and hares. This cestode seems to be more successful in its food chain than the text books of parasitology suggest. Bladderworms are found in over 90 per cent of adult rabbits on the island of Skokholm, off Pembrokeshire; dogs are kept off the island and there are no other carnivores. Infected rabbits there have usually between two and six bladderworms, so the incidence of infection in individuals is small. Infection is possibly transmitted by scavenging birds, which may eat pieces of adult tapeworms found in carnivore faeces on the mainland, transport them to the island and void the eggs, which have passed through their gut unharmed. The cysticercus of *T. serialis* used to occur on Skokholm up to 1960 when Fly, the boatman's lurcher, used to visit the island.

Four other species of taeniid worms have been found in foxes in Britain. *Taenia taeniaeformis* found in Northern Ireland by Ross and Fairley (1969) has larval stages in rats, other rodents and rabbits. Its deep penetration of the intestinal wall sometimes perforates it. Its larval stage is unusual since it is segmented and looks like an adult tapeworm. Williams (1976a) found *Taenia ovis* in 1.3 per cent of 149 foxes from west Wales, and both he and Ross and Fairley in Ireland found *Taenia hydatigena* and *Taenia multiceps*.

*Taenia hydatigena*, commonly a tapeworm of dogs which grows to a length of five metres, has its larval stage in the peritoneum of sheep, goats, cattle and pigs. *Taenia multiceps* is a worm of some economic significance to shepherds in Britain. The adult occurs in dogs and the larval stage usually in sheep. The sheep are infected by grazing pastures infected by eggs passed from adults in the gut of the dog. The adult cestode is no more harmful to dogs than most other taeniids but the larva (*Coenurus cerebralis*) can cause serious disease in the intermediate hosts, where it may grow to the size of a hen's egg in brain tissue. Pressure on the brain in the later stage of growth causes an infected sheep to hold its head at an unusual angle, stagger and sometimes turn in circles. The locomotary symptoms depend upon the location of the cyst in the brain. This condition in sheep is known according to locality as gid, sturdy, staggers or turnstick.

This tapeworm has been recorded only once in foxes in Britain outside Ireland, in one out of 149 foxes from west Wales (Williams, 1976a) but it occurs regularly in continental foxes. The brain cases of most sheep carcases found on hill land are intact – indeed, it would be a formidable task for foxes or dogs to crush the cranium of adult sheep. However, many shepherds consider the fox to be responsible for sheep infection by being host to the adult cestode, a view possibly put forward to draw attention from dogs as the source of infection. Most probably, large dogs capable of crushing the cranium and dogs fed on knackers' carcases are the main sources of infection in sheep, and perhaps horses (see Williams, 1976b and c). However, smaller, less evident larvae in other tissues could be a source of infection, though this has not so far been demonstrated.

The adult stage of *Echinococcus granulosus*, a tapeworm which occurs in dogs, is only about 5mm long. Its larval form, a hydatid cyst, is very large and is found in sheep and other herbivores throughout the world. (In south Wales 34 per cent of a sample of 23,000 sheep were found to be infected.) The larval form sometimes infects man – in one case the hydatid continued to grow for forty-three years; in another the cyst contained 54.5 litres of fluid (Lapage, 1956).

In domestic animals the effect of the hydatid varies according to the size and location of the cyst, but its real significance is the hazard of infection in man via dogs. Sinclair (1956) found adult *Echinococcus* species in five out of eight foxes from Cardiganshire, but he was unable to find any infected foxes in a later, larger sample from the same area (Sinclair, 1957). He suggested that rabbits may have been the intermediate host and that the occurrence of myxomatosis and the drastic reduction of wild rabbits which occurred between the two sampling periods may have been responsible for the negative results of the second survey. On reconsideration, Sinclair suggested that the species he found was *E. multilocularis*, recorded only once in Britain, by Walshe in 1954 (as the hydatid in a woman who had never been out of Britain), but commonly found on the Continent (Vogel, 1957; Coudert *et al.*, 1970), where a vole is the intermediate host. Cook (1965), in an extensive survey of the occurrence of *E. granulosus* in Britain, found a mean number of three per fox in twenty-six adult foxes in a total sample of 319 foxes from England and Wales, i.e. in 8 per cent of the total; 25 per cent of sixty foxes from mid-Wales were infected. As a corollary to his main study, he stated that *E. granulosus* is the only tapeworm that matures and produces eggs in British foxes. Since the adult *E. granulosus* is a very small cestode indeed, being only about 3–5mm long, large cestodes would not easily have been overlooked, yet of three other species of (non-mature) tapeworms found in several hundred foxes, only three examples of these exceeded 100mm in length. He found three taeniid worms in his survey – *T. ovis*, *T. hydatigena* and *T. pisiformis*, but all were small, immature, non-gravid adult stages.

Troitskaya (1955) surveyed the endoparasites of Russian foxes and observed that scolices with only a few segments – without mature proglottids – were often the only tapeworms found in some foxes. She referred to this as destrobilization, or loss of the greater part of the tapeworm, which occurs when there is an abrupt change in the environment of the worm, associated, for example, with diet or hunger. Some species of the tapeworms found were identified by the only evidence of their presence, the scolex.

Many investigations of the incidence of tapeworms in British red foxes are unreported because so few adult worms were found and so few foxes infected. Because the fox is a scavenger at the apex of a food chain, a high incidence of infection is anticipated, but if few tapeworms are found, the sampling method becomes suspect. Investigations are usually carried out on material collected by third parties, and there is inevitably some delay between the death of the fox and its examination. In some instances this delay may be less than twenty-four hours; in others it may be several days. Whether a delay between death and examination has any effect upon the identification of tapeworms is not known, but it would seem to be necessary to establish this to enable confident comparisons to be made between samples and between different reported studies. Cook's material was preserved, in many cases, within twenty-four hours of the death of the fox, yet he found few cestodes larger than *Echinococcus*. Other investigations — those of Williams (1976a) and Walters (1977), for example – found mature cestodes in material examined after a long interval between death and examination.

More recently, my colleague Bernard Williams, has found four cases of infection of *E. granulosus* in a sample of 149 foxes collected from Carmarthenshire and Pembrokeshire, and another veterinary colleague, Tom Walters, found several hundred *Echinococcus* in one individual of a small sample of foxes that I obtained for him from an area within about three kilometres of my home at Builth Wells. In a larger sample (127) from mid-Wales Walters (1977) found twelve infected foxes. Earlier, a large sample of foxes from Wales examined at the Central Veterinary Laboratory did not reveal any *Echinococcus* species, (Olerenshaw, pers. comm.).

The differences in occurrence of *Echinococcus* demonstrated by different workers are almost certainly due to sample differences, either to the state of preservation of the material examined or to its uneven dispersion among fox populations.

*Echinococcus granulosus* and *E. multilocularis*, especially the former, have been the subject of considerable research in recent years, including investigations on experimental transmissions. Gemmel (1959) reported that the dingo and the domestic dog are the only definitive hosts of *E. granulosus* in Australia. One naturally infected fox was found with *E. granulosus*, but the one tapeworm specimen recovered was infertile. Experimental transmission of larvae from sheep to dogs was highly successful, but no fertile adults developed in the experimentally infected foxes. The conclusion is that foxes are not a definitive host of *E. granulosus* in Australia. This confirmed the results of previous attempts by other workers to infect foxes. Evidence accumulated that larval forms of *E. granulosus* from intermediate hosts other than sheep – moose and horses, for example – could successfully reach maturity in foxes, and as a result sub-specific rank was given to larval forms according to their origin, i.e. the intermediate hosts, and the adult worms of some of these exhibit morphological features which distinguish them.

Thus, *E. granulosus equinus*, a 'sub-species' derived from horses in England, was apparently used successfully to infect Australian red foxes. The investigations were terminated before the developing tapeworms reached maturity in the three foxes involved, but their rate of growth suggested that *E. granulosus equinus* from English horses found the environment in the gut of the fox more suitable for its growth and development than was the case with larvae obtained from sheep (Howkins, Gemmell and Smyth, 1965; Williams and Sweatman, 1963). The evidence that *E. granulosus equinus* will reach maturity and produce viable eggs is slender but, assuming that only *E. granulosus equinus* larvae will develop to maturity in foxes, it is difficult to understand where those adults forms observed by Sinclair and by Cook originated, since foxes would only rarely be presented with horse flesh in their diets – except possibly in such areas as the New and Epping Forests and hill lands where ponies range freely under minimal supervision. (In three years, only four carcases of mountain ponies have been found over 427 square kilometres of hill land in the Welsh fox study area.) Forbes (1964) suggested that other mammals such as rabbits, as indicated by Sinclair, may be involved in the tapeworm life cycle. Other herbivores such as deer are infected with larvae of *E. granulosus equinus* also. It seems to be agreed that the adult cestode *E. granulosus granulosus* of dogs is derived from sheep, and that the fox is of little significance in the cycle of events leading to infection in man.

Interest is now centered on the hydatid cysts of horses. A recent survey of the occurrence of hydatids in slaughtered horses (2,133 examined in twenty-two months: Dixon *et al.*, 1973), revealed infection in 62 per cent of the horses slaughtered. Forbes and Cook (1963) found that 40.5 per cent of 84 horses were infected, of which 66 per cent were hunters and 34 per cent were draught horses. This exceeds the highest occurrence of *Echinococcus* larvae recorded in British sheep, cattle and pigs. Thompson and Smyth (1974) indicated that the incidence (percentage of horses infected) of equine *Echinococcus* in Britain has increased spectacularly since 1960, when the incidence was about 7 per cent, to the late 1960s, when it was 62 per cent. They attribute this increase to the feeding of raw meat and offal, including that of horse, to hunting dogs; 29 per cent of fox hounds from twenty-one kennels examined by them were found to be infected. The majority of dogs in Britain are probably fed from tins and packets and on cooked meat, but sporting and farm dogs have access to uncooked meat and these are most likely to be the principal hosts for the adult stages of this and other cestodes.

Smyth and Smyth (1964) have suggested a cline of sub-species of *Echinococcus* between those now regarded as separate species, *E. granulosus* and *E. multilocularis*. The involvement of the fox in all this arose because of the apparent absence of *E. multilocularis* in Britain, the sometimes uncertain identification of adult forms found, and also the intermittent occurrences of adult *Echinococcus* in foxes from one survey to another.

Of *Mesocestoides* species, *M. lineatus* has been found in a Scottish fox (Lapage, 1956) and an unidentified one by Beresford-Jones (1961). Bouvier (1946) considered this tapeworm to be the cause of death in old and ailing foxes in Switzerland. *Hymenolepis nana* has been found only once in Britain.

*Dipylidium caninum* is common in dogs and cats, and in France in foxes, but an adult of this species has not been found in British foxes. The intermediate hosts are the fleas of the dog, cat and human and the dog louse.

*Diphyllobothrium latum*, widespread throughout the world, requires two intermediate hosts, a crustacean and a fish. It is known as the tapeworm of man. The adult of this cestode has been found in foxes in

France but not in any wild mammal in Britain. The adult worm has long been known in Ireland (since 1844) and larva were found in thirty-five perch out of a sample of seventy-nine in Gordice Lake, Eire (Harris and Hickey, 1945), but apart from infection of the adult worm in a boy, there was no evidence that this cestode was completing its cycle in the vicinity of the lake. Perhaps, like the *T. pisiformis* bladderworms of Skokholm rabbits, the infection in the intermediate hosts was a dead end.

In view of the catholic diet of the fox the endoparasites so far listed for British foxes are a poor representation of the potential for infestation. Insects, amphibians, reptiles and birds are apparently of little significance in the life cycles of the helminth parasites of foxes described here. Even the voles, the mainstay of foxes, are hardly implicated as intermediate hosts. It is surprising therefore that in Britain helminths have not exploited the feeding chain more widely than seems to be the case.

Wandeler and Hörning (1972) investigated the relationship between the occurrence of adult tapeworms in foxes and the presence of their larval forms in the intermediate hosts which were commonly eaten by foxes in Switzerland, the most frequent prey species being *Microtus arvalis*, *Microtus agrestis* and *Arvicola terrestris*. The frequency of occurrence of several tapeworm species in the fox was shown to be related to the variety and quantity of the tapeworm intermediate hosts eaten, and by the frequency of occurrence of tapeworm larvae in those hosts. In addition, in some fox prey species (*Apodemus* sp. and *Clethrionomys glareolus*) larval forms of tapeworm species were found which were absent, or did not occur as mature tapeworms, in the fox – which suggests that host specificity influences the maturation of some larval species in the fox. The tapeworms found in the foxes examined are shown in Table 32.

Whether a fox can become infected indirectly from the intermediate host simply by mechanical transmission of infective larvae is not known, but Lapage has indicated that the house-fly (*Musca domestica*), for example, has been shown to have viable eggs of the following species in its gut: *Taenia pisiformis*, *T. hydatigena*, *Hymenolepis nana*, *Dipylidium caninum*, *Ancylostoma caninum* and *Toxocara canis*.

## Other parasites

Two species of *Eimeria* and three *Isospora* have been found in foxes (Lapage, 1956) but whether or not all five occurred in British foxes is not known. Watkins and Harvey (1942) identified *E. vulpis* in silver foxes in Britain, and Beresford-Jones (1961) found oocysts of *Eimeria* and *Isospora* sp. in British wild foxes. Bejšovec (1965) in Czechoslovakia fed birds of prey and foxes with foods containing parasitic protozoa and helminth embryos not normally found in these species. It was found that all nine *Eimeria* unsporulated oocysts and all sixteen helminth larvae were successfully passaged. It was concluded that these predators could act as efficient mechanical carriers of parasites derived from their prey.

Farmer and his colleagues (1978) found *Sarcocystis* spp. in the gut of 17 per cent of forty-one foxes from north Wales. Unsporulated oocysts of *Isospora* spp. found were unidentifiable, probably because the gut had been deep-frozen at −20°C. *Monocystis* spp. observed were indicative of the earthworm and insect diet of the foxes.

A microsporum ringworm infection was found in one fox in a sample of twenty-six by Ross and Fairley (1969). These animals, which had marked loss of hair, had been selected from a much larger sample for sarcoptic mange investigations, so the occurrence of microsporum may indeed be higher than indicated. Other surveys in Britain have not yet revealed ringworm infection in foxes.

A skin infection by the actinomycete *Dermatophilus* has been found in a wild fox by Austwick (1965).

## Skeletal Disorders

Not enough is known about skeletal disorders in foxes.

Osteomalacia, a generalized bone condition, is sometimes found in very young foxes. This is a softening or lack of density, which results in deformity from physical forces exerted on the bone, and it is not likely that foxes with this condition survive into maturity. Rickets, too, is very occasionally seen in cubs, but there is no information available about the condition in adult foxes. (It frequently occurs among foxes kept as pets wherein the first indications are a flat-footed (plantigrade) appearance of the forefeet. In the wild the inclusion of skin and fur (of prey) in the diet probably provides an abundant supply of vitamin D, whereas captive animals deprived of this source require vitamin D additives in their diet.)

Dr Stephen Harris (1977a) has observed the common occurrence of spondylosis deformans among London suburban foxes. This is a disorder of the vertebrae. The centrum, the body of the vertebra lying beneath and along the length of the spinal cord, develops bony growths which may result in the formation of a fused bridge of bone joining adjacent vertebrae. More commonly spurs of bone project forwards or backwards from the borders of the centra over the intervertebral spaces. If these spurs unite they lock the affected vertebrae, but even if they do not unite there may be some restriction of movement of the vertebrae. Any vertebrae can be affected, including those of the tail, and the condition may be general or localized. It is a condition well known in dogs, ancient and modern, having been found in dog skeletons from archaeological sites dating back to as early as 2500 BC (Harcourt, 1971). Harris (1977a) has observed instances of the arthritic fusion of several vertebrae in foxes. He has also observed examples of syndactyly, a variable condition ranging from the fusion of two or more digits by a sheath of skin to the fusion of the bones of the digits. Harris described a 'web-footed' vixen which had all four feet affected. The normally four-toed hindfeet had only three toes, the third and fourth being fused along their entire length. The forefeet had the two middle toes (of the four in contact with the ground) fused along their length except for the bone of the toes bearing the claws, which were separate and splayed at an acute angle to each other. Snow prints of this fox would have confused the expert tracker, just as would those of another 'three-toed fox' dog fox I examined from Kent, which had the two 'middle toes' of the forefeet fused along their entire length. The condition involving bone fusion is not common; the one example I found occurred in 1,600 examined from Wales and south-east England. Another example was reported by Woodhead in 1969.

A description of tooth abnormalities and disorders would be tedious and lengthy, but since many countrymen assign age to foxes according to the condition of the teeth, some mention must be made of teeth. Foxes caught in snares and traps, or held accidentally by fence wire (usually the hindfeet are caught by the two top straining wires), frequently snap and chew remorselessly at the object restraining them – or, indeed, any object – and in so doing fracture their teeth. Also, when moving quickly either as pursued or pursuer, the fox runs the risk of colliding with some obstacle; in the same way the desperate snatch at some prey may sometime result in damage to teeth when some hard object intervenes. Thus the toothless fox which one often hears of has probably incurred this condition accidentally or as a result of dental disease. It is possible to distinguish between new and old damage to teeth by the sharpness of the fractured edge of a tooth.

Swellings and the erosion of bone in the region of the tooth roots are not uncommon among British foxes. These conditions occur most frequently in the lower jaw. In Finland, Rantanen and Pulliainen (1970) found no evidence of dental caries in a survey of dental disorders of foxes, and disease in the region of tooth roots was usually associated with accidental damage to the tooth. The Finnish sample showed that wear of the teeth resulting in the exposure of the underlying dentine was uncommon. The loss of teeth, however, is more common. Apart from those fractured or lost in adult life, teeth may be absent due to nondevelopment of the tooth or to loss early in life. The teeth most commonly lost through either of these causes are the first and second pre-molars, especially in the lower jaw, and the small vestigial third molar of the lower jaw.

Supernumerary teeth sometimes occur among all tooth types, including the canine teeth (Coyler, 1936; Reinwaldt, 1963; van Bree and Sinkeldam, 1969). Non-alignment of pre-molar teeth sometimes occurs, also bilateral asymmetry of distribution of teeth in the row. Usually, however, the teeth of foxes exhibit a perfect 'bite' and whilst undershot jaws are more common than prognathous overshot jaws, these conditions are rarely seen in foxes.

Archaeologists consider the shortening of the muzzle and the tooth row in canids to be indicative of domestication. In this context domestication is synonymous with soft living, and whilst dental disease may be more common among animals that feed on sub-standard or sloppy foods, such compaction suggests that long-muzzled individuals have suffered from an adverse survival rate, or else the condition is not inherited and depends upon the food that the individual eats. Sub-standard food could perhaps result in retarded development. My colleagues and I are beginning to acquire an eye for foxes, and short-muzzled forms are not by any means uncommon among live rural foxes that we have handled.

## Disease

### Miscellaneous diseases

Little was known about the diseases of wild foxes in Britain until interest was stimulated by deaths of large numbers of foxes in the winter and spring of 1960–1. These occurred predominantly in the arable farming areas of Northamptonshire, Lincolnshire, Huntingdonshire, Cambridgeshire, Hertfordshire, Essex and Suffolk. In March of the previous year similar occurrences had been reported (Rothschild, 1963). Huntsmen reported finding 1,300 dead foxes, and there was evidence from other counties of substantial reductions in the number of foxes. Among the suggestions put forward to account for these deaths, naturalists submitted that there was a relationship between the deaths of foxes and those of wood-pigeons and other birds, which subsequently proved to be correct. The cause of death in wood-pigeons and foxes was not positively determined, but field and laboratory evidence suggested that poisoning by chlorinated hydrocarbon compounds was implicated (Taylor and Blackmore, 1961). Blackmore (1964b) later showed that these insecticides were indeed the most common single cause of death, the compounds identified being used to protect winter- and spring-sown cereals against insects. Dieldrin, the insecticide then commonly used, had also been in use for some years, but climate, crop husbandry practices and the quantity of seed eaten by birds may have been different in different years. For whatever reason, the dressed grain was more readily available to birds, or more of them fed on it and died and were eaten by carrion feeders or became impaired and were vulnerable to predation before death actually ensued. Foxes and other species at the apex of this particular food chain ran the risk of secondary poisoning. Blackmore (1963) concluded, from experiments, that insecticidal poisoning in foxes can be suspected if more than one part per million of dieldrin, or more than four parts per million of heptachlor are found in the flesh. The use of dieldrin in agriculture is now much reduced and is being phased out; it is no longer used in sheep dips and dieldrin-dressed seed can only be used when absolutely necessary in the autumn.

This was not the first example of secondary poisoning of foxes. Bouvier, (1946) in a survey of diseases of some wild animals in France from 1942 to 1945, found that one of the principle causes of death in foxes in 1944 was secondary thallium poisoning (thallium was a poison used for the destruction of house mice and field mice). This occurred in many regions but the numbers of foxes found dead is not recorded. In Denmark, Munch, Clausen and Karlog (1974) and Clausen and Karlog (1974) found a high proportion of foxes, badgers and martens (mainly *Martes foina*) to be loaded with thallium; 50 per cent of forty-six stone martens (*M. foina*) were thallium-loaded and 22 per cent were poisoned by thallium. Of 265 foxes and seventeen badgers found dead or sick from 1963 to 1971, forty-five foxes and five badgers were subjected to investigations for thallium poisoning. Thirty-two foxes and two badgers showed the presence of thallium in their tissues, and in twenty foxes and one badger the cause of death was considered to be directly attributable to thallium poisoning. As elsewhere on the Continent, thallium is used for rodent control, but there is no evidence from Denmark to show whether the carnivores ate poisoned bait or suffered secondary poisoning through eating poisoned rodents.

During preliminary research into these mysterious mortalities in Britain the nature of the symptoms of the affected foxes suggested an infective condition, and investigations were undertaken to determine whether or not a viral agent was involved. The results were inconclusive (Bowden *et al.*, 1960). During the course of his investigations into suspected insecticidal poisoning by dieldrin, Blackmore (1964b) surveyed the diseases of foxes found dead in the field and also those of captive animals. Although inadequate, since the sample is small, it is the best information on fox diseases in Britain at present available. Sixty wild foxes were examined; forty were found dead in the field and the others were captive animals, most of which had died within a short time of being taken to the laboratory; 38 per cent of these died of insecticidal poisoning. The other causes of death are shown on page 241.

*Number of cases*

| | |
|---|---|
| Streptococcal infection | 8 |
| Other bacterial infection | 6 |
| Viral infection | 0 |
| Ascardidiasis (cubs) | 2 |
| Pyometretis | 1 |
| Hydrocephalus | 2 |
| Choke and inhalation pneumonia | 1 |
| Traumatic injury | 11 |
| Insecticide poisoning | 23 |
| Undiagnosed | 6 |
| TOTAL | 60 |

In two of the eight animals which succumbed to streptococcal infection, the primary cause of the infection was shot-gun pellets. One adult fox with a streptococcal abscess had several shot-gun pellets in the vicinity of the abscess. Blackmore considered streptococcal infection to be relatively common and that infection occurs via wounds. Secord (1936) considered the fox, in captivity, to be especially vulnerable to septicaemia, even from superficial wounds; 60 per cent of all foxes examined (these included some twenty-one experimental animals which died or were killed) showed evidence of interstitial nephritis, probably due to leptospiral infection. Of other bacterial infections, *Proteus vulgaris* and *Proteus mirabilis* were implicated in the death of a cub and an adult fox respectively. *Pasteurella septica* was recovered from a young cub which died, and another successfully treated cub of eight weeks was found to be infected by an organism serologically similar to *Pasteurella pseudotuberculosis*. *Pasteurella septica* was also observed in a fox cub by Woodford and Cooper (1969); the cub died. *Pasteurella pseudotuberculosis* has been isolated in only one fox in Britain, by Mair (1968), who considered it to be rare in British foxes. The main reservoir of infection is rodents.

Bacteria of the *Salmonella* group have been found in foxes by Taylor (1968). As with leptospirosis, foxes, being predators or scavengers, are likely to contract *Salmonella* infection from many sources but only *S. infantes* has been isolated from British foxes. Taylor considered, however, that *Salmonella* infection in wild small rodents, rabbits and hares is uncommon.

Non-haemolytic *Escherichia coli* was found in the gut of apparently healthy foxes, but this organism was involved in the death of a fox from pyometritis. It was also found in two young cubs which died and exhibited septicaemia, due to non-haemolytic *Escherichia coli*.

Blackmore (1964b) found no evidence of distemper infection, nor of louping-ill antibodies. Large quantities of canine viral hepatitis antibodies were found in closely observed hand-reared foxes which had been in contact with dogs infected with this virus. None of the foxes found dead of Dieldrin poison in the field gave positive reactions, and Blackmore considers that the wild fox has a high degree of resistance to canine viral hepatitis. The 1960–1 fox deaths were at first tentatively attributed to this disease.

One of the two cases of hydrocephalus may have been due to insecticidal poisoning, but this condition has been noted by other workers in wild and ranched foxes in Britain and North America. Blackmore considers that this condition might be a comparatively common congential disease.

Canine viral hepatitis (Rubarth's disease in dogs) is considered to be identical with infective fox encephalitis. Fox encephalitis, described by Green *et al.* (1930) in North America, was not identified in any of the foxes examined by Blackmore and does not appear to have been unequivocally demonstrated in British foxes. Tickner (1932) describes symptoms of hysteria in three wild foxes observed by him near Oxford, which subsequently revealed cerebral lesions of unknown aetiology. In North American ranch foxes death usually occurs within twenty-four hours of the onset of convulsions, but Tickner's observations of the abnormal behaviour of the Oxford foxes showed that they occurred for several days, which suggests a condition of different origin. Infectious hepatitis has been described in foxes in Poland (Czarnowski, 1960).

Routine rabies diagnostic work in Switzerland identified a tick-borne encephalitis virus in a dog suspected of rabies (Grěsiková *et al.*, 1972); subsequent antibody tests on wild foxes in Switzerland revealed that possibly 20 per cent of foxes were or had been infected (Alexander Wandeler, pers. comm.). Of twenty foxes from Georgia, showing signs of encephalitis in the wild, five revealed *Listeria monocytogenes* (Schaltens and Brim, 1964).

Whilst there are no conclusive records of viral infection in British foxes (Blackmore, 1964b), yet another viral infection known as pseudorabies, or Aujeszkys disease, has been found in foxes in Europe, on Polish fur farms (Zwierzchowski, 1960), and in the wild in Denmark (Bitsch and Munche, 1971). Affected animals suffer intense skin irritation; they may mutilate themselves so violently to allay the irritation that death from shock may ensue.

Epidemics of distemper can occur in foxes, causing considerable numbers of deaths locally in Europe (Dr K. Bogel, pers. comm.) and on fur farms (Cakala, 1960). Its sporadic occurrences allows fully distemper-susceptible populations to be built up during the interepizootic phases. There is no record of distemper in wild foxes in Britain. The disease is associated with aggressive behaviour towards other animals and even moving vehicles. Infected foxes foam at the mouth and sometimes become lethargic and oblivious to humans. As with some other diseases (Aujeszkys disease, fox encephalitis and listeriosis, for example), abnormal behaviour may raise a false alarm over the presence of rabies.

Tularemia has been sometimes responsible for widespread deaths of foxes in Voronesh Province, USSR (Chirkova, 1955a).

Warts (of viral origin?) are sometimes found on the lips and eyelids of foxes. The first record of leptospiral infection (*L. icterohaemorrhagiae*) in a fox was in 1926 (Dunkin), but since then many other leptospiral serotypes have been identified. Small mammals, especially rodents, are the chief carriers of leptospires. Twigg *et al.* (1968) found that many foxes which showed positive reactions to leptospire antibody tests gave positive reactions to several serotypes. In one case eight serotypes were observed in one fox. Altogether ten of the fifteen serotypes identified in mammals were found in foxes: these are *L. icterohaemorrhagiae, L. saxkoebing, L. hebdomadis, L. canicola, L. poi, L. autumnalis, L. erinaceiauriti, L. ballum, L. hardjo, L. bataviae*. The first three of this list were also identified by Blackmore in his survey (1964b); in addition he identified *L. bratislava*. The two most common serotypes are *L. icterohaemorrhagiae* (found commonly in brown rats) and *L. canicola* (found in dogs). Twigg and his colleagues pointed out that there would be little stability in a system in which the predator was highly susceptible to the parasites carried by the prey, and the reservoir of leptospires in the wide variety of prey foods eaten commonly by foxes is considerable. Blackmore, however, stated that 61 per cent of adult foxes had kidney lesions and it was animals in this age group which showed evidence of leptospiral infection. *L. icterohaemorrhagiae*, commonly found in rats, is a serotype which usually infects man, in whom the condition is known as Weil's disease. It can be contracted directly from the urine of rats or from water polluted by rats, the spirochaetes being able to penetrate intact skin in some conditions.

Vasennis (1964) reported the occurrence of *Mycoplasma* (PPLO) in the nasoturbinal microflora of 24 per cent of red foxes examined in Finland.

Brucellosis, in Britain a disease primarily of cattle, is commanding more attention now that the first hurdles in the race — to produce pathogen-free milk (eg. tuberculosis eradication) – have been successfully cleared. Farmers have alleged that the fox, a scavenger with an apparent liking for foetal membranes, may interfere with brucellosis eradication campaigns by dragging infected cattle afterbirths from one place to another. They suggest that brucellosis-free pastures may become infected in this way; however, *Brucella abortus* is very delicate when outside the animal body and pastures infected by this means may be infected for a very short period of time only. Whether or not this aspect has any influence upon the spread of brucellosis is not known. McCaughey (1968) recorded antibodies to *Brucella abortus* in two out of five foxes in Northern Ireland, and the organism has been isolated from captive foxes in Russia and wild foxes in Bulgaria. A survey of 112 foxes from a small area of Wales, carried out by the Ministry of Agriculture, Fisheries and Food in 1972, demonstrated *Brucella* antibodies in eight foxes, in one of which *Brucella abortus* was isolated. This was not unexpected, since Bouvier (1963) demonstrated the occurrence of *Brucella* sp. and *Mycobacterium bovis* (bovine tuberculosis) in foxes in Switzerland, probably the direct result of the scavenging of roe-deer carcases. It seems unlikely that foxes play even a minor role in the dissemination of brucellosis in Britain.

Foxes probably play no part either in the spread of foot-and-mouth disease outbreaks, except as potential mechanical carriers of the virus. Foxes have frequently been seen at night by the light of the cattle funeral pyres, attracted to them possibly by the smell of animal matter but they are highly unlikely to gain access to infective material.

The diseases and disorders of captive ranched foxes give some indication of the variety of conditions that may be seen in wild foxes – though, for the reasons stated earlier, the prevalence of any disease or parasite in wild animals will be different from that for farmed animals, as would be the susceptibility of wild and captive animals. Chaddock (1948) reported a ten-year study of the cause of death of 2,482 ranched foxes in North America; the results are shown below. The cause of death in some cases was arbitrarily decided and the causal organism in cases of death from infectious diseases were not known in many cases.

*Parasites*

| | |
|---|---:|
| Hookworms (*Ancylostoma caninum*) | 84 |
| Lungworms (*Eucolius aerophilus*) | 591 |
| Roundworms (*Toxocara*) | 115 |
| Coccidiosis (*Isospora*) | 5 |
| Earmites (*Otodectes cynotis*) | 4 |
| Mange (*Demodex folliculorum*) | 33 |
| Protozoan infection | 1 |
| Trichinosis | 3 |

*Infectious diseases*

| | |
|---|---:|
| Distemper | 210 |
| Encephalitis | 125 |

*Dietary disorders*

| | |
|---|---:|
| Malnutrition | 5 |
| Food poisoning | 27 |
| Enteritis | 35 |

Fatty degeneration of liver                                           173
Gout                                                                    1
Rickets                                                                 1
Chronic dermatitis                                                      2
Obesity                                                                 2
Chastek paralysis (vitamin $B_2$ deficiency)                           22

*Traumatic injuries*
Rupture of various organs                                              60
Perforation of intestine (ingested twig)                               1
Perforation of chest cavity                                            1
Fracture of the cranium                                                6
Fracture of vertebrae                                                  8
Killed by penmates                                                    66
Trauma (undescribed)                                                   5

*Neoplasms*
Carcinomas of the duodenum, spleen, bladder,
colon, lung, tongue and skin                                          19

*Miscellaneous infections*
Generalized infection                                                132
Paratyphoid                                                            5
Streptococcus                                                          4
Staphylococcus                                                         3
Clostridium welchii                                                    2
Escherichia coli                                                       3
Salmonella                                                            12
Meningitis                                                             6
Abscess of the brain                                                   3
Necrotic stomatitis                                                    1
Abscess of the liver                                                   4
Abscess of the neck                                                    2
Peritonitis                                                            4
Abscess of the throat                                                  1
Pneumonia                                                            184
Pleuritis                                                             11
Endocarditis                                                           3
Pericarditis                                                           4
Vegetative endocarditis                                                1
Mastitis                                                               2
Nephritis                                                             65
Pyonephritis                                                          10
Cystitis                                                              70
Gastroenteritis                                                      36

| | |
|---|---|
| Metritis | 16 |

*Miscellaneous causes*

| | |
|---|---|
| Hydrocephalus | 13 |
| Exposure | 2 |
| Suffocation | 6 |
| Exhaustion | 1 |
| Heat prostration | 54 |
| Casualty from vermifuge administration | 63 |
| Mucopurulent pneumonia | 4 |
| Jaundice | 22 |
| Fibrosis of the liver | 3 |
| Ulceration of gastric mucosa | 7 |
| Intestinal intussusception | 9 |
| Torsion of the ileum | 1 |
| Prolapse of the rectum | 3 |
| Diaphragmatic hernia | 6 |
| Umbilical hernia | 1 |
| Strangulated hernia | 2 |
| Cystic calculus | 3 |
| Uremia | 2 |
| Occlusion of ureter | 1 |
| Occlusion of urethra | 11 |
| Dystocia | 7 |
| Toxemia | 12 |
| Anemia | 4 |
| Shot, escaped during storm | 12 |
| Thymustod | 1 |
| Congenital malformations (anal fissure) | 4 |
| Cretin | 7 |

**Rabies**

The red fox is very susceptible to rabies. Because the disease is widespread in the red fox population throughout much of its range in North America, Europe and Asia, and because it is currently in the public eye, it warrants more detailed consideration here than other diseases that affect foxes.

Rabies is a virus disease, commonly transmitted through a bite, when infected saliva enters the wound. All mammals are susceptible to varying degrees. The disease can be transmitted through the inhalation of infected droplets and, in some circumstances, through infected food, but as far as carnivores are concerned, the bite is by far the most common route of transmission. Virus introduced into a wound travels via the nervous system to the brain, where it multiplies. As multiplication proceeds, the virus moves outwards from the brain, along the nerves, to all the tissues and organs served by the nervous system. The salivary glands are infected; virus appears in the saliva a day or two before overt symptoms of rabies are evident in the infected animal.

The development of the classical symptoms of rabies seems to fall into three stages – restlessness, a change in temperament and behaviour and, finally, paralysis. The madness associated with the disease in dogs generally occurs during the second stage, but this is variable. Some affected dogs suffer from the furious form of the disease; a more or less complete derangement of their behaviour may cause them to leave home and to wander aimlessly, biting savagely at other animals and even at inanimate objects. This stage can last up to four or five days before paralysis and death ensue. Only about 25 per cent of affected dogs in the current European epizootic display these symptoms, however; the remainder suffer from the form of the disease known as dumb rabies. With this form the animal becomes increasingly restless and irritable, and though it may show a tendency to snap, it usually obeys its handler and may even seek solace from him. Progressive paralysis occurs at an early stage – the animal walks unsteadily, often in circles, then finally falls down and dies in a coma.

Rabies symptoms in the fox are not as dramatic and the extreme aggressiveness does not occur, but the dumb and furious forms of the disease can be identified. With the furious form the fox will wander aimlessly, without fear of man or his animals, entering towns, houses and farmsteads. Unprovoked attacks are not common, but the fox will attack anything that intercepts or impedes it. In Europe at present about 50 per cent of infected foxes display these symptoms; the others exhibit the progressive paralysis described above. The rabid behaviour – both dumb and furious – may last between one and seven days before total paralysis and death supervene.

The extreme form of mental derangement which occurs with furious rabies is extremely successfully adapted to facilitate transmission of the disease to another animal. The occurrence of the dumb form, which probably plays only a minor role in the transmission of the disease, may be significant as well, however: in order that the survival of the virus should not be jeopardized by the death of all susceptible animals, the effect of the virus on a completely susceptible population may be reduced by the dumb form. Thus, fewer animals are infected than might otherwise be the case, and more survive to build up the population for further outbreaks of rabies. If the virus were capable of being transmitted by all affected animals, it might disappear with the elimination of its hosts. As far as the red fox in Europe is concerned, rabies has a considerable but not a devastating effect on the population. Coupled with the effects of the disease, however, is a greater incentive to kill foxes to

prevent the spread of rabies and to reduce the hazard to man and his livestock. Nevertheless, such is the capacity of the fox to withstand the combined onslaught of disease and control that a mere slackening of control
measures will allow the fox population to increase quite quickly, and it
will regain former levels in a comparatively short period of time.

Epizootics of wildlife rabies in continental Europe in historic times
implicated the fox as a susceptible animal. The rabid wolf was feared,
and observations of the wolf may have diverted attention from occurrences of rabies in foxes. At the present time the wolf is absent from
much of Europe, though it still occurs, in smaller numbers than formerly, in eastern European countries and is still implicated in rabies incidence. Although a small animal, the fox has now supplanted the wolf as
the largest canid in most parts of Europe and is considered the main reservoir of rabies, contributing up to 85 per cent of all cases (Wandeler *et
al.*, 1974). The disease is contracted by other species but cannot be
maintained in the absence of its occurrence in foxes – see Figure 28.

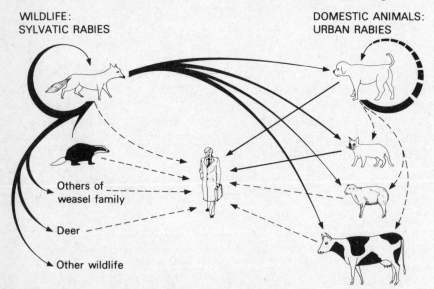

WILDLIFE:
SYLVATIC RABIES

DOMESTIC ANIMALS:
URBAN RABIES

Others of
weasel family

Deer

Other wildlife

**28**   Diagrammatic representation of the cycle of rabies in Europe. (Diagram reproduced
with kind permission of Professor Franz Steck.)

Since 1939, when rabies first occurred in the current epizootic in
Polish foxes, the disease has spread westwards with very little hindrance, reaching France in 1968. (Known cases of rabies in France,
since its first occurrence there, are shown in Table 33.) It commonly
advances at a rate of between twenty and sixty kilometres a year. It is
most prevalent and persistent where there are large populations of foxes
to support it; it has been observed that fox populations at densities of
one fox per square kilometre and over will support it, while one fox per

five square kilometres will not. Somewhere between these values lies a broad range of numbers crucial to the maintenance of the disease. At these higher densities the fox population is reduced, according to different estimates, by 20–60 per cent, which represents not the proportion of susceptible animals in the population (since the fox is very susceptible to rabies infection), but the numbers that become infected and subsequently die.

Rabies in foxes is most pronounced where the disease is advancing into hitherto uninfected areas. It occurs at all times of the year, but there are more occurrences in the late winter and early spring than at other times. This is probably related to the greater opportunity for contact between foxes at the time of the dispersal of juveniles. In the wake of the advancing front rabies occurs sporadically among foxes and other carnivores, but there is some periodicity (three to five years) in infected areas of Europe, as there is in Canada (Johnston and Beauregard, 1969). The disease is still present in foxes in eastern Europe some thirty-seven years after its first appearance there.

In North America, where the number of species of carnivores is greater than in Europe, the epidemiology of wildlife rabies is more complex; although the red fox is involved, it is not the main reservoir of rabies in areas where the skunks and racoons are found. In Canada, however, the role of the red fox is more important.

The disease seems to have been recognized in dogs in Britain throughout the period of recorded history. The occurrence of rabies in sporting dogs and packs of hounds is well documented by Edward, Second Duke of York as early as the fifteenth century, but the possibility that the disease might be transmitted to dogs by wildlife was not considered apparently, even by those who had a wide knowledge of hunting and obvious solicitude for their dogs. Edward observed that 'wolves go mad, and when they bite a man he does not get well, for their biting is venomous on account of the toads they have eaten'. Whether or not this is a reference to rabies is uncertain. Church records of payments of bounties for killing vermin testify to the death of many thousands of carnivores and other species; some parish records include oblique references to rabies ('payment for medicine for the bite of a mad dog, ten shillings'), but there is no known reference to special payments for killing rabid wild animals. Other early references to treatment for rabies are extant: two physicians, Howman (1684) and Mead (1708), each reported a case of human rabies following an attack by a fox. Mead's patient died four months after 'the bite of a mad fox that had been bit by a mad dog', but he omits to mention whether the fox was wild.

Since the fox thrives on variety and prospers in fragmentary habitats, the abundance of the fox today is probably due directly to man's influence on the environment. The habitat over much of Britain up until about 1750 – when the golden age of agriculture was well under way and land clearance and enclosure were extensive – was less well suited to supporting high densities of foxes, and records of bounties administered by the Church from the sixteenth to the eighteenth centuries suggest that the numbers killed were rather small. Although it should not be concluded that densities of foxes up to the early eighteenth century were insufficient to support a rabies epizootic, available evidence suggests that dramatic epizootics among foxes did not occur.

Rabies was particularly prevalent in the nineteenth century. There are few direct references to rabies in wild animals, although Hole (1969) reports outbreaks in three deer herds at a time when the disease was common among dogs in the Midlands and in the London area, and Parker (1943), in an anecdotal account, mentions a possible occurrence of rabies in a Hampshire fox towards the end of the century. Outbreaks of the disease among dogs in the later part of the nineteenth century, however, were considerable; it is surprising that there was no evidence of it in wild carnivores then, nor later from 1918–22, when 319 cases of the disease were recorded in domestic animals. Most occurrences in dogs were in urban areas, where the fox was not entirely excluded, so some contact between dogs and foxes is likely to have taken place. Stray dogs were common in the nineteenth century (121 of 312 rabid dogs were recorded as strays in 1889), and they may have largely occupied the ecological niche of today's urban foxes. If the speculative assumption that rabies was not common among wild animals in Britain, or occurred only locally and sporadically, is correct, it must be concluded that ecological features of the host or the virus were unfavourable to the success of rabies in the larger wild mammals in Britain.

The probability of an outbreak of wildlife rabies in Britain today cannot be assessed. The smuggling of dogs, cats and other mammals, and accidental importations such as landings of animals from foreign ships or stowaways on aircraft, are the most likely source of infection. The wide powers and vigilance of the government Veterinary Service provide good insurance against a major outbreak among domestic animals in the event of an outbreak initiated by a smuggled or an accidentally introduced mammal. The probability of infection of wildlife by a smuggled dog or cat seems to be remote, since contact would have to be made between a diseased domestic animal and a healthy wild animal, but it is a possibility. Most foxes keep a respectful distance from dogs – even dogs that are behaving peculiarly – but friendly associations between dogs and foxes have been observed, mostly in urban areas. The consumption of infected carcases is a more likely route of direct infection; partly eaten dog carcases have been found in suburban fox dens (almost certainly all road casualties). Foxes also eat dead cats, and a rabid cat, especially in the terminal stages of the disease, seems to be a more likely source of infection than a rabid dog.

People often ask why precautionary measures against rabies should not be taken now by reducing the fox population to a low level throughout Britain. Apart from the unwarranted economic and widespread social effects of such a measure, there is no justification for the slaughter of a wild animal on such a scale merely as a precaution against a disease that has not reached Britain and the arrival of which is not inevitable. The risk of an occurrence of wildlife rabies remains very small, but improbable events do occur. Though the chain of transmission from Europe to Britain and from domestic animals to wild animals is slender, anti-rabies vigilance and preparedness must be maintained, not just for the next year or two but, if the experience of eastern Europe, where the disease still persists, is any guide, probably for many scores of years. Thus any undertaking considered must be viewed as an open-ended commitment, whether it be localized or more widespread.

Further key reading on this subject, with particular reference to Europe can be found in Baer, (1975); Bogel *et al*, (1976); Chalmers and Scott, (1969); H.M.S.O. (1971); Irvin, (1970); Kaplan, (1977); Lloyd, (1976, 1977); Kantorovich, (1964); Muller, (1971); Tabel *et al*, (1974); Toma and Andral, (1977) and Wandeler *et al*, (1974a, 1974b).

# Appendix 1
# Field Signs

It is not always possible to distinguish a single fox print from that of a small dog, but generally the toe pads are more elongated in foxes and the print is invariably longer than it is in dogs. Depending on the age and size of the fox and on the surface on which the print is made, a front footprint can be between 50mm and 75mm long and is 6–13mm longer than the print of a hindfoot. The shape of the claws can often be seen in the print, and on smooth mud a print of the inter-digital hair can be seen (see Figure 7).

In snow or sand the prints of a trotting fox are very nearly in a straight line. According to Schlezel (1912), there are, from birth, small differences in length between the left and right limbs of canids, which increase with age and give rise to the circular creeping movement of the new-born and the slightly crabwise gait of the adult. This lopsidedness is less pronounced in foxes, which probably explains the straighter line formed by the prints of the fox.

Print tracks of foxes can be seen clearly in dewy or frosted grass and in areas of laid rank grass. Foxes readily leap over fences, but they often make their way over them at straining posts, where claw marks and scraped lichen or mosses will reveal the regular passage of foxes. Foxes have regular runs through hedges, but since they hunt along hedgerows, they may pass through them at any convenient point. These runs are not as well defined as those of badgers, and they are often no larger than those of brown hares (in many cases hare runs can be distinguished by the jumps on the runs on either side of the hedge). Where foxes regularly pass through a hedge, bramble thicket, barbed-wire fence or other obstruction, fur sooner or later becomes caught on some snag and can be found and identified. Clearly defined fox runs do not often cross open spaces, but they can be seen in overgrown, grassy areas. On hill land foxes often use sheep paths to move from one part of their range to another.

Faeces provide good field evidence of the presence of foxes. They are of vari-able size and colour. If the contents include fur, feathers or other stringy, indi-gestible matter, the faeces may be linked by them and are usually pointed at both ends. They can be distinguished from bird casts by their elongated shape, and when fresh they have a characteristic odour. Old faeces may remain intact for many months, but by then all the soft parts may have been leached out by rainfall.

While the presence of foxes can usually be deduced fairly readily, it is very difficult to obtain a clear indication of numbers by field signs alone. Signs are more clearly seen in some habitats than in others; for example, in areas where fields are small there is a greater chance of finding evidence of the passage of foxes through hedges than in areas where large fields or open areas predominate. If faeces were distributed randomly it would not be too difficult to devise a reliable method of estimating numbers, but they tend to be clumped, or at least unevenly distributed, and more difficult to find in some areas than others, so that simple observation of numbers of faeces cannot be used for this purpose. The number of dens or earths occupied during the cubbing season is an excellent indicator of numbers of foxes per unit area, and this method has been used by many research workers and others. The success of this method, however, depends upon the careful timing of observations, which must be made over a short period of time throughout a large area. It requires some experience in judging signs of occupation of the earths, and in fragmentary habitats, wooded areas and hill land it may require considerable time and effort to obtain reliable counts. The number of fox dens or earths *per se* is no indication of the numbers of foxes in any area.

Whilst the size of a fox seen in the field may give a clue to its sex, size alone is an unreliable indicator. Burrows (1968), and Talbot (1906) before him, affirm that the shape of the head viewed from the front is a clear indicator, the ears being wider apart on the broader dome of the head of the male and set so as to make a W shape in front profile, in contrast to the V shape of the vixen's. There certainly is such a difference, but it is not often easy to distinguish the sexes in isolation. A more reliable guide, given a clear view, is the cream-coloured fur of the scrotum, which readily identifies the dog fox.

Urination postures can provide an indication of sex, but there is no clear-cut difference in the postures as with adult dogs and bitches. Urine is used as a scent marker by both sexes, and it is likely urine marks seen in the field is of the scent-marking kind. When urinating, females squat deeply into a nearly sitting position, with the face parallel to the ground. Dog foxes sometimes stand, but they usually squat (though not as low as the vixen). Both sexes mark objects such as stones, tufts of grass, logs, molehills and other prominent objects; they also mark other scents. If the object marked is above ground level, the sex of the urinating fox can be detected with greater certainty, but such marking is done very quickly and can pass unnoticed by a distant observer. When scent-marking with urine the vixen will turn its rear end to the object, while the male may face or stand astride it. Though it seems that urine is usually deposited, the secretion of the anal glands can be deposited more or less in like fashion, which can lead to some confusion in the field, since both sexes deposit anal-gland secretion in the same way.

Places which have been scent-marked can be detected by the smell which lingers on any permanent object such as a tree, a stone or even a tuft of grass along a path used by foxes, if one is prepared to use one's nose while crawling on all fours. I am uncertain whether the smell is always that of urine, or whether it is sometimes that of the anal-gland secretion. The smell is hard to describe, but it is readily recognized once learned. It is possible to pick up the smell of fox which drifts on the wind across one's path as one walks along a hedge, road or forest ride, but it is often very difficult to detect its precise location.

Traces of meals – or the search for one – are a good indication of the presence of foxes. They scratch out vole nests and rabbit stops, for instance, frequently leaving footprints in excavated soil as evidence. In matted grass round holes up to 50mm in diameter are usually made by foxes investigating vole runs with their noses (they do not often expose and devastate such runs in the manner of mouse-hunting dogs). If a large bird is taken by a fox, the primary wing feathers are sheared cleanly near the base and discarded, and remains such as the head or legs of a domestic hen or of a lamb will usually be partially buried.

Fresh digging at earths from January to March also indicates the presence of foxes in the vicinity. Rabbit burrows are enlarged for tenancy by foxes, characteristically by digging the floor of the burrow, whereas dogs tend to tear down the roof of the burrow, as well as the sides and floor, when hunting for rabbits.

The alarm calls of the jay, magpie and blackbird often indicate the presence of a predator (not necessarily the fox). A more positive sign, however, is the mobbing behaviour of corvids, especially crows and ravens, and of kestrels during their breeding season.

Specialized accounts of field signs of British mammals can be found in Leutscher (1960), Lawrence and Brown (1973) and Bang and Dahlstrom (1974).

# Appendix 2
# Some Field and Laboratory Techniques

## Tagging

One essential feature of any tag used on the fox is that it should be readily visible because whoever tags the animal will usually have to rely upon others to observe the tag, almost invariably after the fox is killed or found dead. Serially numbered aluminium chicken wing tags 2cm long (made by Ketchum Ltd) have been used, but these do not clench as satisfactorily as tags made in monel metal (available from the National Band and Tag Co., Newport, Kentucky, 41072, USA – size 4, style 1005 or from 1.Ö, Mekaniska, Bankeryd, Sweden). Both ears should be tagged (Fairley, 1969b; Hubert *et al.*, 1976). Dalton plastic Roto tags are equally effective, and have the advantage of being brightly coloured and more easily seen.

Sheldon (1949a) describes a light spring-metal collar for fitting to the neck of a fox. It has the advantage that it can be seen at a distance and that reflective Scotchlite tape can be attached to it to enable colour coding for field identification of individual foxes. Also, there is provision in this design for increase in neck size; thus, a juvenile could be fitted with a collar without fear of damage to the fox as it grows. Tags attached to the Achilles tendon have been used (Cook, 1943), but their use is unnecessary since ear tags are satisfactory.

So far as is known, self-attaching snares, such as those used for deer and hares (Romanov, 1956: Verme, 1962), have not been used for foxes; nor is there any record of freeze-branding having been used.

Plastic coloured ear tags (such as Roto tags) have been used for field identification but these are of limited use except when viewed at close quarters.

David Macdonald has used Beta lights (radio-active, tritium-light-emitting devices) on foxes fitted with radio collars to aid identification in the field at night. For methods of estimating numbers of foxes, consult Chapter 4, on Population Dynamics.

I have used Durafur Black B dye (ICI) to aid the identification of captive foxes. It could be used with free-range foxes for visual identification in daytime, but the total number of identification codes would be few – and it would only last until the next moult.

Brightly flashing lights, such as LED displays attached to collars (as used for beavers by Brooks and Dodge, 1978), if fitted to foxes, might put them at a disadvantage when hunting such species as rabbits, for example.

## Age Determination

### Live foxes

In the field, problems of assigning ages to foxes begin when they are about eight months of age. In Britain a well conditioned fox weighing less than 4kg will usually be juvenile. In young animals between nine and fifteen months old the teeth are very clean, the cusps of the pre-molars and molars are pointed, the canines are sharp and the 'fleur de lys' of the upper incisors are well marked. There is no difference between the pellage of young foxes of nine months of age upwards and that of older foxes — the belly hair of juveniles is not darker, as is commonly stated. The ulnar protuberance (at the epiphysis) is well marked up to nine months of age (as in hares and rabbits), and the epiphyseal notch at the head of the tibia can be felt by the thumb nail up to about six months. Reilly and Curren (1961) developed a field technique for feeling the epiphyseal notch of the humerus, which closes at between nine and nine and a half months.

The teeth of the fox continue to erupt because a slight deposition of cementum surrounding the dentine occurs throughout life (thus pushing the tooth up) and because of retraction of the gums. This is revealed in older foxes by exposed dentine between the enamel line and the gum. Ageing by the degree of exposure of dentine is more useful when applied to dead foxes but serves only to give a rough indication of age.

If X-ray facilities are available, the epiphyses of the long bones can be examined in more detail, as described by Sullivan and Haugen (1950). In addition, the pulp cavity of the canine teeth of the fox up to about fifteen months of age, as revealed by X-ray, is larger than in adults. This method was first described by Smirnov in 1960, and has been used by Jensen (pers. comm.). D. H. Johnston (pers. comm.) removes the first pre-molar tooth on the live animal, and ages it by microscopic examination of the cementum.

The nipples of a vixen that has suckled a litter are larger than those of a virgin animal, and there is usually a dark spot in the centre of the nipple.

### Dead foxes

At autopsy three main methods of age determination are available. The weight of dried eye lenses will clearly differentiate between foxes older and younger than fifteen months of age (Friend and Linhart, 1964) but the technique is not as useful for determining the ages of adult animals. A more useful technique is that described by Churcher (1960), which is based on changes that take place with age in the sutures of the skull and in shapes of certain bone processes. His criteria are mainly the closure of the basioccipital-basisphenoid suture between one and two years, of the presphenoid-basisphenoid sutures between two and three years, and the degree of closure of the premaxilla/maxilla sutures from four to seven years. The postorbital process also becomes blunt with age. He provides a key for ageing skulls based on these and other criteria, and correlates increasing age with the degree of exposure of dentine between the alveolus (socket) and enamel line. (Allen, 1974, has demonstrated this in red foxes and Macpherson, 1969, in arctic foxes.) Churcher also showed that it was not possible to differentiate the sex of a fox by the dimensions of the sagittal and nuchal crests, but that sex could be differentiated by a consideration of differences in certain skull proportions.

The annulation of the cementum of canine teeth of the fox has been investigated by many workers. Jensen and Nielsen (1968) and Grue and Jensen (1973) reported their development of this technique in canine teeth. This is a particularly useful method of age determination, since it will give absolute ages to within a few months because the breeding season of the fox is well defined – but it does require much time, microscopy and experience in reading the annulations.

The baculum, or os penis, has been examined as a means of age determination in many of those species of mammals which possess this bone – with fairly satisfactory results; but no reports of investigations on the use of the baculum as an age determinant in the fox are known to me. A comprehensive review of age determination in the fox is given by Harris (1978b).

An examination of the uterus for placental scars may provide evidence of previous pregnancy and thus define a minimum age for a vixen. Staining for haemosiderin may reveal the sites of old scars not seen in untreated uteri. For a review of age determination methods for mammals, see Habermehl (1961) and Morris (1973).

## Capturing and Handling Foxes

Methods of capturing foxes have been described in Chapter 7, some of which are applicable to the live capture of foxes for study purposes. To my knowledge, immobilization by narcotic darts has not been used to capture foxes, and the use of narcotic substances in baits is of doubtful legality for mammals in Britain. A method of fox control once used in Norway (but perhaps not now) was to offer bait to which Luminol (a barbiturate) had been added. The baited foxes were tracked in snow to the place where they lay asleep. In conditions where foxes could be tracked and found this technique, where it is not illegal, could be useful with safer narcotics. Tranquillizer tabs have been used in conjunction with untoothed gin traps in North America. When trapped, the captured animal bites at the jaws of the trap and swallows some of the tranquillizer steeped in a pad around the jaws of the trap (Balser, 1965).

Cage traps will catch foxes, but compared with snares and other techniques, the rewards are small. The designs used are numerous and have no common feature except that the more successful ones are usually larger than $1.5 \times 0.5 \times 0.5$m. The most successful traps are permanently sited and very large, e.g. $4 \times 4 \times 2$m. Cage traps should be visited more often than once a day because foxes can cause considerable damage to their teeth in their attempts to break out. For this reason the mesh of the cage should be no greater than 2.5cm square, and light cord rather than wire should be used for the trip mechanism. The cage door should be locked mechanically when sprung. Preferably the traps should be prebaited in the late afternoon, but outside the trap only; when there is evidence that foxes are taking the bait regularly, bait should then be put in the trap only. Any flesh bait will do; my colleague Chris Cheeseman has caught foxes in cages (placed outside badger setts) baited with peanuts and honey.

Alexander Wandeler has used small cage traps (about $0.75 \times 0.3 \times 0.3$m, fitted with a flap-type door under which the animal pushes) to catch fox cubs in Switzerland. The traps are pushed into the den entrances, which are sealed securely.

Bright new snares can be dulled by boiling in water with oak bark.

Bagging an adult fox, whether it be caught in a net, cage or snare, is something of a problem if it is to be done single-handed. Caged animals can be run into a sack placed at an exit, but two people are needed. A netted animal can be caught by the scruff and the net removed (often it has to be cut), but again two people are needed if the animal is not anaesthetized. If the fox is held in a snare, a thumb stick is useful to engage the snare wire and to pin the animal down by running a stick along the wire. A good hold of the scruff should then be taken and *the snare loop round the animal cut with wire cutters*. If two people are at hand, it is a simple matter to hold the scruff and back legs and to put the fox into a loosely woven hessian sack, but this should not be tried by one person alone unless he is experienced.

Whatever is to be done to the animal should be done quickly to avoid stressing it unduly. Most foxes held firmly do not struggle and they usually lie quietly in a sack. When released after being tagged a fox often runs swiftly for a few metres then stops to cast a glance backwards over its shoulders as if wondering – as most shepherds might – why it had been released.

If working single-handed, it may be necessary to anaesthetize the fox, but in general it would be prudent, from the handler's point of view, to consider the advisability of using drugs given by injection for fear of accident when working far from the laboratory. Since I have no first-hand experience of the use of anaesthetics for foxes and there is little available information on field anaesthesia of foxes, experienced veterinary advice should be sought. The consensus of opinion among those who use anaesthetics to handle foxes is that a tranquillizer should be incorporated with the anaesthetic (for example, Ketamine hydrochloride with Acetylpromazine, in the proportion of 9:1. Inhalation anaesthesia with ether has been used with trapped foxes, but on cold nights outdoors the process can be prolonged and possibly hazardous to the fox if it is not kept warm. The fox is more tolerant of anaesthetics than the domestic dog and higher doses per unit weight seem to be required. Blackmore (1964a) and Graham-Jones (1964) have reported on this aspect; general problems of anaesthesia are considered by Croft (1957) and Lumb (1963).

Individuals using anaesthesia for handling and experimental work on wild foxes in the United Kingdom should enquire from the Home Office whether the particular work can be done without licence. For methods of the humane killing of animals see UFAW (1967) and Carding (1977).

## Bait Markers

If, for whatever purpose, something useful can be learned by feeding foxes at bait stations with food containing substances which can be identified in faeces later, many substances are available.

I have used coloured knitting wool in pieces of rabbit to determine the distances that foxes might range from the bait. Each coloured sample was subdivided into 1- 2- and 3-cm lengths, giving a twenty-four item code in all. This was abandoned in favour of a method suggested to me by Alexander Wandeler. He successfully used 6mm Dymo strip plastic markers, and by adopting a letter-and-numeral code was able to label a very large number of baits individually. Six to ten markers should be used per bait; I used only two, with limited success.

Coloured Alcathene beads manufactured by ICI have been used very successfully for tracing badger ranges by my colleague Dr Chris Cheeseman, who also found the markers in fox faeces. Any non-toxic, non-digestible markers which can be put in bait acceptable to foxes would suffice for the purpose, but Wandeler's method offers the greatest scope.

So far as I know, the marking of baits with dyes which colour faeces (used with rodents by Adamczyk and Ryskowski, 1968) has not been reported for foxes. Fluorescent whitening agents which label faeces and urine also offer possible applications. Rhodamine B dye, incorporated in baits intended for dingoes in Australia, was identified in fox faeces (CSIRO, 1974).

The use of substances that can mark faeces requires much time and effort, as the area has to be searched for faeces — but at least the physical markers persist. All these bait-marking methods are also suitable if foxes are caught and killed soon after baiting, when the markings can be identified in the gut. More persistent markers, identifiable in the dead animal, are required if it is not possible to capture the animals soon after baiting. The antibiotic tetracycline has been used, for example, by Linhart and Kennelly (1967). My colleagues and I have used Ledermycin (tetracycline hydrochloride) in baiting trials (250mg per bait), identifying the animals that took the bait by the characteristic yellow fluorescence in the tibia and jaw bone of foxes killed up to six weeks later.

It should be noted that fatty tissues of foxes, especially those in the neck, normally fluoresce a yellow colour when exposed to ultra-violet light. In young foxes especially, tetracycline is incorporated in new bone as it grows and D.H. Johnston (pers. comm.) was able to determine the day the bait was taken by the labelling of von Ebner's lines in the dentine of the teeth of juveniles.

Decachlorbiphenyl is also a persistent marker, identifiable in liver tissue by gas liquid chromatography. The baits were labelled with 10mg doses of the compound. Sudan Black has also been used, quite unsuccessfully.

## Radio Tracking

The use of radio transmitters to follow the movements of foxes is a technique which was first used in North America. Its use for foxes in Britain is described in Taylor and Lloyd (1978) and in North America by Storm (1965). Mech (1967) describes a method of exploiting telemetry as a technique in the study of predation. The accuracy of radio-tracking systems is described by Heezen and Tester (1967).

Radio transmitters can be used for purposes other than for radio-tracking. Rabbit or lamb carcases, for example, can be 'bugged', and during the breeding season this technique has been used in Wales to locate fox breeding dens to which carcases have been carried back to feed cubs. Similar devices can be adapted to indicate when baits are taken, snares (or traps) sprung, etc; by arranging for the transmitter to be switched on when the expected event occurs. In Britain licences for use of radio telemetry are issued by the Home Office.

## Rearing and Keeping Foxes in Captivity

Very young cubs less than fourteen days old (eyes open at about fourteen days) should be fed on warmed cow's milk (with about 30g of sugar per litre added, and much of the cream removed) at three-hourly intervals. The genital region should be stimulated with absorbent material before and after each feed to promote excretion and to keep the cubs clean. After fourteen days more of the cream in the milk can be included and gradually an increasing amount of dried milk (up to about 60g per litre) can be added to the natural milk.

Cubs can be fed at four to six-hourly intervals until four weeks old, when they can be fed about three times a day. The total daily intake at this time is about 300ml each. Solid food can be introduced at four weeks – liver, rabbit embryos or boneless fish. They can take solid foods exclusively at between seven and eight weeks, but cubs up to four months old should be given supplementary vitamin D.

It is essential to keep cubs and their bedding clean.

Cubs can and have been reared by lactating cats and dogs. Lactating cats used to be kept as wet nurses on silver fox farms to rear orphaned or other cubs. A pseudo-pregnant sheepdog bitch near Builth Wells successfully reared a litter of four cubs; they were reared for hunting purposes but their attraction for dogs sealed their fate – they remained captive pet animals.

Foxes should be kept in cages no smaller than 2 × 2 × 1m, with a kennel, preferably above ground level, 0.5 × 0.5 × 0.75m in size with a small entrance at one end. If the animal is to be handled, the kennel should be located outside the cage, with provision for a sliding door at each end. If possible, such a cage should be portable and should be moved regularly to a fresh patch.

The diet of an adult fox should contain plenty of variety and, if possible, should include a regular supply of fur or feather. Cooked cabbage and other vegetables can provide roughage too. Fruit – particularly apples – are acceptable to foxes. Tinned dog or cat food should form only part of their diet.

Bedding should be provided in the kennels and at least part of the run should be sheltered from rain.

The keeping of foxes should not be undertaken lightly.

# Appendix 3
# Fox Hybrids

Aristotle wrote that boar-hunting dogs were derived from dog/fox crosses and other types of dogs from fox/wolf and dog/tiger crosses. It seems that there was (and still is in some parts of the world) a practice of tethering bitches so that they may mate with wild animals – presumably wolves, as in the case of another heterogeneous cross mentioned by Aristotle. Subsequent natural historians in the family tree of plagiary from Aristotle's time to the fourteenth and fifteenth centuries perpetuated these beliefs, and only recently a correspondent declared to me that in the near future he hoped to cross dogs with captive foxes. Albertus Magnus (1560) affirmed that the hyaena was the progeny of wolf/fox crosses. Topsell (1607), describing a beast which he called variously the 'Apish-fox', 'Simivulpa', 'Alopecopithecos' and 'Fuchsasse', identified it as a cross between a fox and an ape – he was probably referring to a South American opossum.

Literature on foxes abounds with 'evidence', and this quotation from Lloyd's *Natural History (Mammalia)* (1896) is not atypical: 'In the Worcester Museum is an animal . . . which is undoubtedly a cross between a fox and a dog. It was shot wild and can only be the result of such a union.' (Landseer, in a collection of animal portraits, depicts the alleged progeny of a cross between a terrier bitch and dog fox.)

A checklist of mammalian hybrids compiled by Annie Gray (1954) cites known cases of heterogeneous crosses involving foxes and other canids. Crosses between the American red fox and arctic foxes are reported, and whilst there is no disputing the cross, there is some difference of opinion about the fertility of the hybrids, which have short guard hairs, rounded ears and a dense underfur similar to that of the arctic fox. Silver foxes artifically inseminated with arctic fox sperm produced offspring (Starkov, 1940). Generally, these crosses are reported to resemble the red fox in size and growth rate, but the offspring are more vicious and stronger than both parental species. The (diploid) number of chromosomes in artic foxes is 52, but only 38 in the red fox (see below, p. 262). The hybrid chromosome number was stated to be 43.

Crosses of dog/jackal and the reciprocal are possible, and also dog/coyote. Hybrids of dog and *Vulpes* (*Vulpes vulpes* and *Vulpes fulva*) have been reported, but they are of doubtful authenticity. Dog and fox have occasionally shown sexual interest in each other. Most instances of this relate to dog foxes being attracted to bitches on heat, but only one possible case of copulation has been reported (by Niemeyer in 1868). At that time German research workers began to show enormous interest in the possibility of dog/fox crosses, an interest which continued and flourished even up to the 1920s. There are no reliable records of fox/coyote and fox/wolf crosses, but there is a suggestion that *Vulpes fulva* and the American grey fox (*Urocyon cinereoargenteus*) may breed (Bezdek, 1944).

A cross between the South American pampas fox, *Dusicyon*, and a dog has been reported, and anecdotal reports that Guayanan Indians mate the crab-eating fox (*Cercodyon*) with domestic dogs may refer to the same cross as that reported by Krieg (1925). In spite of many accounts of alleged dog/fox crosses, such claims are unsubstantiated by good factual evidence.

A naturally occurring hybrid cross between an escaped silver fox and arctic fox in Iceland has been described by Gudmundsson (1945). The offspring were captured and mated, but the two females miscarried, following matings with silver foxes. In North America, Thornton and his colleagues (1971) described evidence for cross-breeding between the red fox and the desert kit fox (*Vulpes macrotis*). These two species have a narrow overlap in their distribution, and the observations leading to the postulation of hybridization are the descriptions of foxes found in this range of overlap. It is believed that hybridization is limited in extent and that the mechanisms precluding regular hybridization are differences in the times of breeding and in habitat preferences or dispersion. Physiological reasons for the improbability of fox/dog crosses are discussed by Creed (1960a).

The diploid chromosome number of the red fox had been given variously as 34 and 42, until Makino (1948), described it as 38. This was subsequently confirmed by two other workers (Lande, 1958 and Gustavsson, 1964), who showed that the complement consists of 32 medium-sized chromosomes, a medium-sized X chromosome and 4 dot-like micro-chromosomes in the female and 5 in the male. One of these was the Y chromosome, which was the smallest of all. Other workers (Moore and Elder, 1965; Gustavsson and Sundt, 1967; Buckton and Cunningham, 1971) have subsequently shown that though the 33 medium-sized chromosomes in the male and 34 in the female were invariable in number, variation in the number of the (autosomic) micro-chromosomes occurred both within and between individuals. Although the most commonly found complement was 38 chromosomes, these workers severally found a range from 35 to 40 chromosomes. Thus it would seem that the micro-chromosomes can vary in number from 1 to 6. The genetics of the red fox in this and other contexts is reviewed by Robinson (1975).

# Appendix 4
# Urban Foxes

In recent years the term 'town fox' or 'urban fox' has become well known, as the city-dwelling fox is a common phenomenon south of Nottingham (and in Glasgow and Edinburgh). There may be some precise administrative definition of the terms urban and suburban, but from the ecological point of view one can merge gradually into the other without clearly defined habitat demarcation, and there can be islands of one within the other. Furthermore, one suburban area may differ markedly from another from the fox's point of view, and the same applies to urban areas. If urban areas are defined as areas where concrete and tarmacadam predominate, then from the fox's point of view towns are poor places to live.

Foxes are found in such places, however, but where they are clearly residential rather than itinerant, the circumstances obtaining tend to emphasise the requirements of town foxes. In the more outlying areas of towns or cities, where the residential areas enjoy household gardens and other open spaces (fields, parks, allotments, industrial complexes, and so on) the fox can find space to live. If such areas contain abundant surface cover and the possibility of some seclusion, the area becomes a highly desirable residential area for the fox – judging by the number of foxes that are encountered.

Although the non-rural fox is located primarily in suburban areas – as described here – in keeping with the current trend it will be referred to as the urban fox.

The distribution of urban foxes is determined by the availability of suitable daytime refuge of whatever form, whether it be a pile of uncut timber in a timber yard, an earth under a garden shed, a lying-up place under the platform of a suburban railway station or an earth in a railway cutting. How far the foxes move during their nocturnal wanderings is not known but, as with rural foxes, doubtless their habits are determined by the availability and distribution of food and by competition for it according to the density of foxes in any area.

One obvious feature of the behaviour of urban foxes is that they are rather more gregarious than foxes in most rural communities. When complaints of fox nuisance in urban areas used to be dealt with by the Ministry of Agriculture (up to 1968) those concerned knew from previous experience where the foxes would probably be found in daytime. Dens and earths not previously known to the control staff were always being discovered, but the distribution of cover was such that the most suitable places would be used year after year, and often several foxes would be taken in a comparatively small area, whether in a single earth in an allotment or garden, or in cover afforded by rhododendron bushes in the grounds of some institution. Clearly, there must be greater social involvement between one fox and another living in such close proximity than there is in the less closely associated rural fox communities, but such close shoulder-rubbing probably exists in high-density rural fox communities, and the situation in urban areas is perhaps no more than a normal behavioural adaptation to circumstances common to both rural and urban dwelling foxes. The entire way of life of urban foxes, including their behaviour, is essentially no different from that of rural foxes. A fox is a fox whether it be urban or rural, British or Japanese, and behavioural or physiological differences observed in different places all seem to fall within the known range of response of the fox to external or environmental stimuli. The features which determine distribution and abundance may be different for urban foxes; food availability is usually the most important limiting factor in most fox communities, but in some urban areas it might be the availability to cover which is at a premium.

The urban fox appears to be less timid than the rural fox, but its temerity in the presence of man is only a matter of degree, inspired by mutual tolerance or, at least in urban areas, by the indifference of the majority of the human species encountered by the fox. Were this to extend to immunity to interference from dogs, whether it be the barking of a frightened miniature lapdog or a chase by a larger dog, its timidity would perhaps be even further suppressed. Secure refuge would be less vital to its survival; food might then have a more direct bearing on the distribution of the urban fox and it could adopt to a greater extent the role of the stray dog or cat, without, however, forfeiting its capacity to live off the land as a predator and scavenger.

Wherever the fox lives it is an opportunist, and its diet in urban areas amply demonstrates this. The urban fox has not abandoned its predatory role – indeed, perhaps town life is not so soft that it could afford to do so. Small mammals (particularly the field vole), birds and earthworms still occur frequently in the diet, but it is augmented by an immense variety of scavenged food, much of which the country fox would scarcely ever encounter. Not a great deal is known about the quantitative aspect of urban fox diet, however; my colleague, R. J. Page, and I abandoned our own studies when it became clear, that in describing the contents of fox stomachs it was not possible to relate foods eaten to what was available, nor to determine how the items described were obtained by the fox. We had no means of telling whether all foxes were equally opportunistic, whether some were relegated by other foxes to eating the least desirable foods whatever they might be, whether some had developed their own individual life-style, nor whether it was essential to the well-being of the fox to eat a certain proportion of natural prey regularly, and so forth. Also, the identification of scavenged material was tedious, often impossible and not attempted unless there were obvious clues. But it was already clear from our colleagues' field reports of foxes visiting bird tables, rummaging in compost heaps and dustbins, pilfering (even in daylight) scraps put out for dogs and cats and visiting factory canteen waste that in due course, had we been able, we would have been able to compile a list of scavenged foods that would have included everything that appears on the kitchen table – and a lot else besides. Evidence at dens and earths highlighted the unusual and included such items as remnants of dog and cat, ornamental ducks, poultry, a cockatoo-like bird, a kestrel and a large part of a cow's rumen. Sawn butcher's bones were common. Though imprecise and superficial, the picture of urban fox diet that has emerged indicates that it is behaving no differently from rural foxes, except that the scene is different. There is no difference between the country fox feeding on a dead calf dumped by a farmer in a ditch and the town fox feeding on a dog killed by a car; and a dustbin provides similar kinds of food whether it be in a caravan park, a country lay-by or an urban back yard. The same controversy over predation on man's livestock exists in both areas, but in urban areas substitute cats for lambs and cage birds for poultry. Possibly the only large-scale difference is the more regular supply of scavengable food in urban areas and the greater availability (though not necessarily an abundance) of earthworms on the short swards of domestic lawns than on the rougher rural pastures.

Current research on urban foxes in Greater London by Dr Stephen Harris (as yet unreported) has revealed an increasing occurrence of sarcoptic mange in foxes since about 1971. In addition, he has demonstrated a deformity of the spinal column, spondylosis deformans, in a very high proportion of urban foxes. Whether or not this condition is exclusive to urban foxes is not yet known, since no one else seems to have examined foxes for this condition. It will be interesting to learn in due course whether or not these conditions are considered to be related to diet.

Litter sizes of cubs born to rural foxes and the proportions of vixens that produce cubs vary from place to place, and sometimes from one year to another in the same place (see Table 17). Some of the apparent variation is real and some is due to variability in sample composition and size. The same applies to urban fox populations. The pattern of reproduction and reproductive productivity in urban areas is probably identical to that in rural areas, and the variability found between and within each of the two areas will be determined by the same environmental restraints on reproduction, such that, for example, populations at high densities will show poorer reproductive performance than those at low densities. This example serves as a generality; doubtless there are features which determine variability even between populations of low density (such as might be the case between a population low in numbers which has reached the maximum that the area will carry and others which may be artificially depressed in number by man or by disease, or which are capable of increasing in numbers when new areas are colonized or when there is some beneficial change in the environment). Thus, although urban foxes from some areas reveal differences in reproductive patterns, sometimes showing better performance, sometimes worse, the differences are within the range of variability that can be found in rural fox populations. In this context especially, other foxes and their abundance and dispersion constitute an important part of the environment.

As with reproduction, the longevity and survival rates of urban fox populations that I have examined differ in certain respects from those of rural fox communities; whilst it is tempting to assign the differences to some overt feature of the environment – say, to disease, road deaths, hunting, control or unsuitable diet – the inference would be unwarranted because the population structure of different communities of urban foxes sampled fall within the range observed in different rural fox populations.

Whilst samples of foxes collected by my colleagues for our studies can be grouped according to geographical areas or distinctly different agricultural areas, the habitat (let alone the environment within these areas) lacks uniformity; in effect, one may be comparing samples from wholly incomparable areas. Without doubt, the non-uniformity of samples obtained for study presents a major difficulty in making correct inferences, and in this respect foxes collected in urban environments may, if one were forced to hazard a guess, be the more reliably representative.

The collection of adequate information on fox numbers is a laborious business and data are as difficult to obtain in urban and suburban areas as elsewhere. My colleague, R.J. Page, benefiting from help given by local authority staff and inhabitants of the Borough of Hillingdon, sought and located fox breeding dens during the breeding season and in this way derived a minimum density of adult foxes of 2.6 foxes per square kilometre . For comparison, by a similar method Insley (1977) estimated fox numbers in the New Forest in 1975 to be 2.2 foxes per square kilometre. On mixed farming land in north Pembrokeshire a similarly based estimate of 3.7 foxes per square kilometre was derived in 1977 (see Table 26). If road sightings of foxes at night are any indication of numbers, the frequent sightings of foxes in the London suburbs and fringe areas and in north Pembrokeshire contrast sharply with the infrequent sightings of foxes on roads in mid-Wales and tend to confirm the experimental evidence of relative numbers in these areas.

There is little available information about the movement of foxes in urban areas. Home-range sizes are not known, but some information on dispersal movements is accruing. Page (pers. comm.) has tagged some 200 cubs in a suburban and urban London area. Those that have been recovered as a result of accidental death, natural mortality or control effort reveal that males disperse about eight kilometres from their place of birth and females about 2.5 kilometres. These figures are likely to change as more foxes are recovered, but it is unlikely that the discrepancy between males and females will alter markedly. Railways probably provide easy dispersal routes.

It is popularly assumed that the urban fox is a comparatively new phenomenon. Perhaps it is, as there is little evidence to suggest that they were in urban areas some sixty or seventy years ago. They were certainly found in urban areas before the first outbreak of myxomatosis (in 1953), however, and in some areas before 1939. They did not, apparently, derive from a spread of foxes from rural areas following an increase in reproductive productivity and increased survival of cubs promoted by an abundance of food during the 1954-55 myxomatosis epizootic, as seems to have been the case in some rural areas of Scotland (Hewson and Kolb, 1973), though such infiltration could have been a contributory cause of an increase in numbers of foxes which was reported in the late 1950s. The first irruptions of urban foxes were probably due not so much to an influx of foxes as to extensive housing development in the suburban fringes in the 1920–40 period. The fragmentary sprawl of residential areas into the Green Belts left many islands of agricultural land which could have been the foci for recolonization of the developed areas. Whether this was a contributory factor any more than the decline in the numbers of gamekeepers or sporting estates in the suburban fringes is conjectural. It would perhaps be nearer the truth to say that many contributory factors probably led to the colonization of urban areas –

whatever the cause, the effect is persistent.

In Europe the urban fox is almost unique to Britain. Foxes do not apparently occur in heavily built-up and residential areas except in Copenhagen, where they seem to have adopted a mode of life similar to that of British urban foxes. In Copenhagen the petrol crisis of the mid-1970s revealed the presence of foxes well inside the urban areas. Weekend motoring was prohibited to conserve petrol, and when the roads were again thronged with traffic, foxes which had quickly become used to the quiet weekends, fell victim to the sudden surge of traffic. Those killed were probably outside their accustomed range.

Foxes are apparently found in the fringe of residential areas in only a few European cities. But foxes in continental Europe do feed on human waste, in some situations, possibly, to a greater extent than urban foxes in Britain. In Switzerland, for example, rural foxes scavenge in the vicinity of human dwellings, probably because farmsteads and other dwellings are scattered in open areas near to the ever-present coniferous woodland where foxes find daytime refuge. Wandeler (pers. comm.) found human waste in the diet of over 50% of rural foxes examined in Switzerland.

# Tables

**Table 1  Linear dimensions of foxes** (mm: range shown in brackets)

|  | Head and body | Tail | Hind foot | Ear |
|---|---|---|---|---|
| Wales | ♂ 666 | 411 | 154 | 90 |
| (samples: 50) | (570–747) | (350–465) | (130–172) | (83–102) |
|  | ♀ 622 | 380 | 142 | 86 |
|  | (560–730) | (330–420) | (130–155) | (82–98) |
| England | ♂ 671 | 412 | 152 | 93 |
| Hattingh, 1956 |  |  |  |  |
| (sample: 31–45) | ♀ 627 | 385 | 141 | 89 |
| Scotland | ♂ 712 | 436 | 167 | 95 |
| Kolb and Hewson, | (659–750) | (388–493) | (143–178) | (87–106) |
| 1974 |  |  |  |  |
| (sample: 39 males, | ♀ 679 | 411 | 159 | 94 |
| 30 females) | (574–732) | (277–491) | (143–168) | (89–102) |
| Northern Ireland | ♂ 723 | 367 | 161 | 104 |
| Fairley, 1970a | (635–777) | (222–429) | (109–173) | (94–113) |
| (sample: 42) |  |  |  |  |
|  | ♀ 677 | 348 | 151 | 99 |
|  | (614–744) | (289–410) | (134–166) | (56–110) |

**Table 2 Mean live weights of foxes**

| | Males | | Females | | | Ratio of weight of ♀♀ to ♂♂ |
|---|---|---|---|---|---|---|
| | No. in sample | Mean weight (g) | No. in sample | Mean weight (g) | | |
| Kansas USA | 24 | 4630 | 7 | 3770 | (Stanley, 1963) | 1·228 |
| Indiana USA (winter) | 47 | 5250 | 52* | 4210 | (Hoffman and Kirkpatrick, 1954) | 1·254 |
| Norway | 193 | 5900 | 107 | 5100 | (Lund, 1959) | 1·156 |
| Netherlands | 100 | 5960 | 100* | 5100 | (van Haaften, 1970) | 1·168 |
| England (Westmorland) | 7 | 6260 | — | | (Hattingh, 1956) | |
| Australia | 84 | 6300 | 60* | 5500 | (McIntosh, 1963b) | 1·145 |
| Wales | 463 | 6401 | 610 | 5540 | (Lloyd and Page, unpublished) | 1·168 |
| SE England | 262 | 6446 | 234 | 5540 | (Lloyd and Page, unpublished) | 1·160 |
| Southern England (Feb. to May) | 33 | 6670 | 29* | 5410 | (Hattingh, 1956) | 1·232 |
| Scotland | 6 | 6720 | 5* | 5720 | (Hattingh, 1956) | 1·174 |
| East Germany | 59 | 6872 | 39 | 5700 | (Stubbe and Stubbe, 1977) | 1·205 |
| Ireland | 207 | 6900 | 159 | 5700 | (Fairley, 1970a) | 1·210 |
| Scotland (Fife) | 26 | 7225 | 34 | 5950 | (Lloyd, unpublished) | 1·214 |
| Scotland (NE and Argyll) | 39 | 7300 | 30† | 6200 | (Kolb and Hewson, 1974) | 1·177 |
| England (fell foxes, Cumberland) | 14 | 7380 | 14 | 6485 | (Ian Gray, pers. comm.) | 1·144 |
| Denmark (Jutland) | 252 | 7600 | 198 | 6100 | (Birger Jensen, pers. comm.) | 1·246 |

† may include pregnant vixens
* includes pregnant vixens in samples

**Table 3 Skull measurements – mean and range** (mm: range shown in brackets)

| | Scotland[1] ♂(6) | England[2] ♂(9) | SE England[3] ♂(16) | SE England[3] ♀(12) | Wales[3] ♂(10) | Wales[3] ♀(10) |
|---|---|---|---|---|---|---|
| Condylo-basal length | 150·7 (138·5–157·0) | 144·6 (135·0–151·5) | 144·7 (137·8–152·8) | 136·2 (129·6–141·1) | 146·4 (135·4–154·0) | 136·0 (132·2–139·8) |
| Zygomatic width | 83·2 (81·0–85·5) | 81·9 (76·0–86·0) | 84·1 (79·7–90·7) | 78·5 (74·8–81·8) | 82·0 (75·9–86·5) | 76·1 (70·3–80·0) |
| Inter-orbital width | 39·6 (27·5–33·0) | 30·3 (22·0–32·5) | 31·3 (27·9–34·5) | 28·9 (27·4–31·4) | 29·8 (27·2–35·0) | 27·6 (24·6–30·2) |
| Post-orbital width | — — | — — | 21·4 (18·6–24·2) | 21·9 (18·3–24·6) | 22·4 (18·5–27·9) | 21·9 (20·5–24·1) |
| Mandible | 118·8 (113·0–124·5) | 112·5 (103·5–117·5) | 112·2 (104·6–117·2) | 105·2 (99·8–109·8) | 112·6 (103·1–119) | 104·5 (100·8–108·8) |
| Maxillary tooth row | 69·3 (66·5–72·5) | 64·9 (61·0–69·0) | | | | — |
| Mandibular tooth row | 78·5 (72·5–82·0) | 73·1 (69·0–77·0) | 78·3 (74·3–81·8) | 73·4 (69·5–75·9) | 79·0 (74·4–84·0) | 74·2 (72·5–77·3) |
| Length of upper tooth row | — | — | 76·6 (73·0–83·8) | 72·2 (67·3–77·4) | 77·9 (71·4–83·0) | 72·8 (71·2–75·0) |

[1] Tetley (1940)  [2] Hattingh (1956)  [3] Page and Lloyd (unpublished)

**Table 4  Mean body weights of male and female foxes from six Welsh counties.** Duration of sampling period shown ( )

| | Males | | Females (Dec., Jan., Feb. only) | | Ratio of weights: |
|---|---|---|---|---|---|
| | No. of foxes | Mean weight (kg) | No. of foxes | Mean weight (kg) | females = 100 |
| Pembrokeshire (4 years) | 131 | 6·07 | 75 | 5·05 | 120·2 |
| Carmarthenshire (2 years) | 62 | 6·14 | 48 | 5·35 | 114·8 |
| Breconshire (4 years) | 138 | 6·54 | 108 | 5·47 | 119·6 |
| Cardiganshire (2 years) | 49 | 6·63 | 36 | 5·76 | 115·1 |
| Radnorshire (3 years) | 41 | 6·81 | 33 | 5·76 | 118·2 |
| Montgomeryshire (3 years) | 42 | 6·84 | 44 | 5·99 | 114·2 |
| Totals | 463 | 6·42 | 344 | 5·47 | 117·4 |

Mean weight of all vixens in Wales (610) = 5.85kg
Mean weight of all vixens in SE England (234) = 5.85kg
Mean weight of vixens, Dec.-Feb., in Wales (344) = 5.47kg
Mean weight of vixens, Dec.-Feb., in SE England (127) = 5.54kg
Mean difference in weight between female and male foxes in entire sample (1,569 foxes) = female: male 1:1.16, males being a mean of 16.4 % heavier than vixens.


**Table 5  Seasonal body weights of male foxes**

| Month | SE England (1966–9 inclusive) | | Wales (6 counties 1966–9 inclusive) | |
|---|---|---|---|---|
| | No. of foxes | Mean weight (kg) | No. of foxes | Mean weight (kg) |
| J | 58 | 6·53 | 169 | 6·53 |
| F | 45 | 6·35 | 105 | 6·49 |
| M | 62 | 6·40 | 69 | 6·27 |
| A | 9 | 6·21 | 36 | 6·31 |
| M | 3 | 6·53 | 12 | 6·08 |
| J | 1 | 6·81 | 3 | 6·35 |
| J | 2 | 7·04 | — | — |
| A | 7 | 5·67 | — | — |
| S | 14 | 6·58 | — | — |
| O | 8 | 6·58 | 4 | 6·35 |
| N | 16 | 6·62 | 16 | 6·31 |
| D | 37 | 6·63 | 47 | 6·31 |
| Totals | 262 | 6·45 | 461 | 6·43 |

**Table 6  Weights of foxes according to age***

| | Suburbia | | | | | Elsewhere | | | | |
| | Males | | | Females | | Males | | | Females | |
| | No. of foxes | LW (g) | PW (g) | No. of foxes | PW (g) | No. of foxes | LW (g) | PW (g) | No. of foxes | PW (g) |
|---|---|---|---|---|---|---|---|---|---|---|
| 1–11 months | 53 | 6430 | 5980 | 44 | 5020 | 141 | 6240 | 5810 | 168 | 4910 |
| 1·0–1·11 years | 45 | 6768 | 6230 | 41 | 5130 | 145 | 6590 | 6100 | 184 | 5060 |
| 2·0–2·11 years | 26 | 6850 | 6380 | 24 | 5370 | 77 | 6750 | 6290 | 97 | 5330 |
| 3·0–3·11 years | 13 | 7130 | 6640 | 15 | 5500 | 40 | 6910 | 6390 | 58 | 5290 |
| 4·0–4·11 years | 10 | 7470 | 6850 | 5 | 5850 | 31 | 7050 | 5650 | 25 | 5260 |
| 5·0–5·11 years | 3 | 7180 | 6570 | 2 | 5490 | 6 | 6720 | 6190 | 13 | 5170 |
| 6·0–6·11 years | 1 | 5890 | 5440 | 4 | 5100 | 1 | 5890 | 5440 | 8 | 5130 |
| 7·0–7·11 years | 1 | 5890 | 5210 | 1 | 7640 | 4 | 6510 | 6010 | 3 | 5950 |
| 8·0–8·11 years | — | — | — | — | — | — | — | — | 1 | 4310 |
| 9·0–9·11 years | — | — | — | — | — | — | — | — | 1 | 4540 |

* Data mostly refers to the period October–April inclusive
LW = live weight
PW = paunched weight: stomach gut (and uterus) removed

**Table 7  Mean weights of 450 foxes (*Vulpes vulpes*) collected in south Jutland, Denmark, mid-October 1967—end January 1968\***

| Age | Males | Females |
|-----|-------|---------|
| | (sample size in brackets) | |
| 1 year | 7·4kg (189) | 6·0kg (148) |
| 1–2 years | 7·9kg (27) | 6·4kg (24) |
| 2 years | 8·2kg (36) | 6·6kg (26) |
| Totals | 7·6kg (252) | 6·1kg (198) |

\* Jensen, pers. comm.

**Table 8  Ratio of length to body weight**

| | Mean Head and body length (mm) | Mean Weight (g) | Ratio or length/ weight factor |
|---|---|---|---|
| *Males* | | | |
| Wales | 666 | 6460 | 9·7 |
| England (Hattingh, 1956) | 671 | 6670 | 9·9 |
| Ireland (Fairley, 1970a) | 723 | 6900 | 9·5 |
| Scotland (Kolb and Hewson, 1974) | 712 | 7300 | 10·3 |
| *Females* | | | |
| Wales | 622 | 5340 | 8·6 |
| England (Hattingh, 1956) | 627 | 5410 | 8·6 |
| Ireland (Fairley, 1970a) | 677 | 5700 | 8·4 |
| Scotland (Kolb and Hewson, 1974) | 679 | 6200 | 9·1 |

**Table 9  Fox diet before and after the first outbreak of myxomatosis: percentage occurrence of main items**

| | a* | b* | c* | d† | e† | f† | g† | h† | i† | j* | k† |
|---|---|---|---|---|---|---|---|---|---|---|---|
| No. of stomachs with contents | 26 | 25 | 17 | 340 | 163 | 106 | 372 | 67 | 64 | 30 | 120 |
| Small rodents | 23 | 16 | ⎱ 18 | 6 | 1 | 52 | 48 | 45 | 34 | 39 | 46 |
| Rat | — | — | ⎰ | 17 | 16 | 6 | 12 | 9 | 13 | — | — |
| Lagomorph | 49 | 68 | 47 | 45 | 59 | 34 | 25 | 30 | 13 | 59 | 42 |
| Sheep | 38 | 4 | 65 | 9 | 6 | 33 | 9 | 51 | 9 | 0 | 5 |
| Birds – wild and domestic | 27 | 40 | 29 | 42 | 35 | 40 | 63 | 30 | 45 | 53 | 54 |

\* before myxomatosis  † after myxomatosis
a adults, hill land, Wales 1939 (Southern and Watson, 1941)
b adults, lowland, England 1939 (Southern and Watson, 1941)
c adults, England 1955 (Lever, 1959)
d adults, Northern Ireland, 1966-8 (Fairley, 1970a)
e cubs, Northern Ireland, 1966-8 (Fairley, 1970a)
f adults, hill land, England, Wales and Scotland, 1955-8 (Lever, 1959)
g adults, lowland, mainly England, 1955-8 (Lever, 1959)
h adults, hill land, Wales, 1966 (Lloyd, unpublished)
i adults, Kent, 1966 (Lloyd, unpublished)
j adults, Gotland, Sweden, 1961 (Englund, 1965b)
k adults, Gotland, Sweden, 1961-2 (Englund, 1965b)

**Table 10  Fox stomach analysis***

| | Adults—Wales (Jan.–March only) | | Adults—Kent (Jan.–March only) | | Cubs—Wales (March–June) | |
|---|---|---|---|---|---|---|
| No. of stomachs | 84 | | 102 | | 82 | |
| No. empty | 17 | | 38 | | 6 | |
| No. with contents | 67 | | 64 | | 76 | |
| | | % | | % | | % |
| No. with: (= frequency of occurrence) | | | | | | |
| Microtus | 23 | 34·3 | 17 | 26·5 | 30 | 36·5 |
| Clethrionomys | 4 | 5·9 | 2 | 3·1 | 2 | 2·6 |
| Apodemus | 3 | 4·5 | 3 | 4·6 | 10 | 13·1 |
| Lagomorph | 20 | 29·8 | 25 | 39·0 | 15 | 26·2 |
| Rat | 6 | 8·9 | 8 | 12·5 | | |
| Sheep | 34 | 50·7 | 8 | 12·5 | 36 | 47·3 |
| Shrew | 1 | 1·5 | 6 | 9·3 | 21 | 27·6 |
| Badger | 1 | 1·5 | 0 | 0 | | |
| Roe deer | 0 | 0 | 2 | 3·1 | | |
| Hedgehog | 0 | 0 | 1 | 1·5 | | |
| Pig | 1 | 1·5 | 2 | 3·1 | | |
| Fat | 1 | 1·5 | 2 | 3·1 | | |
| Unidentified fur | 1 | 1·5 | 4 | 6·2 | | |
| Unidentified bird remains | 3 | 4·5 | 5 | 7·8 | | |
| Beetles | 10 | 15·0 | 4 | 6·2 | | |
| Other insects | 2 | 3·0 | 4 | 6·2 | | |
| Blowfly maggots | | | | | 4 | 5·2 |
| Grass | 8 | 11·9 | 12 | 18·7 | | |
| Other plant matter | 1 | 1·5 | 5 | 7·8 | | |
| Apples and pears | 0 | 0 | 6 | 9·3 | | |
| Earthworms | 1 | 1·5 | 0 | 0 | | |
| Cardboard, cloth, leather, polythene, cellophane etc. | 0 | 0 | 10 | 15·6 | | |
| Birds | | | | | 5 | 6·5 |
| Passeriformes (song birds) | 6 | 8·9 | 9 | 14·0 | | |
| Galliformes (game birds and poultry) | 10 | 14·9 | 12 | 18·7 | | |
| Columbiformes (pigeons) | 1 | 1·5 | 5 | 7·8 | | |
| Anseriformes (ducks and geese) | 2 | 3·0 | 1 | 1·5 | | |
| Charadriformes (waders) | 1 | 1·5 | 0 | 0 | | |
| Ralliformes (rails, coots) | 0 | 0 | 2 | 3·1 | | |
| Mollusc shells | | | | | 1 | 1·0 |

* Lloyd and Page (unpublished)

275

## Table 11  Fox diet in an arid area of Australia*

| | % occurrence (55 stomachs) |
|---|---|
| Red kangaroo | 6·9 |
| (much carrion in sampling area) | |
| Rabbit | 34·5 |
| Goat | 3·6 |
| Sheep | 10·9 |
| Marsupial mouse | 1·8 |
| Emu | 16·0 |
| Other birds (4 species) | 7·3 |
| Geckos, lizards, snakes and skinks | 38·2 |
| Water-holding frog | 12·2 |
| Centipedes | 20·0 |
| Grasshoppers | 10·9 |
| Beetles | 52·7 |
| (one stomach contained 143 individuals of a beetle species occupying 200 ml) | |
| Moths, adult and caterpillar | 20·0 |
| Scorpions and spiders | 24·5 |

* After Martensz (1971)

## Table 12  Fox stomach analysis: Missouri, 1949–54*

| | % occurrence (1006 adult foxes) |
|---|---|
| Rabbits and hares | 39·3 |
| Mice, voles and rats | 51·4 |
| Other mammals (including squirrels, opossum cat, raccoon, skunk, woodchuck, muskrat, pocket gophers, shrew and mole traces only) | 10·4 |
| Poultry including ducks | 13·6 |
| Pig | 5·2 |
| Sheep | 1·9 |
| Calf and goat | 0·4 |
| Birds | 14·7 |
| Song birds | 7·7 |
| Quail | 2·4 |
| Beetles, grasshoppers and traces of other insects | 6·1 |
| Fish and reptiles | 0·8 |
| Grass | 13·8 |
| Fruit and nuts | 2·7 |

* Korschgen (1959)

**Table 13   Fox stomach analysis: Finland***

|                                                              | % occurrence (325 stomachs) |
| ------------------------------------------------------------ | --------------------------- |
| Game animals (mainly alpine hares, squirrels and muskrats)   | 14·0                        |
| Game birds                                                   | 10·3                        |
| Poultry                                                      | 9·1                         |
| Small rodents                                                | 18·5                        |
| Cats                                                         | 1·4                         |
| Hedgehogs                                                    | 1·4                         |
| Rats                                                         | 2·0                         |
| Non-game birds                                               | 2·3                         |
| Insects                                                      | 1·1                         |
| Fruit and vegetables                                         | 3·2                         |

* From Lampio (1953)

**Table 14   Fox stomach analysis: Bulgaria***

|                             | % occurrence (320 adults) |
| --------------------------- | ------------------------- |
| *Muridae* (voles and mice)  | 24·1                      |
| Poultry                     | 21·4                      |
| Hares                       | 17·6                      |
| Birds                       | 8·7                       |
| Insects                     | 11·2                      |
| Fawns                       | 0·4                       |
| Polecat                     | 0·1                       |
| Tortoise                    | 0·3                       |
| Fish                        | 0·1                       |
| Lizard                      | 0·3                       |
| Frog                        | 0·2                       |
| Pig                         | 0·1                       |
| Carrion                     | 7·3                       |
| Unidentified                | 6·5                       |

* After Peshev (1963)

Table 15 Foods of stoats and weasels after myxomatosis: Britain*

| | % occurrence | | | | |
| | Stoats | | Weasels | | |
| | A | C | A | B | C |
|---|---|---|---|---|---|
| *Microtus* (field voles) | 9·5 | 1·7 | 26·0 | 41·3 | 32·2 |
| *Clethrionomys* (bank voles) | 4·5 | — | 9·0 | 16·0 | 6·9 |
| *Apodemus* (wood mice) | 4·0 | 3·4 | 8·5 | 0·5 | 2·1 |
| *Mus* (house mice) | — | | 2·5 | — | 1·4 |
| Unidentified small rodents | 3·5 | 3·5 | 8·5 | 11·2 | 11·1 |
| *Rattus* (rats) | 3·0 | | 2·5 | — | — |
| *Insectivores* (shrews or moles) | 0·5 | | 1·5 | 2·4 | 1·4 |
| Squirrels | 1·5 | | — | — | — |
| Lagomorphs (hares or rabbits) | 28·0 | 56·0 | 19·0 | 13·1 | 7·6 |
| Birds | 33·0 | 25·2 | 14·5 | 12·6 | 27·1 |
| Eggs | — | 10·4 | — | 2·4 | 4·2 |
| Insects | 3·5 | — | 4·0 | — | — |
| Invertebrates | 0·5 | — | 1·5 | — | — |
| Plant remains | 7·0 | — | 2·0 | — | — |

* From Day (1968) (A); Moors (1975) (B); Tapper (1976) (C). This table is presented as a general comparison of the diets of foxes and these two small mustelids. The diets of all three species are not unlike qualitatively but differ quantitatively. This is partly due to the way of life of the three species and to the availability of the different foods in the areas where the studies were made. More food is potentially available to the fox than to stoats and weasels, since it is capable of taking larger prey and feeds on carrion.

**Table 16　Occurrences of barren vixens**

| | No. of ovulated vixens | (a) direct observation of dead embryos | (b) by inference | Pseudo-pregnant or non-fecund vixens | Total | % barren |
|---|---|---|---|---|---|---|
| **1966** | | | | | | |
| Mid-Wales | 27 | 0 | 3 | 2 | 5 | 18·5 |
| SE England | 24 | 2 | 1 | 3 | 6 | 25·0 |
| **1967** | | | | | | |
| Mid-Wales | } 73 | 1 | 0 | 0 | 1 | } 19·2 |
| West Wales | | 3 | 5 | 5 | 13 | |
| SE England | 35 | 2 | 0 | 1 | 3 | 8·6 |
| **1968** | | | | | | |
| Mid-Wales | 26 | 1 | 0 | 5 | 6 | 23·0 |
| **1969** | | | | | | |
| Mid-Wales | } 102 | 3 | 3 | 8 | 14 | } 24·5 |
| West Wales | | 7 | 1 | 3 | 11 | |
| Total | *287 | 19 (6·6%) | 13 (4·5%) | 27 (9·4%) | 59 20·5% | 20·5 |

* Includes 5 non-ovulated anoestrus vixens
Death of all embryos by inference (b) includes abortions and post-natal deaths of young

**Table 17　Mean number of embryos per pregnant vixen at five stages of gestation**

| | No. of pregnant vixens | Tubal ova | Blasto-cysts | Less than 30 days | 30–41 days | 42–53 days |
|---|---|---|---|---|---|---|
| **Wales** | | | | | | |
| 1966 | 19 | 5·3 | 5·6 | 6·0 | 5·8 | 3·0 |
| 1967 | 62 | 4·6 | 4·5 | 4·2 | 4·1 | 4·4 |
| 1968 | 21 | 5·0 | 5·0 | 6·0 | 6·2 | 6·5 |
| 1969 | 100 | 4·2 | 3·8 | 5·0 | 5·1 | 4·9 |
| Total | 202 | 4·5 | 4·2 | 5·1 | 5·1 | 4·7 |
| | | | | | | |
| **Kent and SE England** | | | | | | |
| 1966 | 21 | 5·3 | 6·0 | 5·0 | 4·0 | 5·7 |
| 1967 | 33 | 5·1 | 4·3 | 4·9 | 4·6 | 6·0 |
| 1969 | 21 | 5·7 | 5·0 | 4·3 | 4·8 | 4·7 |
| Total | 75 | 5·2 | 5·1 | 4·8 | 4·5 | 5·4 |

**Table 18   Mean number of corpora lutea and birth litter size**

| | No. of corpora lutea ovary | | | No. of vixens ovulated | Mean no. of corpora lutea | Mean birth litter size |
|---|---|---|---|---|---|---|
| | Left | Right | Total | | | |
| Wales | | | | | | |
| 1966 | 71 | 83 | 154 | 27 | 5·7 | 3·0 |
| 1967 | 193 | 206 | 399 | 73 | 5·5 | 4·4 |
| 1968 | 91 | 87 | 178 | 26 | 6·8 | 6·5 |
| 1969 | 263 | 297 | 560 | 102 | 5·5 | 4·9 |
| Total | 618 | 673 | 1291 | 228 | 5·7 | 4·7 |
| | (47·9%) | (52·1%) | (100%) | | | |
| Kent | | | | | | |
| 1966 | 69 | 81 | 150 | 24 | 6·2 | 5·7 |
| 1967 | 90 | 88 | 178 | 35 | 5·1 | 6·0 |
| 1969 | 68 | 80 | 148 | 28 | 5·3 | 4·7 |
| Total | 227 | 249 | 476 | 87 | 5·5 | 5·4 |
| | (47·7%) | (52·3%) | (100%) | | | |

**Table 19   Distribution of litter sizes of the last 10 days of gestation (42-53 days) in 114 vixens: Wales**

| No. of embryos | No. of examples | % frequency |
|---|---|---|
| 1 | 4 | 3·5 |
| 2 | 8 | 7·0 |
| 3 | 20 | 17·5 |
| 4 | 24 | 21·0 |
| 5 | 36 | 31·5 |
| 6 | 10 | 8·7 |
| 7 | 8 | 7·0 |
| 8 | 2 | 1·7 |
| 9 | 0 | — |
| 10 | 2 | 1·7 |

Most common (mode) litter size = 5;
  mean = 4·7

**Table 20  Weights and crown-rump lengths of fox embryos from 33 days' gestation***

| Age (days) | Weight (g) | Crown-rump length (mm) |
|---|---|---|
| 33 | 0·8 | — |
| 34 | 1·4 | 10 |
| 35 | 2·4 | 26 |
| 36 | 3·6 | 36 |
| 37 | 5·2 | 46 |
| 38 | 7·0 | 53 |
| 39 | 9·8 | 59 |
| 40 | 12·8 | 66 |
| 41 | 16·4 | 71 |
| 42 | 20·6 | 76 |
| 43 | 25·4 | 81 |
| 44 | 30·9 | 86 |
| 45 | 37·2 | 91 |
| 46 | 44·3 | 96 |
| 47 | 52·3 | 101 |
| 48 | 61·2 | 106 |
| 49 | 70·9 | 111 |
| 50 | 81·7 | 116 |
| 51 | 93·6 | 121 |
| 52 | 106·4 | 126 |
| 53 | 120·0 | 131 |

* Based on Figures 15 and 16

**Table 21  Mean daily weights of captive fox cubs, 28–82 days ($\pm$ 2 days)**

| Age (days) | Weight (g)* ♂ | Weight (g)* ♀ | Age (days) | Weight (g)* ♂ | Weight (g)* ♀ |
|---|---|---|---|---|---|
| 28 | 620 | 570 | 44 | 1241 | 1056 |
| 29 | 646 | 593 | 45 | 1296 | 1113 |
| 30 | 679 | 609 | 46 | 1347 | 1155 |
| 31 | 703 | 634 | 47 | 1425 | 1220 |
| 32 | 748 | 666 | 48 | 1483 | 1263 |
| 33 | 769 | 684 | 49 | 1545 | 1329 |
| 34 | 795 | 702 | 50 | 1619 | 1397 |
| 35 | 830 | 727 | 51 | 1676 | 1449 |
| 36 | 880 | 762 | 52 | 1786 | 1532 |
| 37 | 945 | 802 | 53 | 1868 | 1606 |
| 38 | 1024 | 858 | 54 | 1960 | 1688 |
| 39 | 1089 | 901 | 55 | 1997 | 1731 |
| 40 | 1154 | 931 | 61 | 2429 | 2029 |
| 41 | 1169 | 947 | 67 | 2729 | 2329 |
| 42 | 1188 | 975 | 74 | 3206 | 2700 |
| 43 | 1210 | 1031 | 82 | 4100 | 3000 |

* The weights shown are smoothed $\dfrac{a + b + c}{3}$ for the 4 cubs involved.

The mean daily weight gain for the period shown is 63g for males and 45g for females. The mean daily gain for the first ten days and last fifteen days of the period shown are 44g and 91g respectively for males and 29g and 45g respectively for females.

Vogtsberger and Barrett (1973) have investigated the growth rate and bioenergetics of captive red foxes. They found that the mean growth rate was 23g per day from ninety-one days, which represents the second, slower phase of growth of juveniles. The efficiency of assimilation of ingested food was found to be 91%, of which 4% was used for growth (from thirteen weeks) and the remaining 87% for maintenance. The daily intake of energy was calculated to be 223Kcal per day.

Sargeant (1978), in a study of food intake by juvenile foxes, found that the daily weight gain averaged 31-34g per day from twenty-eight to eighty-four days. This finding, and the observations of Vogtsberger and Barrett, are very different from those shown in this table, but the N. American fox is much smaller than the European form—see Table 2.

Table 22    Age structure of a sample of 154 foxes taken from 1400 hectares in Pembrokeshire, January–March 1971 and 1972*

| Age | No. of foxes | % |
|---|---|---|
| $\frac{3}{4}$–1 year | 66 | 42·9 |
| $1\frac{3}{4}$–2 | 36 | 23·4 |
| $2\frac{3}{4}$–3 | 20 | 13·0 |
| $3\frac{3}{4}$–4 | 17 | 11·0 |
| $4\frac{3}{4}$–5 | 4 | 2·6 |
| $5\frac{3}{4}$–6 | 7 | 4·5 |
| $6\frac{3}{4}$–7 | 1 | 0·6 |
| $7\frac{3}{4}$–8 | 2 | 1·3 |
| $8\frac{3}{4}$–9 | 1 | 0·6 |
| Total | 154 | 99·9 |

* Ratio of adults : sub-adults = 1 : 0.75

Table 23   Composition of adults and sub-adults in five samples, including two from Ohio, USA*

| | Pembrokeshire | Mid-Wales | Skye | Ohio areas with little control (a) | Ohio areas with intensive control (b) |
|---|---|---|---|---|---|
| Ratio of adults: sub-adults | 1:0·75 | 1:1·35 | 1:2·03 | 1:2·56 | 1:5·59 |
| Proportion of sub-adults in sample (%) | 43 | 57 | 67 | 72 | 85 |
| Annual mortality rate adults (%) | 43 | 57 | 67 | | |
| Annual survival rate adults (%) | 57 | 43 | 33 | | |

* Phillips (1970)
(a) Area covered 280 square kilometres. Number of foxes killed (81) = 0.29 foxes per km$^2$
(b) Area covered 3500 square kilometres. Number of foxes killed (3325) = 0.95 foxes per km$^2$

## Table 24  Number of foxes surviving per 100 foxes aged* ¾–1 year old.

| Age (years) | Pembrokeshire | Mid-Wales | Skye |
|---|---|---|---|
| ¾–1 | 100·0 | 100·0 | 100·0 |
| 1¾–2 | 58·1 | 43·0 | 33·0 |
| 2¾–3 | 31·6 | 18·4 | 10·9 |
| 3¾–4 | 18·3 | 7·9 | 3·5 |
| 4¾–5 | 10·4 | 3·3 | 1·1 |
| 5¾–6 | 6·0 | 1·4 | |
| 6¾–7 | 3·4 | | |
| 7¾–8 | 1·8 | | |

\* Foxes aged by cementum annulation examination

## Table 25  Age structure: percentage in year groups

| Year group | 1 | 2 | 3 | 4 | 5 | 6 | 7 | 8 | 9 | 10 |
|---|---|---|---|---|---|---|---|---|---|---|
| West Wales | 43·0 | 23·0 | 13·0 | 11·0 | 2·5 | 4·5 | 0·6 | 1·3 | 0·6 | |
| Mid-Wales | 59·0 | 24·5 | 10·5 | 4·5 | 2·0 | 0·8 | | | | |
| Mid-Wales (by tagging returns) | 60·0 | 22·0 | 11·0 | 5·0 | 1·5 | | | | | |
| Isle of Skye | 67·0 | 19·0 | 9·5 | 3·4 | 0·8 | | | | | |
| Ireland (Fairley, 1969b) (assuming 50% mortality annually) | 50·0 | 25·0 | 13·0 | 6·0 | 3·0 | 1·5 | | | | |
| Denmark (Jensen and Nielsen, 1968) | 75·0 | 11·0 | 7·0 | 3·0 | 1·0 | 1·5 | 0·8 | | | |
| London (Harris, 1977b) | 52·0 | 26·0 | 10·0 | 5·0 | 3·5 | 2·5 | 0·5 | 0·5 | | |
| Switzerland (Wandeler et al., 1974b) | 70·0 | 13·0 | 7·0 | 4·0 | ——6·0→? | | | | | |
| USSR (Chirkova, 1955b: by tagging returns) | 90·0 | ——10·0→? | | | | | | | | |
| France (Artois, pers. comm.) | 49·0 | 24·0 | 10·0 | 11·0 | 7·0 | | | | | |
| USA (Phillips, 1970) | 72·0 | ——28·0→? | little control | | | | | | | |
| | 85·0 | ——15·0→? | intensive control | | | | | | | |

\* Animals aged by dental or skeletal examination except where indicated, and figures rounded to nearest decimal place

284

**Table 26  Fox population densities**

| | Number of foxes per km² | Number of litters found per km² |
|---|---|---|
| New Forest, 1975 (Insley, 1977) | 2·18 | 0·76 |
| North Pembrokeshire, Fishguard area, 1977 (Lloyd, unpublished) | 3·7 | 1·3 |
| North Pembrokeshire, Hayscastle area, 1977 (Lloyd, unpublished) | 3·7 (minimum, by number of foxes killed in 3 weeks over 15km²) | — |
| Greater London, 1976 (R. Page, pers. comm.) | 2·5 | 1·0 |
| Mid-Wales study area, 1971–73, 580km² (Lloyd, unpublished) | 1·2 | 0·5 |
| North Wales fox destruction society area, 1971–74, 183km² (Lloyd, unpublished) | 1·6 (no. of adult foxes killed) | — |
| Mid-Wales fox destruction society area, 1972–74, 160km² (Lloyd unpublished) | 0·9 (no. of adult foxes killed) | — |
| *Denmark, 1965–70, 30km² (B Jensen) | ⎫ | 0·5 |
| *Switzerland, Canton Berne, 1970–72 (Alexander Wandeler) | ⎬ Estimated range of population densi- ties of adults | 0·16–0·24 |
| *Dutch National Park, 1972, 45km² (J. L. van Haaften) | ⎭ 0·5–1·8 | 0·5–0·6 |

\* In Lloyd *et al.* (1976)

**Table 27  Recoveries of tagged cubs***

| | West Wales | Mid-Wales |
|---|---|---|
| Fox population density | High | Medium to low |
| Hunting pressure | Minimal | High |
| Number of fox earths | Few | Many |
| Mean number of occupied earths (1971) | 1 in 15 tenanted in breeding season | 1 in 80 tenanted in breeding season |
| Home-range sizes | 40–100 hectares | 200–600 hectares |
| Food supply | Much variety – providing buffer against shortage | Less variety; abundance tends to be seasonal, e.g. carrion and ground-nesting birds |
| Climate | Mild – little frost and snow | Harsh, cold and wet; frosts frequent Oct.-April; intermittent snow lies for 2-3 weeks per annum |
| Dense ground cover | In close proximity to most open spaces | Except in or near forests, dense cover not available |
| Mean distance emigrated (km) | ♂ 4·7 ♀ 1·9 | ♂ 13·7 ♀ 2·25 |
| Proportion of vixen cubs moving less than 1·6km (%) | 66 | 69 |
| Proportion of male cubs travelling more than 9·6km (%) | 11 | 39 |
| Proportion of male cubs travelling more than 19·3km (%) | Nil | 11 |
| Mean age at recapture (months) | 18·6 | 8·5 |
| Tagged cubs recovered under 12 months old as a proportion of all cubs recovered (killed) (%) | 37 | 62 |
| Tagged cubs recovered over two years old as a proportion of all cubs recovered (%) | 23 | 18 |
| Recoveries of tagged cubs (%) | 28 | 47 |

* These data are all subject to change as further tagged foxes, still at large, are recovered

**Table 28  Ministry of Agriculture, Fisheries and Food June agricultural census returns***

| Year | Total acreage | Grass acreage | Acreage rough grazing and common | Acreage woodland | No. of workers employed by occupiers | No. of holdings |
|---|---|---|---|---|---|---|
| 1940 | 22,200 | 1720 | 20,480 | Not recorded | 50 | 29 |
| 1949 | 22,200 | 1300 | 20,300 | 600 | 35 | 30 |
| 1962 | 22,200 | 1300 | 16,490 | 4410 | 18 | 23 |
| 1970 | 22,200 | 1350 | 13,410 | 7440 | 8 | 14 |

| Year | Total sheep | No. breeding ewes | No. lambs | Lambing % | Yearling ewes | Rams | Dry ewes and wethers | Subsidy (full rate) |
|---|---|---|---|---|---|---|---|---|
| 1940 | 29,232 | 10,420 | 9220 | 88 | 2031 | 425 | 7136 | 12½p |
| 1949 | 17,824 | 5722 | 6199 | 108 | 2051 | 225 | 3627 | 25p |
| 1962 | 18,585 | 6733 | 5991 | 89 | 2466 | 278 | 3117 | 37p |
| 1970 | 13,517 | 5544 | 4413 | 80 | 1586 | 197 | 1777 | £1·60 |

| | Mean no. sheep per holding | | | Overall sheep density per acre | | | | No. of sheep per worker |
|---|---|---|---|---|---|---|---|---|
| Year | Total | Ewes | Lambs | All sheep, ex-cluding lambs | Ewes | Yearling Ewes | Lambs | |
| 1940 | 1008 | 359 | 317 | 0·90 | 0·469 | 0·092 | 0·415 | 370 |
| 1949 | 594 | 190 | 206 | 0·533 | 0·265 | 0·094 | 0·287 | 274 |
| 1962 | 808 | 292 | 260 | 0·859 | 0·378 | 0·139 | 0·336 | 453 |
| 1970 | 965 | 396 | 315 | 0·616 | 0·375 | 0·107 | 0·298 | 614 |

* Records refer to two parishes in a Welsh hill area; original data retained

287

**Table 29    Intercanine gaps of potential lamb predators***

|  | Upper canines (mm) | Lower canines (mm) |
|---|---|---|
| Polecat | 11·5 | 10·5 |
| Mink | 12·5 | 10·5 |
| Badger | 26·0 | 24·5 |
| Otter | 29·0 | 27·0 |
| Fox | 30·0 | 26·0 |
| Small dog | 22·0 | 17·0 |
| Medium dog (10kg) | 30·0 | 26·0 |
| Labrador dog (30kg) | 53·0 | 45·0 |
| Alsatian dog (35kg) | 55·0 | 46·0 |

* After Swire (1978)

**Table 30  Cost of fox control to the Forestry Commission, 1971–72**

| Conservancy | Subscriptions to fox destruction societies £ | Foxes killed by FC Adult | Cub | Bonuses paid by FC Adult £ | Cub £ | Staff employed on fox control operations Ranger/years (approx.) | Average wages paid (approx.) £ | Total expenditure on fox destruction £ |
|---|---|---|---|---|---|---|---|---|
| NW (E) | — | 76 | 41 | 13 | 5 | 0·6 | 655 | 673 |
| NE (E) | — | 284 | 147 | — | — | 0·5 | 546 | 546 |
| E (E) | — | 26 | 21 | — | — | — | — | — |
| SE (E) | — | 50 | 21 | — | — | — | — | — |
| SW (E) | — | 19 | 9 | — | — | — | — | — |
| N (S) | 417 | 549 | 132 | 549 | 66 | 7 | 7644 | 8676 |
| E (S) | 9 | 448 | 142 | 358 | 43 | 3 | 3276 | 3686 |
| S (S) | — | 568 | 252 | 565 | 125 | 4 | 4368 | 5058 |
| W (S) | 280 | 379 | 109 | 379 | 54 | 4·5 | 4914 | 5627 |
| N (W) | 811 | 476 | 286 | 318 | 137 | 10 | 10,920 | 12,187 |
| S (W) | 316 | 310 | 64 | 276 | 24 | 1 | 1092 | 1708 |
| Total | 1833 | 3185 | 1224 | 2458 | 454 | 30·6 | 33,415 | 38,161 |

4,409

(E) = England
(S) = Scotland
(W) = Wales

**Table 31  Number of foxes known to be killed per annum***

| | No. of foxes killed | Area (km²) | Kills : total area(km²) |
|---|---|---|---|
| Bulgaria | 60,700 | 108,780 | 1:1·8 |
| Denmark | 50,000 | 47,267 | 1:0·8 |
| France | 93,000 | 550,789 | 1:5·7 |
| Sweden | 80,000 | 414,845 | 1:5·2 |
| Wales | 10,000 | 207,640 | 1:2·1 |
| Mid-Wales | 502 (all ages) | 906 | 1:1·8 |
| Norway | 25,000 | 323,750 | 1:13·0 |
| Michigan | 26,964 | 147,630 | 1:5·4 |
| Ohio, USA | 26,000 (p.a. over 13 years) | 550,260 | 1:20·0 |
| Iowa, USA (parts of 3 counties) | 3325 | 3496 | 1:1·0 |
| Canada | 61,000 pelts taken, 1970–71 | | |
| USSR | 55,000 wild skins exported, 1970 | | |
| USA | 187,000 skins sold in 40 states excluding Alaska, 1969–70 | | |

* The records, obtained from hunters and from bounty payments, represent the minimum number of foxes killed.

**Table 32  Nematode and cestode parasites of foxes**

| Species | a | b | c | d | e | f | g | h | i |
|---|---|---|---|---|---|---|---|---|---|
| **Nematodes** | | | | | | | | | |
| *Toxocara canis* | √ | √ | √ | | √ | √ | | √ | √ |
| *Toxocara mystax* | | | | } Sp | √ | | | | |
| *Toxascaris leonina* | √ | √ | √ | only | | | | √ | √ |
| *Uncinaria stenocephala* | √ | √ | √ | | √ | √ | | √ | √ |
| *Ancylostoma* sp. | | √ | | | | | | | √ |
| *Trichinella spiralis* | | √ | | | | √(Eucoleus | | | |
| *Capillaria aerophila* | √ | √ | | | √ | √ | √ aerophilus) | | |
| *Capillaria plica* | √ | √ | | | √ | √ | √ | | |
| *Crenosoma vulpis* | √ | √ | | | | √ | | | |
| *Physaloptera sibirica* | √ | | | | | | | | |
| **Cestodes** | | | | | | | | | |
| *Taenia serialis* | √ | √ | √ | √ | √ | | | √ | √ |
| *Taenia pisiformis* | √ | | √ | | √ | √ | | | √ |
| *Taenia taeniaeformis* | √ | | √ | | | | √ ? | √ | |
| *Taenia hydatigena* | √ | | √ | | | | | | √ |
| *Taenia multiceps* | √ | | √ | √ | | | | | √ |
| *Taenia crassiceps* | √ | | | √ | | | √ | | |
| *Taenia polycantha* | √ | | | √ | | | √ | | |
| *Taenia ovis* | | | | | | | | √ | √ |
| *Echinococcus granulosus* | | | | √ | | | | | √ |
| *Echinococcus multilocularis* | | | | √ | | | √ | | |
| *Mesocestoides* sp. | √ | √ | | √(M. litteratus) | | | √(M. lineatus) | | |
| *Diphyllobothrium latum* | | | | √ | | | √ | | |
| *Diphyllobothrium erinacei* | | | | | | | | √ | |
| *Hymenolepis nana* | | √ | | | | | | √ | |
| *Dipylidium caninum* | √ | √* | | √ | | | √ | √ | |
| *Euparyphium melis* | | √ | | | | | | | |
| *Eristalis* sp. (larva) | | √ | | | | | | | |
| *Acanthocephala* | | | | | | | | | |
| *Macracanthorhynchus catulinus* √ | | | | | | | | | |

a  USSR (Troitskaya, 1955)
b  England, Wales and Scotland (Beresford-Jones, 1961)
c  N. Ireland (Ross and Fairley, 1969)
d  France (Joyeux and Boer, 1936)
e  England (Blackmore, 1964b)
f  England: farm and wild (Watkins and Harvey, 1942)
g  Switzerland (Wandeler and Hörning, 1972)
h  Australia (Pullar, 1946)
i  West Wales (Williams, 1976a, b, c)

* egg capsules only

291

**Table 33  Number of known cases of rabies in wild and domestic animals in France; 26 March 1968 to 1 February 1979**

| | |
|---|---:|
| Fox | 12038 |
| Badger | 199 |
| Deer | 73 |
| Otters (martens, polecats etc) | 247 |
| | |
| Cattle | 1519 |
| Dog | 360 |
| Cat | 558 |
| Sheep and goats | 335 |
| Horses | 94 |
| Pigs | 9 |
| Others | 2 |

# Bibliography

Ables, E. D. (1965). An exceptional fox movement. *J. Mammal.*, *46:* 102.

Ables, E. D. (1969a). Home range studies of red foxes (*Vulpes vulpes*). *J. Mammal.*, *50:* 108–20.

Ables, E. D. (1969b). Activity studies of red foxes in southern Wisconsin. *J. Wildl. Mgmt.*, *33:* 145–53.

Ables, E. D. (1975). Ecology of the red fox in North America, in M. V. Fox, ed., *The Wild Canids – their systematics, behavioural ecology and evolution*. New York: Van Nostrand Reinhold.

Adamczyk, K. and Ryszkowski, L. (1968). Estimation of the density of a rodent population using stained bait. *Acta. theriol.*, *13:* 295–311.

Afshar, A. and Bahmanyar, M. (1978). Non-fatal rabies virus infections. *The Veterinary Bulletin* (Commonwealth Bureau of Animal Health) *48:* 553–9.

Albone, E. S. (1975). Dihydroactinidiolide in the supracaudal scent secretion of the red fox. *Nature*, Lond., *256:* (5518), 575.

Albone, E. S. (1977). Ecology of mammals – a new focus for chemical research. *Chemistry in Britain*, *13:* 92–9.

Albone, E. S. and Fox, M. W. (1971). Anal gland secretion of the red fox. *Nature*, Lond., *233:* (5321), 569–70.

Albone, E. S. and Flood, P. F. (1976). The supracaudal scent gland of the red fox, *Vulpes vulpes*. *J. Chem. Ecol.*, *2:* 167–75.

Albone, E. S., Robins, S. P. and Patel, D. (1976). 5—amino-valeric acid – a major free amino acid component of the anal sac secretion of the red fox *Vulpes vulpes*. *Comp. Biochem. Physiol.*, *55B:* 483–6.

Albone, E. S. and Perry, G. C. (1976). Anal sac secretion of the red fox *Vulpes vulpes*. *J. Chem. Ecol.*, *2:* 101–11.

Alexander, G., Peterson, J. E. and Watson, R. H. (1959). Neonatal mortality in lambs. *Aust. vet. J.*, *35:* 433–41.

Alexander, G., Mann, T., Mulhearn, C.J., Rowley, I. C. R., Williams, D. and Winn, D. (1967). Activities of foxes and crows in a flock of lambing ewes. *Aust. J. Expt. Agric. & Anim. Husb.*, *7:* 329–36.

Allen, S. H. (1974). Modified techniques for ageing the red fox using canine teeth. *J. Wildl. Mgmt.*, *38:* 152–4.

Allen, S. H. and Sargeant, A. B. (1975). A rural mail-carrier index of North Dakota red foxes. *Wildl. Soc. Bulletin*, *3:* 74–7.

Andrews, R. D., Storm, G. L., Phillips, R. L. and Bishop, R. A. (1973). Survival and movements of transplanted and adopted red fox pups. *J. Wildl. Mgmt.*, *37:* 69–72.

Apfelbach, R. (1973). Olfactory sign stimulus for prey selection in polecats. *Z. Tierpsychol.*, *33:* 270–3.

Arnold, D. A. and Schofield, R. D. (1956). Home range and dispersal of Michigan red foxes. *Michigan Acad. Sci. Arts & Let.*, *41:* 91–7.

Arthur, D. R. (1963). *British ticks*. London: Butterworth.

Aubert, M. F. A. (1975). Contribution à l'étude du parasitisme du renard (*Vulpes vulpes* L.) par les *Ixodidae (Acarina)* dans le nord-est de la France. *Acarologia*, *17:* 452–79.

Aubert, M. F. A. and Beaucournu, J. C. (1976). Contribution à l'étude du parasitisme du renard (*Vulpes vulpes* L.). *Ann. Parasitol. Hum Comp. Fr.*, *51:* 143–56.

Austwick, P. K. C (1965). Mycotic infections. *Symp. zool. Soc. London.*, *24:* 256.


Baer, G. M. (ed) (1975). *The Natural History of Rabies*. Vol 1 and 2. New York: Academic Press.

Bagnall, R. S. (1932). On Mallophaga affecting the mammals of Northumberland and Durham. *Vasculum*, *18:* 14–8.

Balser, D. S. (1964). Management of predator populations with anti-fertility agents. *J. Wildl. Mgmt.*, *28:* 352–8.

Balser, D. S. (1965). Tranquilizer tabs for capturing wild carnivores. *J. Wildl. Mgmt.*, *29:* 438–42.

Bang, P. and Dahlstrom, P. (1974). *Collins guide to animal tracks and signs* London: Collins.

Bassett, C. F. (1946). The effect of artificially altered length of day on moult in the silver fox. *Ann. N.Y. Acad. Sci.*, *48:* 239–54.

Bassett, C. F. and Leekley, B. S. (1942). Determination of estrum in the fox vixen. *N. Amer. Veterinarian*, July 1942: 454–7.

Bateman, M., ed. (1969). *This England*. Harmondsworth: Penguin Books.

Beames, I. (1972). The spread of the fox in the London area. *Ecologist*, *2:* 25–6.

Beaucournu, J. C. (1973). Notes sur les Siphonaptères parasites de carnivores en France. *Ann. Parasitol. Hum. Comp. Fr.*, *48:* 497–516.

Beckford, P. (1810). *Thoughts on hunting*. London: Albion Press.

Behrendt, G. (1955). Beiträge zur Ökologie des Rotfuchses (*Vulpes vulpes* L). *Zeit. Jagdwissen.*, *1:* 161–83.

Bejšovec, J. (1965). The importance of raptorial birds, owls, rooks and the common fox for the transmission of endoparasites of production animals and small rodents. *Ceskoslovenska parazitologie*, *12:* 81–91.

Beresford-Jones, W. P. (1961). Observations on the helminths of British wild red foxes. *Vet. Rec.*, *73:* 882–3.

Berg, G. (1950–1). Wooden traps. *Ur. Folk-Liv*, 31–59.

Bergman, G. (1966). Occurrence and living habits of the fox (*Vulpes vulpes* ) in Finnish island areas, and its effects on birds. *Suomen Riista*, *18:* 39–48.

Berkeley, Grantley F. (1854). *Reminiscences of a huntsman*. London: Longman.

Bernard, J. (1959). Note sur le période de reproduction du renard (*Vulpes vulpes* L.) dans le Luxembourg belge. *Saugetierk. Mitt.*, *7:* 110–13.

'Berwin' (1965). What do foxes eat? *Gamekeeper & Countryside*, *812:* 214–15.

Bezdek, H. (1944). A red-grey fox hybrid. *J. Mammal.*, *25:* 90.

Bezeau, L. M. and Gallant, T. B. (1950). Experiments on self-selection of diets by foxes. *Sci. Agric.*, *30:* 150–6.

Bishop, D. W. (1942). Germ cell studies in the male fox (*Vulpes fulva*). *Anat. Rec.*, *84:* 99–115.

Bitsch, V. and Munche, B. (1971). On pseudorabies in carnivores in Denmark. 1. The red fox. *Acta. vet. Scand.*, *12:* 274–84.

Blackmore, D. K. (1963). The toxicity of some chlorinated hydrocarbon insecticides to British wild foxes (*Vulpes vulpes*). *J. Comp. Path. & Therapeutics*, *73:* 391–408.

Blackmore, D. K. (1964a). Problems encountered in attempting to anaesthetise and sedate British wild foxes. *Small Animals Anaesthesia Symp.* (1965), 191–4.

Blackmore, D. K. (1964b). A survey of disease in British wild foxes (*Vulpes vulpes*). *Vet. Rec.*, *76:* 527–33.

Blaine, Delabere P. (1880). *An encyclopaedia of rural sports*. London: Longman.

Bögel K., Moegle, H., Knorpp, F., Arata, A., Dietz, K. and Dielthelm, P. (1976). Characteristics of the spread of a wildlife rabies epidemic in Europe. *Bull. World Health Organ.*, *54:* 433–47.

Bothma, J. Du P. (1966). Food of the silver fox, *Vulpes chama*. *Zool. Afr.*, *2:* 205–10.

Bouchud, J. (1951). Etude paléontologique de la fauna d'Isturitz. *Mammalia*, *15:* 184–203.

Bougerol, C. (1968). Les destructions des petits carnivores en France. *Mammalia*, *32:* 525–7.

Bouvier, G. (1946). Observations sur les maladies du gibier, de quelques animaux sauvages et des poissons. *Schweiz. Arch. Tierheilk.*, *88:* 268–74.

Bouvier, G. (1963). Possibilities of transmission of tuberculosis and brucellosis in game to man, and domesticated and wild animals. *Bull. Off. Int. Epizoot.*, *59:* 433–6.

Boville, E. W. (1962). *English country life 1780–1830*. London: OUP.

Bowden, R. S. T., Hodgman, S. F. J. and Hart, C. F. (1960). Some observations on the present mortality in wild foxes. *J. Small Anim. Practice*, *1:* 94–100.

Bradbury, K. (1977). Identification of earthworms in mammalian scats. *J. Zool.*, Lond. *183:* 553–5.

Brambell, F. W. R. (1942). Intra-uterine mortality of the wild rabbit, *Oryctolagus cuniculus* (L.). *Proc. Roy. Soc. B.*, *130:* 462–79.

Bree, P. J. H. van, and Sinkeldam, E. J. (1969). Anomalies in the dentition of the fox (*Vulpes vulpes*), from continental western Europe. *Bijdragen tot de dierkunde*, *39:* 3–5.

Brooks, R. P. and Dodge, N. E. (1978). A night identification collar for beavers. *J. Wildl. Mgmt.*, *42:* 448–52.

Brown, J. L. and Orians, G. H. (1970). Spacing patterns in mobile animals. *Ann. Rev. Ecol. Systematics*, *1:* 239–62.

Brunner, H. and Coman, B. (1976). *The identification of mammalian hair*. Victoria: Inkata Press.

Buckton, K. E. and Cunningham, C. (1971). Variation of the chromosome number in the red fox. *Chromosoma (Berl.).*, *33:* 268–72.

Burrows, R. (1968). *Wild fox*. Newton Abbot: David and Charles.

Butler, L. (1945). Distribution of genetics of the colour phases of the red fox in Canada. *Genetics, 30:* 39–50.

Butler, L. (1947). The genetics of the colour phases of the red fox in the Mackenzie River locality. *Can. J. Research, D.25:* 190–215.

Butler, L. (1951). Population sizes and colour phase genetics of the coloured fox in Quebec. *Canad. J. Zool., 29:* 24–41.

Cakala, S. (1960). Distemper in foxes. *Med. Wet. Warszawa. 16:* 153–9.

Calhoun, J. B. (1950). Population cycles and gene frequency fluctuations in foxes of the genus *Vulpes* in Canada. *Can. J: Research D. 28:* 45–57.

Carding, T. (1977). Euthanasia of dogs and cats. *Animal Regulation Studies. 1:* 5–21.

Chiasson, R. B. (1953). Fluctuations of some Illinois fox populations. *Ecology, 34:* 617–9.

Chaddock, T. T. (1948). Veterinary problems of the fur ranch. *Veterinary Medicine, 43:* 13.

Chaddock, T. T. and Carlson, B. A. (1950). Fox encephalitis (infectious canine hepatitis) in the dog. *N. Amer. Vet., 31:* 35–41.

Chalmers, A. W. and Scott, G. R. (1969). Ecology of rabies. *Trop. Anim. Hlth. Prod., 1:* 33–5.

Chirkova, A. F. (1941). Methods for forecasting changes in the common fox (*Vulpes vulpes*). *Trudi Tsentral'noi Laboratorii Biologii i Ochotnichego Promisla, 5:* 78–99. Translation by J. D. Jackson, for Bureau of Animal Population, Oxford, 1943, TRANS. 132 PER.

Chirkova, A. F. (1955a). The dynamics of fox numbers in Voronesh Province and forecasting of fox harvests. *Voprosy Biologii Pushnykh Zverery, Moscow, 13:* 20.

Chirkova, A. F. (1955b). Fox tagging studies. *Voprosy Biologii Pushnykh Zverery, Moscow, 14:* 191.

Chirkova, A. F. (1967). The relationships between the arctic fox and red fox in the Far North. (translation of *Problemy Severa,* Problems of the north). *Nat. Res. Council Canada, 11:* 129–31.

Churcher, C. S. (1959). The specific status of the New World red fox. *J. Mammal., 40:* 513–20.

Churcher, C. S. (1960). Cranial variation in the North American red fox. *J. Mammal., 41:* 349–60.

Clausen, B. and Karlog, O. (1974). Loading with thallium among wild animals of the marten genus and badgers in Denmark. *Nord. Vet-Med. 26:* 339–50.

Coman, B. J. (1973a). Helminth parasites of the red fox (*Vulpes vulpes*) in Victoria. *Aust. Veter. J., 49:* 378–84.

Coman, B. J. (1973b). The diet of red foxes *Vulpes vulpes* L. in Victoria. *Aust. J. Zool. 21:* 391–401.

Cook, A. R. (1943). A technique for marking mammals. *J. Mammal., 24:* 45–7.

Cook, B. R. (1965). Incidence and epidemiology of *Echinococcus granulosus* in Great Britain (Ph.D. thesis). University of Liverpool.

Cook, D. B. and Hamilton, W. J. (1944). The ecological relationship of the red fox food in eastern New York. *Ecology, 24:* 91–104.

Cook, R. M. L. (1964). Old vermin traps on south-west Dartmoor. *Devon Assoc. for the Advancement of Science, 96:* 190–201.

Corridan, J. P., O'Rourke, J. F. and Verling, M. (1969). *Trichinella spiralis* in the red fox (*Vulpes vulpes*) in Ireland. *Nature,* Lond., *222:* 1191.

Corridan, J. P., and Gray, J. J., (1969). Trichinosis in south-west Ireland. *Br. Med. J.,* 21 June, 727.

Coudert, J., Euzeby, J. and Garin, J. P. (1970). Fréquence de *E. multilocularis* chez le renard commun (*Vulpes vulpes*) dans le secteur nord-est de la France. *Lyon Médical, 32:* 293–8.

Cowan, I. McT. (1949). Rabies as a possible population control of arctic canidae. *J. Mammal., 30:* 396–8.

Coyler, F. (1936). *Variations and diseases of the teeth of animals.* London: Bale, Sons and Damelsson.

Crawford, J. S. and Veitch, A. G. (1959). Organised drives will control foxes. *J. Agric. W. Aust., 8:* Bull. No. 2604.

Creed, R. F. S. (1960a). Observations on reproduction in the wild red fox (*Vulpes vulpes*). An account with special reference to the occurrence of fox—dog crosses. *Br. Vet. J., 116:* 419–26.

Creed, R. F. S. (1960b). Gonad changes in the wild red fox (*Vulpes vulpes*). *J. Physiol., 151:* 19–20.

Creed, R. F. S. (1972). Aspects of reproduction and early development in *Vulpes vulpes,* L. (Ph.D. thesis). University of London.

Croft, P. G. (1957). Anaesthesia and euthanasia. UFAW *Handbook on the Care and Management of Laboratory Animals.* London: Universities Federation for Animal Welfare.

Cromwell, H. W., Sweebe, E. E. and Camp, T. C. (1939). Bacteria of the *Listerella* group isolated from foxes. *Science 89:* 293.

Cross, E. C. (1940). Periodic fluctuations in the numbers of the red fox in Ontario. *J. Mammal., 21:* 294–306.

Crowcroft, P. (1957). *The life of the shrew.* London: Reinhardt.

CSIRO (1974). Division of Wildlife Research Report, 1972–4. Melbourne, Australia.

Cuthbert, J. H. (1973). Some observations on scavenging of Salmon, *Salmo salar,* carrion. *Western Naturalist, 2:* 72–4.

Czarnowski, A. (1960). Infectious hepatitis in foxes. *Med. Wet. Warszawa. 16:* 14–16.

Danell, K. (1978). Population dynamics of the musk rat in a shallow Swedish lake. *J. Anim. Ecol., 47:* 697–709.

Darrow, R. W. (1945). Relation of buffer species abundance to fox predation on grouse nests. *Trans. N. Amer. Wildlife Conf., 10:* 270–3.

Davis, S. (1977). Size variation of the fox, *Vulpes vulpes,* in the palaearctic region today, and in Israel during the late Quarternary. *J. Zool.,* Lond., *182:* 343–51.

Day, M. G. (1968). *Food habits of British stoats (Mustela erminea) and weasels (Mustela nivalis). J. Zool,* Lond., *155:* 485–7.

Debbie, J. G., Abelseth, M. K. and Baer, G. M. (1972). The use of commercially available vaccines for the oral vaccination of foxes against rabies. *Am. J. Epidemiology*, *96:* 231–5.

Dennis, S. M. (1965a). Why did these lambs die? *J. Agric. W. Aust.*, *6:* Bull. No. 3321.

Dennis, S. M. (1965b). More light on lamb losses. *J. Agric. W. Aust.*, *6:* Bull. No. 3387.

Déschambre, E. (1951). À propos des évolutions convergentes et parallels. *Mammalia*, *15:* 173–83.

Dixon, J. B., Baker Smith, J. K. and Greatorex, J. C. (1973). The incidence of hydatid cysts in horses in Great Britain. *Vet. Rec.*, *93:* 255.

Dunkin, G. W. (1926). Jaundice in a wild fox due to *Leptospira icterohaemorragaiae*. *Vet. Journal*, *82:* 147–9.

Elton, C. S. (1942). *Mice, voles and lemmings*. Oxford: Clarendon Press.

Englund, J. (1965a). Studies on the food ecology of the red fox (*Vulpes vulpes*) in Sweden. *Viltrevy*, *3:* 377–485.

Englund, J. (1965b). The diet of foxes (*Vulpes vulpes*) on the island of Gotland since myxomatosis. *Viltrevy*, *3:* 507–30.

Englund, J. (1969). The diet of fox cubs (*Vulpes vulpes*) in Sweden. *Viltrevy*, *6:* 1–39.

Englund, J. (1970). Some aspects of reproduction and mortality rates in Swedish foxes. *Viltrevy*, *8:* 1–82.

Errington, P. L. (1935). Food habits of mid-west foxes. *J. Mammal.*, *16:* 192–200.

Errington, P. L. (1937). Food habits of Iowa red foxes during a drought summer. *Ecology*, *18:* 53–61.

Errington, P. L. and Berry, R. M. (1937). Tagging studies of red foxes. *J. Mammal.*, *18:* 203–5.

Evans, A. D. and Lennox, M. (1953). *Trichinella* in rats and pigs. *Br. Med. J.*, 18 July, 131.

Evans, G. O. (1951). The seasonal incidence of *Ixodes ricinus* L. on cattle in mid-Wales. *Bull. ent. Res.*, *41:* 459–68.

Fairley, J. S. (1965). The food of the fox in Co. Down. *Ir. Nat. J.*, *15:* 2–5.

Fairley, J. S. (1969a). A critical examination of the Northern Ireland fox-bounty figures. *Ir. Nat. J.*, *16:* 213–25.

Fairley, J. S. (1969b). Tagging studies of the red fox *Vulpes vulpes* in north-east Ireland. *J. Zool. Lond.*, *159:* 527–32.

Fairley, J. S. (1970a). The food, reproduction, form, growth and development of the fox *Vulpes vulpes* (L.) in N.E. Ireland. *Proc. Roy. Irish Acd.*, *69*(B): 103–37.

Fairley, J. S. (1970b). More results from tagging studies of foxes (*Vulpes vulpes* L.) *Ir. Nat. J.*, *16:* 392–3.

Farmer, J. N., Herbert, I. V., Partridge, M. and Edwards, G. T. (1978). The prevalence of *Sarcocytes* sp. in dogs and red foxes. *Vet. Rec.*, *102:* 78–80.

Fenner, F. and Chapple, P. J. (1965). Evolutionary changes in myxoma virus in Britain. *J. Hyg.*, *63:* 175–85.

Fennessy, B. V. (1966). The impact of wildlife species on sheep production in

Australia. *Proc. Aust. Soc. Anim. Prod.*, 6: 148–56.

Forbes, L. S. (1964). Hydatid infections in New Zealand and the United Kingdom. A review. *Vet. Rec.*, 76: 597–603.

Forbes, L. S. and Cook, B. R. (1963). Hydatid disease in the United Kingdom. *Trans. Roy. Soc. Trop. Med. Hyg.*, 57: 5.

Forbes, T. O. A. and Lance, A. N. (1976). The contents of fox scats from Western Irish Blanket bog. *J. Zool.*, Lond., *179:* 224–6.

Fox, M. W. (1971). *Behaviour of wolves, dogs and related canids.* London: Jonathan Cape.

Fox, M. W., (ed). (1975). *The wild canids.* N. York: Van Nostrand Reinhold.

Friend, M. and Linhart, S. B. (1964). Use of the eye lens as an indicator of age in the red fox. *N.Y. Fish and Game J.*, 11: 58–66.

Furnell, M. G. J. (1957). *Trichinella spiralis* in rats and cats in Limerick. *Ann. Rep. Med. Res. Counc. Ir.*

Gemmel, M. A. (1959). The fox as a definitive host of *Echinococcus* and its role in the spread of hydatid disease. *Bull. Wld. Hlth. Org.*, *20:* 87–99.

Gier, H. T. (1947). Populations and reproductive potentials of foxes in Ohio. *Ninth Midwest Wildlife Conf.* 9–11 December, 1947. Indianapolis: Lafayette.

Gilmore, R. M. (1946). Mammals in archeological collections from southwestern Pennsylvania. *J. Mammal.*, 27: 227–35.

Gilmore, R. M. (1949). The identification and value of mammal bones from archeological excavations. *J. Mammal.*, *30:* 163–9.

Gosden, P. E. and Ware, G. C. (1976). The aerobic flora of the anal sac of the red fox. *J. Appl. Bact.*, *41:* 271–6.

Goszczynski, J. (1974). Studies on the food of foxes. *Acta. theriol.*, *19:* 1–18.

Gould, S. E. (1970). *Trichinosis in man and animals.* Springfield, Illinois: Thomas.

Gouldsbury, P. A. (ed). (1973). *Predatory mammals in Britain.* Council for Nature Publication. London: Seel House Press.

Graham-Jones, O. (1964). Restraint and anaesthesia of some captive wild mammals. *Vet. Rec.*, *76:* 1216–48.

Gray, A. (1954). *A check list of mammalian hybrids.* Commonwealth Agric. Bureau Pub., Farnham Royal, Bucks, England.

Grešiková, M., Sekeyová, M., Weidnerová, K., Blasković, Steck, F. and Wandeler, A. (1972). Isolation of tick-borne encephalitis virus from the brain of a sick dog in Switzerland. *Acta. virol.*, *16:* 88–9.

Grue, H. and Jensen, B. (1973). Annular structures in canine tooth cementum in red foxes (*Vulpes vulpes* L.) of known age. *Dan. Rev. Game Biol.*, 8:(7), 12pp.

Gudmundsson, B. (1945). Hybrids between Silver fox and Mountain fox at Loue, Keldichverfi. *Natturnfroedingurinn*, *15*: 108–12 (Animal Breeding Abstracts, *16:* 607).

Gunn, R.G. (1968). Relationships between environment, management, and the life-time production of hill sheep. *Proc. Symp. on Hill Land Productivity, European Grassland Federation*, July 1968, 177–83.

Gunn, R.G. and Robinson, J.F. (1963). Lamb mortality in Scottish hill flocks. *Anim. Production*, 5: 67–76.

Gustavsson, I. (1964). Karyotype of the fox. *Nature*, Lond., *201*: 950–1.

Gustavsson, I. and Sundt, C.O. (1967). Chromosome elimination in the evolution of the silver fox. *J. Hered.*, *58*: 75–8.

Haaften, J. van (1970). Fox ecology in the Netherlands. *Trans. IX Internat. Cong. Game Biologists*, Moscow.

Habermehl, K.H. (1961). *Altersbestimmung bei Haustieren, Pelztieren und beim jagdbaren Wild (Age determination of domestic, fur-bearing and game animals)*. Berlin and Hamburg: Parey.

Haglund, B. (1966). De stora roudjuvens vintervanor. *Viltrevy*, *4*: 81–308.

Halahan, P.C. (1936). A non-injurious animal trap. *Field* (London), *168*: 1501.

Haldane, J.B.S. (1942). The selective elimination of silver foxes in eastern Canada. *J. Genetics*, *44*: 296–304.

Hall, E.R. (1940). Supernumerary and missing teeth in wild mammals – insectivora and carnivora – with some notes on disease. *J. dent. Res.*, *19*: 103–19.

Haltenorth, T., (1938). Neue Write und Verbreitungsgebiete. *Sitzber Ges. Naturf. Fr. Berl.*, 1937: 77–80.

Haltenorth, T. and Roth, H.H. (1967). Short review of the biology and ecology of the red fox. *Sauge Tierkundliche Mitteilungen* (1967–8), 339–52.

Hamilton, W.J. Jr. (1939). *American mammals*. New York: McGraw-Hill.

Harcourt, R.A. (1971). The paleopathology of animal skeletal remains. *Vet. Rec.*, September 1971, 267–72.

Harris, J.R. and Hickey, M.D. (1945). Occurrence of the *Diphyllobothriidae* in Ireland. *Nature*, Lond., *156* (3963): 447.

Harris, S. (1975). Syndactyly in the red fox, *Vulpes vulpes*. *J. Zool.*, Lond., *176*: 282–7.

Harris, S. (1977a). Spinal arthritis (spondylosis deformans) in the red fox, *Vulpes vulpes*, with some methodology of relevance to zooarchaeology. *J. Archaeolol. Sci.*, *4*: 183–95.

Harris, S. (1977b). Distribution, habitat utilization and age structure of a suburban fox *(Vulpes vulpes)* population. *Mammal Rev.*, 7: 25–39.

Harris, S. (1978a). Injuries to foxes *(Vulpes vulpes)* living in suburban London. *J. Zool.*, Lond., 186: 567–72.

Harris, S. (1978b). Age determination in the red fox *(Vulpes vulpes)*: an evaluation of technique as applied to a sample of urban foxes. *J. Zool.*, Lond., *183*: 91–117.

Harris, S. (1979). Age-related fertility and productivity in Red foxes, *Vulpes vulpes*, in suburban London. *J. Zool.*, Lond., 187: 195–9.

Harrison, D.L. (1962). An unusual mutant fox. *The Naturalist*, 113–14.

Hattingh, I. (1956). Measurements of foxes from Scotland and England. *Proc. Zool. Soc. Lond.*, *127*: 191–9.

Hauk, E. (1950). Abstammung Ur und Frühgeschichte des Hauschunds. *Prähist. Forschungen, Wein 1*: 164.

Hediger, H. (1955). *Studies of the psychology and behaviour of animals in zoos and circuses*. London: Butterworth.

Heezen, K.L. and Tester, J.R. (1967). Evaluation of radio-tracking by triangulation with special reference to deer movements. *J. Wildl. Mgmt. 31*: 124–41.

Helminen, M. (1961). On the occurrence of the Samson character in wild foxes.

*Suomen Riista, 14:* 143–57.

Henry, J.D. (1977). The use of urine marking in the scavenging behaviour of the red fox. *Behaviour, 61:* 82–106.

Hewson, R. and Kolb, II.II. (1973). Changes in numbers and distribution of foxes (*Vulpes vulpes*) killed in Scotland from 1948–1970. *J. Zool.*, Lond., *171:* 285–92.

Hewson, R., Kolb, H.H. and Knox, A.G. (1975). The food of foxes in Scottish forests. *J. Zool.*, Lond., *176:* 287–92.

Hewson, R. and Kolb, H.H. (1976). Scavenging on sheep carcases by foxes (*Vulpes vulpes*) and badgers (*Meles meles*). *J. Zool.*, Lond., *180:* 496–8.

Hildebrand, M. (1952). An analysis of body proportions in the *Canidae. Amer. J. Anat., 90:* 217–56.

Hildebrand, M. (1954). Comparative morphology of the body skeleton in recent *Canidae. Univ. of California Pub. in Zoology, 52:* 399–470.

Hinaidy, H.K. (1976). Ein weiterer Beitrag zur Parasiten fauna des Rotfuchses (*Vulpes vulpes*) in Österreich. *Zbl. Veter. Med., 23:* 66–73.

HMSO (1971). Report of the committee of inquiry on rabies. *Cmnd. 4696.* London.

Hodgeman, S.L.F. and Bowden, R.S.T. (1960). Virus disease in wild foxes. *Vet. Rec., 72:* 168.

Hoffman, R.A. and Kirkpatrick, C.M. (1954). Red fox weights and reproduction in Tippecanoe County, Indiana. *J. Mammal., 35:* 504–9.

Hope Jones, P. (1974). Wildlife records from Merioneth parish documents. *Nature in Wales, 14:* 35–43.

Hörning, B. (1965). Weitere Trichinenfunde in der Schweiz. *Schweiz. Arch. Tierheilk, 107:* 335–40.

Howard, W.E. (1967). *Biological control of vertebrate pests.* Proc. 3rd Vertebrate Pests Conf., San Francisco. 137–157. Davis, University of California.

Howkins, A.B., Gemmel, M.A. and Smyth, J.D. (1965). Experimental transmission of *Echinococcus* from horses to foxes. *Ann. Trop. Med. Parasit., 59:* 457–62.

Hubert, G.F., Storm, G.L., Phillips, R.L. and Andrews, R.D. (1976). Ear tag loss in red foxes. *J. Wildl. Mgmt., 40:* 164–7.

Huggett, A. St. G. and Widdas, W.F. (1951). The relationship between mammalian foetal weight and conception age. *J. Physiol., 114:* 306–17.

Hughes, R. Elfyn, Dales, J., Williams, I. Ellis and Rees, D.I. (1973). Studies in sheep population and environment in the mountains of north west Wales. 1. Studies of sheep since mediaeval times. *J. appl. Ecol., 10:* 113–37.

Huson, L.W. and Page, R.J.C. (1979). A comparison of fox skulls from Wales and South-East England. *J. Zool.*, Lond., *187:* 465–70.

Insley, H. (1977). An estimate of the population density of red fox (*Vulpes vulpes*) in the New Forest, Hampshire. *J. Zool.*, Lond., *183:* 549–53.

Irvin, A.D. (1970). The epidemiology of wildlife rabies. *Vet. Rec., 87:* 333–48.

Isley, T.E. and Gysel, L.W. (1975). Sound source localization by the red fox. *J. Mammal., 56:* 397–404.

Jenkins, D., Watson, A. and Miller, G.R. (1964). Predation and red grouse populations. *J. appl. Ecol.*, *1*: 183–95.

Jensen, B. (1973). Movements of the red fox (*Vulpes vulpes* L.) in Denmark investigated by marking and recovery. *Dan. Rev. of Game Biology*, *8*: (3) 1–20.

Jensen, B. and Nielsen, L.B. (1968). Age determination in the red fox (*Vulpes vulpes* L.) from canine tooth sections. *Dan. Rev. Game Biol.*, *5*(6): 3–15.

Johansson, I. (1938). Reproduction in the silver fox. *Ann. Agric. Coll. of Sweden*, *5*: 179–200.

Johansson, I. (1941). Oestrus and mating in the silver fox. *Lantbr. Högskol. Ann.* [Uppsala], *5*: 179–200.

Johnson, D.R. (1968). Coat-colour polymorphism in North Plains red fox populations. *Can. J. Zool.*, *46*: 608–10.

Johnston, D.H. and Beauregard, M. (1969). Rabies epidemiology in Ontario. *Bull. Wildlife Disease Assoc.*, *5*: 357–70.

Jones, E.D. (1949). Robert Vaughan of Hengwrt. *J. Mer. Hist. and Record Soc.*, *1*: 21–30.

Jorgenson, J.W., Novotny, M., Carmack, M., Copland, G.B., and Wilson, S.R. (1978) in *Science*, *199*: 796–8.

Joyeux, C.H. and Boer, J.G. (1936). *Faune de France*, No. 30. Cestodes. Paris.

Kadlec, J.A. (1971). Effects of introducing foxes and raccoons on herring gull colonies. *J. Wildl. Mgmt.*, *35*: 625–35.

Kaikusalo, A. (1971). On the breeding of the arctic fox in N.W. Enontekio, Finnish Lapland. *Suomen Riista*, *23*: 7–16.

Kantorovich, R.A. (1964). Natural foci of rabies-like infections in the far north. *J. Hyg. Epi, Micro. and Immunol.*, *8*: 100–110.

Kaplan, C. (ed.), (1977). *Rabies, the facts.* London: Oxford University Press.

Keeler, C.E. (1964). Coat colour gene synthesis of tame behaviour in the rat, mink and fox. *Mind over Matter*, *9*: 16–30.

Keeler, C.E., Mellinger, T., Fromm, E. and Wade, L. (1970). Melanin, adrenalin and the legacy of fear. *J. Hered.*, *61*: 81–8.

Kellogg, C.E. (1941). Inheritance of degree of silvering in foxes. *U.S. Fish and Wildlife Service; Wildlife Leaflet No. 178.*

Kleiman, D. (1966). Scent marking in *Canidae. Symp. Zool. Soc. Lond. 18*: 167–77.

Klenk, K. (1971). Das aktivitätsmuster des Rotfuches in einen Freilandgehege mit Künstlichen Ban. *Sonderdrücke auz Z. f. Saugetierkunde*, *Bd.*, *36*, 5: 257–79.

Kolb, H.H. and Hewson, R. (1974). The body size of the red fox (*Vulpes vulpes*) in Scotland. *J. Zool.*, Lond., *173*: 253–5.

Korschgen, L.J. (1959). Food habits of the red fox in Missouri. *J. Wildl. Mgmt.*, *23*: 168–76.

Korytin, S.A. and Solomin, N.N. (1969). Materialy po etiologii psovykh. *Sb. Trud. vses. nauchno-issled. Inst. Zhirotnogo Syr'ya Pus Hniny*, *22*: 223–34.

Krieg, H. (1925). Biologische Reisenstudien in Südamerika. Bastard zwischen Hund und Pampafuchs (*Pseudoalopex [canis] agorae*). *Z. Morph. Okel. Tiere.*, *4*: 702–10.

Kruuk, H. (1964). Predators and anti-predator behaviour of the black-headed gull (*Larus ridibundus* L.). *Behaviour Suppl., 11*: 128pp.

Kurten, B. (1968). *Pleistocene mammals of Europe*. London: Weidenfeld and Nicolson.

Lampio, T. (1953). On the food of the fox. *Suomen Riista, 8*: 156–64.

Lamprecht, J. (1978). The relationship between food, competition and foraging group size in some larger carnivores. *Z. Tierpsychol, 46*: 337–43.

Lande, O. (1958). Chromosome number in the silver fox. *Nature, Lond., 181*: 1353–4.

Lapage, G. (1956). *Veterinary parasitology*. London: Oliver and Boyd.

Lascelles, G. (1915). *Thirty-five years in the New Forest*. London: Arnold.

Latham, R. M. (1952). The fox as a factor in the control of weasel populations. *J. Wildl. Mgmt., 16*: 516–17.

Lawrence, M. J. and Brown, R. W. (1973). *Mammals of Britain: their tracks, trails and signs*. London: Blandford.

Layne, J. N. and McKeon, W. H. (1956a). Some aspects of red fox and grey fox reproduction in New York. *N. Y. Fish & Game J., 3*: 44–74.

Layne, J. N. and McKeon, W. H. (1956b). Notes on the development of the red fox foetus. *N. Y. Fish & Game, J., 3*: 120–8.

Lederer, E. (1950). Odeurs et parfums des animaux. *Fortschr. Chem. organ. Naturstoffe, 6*: 87.

LeDune, E. K. (1937). Sarcoptic mange in a wild red fox. *Vet. Med., 32*: 556–7.

Leutscher, A. (1960). *Tracks and signs of British animals*. London: Cleaver-Hume Press.

Lever, J. A. W. (1959). The diet of the fox since myxomatosis. *J. Anim. Ecol. 28*: 359–75.

Lever, R. A., Armour, C. J. and Thompson, H. V. (1957). Myxomatosis and the fox. *Agriculture, 64*: 105–11.

Linhart, S. B. (1960). Rabies in wildlife and control methods in New York State. *N. Y. Fish & Game J., 7*: 1–13.

Linhart, S. B. (1964). Acceptance by wild foxes of certain baits for administering antifertility agents. *N. Y. Fish & Game J., 11*: 69–77.

Linhart, S. B. (1968). Dentition and pelage in the juvenile red fox (*Vulpes vulpes*). *J. Mammal., 49*: 526–8.

Linhart, S. B. and Enders, R. K. (1964). Some effects of diethylestilboestrol on reproduction in captive red foxes. *J. Wildl. Mgmt., 28*: 358–63.

Linhart, S. B. and Kennelly, J. J. (1967). Fluorescent bone labelling of Coyotes with dimethylchlortetracycline. *J. Wildl. Mgmt., 31*: 317–21.

Litvartis, J. A. and Mantz, W. H. (1976). Energy regulation of the diet fed to a captive red fox. *J. Wildl. Mgmt.; 40*: 365–8.

Lloyd, H. G. (1963). Intra-uterine mortality in the wild rabbit, *Oryctolagus cuniculus* L. in populations of low density. *J. Anim. Ecol., 32*: 549–63.

Lloyd, H. G. (1968). The control of foxes (*Vulpes vulpes* L.). *Ann. appl. Biol., 61*: 334–45.

Lloyd, H. G. (1976). Wildlife rabies in Europe and the British situation. *Trans. Roy. Soc. Trop Med. Hyg. 70*: 179–87.

Lloyd, H. G. (1977). Wildlife rabies: prospects for Britain, in Kaplan, ed.,

*Rabies, the Facts*. London: Oxford University Press.

Lloyd, H. G. and Englund, J. (1973). The reproductive cycle of the red fox in Europe. *J. Reprod. Fert., Suppl., 19*: 119–30.

Lloyd, H. G., Jensen, B., van Haaften, J. L., Niewold, F. J. J., Wandeler, A., Bogel, K. and Arata, A. A. (1976). Annual turnover of fox populations in Europe. *Zbl. Vet. Med., B. 23*: 580–9.

Lockie, J. D. (1959). The estimation of the food of foxes. *J. Wildl. Mgmt. 23*: 224–7.

Lockie, J. D. (1964). The breeding density of the golden eagle and fox in relation to food supply in Western Ross, Scotland. *The Scottish Naturalist, 71*: 67–77.

Longley, W. H. (1962). Movements of red fox. *J. Mammal., 43*: 107.

Lord, R. D. (1961). A population study of the grey fox. *Amer. Midland Nat., 66*: 87–109.

Lumb, W. V. (1963). *Small animal anaesthesia*. Philadelphia: Lea and Febiger.

Lund, Hj. Munthe-Kaas (1959). The red fox in Norway. 1. Survey of 551 red foxes, their size and sex ratio. *Norwegian State Game Research: 2* (5): 1–57.

Lund, Hj. Munthe-Kaas (1962). The red fox in Norway. 2. The feeding habits of the red fox in Norway. *Norwegian State Game Research, 2*, (12): 1–79.

Lundberg, G. (1937). Vart villebrad Raven. *Skogen, 6*: 133–6.

Lups, P., Neuenschwander, A. and Wandeler, A. (1972). Gebissentwicklung und Gebissanomalien bei Fuchsen (*Vulpes vulpes* L.) aus dem schweizerischen Mittelland. *Revue Suisse de Zoologie, 79*: 1090–1103.

Lydekker, R. (1896). *Lloyd's Natural History: A Hand-book to the British Mammalia*. London: Edward Lloyd.

Macdonald, D. W. (1976). Food caching by red foxes and some other carnivores. *Z. Tierpsychol., 42*: 170–85.

Macdonald, D. W. (1977a). On food preference in the red fox, *Mammal. Rev., 7*: 7–23.

Macdonald, D. W. (1977b). The behavioural ecology of the red fox in Kaplan, ed., *Rabies, the facts*. London: Oxford University Press.

Macpherson, A. H. (1964). A northward range extension of the red fox in the eastern Canadian arctic. *J. Mammal., 45*: 138–40.

Macpherson, A. H. (1969). The dynamics of Canadian arctic fox populations. *Can. Wildl. Serv. Rep. Ser., 8*: 52pp.

Magnus, Olaus (1555). *Gentium Septentrionalis Historiae Brevium*. Amsterdam.

Mair, N. S. (1968). Pseudo-tuberculosis in free living wild animals. *Symp. zool. Soc. Lond., 24*: 107–17.

Makino, S. (1948). Notes on the chromosomes of four species of small mammals. *J. Fac. Sci. Hokkaido Univ., 9*: 345–57.

Maples, J. C. (1941). Fox-dog hybrids. *Field* (London), *178*: 752.

Marcström, V. (1968). Tagging studies on red fox (*Vulpes vulpes*) in Sweden. *Viltrevy, 5*: 103–17.

Marlow, B. J. (1958). A survey of the marsupials of New South Wales. *CSIRO Wildl. Res., 3*: 71–114.

Marsh, D. B. (1938). The influx of the red fox and its color phases into the Barren Lands. *Canad. Field-Naturalist 52*: 60–1.

Martensz, P. N. (1971). Observations on the food of the fox *Vulpes vulpes* (L) in an arid environment. *CSIRO Wildl. Res., 16*: 73–5.

Matthews, L. Harrison (1951). A large Scottish fox. *Proc. zool. Soc. Lond., 120*: 679–81.

Mayr, E. (1963). *Animal species and evolution*. Cambridge, Mass.: Harvard University Press.

McCaughey, W. J. (1968). Brucellosis in wildlife. *Symp. zool. Soc. Lond., 24*: 102.

McEwen, E. H. and Scott, A. (1957). Pigmented areas in the uterus of the Arctic fox (*Alopex lagopus*). *Proc. zool. Soc. Lond., 128*: 347–8.

McFarlane, D., (1964). The effect of predation on perinatal lamb losses in the Morano, Oberon and Canberra districts. *Wool Technology and Sheep Breeding, 11*: 11–13.

McFarlane, D. (1965). Perinatal lamb losses. 1. An autopsy method for the investigation of perinatal losses. *N. Z. Vet., J., 13*: 116–35.

McHugh, J. F. and Edwards, M. S. H. (1958). Lamb loss investigations at Rutherglen Research Station. *J. Agric. Vict. Dep. Agric., 56*: 425–38.

McIntosh, D. L. (1963a). Food of the red fox in the Canberra district. *CSIRO Wildl. Res., 8*: 1–20.

McIntosh, D. L. (1963b). Reproduction and growth of the fox in the Canberra district. *CSIRO Wildl. Res., 8*: 132–41.

McKeon, W. (1952). Rabies control project report. *N. Y. State Cons. Dept., Div. Fish and Game* (mimeo), 4pp.

McNab, B. K. (1963). Bio energetics and the determination of home range size. *Amer. Nat., 97*: 133–40.

Mech, L. D. (1967). Telemetry as a technique in the study of predation. *J. Wildl. Mgmt., 31*: 492–6.

Mellanby, K. (1943). *Scabies*. London: Oxford University Press.

M'Fadyean, J. (1898). Sarcoptic mange in foxes. *J. Comp. Pathology, 11*: 92–3.

Middleton, A. D. (1935). Factors controlling the population of the partridge (*Perdix perdix*) in Great Britain. *Proc. zool. Soc. Lond.,* 795–815.

Middleton, A. D. (1966). Predatory mammals and the conservation of game in Great Britain. *Game Res. Assoc. Ann. Report,* 14–21.

Millard, F. W. (1906). *Game and foxes,* London: Horace Cox.

Millais, J. G. (1904). *The mammals of Great Britain and Ireland.* Vol. 1. London: Longmans Green.

Monson, R. A., Stone, W. B. and Parks, E. (1973). Ageing red foxes (*Vulpes fulva*) by counting the annular cementum rings of their teeth. *N. Y. Fish Game J., 20*: 54–61.

Montgomery, G. G. (1974). *Communication in red fox diads: A computer simulation study. Smithsonian Contribution to Zoology: 187.* Washington, D.C. Smithsonian Institution Press.

Moore, N. W. (1956). Rabbits, buzzards and hares, two studies on the indirect effects of myxomatosis. *Terre et la Vie, 103*: 220–5.

Moore, P. (ed). (1965). *Against hunting.* London: Gollancz.

Moore, R. W., Donald, I. M. and Messenger, J. J. (1966). Fox predation as a cause of lamb mortality. *Proc. Aust. Soc. Anim. Prod., 6*: 157–60.

Moore, W. and Elder, R. L. (1965). Chromosomes of the fox. *Jour. Hered. 56*: 142–3.

Moors, P. J. (1975). The food of weasels (*Mustela nivalis*) on farmland in north-east Scotland. *J. Zool.*, Lond., *177*: 455–61.

Morris, P. (1973). A review of mammalian age determination methods. *Mammal Rev.*, *2*: 69–104.

Morse, M. A. and Balser, D. S. (1961). Fox calling as a hunting technique. *J. Wildl. Mgmt.*, *25*: 148–54.

Müller, J. (1971). The effect of fox reduction on the occurrence of rabies. *Bull. Off. int. Epiz.*, *75*: 763–76.

Muller-Schwartz, D. (1972). Responses of young black-tailed deer to predator odours. *J. Mammal.*, *53*: 392–4.

Munch, B., Clausen, B. and Karlog, O. (1974). Thallium poisoning in red foxes (*Vulpes vulpes*) and badgers (*Meles meles*) in Denmark. *Nord. Vet.-Med.*, *26*: 323–38.

Murie, A. (1944). The wolves of Mount McKinley, *U.S. Dept. Int. Natl. Park Serv.* Fauna Series No. 5. Washington DC.

Murton, R. K. (1971). The significance of a specific search image in the feeding behaviour of the wood-pigeon. *J. Zool.*, Lond., *165*: 53–84.

Nairn, R. G. W. (1977). Fox (*Vulpes vulpes*) feeding on Sand eels (*Ammodytes* sp.) *Ir. Nat. J.*, *19*: 132.

Nemeseri, L. (1962). Trichinosis in Hungary. *Proc. 1st Int. Conf. on Trichinellosis, Warsaw*, 96–8.

Nicoll, W. (1923). A reference list of the Trematode parasites of British mammals. *Parasitology*, *15*: 236–52.

Niemeyer, W. (1868). Zuchtungesfalge im Zoologischen Garten zu Hanover. *Zool. Gart. (Frankfurt)*, *9*: 68–72.

Niewold, F. J. J. (1973). Various movements of the red fox (*Vulpes vulpes*) determined by radio-tracking. *Proc. 11th Congress of Int. Union of Game Biol.* Stockholm.

Noirot, E. (1966). Ultrasounds in young rodents. 1. Changes with age in albino mice. *Anim. Behav.*, *14*: 459–642.

Norman, F. I. (1971). Predation by the fox (*Vulpes vulpes*) on colonies of short-tailed shearwater (*Puffinus tenuirostris* (Temminck)) in Victoria, Australia. *J. appl. Ecol.*, *8*: 21–32.

Nyholm, E. S. (1971). Ecological observations on the snow hare (*Lepus timidus* L.) on the islands of Krunnit and Kuusamo. *Suomen Riista*, *23*: 115.

Ognev, S. I. (1931). Mammals of eastern Europe and northern Asia, Vol. 2 (National Science Foundation translation) 1962. PST Cat. No. 230.

Oldham, C. (1931). Payments for vermin by some Hertfordshire churchwardens. *Trans. E. Herts. Nat. Hist. Field Club*, *19*: 79–112.

Oldham, J. N. and Beresford-Jones, W. P. (1957). *T. spiralis* in the wild red fox in England. *Br. vet. J.*, *113*: 34–5.

Oleyar, C. M. and McGinnis, B. S. (1974). Field evalution of diethylstilboestrol for suppressing reproduction in foxes. *J. Wildl. Mgmt.*, *38*: 101–6.

Olive, J. R. and Riley, C. V. (1948). Sarcoptic mange in the red fox in Ohio. *J. Mammal.*, *29*: 73–4.

O'Rourke, F. J. and Verling, M. (1971). *Trichinella spiralis* in the foxhound in Ireland. *Vet. Rec.*, *90*: 704.

Osterholm, H. (1964). The significance of distance receptors in the feeding behaviour of the fox, *Vulpes vulpes* L. *Acta Zoologica Fennica*, *106*: 1–31.

Owen, H. J. (1950). *The treasures of the Mawddach*. Bala: Evans.

Parker, E. (1943). *Oddities of natural history*. London: Seeley Service.

Patterson, I. J. (1977). The control of fox movement by electric fencing. *Biol. Conserv.*, *11*: 267–78.

Pavloff, M. P., (1953). Mass diseases of foxes in the Crimea. *Voprosy Biologii Pushnykh Zverey*, Moscow, 13: Translation in Russian Game Reports 3, Canad., Dept. of Northern Affairs & Nat. Resources 1958.

Pearson, O. P. and Enders, R. K. (1943). Ovulation, maturation and fertilization in the fox. *Anat. Rec.*, *85*: 69–83.

Pearson, O. P. and Bassett, C. F. (1944). Size of the vulva and·its relation to fertility in foxes. *Amer. Fur Breeder*, *17*: 12.

Pearson, O. P. (1964). Carnivore-mouse predation: an example of its intensity and bioenergetics. *J. Mammal.*, *45*: 177–88.

Pearson, O. P. (1966). The prey of carnivores during one cycle of mouse abundance. *J. Anim. Ecol.*, *35*: 217–33.

Peshev, Z. (1963). The food of the fox (*Vulpes vulpes*) in some parts of Bulgaria. *Annuaire de l'Université de Sofia*, *58*: 88–119.

Peterson, R. L., Standfield, R. O., McEven, E. H. and Brooks, A. C. (1953). Early records of the red and grey fox in Ontario. *J. Mammal.*, *34*: 126–7.

Phillipe, L. (1950). Le renard roux (*V. fulva fulva*) et son influence écologique et économique durant la saison hivernal sur une partie de l'Ile de Montréal. *Le Naturaliste Canadien*, *78*: 5–43.

Phillips, R. L. (1970). Age ratios of Iowa foxes. *J. Wildl. Mgmt.*, *34*: 52–6.

Phillips, R. L. and Meck, L. D. (1970). Homing behaviour of a red fox. *J. Mammal.*, *51*: 621.

Phillips, R. L., Andrews, R. D., Storm, G. L. and Bishop, R. A. (1972). Dispersal and mortality of red foxes. *J. Wildl. Mgmt.*, *36*: 237–48.

Preston, E. M. (1975). Home range defense in the red fox (*Vulpes vulpes* L.) *J. Mammal* 56: 645–52.

Pucek, Z., Ryszkowski, L. and Zejda, J. (1969). Estimation of average length of life in the bank vole, *Clethrionomys glareolus*. [In *Energy flow through small mammal populations*.] *Polish Sci. Publ.*, 187–201.

Pullar, E. M. (1939). The fox (*Vulpes vulpes* L. 1758) as a definitive host of *Taenia ovis*. *Aust. Veter. J.*, *15*: 123–5.

Pullar, E. M. (1946). A survey of Victorian canine and vulpine parasites. *Aust. Vet. J.*, *22*: 12–21; 40–8; 85–91; 123–5.

Purser, A. F. and Young, G. B. (1959). Lamb survival in two hill flocks. *Anim. Prod.*, *1*: 85–91.

Ralls, K. (1967). Mammalian scent marking. *Anim. Behaviour*, *15*: 123–8.

Ralls, K. (1971). Mammalian scent marking. *Science*, *171*: 443–9.

Rantanen, A. V. and Pulliainen, E. (1970). Dental conditions of wild red foxes (*Vulpes vulpes* L.) in northeastern Lapland. *Ann. Zool. Fennic.*, 7: 290–4.

Ratcliffe, F. N. (1956). The ecological consequences of myxomatosis in Australia. *Terre et la Vie*, *103*: 153–66.

Redahan, E. (1967). A search for *Trichinella spiralis* in pigs and rats in Ireland. *Irish Vet. J.*, *21:* 168.

Reilly, R. J. and Curren, W. (1961). Evaluation of certain techniques for judging the age of red foxes (*Vulpes fulva*). *N.Y. Fish and Game J.*, *8:* 122–9.

Reinwaldt, E. (1963). Ueber einige Anomalien im Gebiss des Rotfuches, *Vulpes vulpes*. *Arkiv Zool.* (A.S.), *15:* 371–5.

Retzius, A. (1848). Om en egen Kortelbildning has nagra arter af Statet. *Canis. Kongl. Wet. Akad. Handl*, 2.

Richards, S. H. and Hine, R. C. (1953). Wisconsin fox populations. *Wis. Cons. Dept. Tech. Wildl. Bull.*, *6:* 78pp.

Rieck, W. (1965). Gibt es ein Eheverhältnis beim Fuchs? *D. Dtsh. Jäger.*, *83:* 139.

Robinson, R. (1975). The red fox, *Vulpes vulpes*, in R. C. King ed., *Handbook of genetics*, Vol. 4. London: Plenum Press.

Robinson, W. B. (1952). Some observations of coyote predation in Yellowstone National Park. *J. Mammal.*, *33:* 470–6.

Rodonaya, T. E. (1965). The inter-relationships between *T. spiralis* and *Echinococcus multilocularis*. *Soobshch. Akad. Nauk. Gruz SSR*, *40:* 437–40.

Rolls, E. C. (1969). *They all ran wild*. Sydney: Angus and Robertson.

Romanov, A. N. (1956). Automatic tagging of wild animals and prospects for its use. *Zoologicheskii zhurnal*, *35:* 1902–5.

Ross, J. G. and Fairley, J. S. (1969). Studies of disease in the red fox (*Vulpes vulpes*) in Northern Ireland. *J. Zool.*, Lond., *157:* 375–81.

Rothschild, M. (1963). A rise in the flea index of the hare, with relevant notes on the fox and woodpigeon, at Ashton, Peterborough. *Proc. zool. Soc. Lond.*, *140:* 341–6.

Rowlands, I. W. and Parkes, A. S. (1935). The reproductive processes of certain mammals. VIII: Reproduction in foxes (*Vulpes* sp.). *Proc. zool. Soc. Lond.*, *105:* 823–41.

Rowley, I. (1970). Lamb predation in Australia: incidence, predisposing conditions and the identification of wounds. *CSIRO Wildl. Res.*, *15:* 79–123.

Ryan, G. E. (1976). Observations on the reproduction and age structure of the fox *Vulpes vulpes* L. in New South Wales. *Aust Wildl. Res.*, *1:* 11–20.

Ryan, G. E. and Croft, J. D. (1974). Observations on the food of the fox *Vulpes vulpes* (L.) in Kinehega National Park, Menindee, NSW. *Aust. Wild. Res.*, *1:* 89–94.

Ryszkowski, L., Wagner, C. K., Goszczynski, J. and Truszkowski, J. (1971). Operation of predators in a forest and cultivated fields. *Ann. Zool. Fennici.*, *8:* 160–8.

Ryszkowski, L., Goszczynski, J., and Truszkowski, J. (1973). Trophic relationships of the common vole in cultivated fields. *Acta. theriol.*, *18:* 125–65.

Sargeant, A. B. (1972). Red fox spatial characteristics in relation to waterfowl predation. *J. Wildl. Mgmt.*, *36:* 225–36.

Sargeant, A. B. (1975). A spring aerial census of red fox in North Dakota. *J. Wildl. Mgmt.*, *39:* 30–9.

Sargeant, A. B. (1978). Red fox prey demands and implication to prairie duck production. *J. Wildl. Mgmt.*, *42*: 520–7.

Sargeant, A. B., Knese, A. D. and Afton, A. D. (1974). Use of small fences to protect ground bird nests from mammalian predators. *Prairie Nat.*, *6*: 60–3.

Sargeant, A. B. & Eberhardt, L. E. (1975). Death feigning by ducks in response to predation by red foxes, (*Vulpes fulva*). *Amer. Mid. Nat.*, *94*: 108–19.

Schaltens, R. G. and Brim, A. (1964). Isolation of *Listeria monocytogenes* from foxes suspected of having rabies. *J. Amer. Vet. Ass.*, *145*: 466–9.

Schlezel, F. R. (1912). Die Extremitäten der Caniden, ihre Beziehungen zur Korpersymmetrie und die Verhaltnisse ihrer relativen Proportionen. *Arch. f. Naturg.*, *Abt. A. (11)*: 1–29.

Schmook, A. (1960). *Der Fuchs, wie er lebt, jagt, gejagt wird*. Thun-München: Ott–Verl.

Schofield, R. D., (1958). Litter size and age ratios of Michigan red foxes. *J.Wildl. Mgmt.*, *22*: 313–315.

Schofield, R. D. (1960). A thousand miles of fox trails in Michigan's ruffed grouse range. *J. Wildl. Mgmt.*, *24*: 432–4.

Scholander, P. F., Hock, E., Walters, V., Johnson, F. and Irving, L. (1950). Heat regulation in some arctic and tropical mammals and birds. *Biological Bull.* *99*: 237–58.

Schoonmaker, W. J. (1938). Notes on mating and breeding habits of foxes in New York State. *J. Mammal.*, *19*: 375–6.

Scott, T. G. (1941a). A method for estimating red fox populations. *Iowa State Coll. Journal of Science*, *14*: 155–9.

Scott, T. G. (1941b). Methods and computation in faecal analyses with reference to the red fox. *Iowa State Coll. J. Sci.*, *15*: 279–85.

Scott, T. G. (1943). Some food coactions of the northern plains red fox. *Ecol. Monog.*, *13*: 427–79.

Scott, T. G. and Klimstra, W. D. (1955) Red foxes and a declining prey population. *Monogr. Univ. S. Ill. No. 1*, 123pp.

Secord, A. C. (1936). Diseases of fur bearing animals. *Vet. Med.*, *31*: 532–49.

Seton, E. Thompson (1925). *Lives of game animals*, Vol. 1, 467–552. New York: Doubleday Doran.

Sheail, J. (1971) *Rabbits and their history*. Newton Abbot and London: David and Charles.

Sheldon, W. G. (1949a). A trapping and tagging technique for wild foxes. *J. Wildl. Mgmt.*, *13*: 309–11.

Sheldon, W. G. (1949b). Reproductive behaviour of foxes in New York State. *J. Mammal.*, *30*: 236–46.

Sheldon, W. G. (1950). Denning habits and home range of red foxes in New York State. *J. Wildl. Mgmt.*, *14*: 33–42.

Sheldon, W. G. (1953). Returns of banded red and gray foxes in New York State. *J. Mammal.*, *34*: 125–6.

Sinclair, K. B. (1956). *Echinococcus* infection in the fox. *Vet. Rec.*, *68*: 104.

Sinclair, K. B. (1957). *Echinococcus* infection in the fox. *Vet. Rec.*, *69*: 1076.

Skrobov, V. D. (1960). Relationship between arctic and red foxes in the tundra of the Nenetskii National Okrug. *Zool. zhurn.*, *39*: 469–71.

Smirnov, V. S. (1960). The determination of the age and sex ratio of mammals using the squirrel, muskrat, and five kinds of predators as examples. *Acad. Nauk., USSR, 14*: 97–112.

Smit, F. G. A. M. (1957a). The recorded distribution and hosts of *Siphonaptera* in Britain. *Ent. Gaz., 8*: 47–75.

Smit, F. G. A. M. (1957b). *Handbook for the identification of British insects*, Vol. 1, Part 16: *Siphonaptera*. Royal Entomological Society of London.

Smith, G. Ennis (1939) Growth of fox foetus and length of gestation period. *Canad. Silver Fox & Fur* (March).

Smith, I. D. (1964). Ovine neo-natal mortality in western Queensland. *Proc. Aust. Soc. Anim. Prod., 5*: 100–6.

Smyth, J. D. and Smyth, M. M. (1964). Natural and experimental hosts of *Echinococcus granulosus* and *E. multilocularis*, with comments on the genetics of speciation in the genus *Echinococcus*. *Parasitology, 54*: 493–514.

Smythe, R. H. (1961). *Animal vision*. London: Jenkins.

Soulsby, E. J. L. (1965). *Textbook of Veterinary Clinical Parasitology*. Vol. 1. Helminths. Oxford: Blackwell.

Southern, H. N., ed. (1964). *Handbook of British mammals*. Oxford: Blackwell.

Southern, H. N. and Watson, J. S. (1941). Summer food of the red fox (*Vulpes vulpes*) in Great Britain: a preliminary report. *J. Anim. Ecol., 10*: 1–11.

Spannhof, I. (1969). The histophysiology and function of the anal sac of the red fox (*Vulpes vulpes* L.). *Forma et functic, 1*: 26–45.

Stains, H. J. (1967). Carnivores and pinnipeds in S. Anderson and J. Knox-Jones, eds, *Recent mammals of the world*. New York: Ronald Press.

Stanley, W. C. (1963). Habits of the red fox in northeastern Kansas. *State Biol. Surv. of Kansas* – Misc. Pub. No. 34: 1–31.

Starkov, I. D. (1937). The sexual cycle of the silver fox. *Usp. zooteh. Nauk, 3*: 385–401 (*Animal Breeding Abstracts, 6*: 38).

Starkov, I. D. (1940). Liso pescovyi gibrid (A silver fox – arctic fox hybrid). *Sovetsk. Zooteh., 11/12*: 119 (*Animal Breeding Abstracts, 9*: 339).

Steck, F., Addy, P., Schipper, E. and Wandeler, A. (1968) Der bisherige Verlauf des Tollwutseuchenzuges in der Schweiz. *Schweiz. Arch. Tierheilk., 110*: 597–616.

Stephenson, J. (1928). Translation of the zoological section of the Nuzhati-L-Qutub of Hamdullah Al Mustaufi Al-Quzwini. *Royal Asiatic Society Oriental Translation Series*, xxx.

Stone, W. B., Parks, E., Weber, B. L. and Parks, F. J. (1972). Experimental transfer of sarcoptic mange from red foxes and wild canids to captive wildlife and domestic animals. *N.Y. Fish & Game J. 19*: 1–11.

Storm, G. L. (1965). Movements and activities of foxes as determined by radio-tracking. *J. Wildl. Mgmt., 29*: 1–13.

Storm, G. L. and Dauphin, K. P. (1965). A wire ferret for use in studies of foxes and skunks. *J. Wildl. Mgmt., 29*: 625–6.

Storm, G. L. and Ables, E. D. (1966). Notes on new born and full-term wild red foxes. *J. Mammal, 47*: 116–8.

Storm, G. L. and Sanderson, G. C. (1969). Results of a field test to control striped skunks with diethylstiboestrol. *Trans. Ill. State Acad. Sci., 62*: 193–7.

Storm, G. L., Andrews, R. D., Phillips, R. L., Bishop, R. A., Siniff, D. B.

and Tester, J. R. (1976). Morphology, reproduction, dispersal and mortality of mid-western red fox population. *Wldl. Monograph (The Wildlife Society)* No. *49*, 82pp.

Stubbe, M. (1967). Zur Populationbiologie des Rotfuchses, *Vulpes vulpes* (L.). *Sonderdruck aus 'Hercynia'* Bd *4*: (1): 1–10.

Stubbe, M. and Stubbe, W. (1977). Zur Populationbiologie des Rotfuchses *Vulpes vulpes* (L.). *Hercynia* N.F. *4*: 161–77.

Stuht, J. N. and Youatt, W. G. (1972). Heartworms and lung flukes from red foxes in Michigan. *J. Wildl. Mgmt.*, *36*: 166–70..

Sullivan, E. G. and Haugen, A.O. (1950). Age determination of foxes by x-ray of forefeet. *J. Wildl. Mgmt.*, *20*: 210–12.

Swire, P. W. (1978). Laboratory observation on the fox (*Vulpes vulpes*) in Dyfed during the winters of 1974/75 and 1975/76. *Br. Vet. J.*, *134* : 398–405.

Switzenberg, D. F. (1950). Breeding productivity in Michigan red foxes. *J. Mammal.*, *31*: 194–5.

Szuman, J. (1960). Untersuchungen über Veränderungen der zytologischen Bestandteile des Vaginalsekrets beim Silber-und Blaufuchs bei anormaler Ranz und Begattung. *Archiv fur Beflügelzucht und Kleintierkunde*, 9 (1): 21–9.

Szuman, J. and Skrzydlewski, A. (1962). Uber die Durchgangszeit des Futters durch den Magen-Darm-Kanal beim Blaufuchs. *Arch. Tierernährung*, *12*: 1–4.


Tabel. H., Corner, A. H., Webster, W. A. and Casey, C. A. (1974). History and epizootiology of rabies in Canada. *Can. Vet. J.*, *15*: 271–81.

Talbot, J. S. (1906). *Foxes at home*. London: Horace Cox.

Tansley, K. (1965). *Vision in vertebrates* (Science Paperbacks). London: Chapman and Hall.

Tapper, S. C. (1976). The diet of weasels, *Mustela nivalis*, and stoats *Mustela erminea* during early summer, in relation to predation on gamebirds. *J. Zool.*, Lond., *179*: 219–24.

Tate, W. E. (1960) *The Parish Chest*. London: Cambridge University Press.

Taylor, J. (1968). *Salmonella* in wild animals. *Symp. zool. Soc. Lond.*, *24*: 51–73.

Taylor, J. C. and Blackmore, D. K. (1961). A short note on the heavy mortality in foxes during the winter 1959–60. *Vet. Rec.*, *73*: 232–3.

Taylor, K. D. and Lloyd, H.G. (1978). The design, construction and use of radio-tracking for some British Mammals. *Mammal Rev.*, *8*: 117–141.

Teagle, W. G. (1967). The fox in the London suburbs. *Lond. Nat.*, 46: 44–68.

Tembrock, G. (1957). Zur Ethologie des Rotfuchses (*Vulpes vulpes* (L.)) unter besondere Berücksichtigung der Fortpflanzung. *Zool. Gart. Lpzg.*, *23*: 289–532.

Tembrock, G. (1963). Acoustic behaviour of mammals, In R. G Busnel, ed., *Acoustic behaviour of animals*. Amsterdam: Elsevier.

Tembrock, G. (1968). in T. A. Sebeok, ed., *Animal communication*. Bloomington, Indiana: Indiana University Press.

Tetley, H. (1941). On the Scottish fox. *Proc. zool. Soc. Lond.*, *111B* : 23–35.

Thompson, R. C. A. and Smyth, J. D. (1974). Potential danger of hydatid disease of horse/dog origin. *Br. Med. J.*, *3*: 807.

Thomson, A. M. and Thomson, W. (1949). Lambing in relation to the diet of the pregnant ewe. *Brit. J. Nutr.*, 2: 290–305.

Thornton, W. A., Creel, G. C. and Trimble, R. E. (1971). Hybridization in the fox genus *Vulpes* in west Texas. *Southwestern Naturalist*, 15: 473–83.

Tickner, G. (1932). A nervous disease among foxes. *J. Anim. Ecol.*, 1: 83–4.

Tinbergen, N. (1975). The Functions of Territory. *Bird Study*, 4: 14–27.

Todd, N. B. (1962). Inheritance of the catnip response in domestic cats. *J. Hered.* 53: 54–5.

Toldt, K. (1907–8). Studien über das Haarkleid von *Vulpes vulpes* L. *Wien, Ann. Naturhist. Hofmuseum*, 22: 197–269.

Toma, B. and Andral, L. (1977). Epidemiology of fox rabies. *Advances in virus research*, 21: 1–36.

Topsell, Edward (1607). *The historie of foure-footed beastes*. London: William Iaggard.

Troughton, E. (1957). *Furred animals of Australia*. Sydney: Angus and Robertson.

Troitskaya, A. A. (1955). Helminths in red foxes in the Tatar, ASSR, USSR. *Voprosy, Biologii Pushnykh. Zverery, Moscow*, 14: 158.

Trut, L. N. (1969). Some new data on selection of silvery-black foxes (*Vulpes fulvus* Desm.) in accordance with their defensive behaviour characteristics. *Jene tika Poredeniya*, Nauk Leningrad: 107–119 (in Russian).

Trut, L. N. and Beljaer, D. K. (1969). Role of behaviour in regulation of the reproductive function in some representatives of the Canidae family. *VI Cong. Inter. Reprod. Amin. Insem. Artif.* Paris (1968) 2: 1677–80.

Twigg, G. I., Cuerden, C. M. and Hughes, D. M. (1968). Leptospirosis in British wild mammals. *Symp. zool. Soc. Lond.*, 24: 75–98.

Twigg, G. I. and Cox, P. J. (1976). The distribution of leptospires in the kidney tubules of some British wild animals. *J. Wildl. Dis.*, 12: 318–21.

Valen, L. van (1964). Nature of supernumerary molars of *Otocyon*. *J. Mammal.*, 45: 284–6.

Varty, K. (1967). *Reynard the Fox*. London: Leicester University Press.

Vasennis, H. (1964). Microflora of foxes in Finland. *Suomen Riista*, 17: 161–3.

Vaughan, H. E. N. and Vaughan, J. A. (1968). Some aspects of the epizootiology of myxomatosis. *Symp. zool. Soc. Lond.*, 24: 298–309.

Veale, E. M. (1957). The rabbit in England. *Agric. Hist. Rev.*, 5: 85–90.

Verling, M. (1972). *Trichinella spiralis* in the 'pasture type' brown rat (*Rattus norvegicus*) in Ireland. *Irish Vet. J.*, 26: 207.

Verme, L. J. (1962). An automatic tagging device for deer. *J. Wildl. Mgmt.*, 26: 287–392.

Vincent, R. E. (1958). Observations of red fox behaviour. *Ecology*, 39: 755–7.

Vogel, H. (1957). Uber den *Echinococcus multilocularis. Süddeutschlands, Z. Tropenmedizin und Parasitologie*, 8: 404–54.

Vogtsberger, L. M. and Barrett, G. W. (1973). Bioenergetics of captive red foxes. *J. Wildl. Mgmt.*, 37: 495–500.

Walshe, J. M. (1954). *Echinococcus alveolaris* of the liver. *J. Path. Bact.*, 67: 371.

Walters, T.M.H. (1977). Hydatid disease in Wales. *Trans. Roy. Soc. Trop. Med. Hyg. 71:* 105–8.

Walton, C. L. (1918). Some results of a survey of the agricultural zoology of the Aberystwyth area. *Parasitology, 10:* 206–31.

Wandeler, A. and Hörning, B. (1972). Aspekte des Cestodenbefalles bei bernischen Fuchsen. *Jahrbuch des Naturhistorischen Museums der Stadt Bern, 4:* 231–52.

Wandeler, A., Muller, G., Wachendorfer, G., Schale, W., Forster, U. and Steck, F. (1974b). Rabies in wild animals in central Europe. 3. Ecology and biology of the fox in relation to control operations. *Zbl. Veter. Med.,* B, 21: 765–73.

Wandeler, A., Wachendorfer, G., Forster, U., Krekel, H., Schale, W., Muller, J. and Steck, F. (1974a). Rabies in wild carnivores in central Europe. 1. Epidemiological studies. *Zbl. Veter. Med.,* B, *21:* 735–56.

Warwick, B. L. and Hanson, K. B. (1937). *Yearbook of agriculture,* 1388–94. Washington, DC.: US Dept. Agric.

Watkins, C. V. and Harvey, L. A. (1942). On the parasites of silver foxes on some farms in the south-west. *Parasitology, 34:* 155–79.

Wetmore, A. (1952). The gray fox (*Urocyon*) attracted by a crow call. *J. Mammal., 33:* 244–5.

Wildman, A. B. (1954. *The microscopy of animal textile fibres.* Leeds: Wool Industries Research Association.

Williams, B. M. (1976a). The intestinal parasites of the red fox in south west Wales. *Br. Vet. J., 132:* 309–12.

Williams, B. M. (1976b). The epidemiology of adult and larval cestodes in Dyfed (UK): 1. The cestodes of farm dogs. *Vet. Parasitology, 1:* 271–6.

Williams, B. M. (1976c). The epidemiology of adult and larval cestodes in Dyfed (UK): 2. The cestodes of foxhounds. *Vet. Parasitology, 1:* 277–80.

Williams, R. J. and Sweatman, G. K. (1963). On the transmission, biology and morphology of *Echinococcus granulosus equinus,* a new subspecies of hydatid tapeworm in horses in Great Britain. *Parasitology, 53:* 391.

Wilson, O. E. and Bossert, W. H. (1963). Chemical communication among animals. *Recent Progr. Hormone Res., 19:* 673–716.

Wood, J. E. (1959). Relative estimates of fox population levels. *J. Wildl. Mgmt., 23:* 53–63.

Wood, J. E. and Odum, E. P. (1964). A nine year history of fur bearing populations on the AEC Savannah river plant area. *J. Mammal, 45:* 540–51.

Woodford, M. H. and Cooper, J. E. (1969). A case of exudative pleurisy in a wild fox. *J. Zool.,* Lond., *158:* 203–4.

Woodhead, G. (1969). Three-toed vixen. *Shooting Times,* (15 November), *4541:* 1863.

Zeuner, F. E. (1963). *A history of domesticated animals.* London: Hutchinson.

Zwierzchowski, J. (1960). Aujesky's disease in foxes and mink. *Roczn. Nauk. rol.* (Series E), *70:* 245.

# Index